HISTORY OF EDUCATION IN INDIA

DR. RAM NATH SHARMA
DR. RAJENDRA K. SHARMA

ATLANTIC
PUBLISHERS & DISTRIBUTORS (P) LTD

Published by

ATLANTIC

PUBLISHERS & DISTRIBUTORS (P) LTD

7/22, Ansari Road, Darya Ganj, New Delhi-110002
Phones : +91-11-40775252, 40775214, 23273880, 23275880
Fax: +91-11-23285873
Web: www.atlanticbooks.com
E-mail: orders@atlanticbooks.com

Printed & bound in India by Atlantic Print Services

PREFACE

This book traces the History of Education in India since ancient Vedic, Post-Vedic and Buddhist period to the Islamic, the British period and Education in India today. It describes in details the activities and recommendations of various Educational Committeesand Commissions. It narrates the proceedings of important seminars on education. It describes the growth of education in India during 1835- 1853; 1854-1882; 1882-1900; 1900-1920; 1921-1937; 1921-1944; 1939-1953 and in the present times. It discusses the progress and problems of education in Primary and Basic, Secondary and Higher education and also suggests remedies.

Based on authortic government reports and important publications, this book has been planned as an ideal textbook on the subject for students of all the Indian universities. Suggestions for improvement are most welcome.

RAM NATH SHARMA
RAJENDRA K. SHARMA

PREFACE

Contents

CHAPTER 1

ANCIENT INDIAN VEDIC EDUCATION

IDEALS OF VEDIC EDUCATION

1. **Liberation.** The aim of ancient Indian education was initially laid down by the Vedas. According to Vedic world view the world is pervaded by divinity and the aim of every living being is to achieve liberation. Thus according to the Vedas the aim of education is liberation. According to a famous statement, "That is knowledge which gives liberation." Therefore, A. S. Altekar has rightly pointed out, "The knowledge is a third eye of man, which gives him insight into all affairs and teaches him how to act. In the spiritual sphere it leads to our salvation, in the mundane sphere it leads to all round progress and prosperity. The illumination given to us by education shatters illusions, removes difficulties and enables us to realise the true values of life."
2. **Control of Mind.** The cause of liberation and bondage, according to Vedic thinkers, is the mind or chitta. Therefore, liberation is possible only through the control of the mind. This was known as the technique of *chittavratti nirodh*. The Indian philosophers developed a whole technique for the control of the mind. Equanimity of the mind leads to self-realisation. This self-realisation is neither of the individual nor of the social self but Brahman which is the essence of the individual and the society. The Vedic axiology does not distinguish between the social and the individual values since according to it both are part of fundamental universal values.

The ancient Indian education was even more developed by the Upanishads. While in the field of religion the Upanishads were more introvert and monistic, they continued the tradition of the Vedas. This tradition was oral. In the words of Radhakumud Mukerji, "For thousands of years, even up to the time of Kumarila (8th century A. D.) it was considered a sacrilege to reduce the Veda to writing, for learning was not reading but realisation, and knowledge was to be in the blood, as an organic part of one's self. Another point to be noted in this connection is that sabda or word by itself has its own potency and value, apart from its sense, and its intrinsic attributes, its rhythm, and vibrations should be captured. Sabda is Brahma."

AGENCIES OF EDUCATION

According to ancient Indian philosophy knowledge may be gained by three steps, *Shravana* or hearing, *Manan* or Meditation and *Nididhyasan* or realisation.

Shravan or hearing was further categorised into six types:

(i) *upakrama,* a formal ceremony performed preceding the study of Veda,
(ii) *abhyasa,* recitation of the texts,
(iii) *apurvata,* a ready grasp of the meaning,
(iv) *phala,* a comprehension of the outcome,
(v) *arthavada,* the reading of elucidatory books, and
(vi) *upapatti,* attainment of final conclusion.

Describing the condition of education in ancient India, P.N. Prabhu has said, "Education in ancient India was free from any external control like that of the state or Government or any party politics. It was the one of the king's duties to see that the learned pundits pursued their studies and their duty of imparting knowledge without interference from any source whatever. So also education did not suffer from any communal interest or prejudices in India." There were three agencies of education:

1. **Gurukula.** This, as the name indicates, was the family of the teacher and his residence where the students used to stay during the period of study. Gradually, the gurukulas were extended to include a number of buildings. However, the institution was built up around the family of the teacher. The primary duty of the student was to serve the teacher and his family. The students were like sons of the teacher and the whole institution lived like a family.

2. **Parishad.** These were bigger educational institutions where several teachers used to teach different subjects. This may be compared to a college.
3. **Sammelan.** Sammelan literary means getting together for a particular purpose. In this type of educational institutions scholars gathered at one place for discussions and competitions generally on the invitation of the king.

DISCIPLINE

The Vedic system of education very much emphasized the importance of discipline in the attainment of knowledge. This, however, was self-discipline. In fact it was self-control which was realised by observance of rules of the Brahmacharya ashram. The parishads or the local academies were initiated by the king. Therefore the scholars and the aspirants of knowledge gathered at the parishads with a perfect academic order. There was hardly any need for insisting upon rules and regulations as these were laid down by scriptures. No one questioned the scripture's command concerning discipline. Therefore, discipline was self-imposed as a part of self-culture.

Vedic Rishis spread the knowledge not only in India but in the whole world. They brought the humanity from the darkness of ignorance to the light of knowledge throughout the world. Indian education system is the oldest in the world. It had peculiarities which were not found anywhere else in the world.

In *'Chhandogya Upanishad'* Narada told Sanatkumars, "I have read all the Vidyas." He had counted them in these words "O lord! I read Rigveda, Samaveda, Yajurveda, Atharvaveda and fifth the Itihas and Puranas, which is Veda of Vedas." Thus the Vedas are the oldest texts available in the world. They are creation of Indian Rishis. Beyond doubt education started first in India. The tradition of earning knowledge was in existence even in the Vedic Age.

THE AIMS OF EDUCATION

1. **Religion.** The literature and culture of ancient India was mostly the means of preaching religion. Religion was predominant in every sphere of life. So it may be said, that ancient India was built up in religious much more than in political, economic and social field. The ancient Indian literature was the vehicle of religions. As has been observed

by Macdonell, "Since the birth of the oldest Vedic poetry we find Indian literature for a period of more than a thousand years bearing an exclusively religious stamp, *i.e.* even those latest productions of the Vedic age which cannot be called directly religious, are yet meant to further religious ends. This is, indeed, implied by the term Vedic, for Veda, primarily signifying knowledge, designates "sacred lore as a branch of literature".

2. **Literature.** Even the literature which was not purely religious had the trend of religious publicity. Ancient Indian education system also developed on the same line. In India the knowledge was not gained only for the sake of knowledge, but it was a means of gaining 'salvation' (Moksha). To quote R. K. Mukerji "Learning in India through the ages had been prized and pursued not for its own sake, if we may so put it but for the sake and as a part of religion. It was sought as the means of salvation or self-realisation, as the means of highest end of life, *viz.*, Mukti or Emancipation." Indeed the ultimate aim of human society of that age was the achievement of Absolute (Brahman), which he himself is, and it was recognised that the entire visible world is fully pervaded with the Absolute (Brahman).
3. **Removal of Ignorance.** It is said that the difference of soul and Absolute is false, it is based on ignorance. A man should engage in Karmopasana *i.e.* worship of work and thus purify his inner senses and attain the 'Absolute'. The welfare of the soul is possible only when the oneness of soul and Absolute is achieved. The ignorance of the relation of Absolute with soul and the world is real ignorance. The soul, though an integral part of the Absolute, has forgotten the whole so it has to be born and die in the world. It is a bondage which cannot be unfastened without full self-realisation and oneness with the Absolute. The souls of all the animate Beings, come in this world to face the consequences of their good or bad deeds. These forget the Absolute, due to ignorance and illiteracy and so bad suffer the miseries. The 'Upanishads' teach the way of 'Salvation' and oneness with Absolute by the destruction of ignorance, which is the cause of all the worldly sufferings. They say that only Absolute is true, and the whole world is false. In this reference Dr. R. K. Mukerji

says, "Theory is that the mind seeking external knowledge contacts and is contaminated and transformed by matter and communicates this contamination to the soul."

4. **Brahman Realisation.** It should also be remembered that according to ancient Indians, education is for the realisation of Brahman in the material world. Material type of knowledge pollutes the soul and thus it forgets its real form. This is the reason that physical knowledge has been called ignorance, which diverts the soul away from the real knowledge of Absolute. Real knowledge is possible only with 'inner meditation' and 'self-realisation'. This knowledge should be heard from the Guru and then it should be meditated over through Nididhyasan. Enlightenment of soul is the way of gaining real knowledge. Thus, finally being set up in his form of self-realisation, man realises the Absolute and achieves the Salvation.
5. **Spiritual Knowledge.** It has been said, "If we really think cool-mindedly, then we find this as the ultimate aim of human life and it is the consequence of the real education." Lord Krishna himself said, "lam the spiritual knowledge among all the knowledge." This knowledge had been taught by the Upanishads. Mundakopanishad says "Ultimate knowledge is that only, which enables one to realise the Absolute. Being acquainted with the Absolute, the soul gets rid of all the worldly sufferings, even the sufferings of taking birth and undergoing death". Various Upanishads have declared their aims in different 'Sutras'. Thus, the central idea of all the Vedic teachings was to follow the action approved by Shastras in the world of duties. The development of Vedic education was based on an organised and thought out scheme with a message to humanity. They were the sources of real education and culture which enabled the proper development of the humanity.

THE FORM OF EDUCATION

Meaning of Vedic Education

Vedic literature includes the Vedic Samhitas, Brahmanas and Aryanyakas (Upanishads) but while considering the Vedic education, it is proper to think over the Vedas only. In his *'Discovery of India'* Pt. Jawaharlal Nehru said, "The Rigveda, the first of the Vedas is probably the earliest book that humanity possesses." The period of Vedic age is now fully recognised by the scholars as about 1500 B. C. to 600 B. C.

Meaning of Vedas

The literal meaning of 'Vedas' is the knowledge and the word is derived from 'Vid' root meaning 'to know'. Thus 'Veda' means the knowledge of various types. Vedas are composed in verses, but some portion of it is written in prose also. Knowledge of Aryan culture is stored in them. Vedic prose is called 'Yajush', verses 'Richa' or 'Rita' and melodious verse Sama. Due to these varieties they are called three Vedas *i.e.* 'Vedatrayee'. Richas and Samasare also called 'Sooktas' meaning fine expression. No doubt they are full of such fine expression.

The Four Vedas

It is said that Vedas were not written in ancient times, and they were traditionally inherited by disciples and also by sons from their teachers (gurus) and fathers. Thus they were preserved orally. Later on in Mahabharat age, they were compiled by 'Krishnadvaipayan' who is also called 'Veda-Vyasa'. He compiled four 'Samhitas', namely 'Rigveda', 'Yajurveda, 'Samaveda' and 'Artharvaveda'. By concluding these their number became 1028. 'Rigveda' is divided into 10 'Mandals' and the name of 'Rishi' and Gods is also given with every 'Sukta'. The general meaning of Rishi is 'mantradrashta'. The seers of hymns were chosen who realised the sense of hymns. Vedic Gods means the Gods who were worshipped along with those particular hymns. The important amongst the 'Rishis of RigVeda' are Gritsamad, Vishwamitra, Vamadeva, Attri, Bharadwaja and Vashishtha, Vaivawasta, Manu, Shiva, Aushinar, Madhuchandra, etc. Amongst the 'Rishis' of 'Vedas' there were some women amongst whom Lopamudra is famous.

Two Branches of Yajurveda

The two branches of 'Yajurveda', namely 'Shukla Yajurveda' and 'Krishna Yajurveda' are available at present. 'Shukla Yajurveda' is also called 'Vajsaneyee Samhita' having two branches as 'Kanva' and 'Madhyandhiya'. Krishna Yajurveda has its four branches as 'Katha Samhita', 'Kapsthal Samhita', 'Maitreyee Samhita' and 'Taittariya Samhita'. Due to the variety of the branches, there are some differences in the hymns, even though, they are compiled separately in the performance of various rituals. The last portion of 'Yajurveda' is 'Ishopanishad' which is related to spiritual meditation instead of performances of the rituals.

Branches of Samaveda

Though 'Puranas' speak of one thousand branches of 'Samaveda', but at present only three — 'Kauthum', 'Shanarniya' and 'Jaimini' are available. Modern scholars recognised the 'Kauthum' branches as more current and reliable. The two parts of 'Samaveda' namely — 'Architaka' and 'Uttararchitaka' have 1,810 hymns, but many of them are repeated and 1,947 hymns are found in 'Rigveda', also. 'Samaveda' has only 75 hymns of its own. Possibly, only those hymns were separately compiled in 'Samaveda' which were sung.

Branches of Atharvaveda

'Atharvaveda' has 'Shaunak' and 'Pippalad' as two branches, in which 'Shaunak' is considered famous and reliable. It has 20 chapters and 731 Suktasand hymns numbering 6,000 but many of them are found even in Rigveda.

SCHEME OF EDUCATION

Since Vedic age education had been put thus "The education is the source of knowledge which shows the real way in the various fields of life". This is approved by the Rigveda statement: "If any one is greater than the other, that does not mean that he has extra bodily organs, but he is great because his intellect and mind have become enlightened and completed by real education." Education system of Vedic age aimed at proper and all round development of humanity.

Composition and Preservation of Hymns

Though Vedic education was carried on verbally, but there were two methods of Vedic education — (i) in first the Rigvedic hymns were composed and (ii) in second they were preserved. The first was based on the inward meditation, which enabled the formation of the hymns and second was based on outward learning method, which enabled the presentation of those hymns. The Rishis, who brought the hymns in spiritual beings were enlightened with the inner light and eternal knowledge. In Vedic age, they were recognised as 'Deva'. In Rigveda, Acharya Guru is called 'Agnipracheta' which means specially learned, Vishvavida *i.e.*

knowing everything (sarvagya), 'Satya-janma' *i.e.* one who knows every thing that is born, Vishwani Deva Yoyunani Vidvan *i.e.* knowing everything, Dhiman Yanta *i.e.* one who gives progress to intellect, etc. These were the qualities attached to the 'Gurus'. Their boundless learning is proved with the fact that they composed the hymns and enabled the development of various knowledge and philosophies. It should also be noted that the symbols of Acharyas were Indra, Agni, etc.

In the beginning Vedic hymns were the traditional heritage of the various families of the Rishis. Thus these hymns were verbally preserved in the families of Vamadeva, Attri, Bhardwaja, Vashishtha, etc.

CENTRES OF EDUCATION

Since the very beginning there were two forms of Vedic education—(i) verbal self-study and (ii) meditation. Vedic hymns were preserved for hundreds of year Vedic Rishis used to cause their sons and grandsons learning hymns by heart. The families of the Rishis were the pathshalas where their sons and grandsons studied. The shape and form of the rituals developed gradually and various methods and systems were introduced, resulting in the admission of other children also as disciples. These were considered as good as their sons. This spiritual education was aided by the ideal background of practical knowledge.

METHODS OF TEACHING

Vedic system of education was psychological. Verbal education was imparted in such a way that it could be preserved for thousands of year In his book *'A Survey of Indian History'* Mr. K. M. Kam said, "A unique degree of verbal authority had been maintained up to this time in the form of the utterances and the 'mantras' of the sacred texts". The hymns were learnt by remembering and they were realised through meditation. The 'Acharya' used to produce the hymns correctly and the students repeated them. Their mistakes were corrected. The sound (Dhvani), words (Shabda) and verses (Chhanda) were pronounced in their original form. Practice made them perfectly efficient, not only in learning the hymns but also in the systematic line of learning.

1. **Correct Pronunciation.** 'Samhitapath', 'Nadpath', 'Jaypath' and 'Gyan path' were practised to keep the hymns entirely correct. There were 52 Dhvanis (sounds) —13 vowels and

39 consonants. The correct pronunciations of all these were attained. Dattatreya Brahman described the three methods of pronunciation as free words, double words and gradual pronunciations.

The people of Vedic age believed that incorrect pronunciation of the hymns caused sin and destroyed their effect. Even an ordinary alteration of sounds or accents alters the actual meaning. *'Panini Shiksha'* mentions that in the sacrifice (Yajna) of Indra or killing Vritrasur, the sound of the hymns were incorrectly pronounced which resulted adversely. Thus due to this definite system of learning of Vedic hymns orally the Mantras were found in their unaltered and original form.

2. **Meditation.** The word 'mantras' means 'born of meditation'. Thus meditation helped preservation of the meanings of the 'mantras' and development of the sound of the disciple. The disciple tried to understand the sense and the echo of the scene by meditation of every word of the hymns. Thus they realised the spiritual elements and their experience. There were students who remembered the hymns by hearing only once and they were called 'Shrudharis'. The hymn says that "I had met such people by myself." The students spent regulated disciplined life in which they kept their senses diverted away from worldly attraction and concentrated on the ultimate knowledge of Absolute. They realised the real light of spiritual knowledge. Being enlightened they entered the society as the 'Guru' of the people.

In Vedic education, meaningless outwardly knowledge has been condemned. A person having meaningless outwardly knowledge has been compared to a donkey loaded with 'Chandan wood'. The mere crammer of Vedic texts has been condemned as Arvak by Rigveda. To maintain the meditation system well the meritorious students were taught its techniques.

Courses of Study

In Vedic period, the courses of study were not limited to religion only. Disciples were also taught Shiksha, Kalpa, Vyakaran, Jyotish, Chhanda and Nirukta, etc. Besides, logic was taught and with its assistance the knowledge of truth was gained. Subjects, which enabled the realisation of self, were mainly taught in these days.

Brahman Sangh

There were the organisations where meritorious students were given chances to fulfil their quest of higher knowledge. These sanghas may be compared to the seminars of the modem times as they had all the traits of these seminars.

Education of other Castes

Vedic education was free to every one. There is mention of such families in which the father is Vaishya, the son Vedic poet, and the mother is a labourer doing grinding. Thus it is clear that the members of all the castes were free to gain their higher education and this statement is supported even by Yajurveda. Similarly there are also evidence in Rigveda that many Rishis of Rigveda were Kshatriyas such as Ambreesh, Trasadayu and Answamedha, etc. The composer of Dattatreya Brahman, Mahidas was the son of a Shudra mother. In short all the four castes were eligible for gaining education in Vedic period. As Mukerji says, "The non-Aryans and depressed classes of these days must have had considerable access to Vedic learning to be able to take part of these sacrifices."

Woman Education

According to Dr. A. S. Altekar, "Home, of course, was the main centre of the education of girls in the domestic science. Women were taking part in every ritual with their husbands. Education of girls were looked after in the same way as that of the boys and many amongst them gained highest education. These were called 'Brahman Vadim' and achieved the status of 'Rishika'. Some of the women were regarded as 'Devis', women even composed hymns. Apala, Homasha, Shashpati, Ghoshala, Mamata, Lopamudra were notable among Vedic scholars."

Women were also given practical and useful education such as spinning, weaving, etc. which is mentioned in 'Rigveda' and 'Atharvaveda'. Word 'Duhita' used for daughter is derived from 'Duh' root and means one who milks the cows, etc. Thus it is clear that women were given 'Shastriya' as well as practical education.

CHARACTERISTICS OF EDUCATION IN VEDIC AGE

1. **Gurukula.** R. N. Tagore says, "A most wonderful thing we notice in India is that here the forest not the town is the foundation of all its culture." In Vedic age, the words

were sent to 'Gurukulas' or the homes of the 'Acharyas' for education, just after the Upanayan' ritual they were called 'Antevasin' or Gurukula wasee. Now they led a life of chastity and purity serving the Acharya and gaining knowledge. Naturally they acquired many qualifications of the teacher. Only 'Brahmacharis' were allowed in 'Gurukulas'. The Gurukulas were free from the Government control and influence. Dr. A. S. Altekar remarked, "The Gurukula system which necessitated the stay of the student away from his home at the home of the teacher or in boarding house of established reputation, was one of the most important features of ancient Indian education."

2. **Ideal of Teacher.** Teachers in the Vedic age were men of the highest caliber from the point of view of knowledge and spiritual progress. They possessed the influence like fire (Agni) and chivalry like 'Indra'. They emerged in high reputation. Living in their 'Ashramas' they paid attention to the spiritual development of student's thoughts. They kept them like their sons. They managed for their food and lodging. They helped them in need. Thus, the teachers owned every responsibility of the taught. Gurus always tried to develop the qualities of his students to make them higher than himself.
3. **Duties of Disciples (Shishyas).** Following were the duties of the students who lived in Gurukula: (a) A student had to do the service of the 'Guru' and necessary jobs of keeping the 'Gurukula' tidy. He also prepared the necessities for the rituals (Yajnas) and grazed the cows of the 'Gurus'. (b) He had to go out for alms. This created the spirit of meekness and generosity in them, (c) Living in 'Gurukulas' the students slept on the ground, took simple food and obeyed the 'Guru' in all respects, (d) His main duty was to study and they very gently learnt and attended to the instructions of the 'Guru'.

   Thus it is clear that while living in 'Gurukula' the student life was of an ideal student, a simple and well regulated life.
4. **'Guru' and 'Shishyas' Relation.** In Vedic age, the relation between the Guru and the Shishyas was just like that of father and son. "Guru, very affectionately looked after his taughts." He never let them suffer in any way and always

tried for their all round development and the students also tried to satisfy the teacher and so far as possible did not give any ground for displeasure to him.

5. **Suitable Age of Education.** Dr. A. S. Altekar says, "Ancient Indians were convinced that no good result could follow if education is begun late in life therefore, they insisted that education ought to commence in childhood." In Vedic period education started in early life. They thought it essential to begin the education in early age, for the full development of inner and outer talents of the students.
6. **Perfection in Education.** The full knowledge of particular subject was aimed at after the general knowledge of various needful subjects.
7. **Multiple Course of Study.** The Vedic students were taught the four Vedas by heart. Side by side they studied Shiksha, Kalpa, Vyakaran, Jyotish, Chhanda, Nirukta and logic in general. They specialised in one subject. From the view of courses of study Vedic education was pluralistic.
8. **Prominence of Religious Education.** About Vedic education, T. N. Siqueira says, "Education was meant to be a religious initiation. The teacher had to teach the pupil how to parry, to offer sacrifice, to perform his duties according to his stage of life. Indian education was essentially religious and personal." Ancient education was dominated by religion. The courses of study were mostly related to religion aiming at generation of kindness, forgiveness, perseverance, nobleness, etc. in students.
9. **Emphasis on Character Building.** Vedic teacher thought that if the students would learn good habits from their early life, their future would be peaceful and happy. Regulated daily routine was considered essential for the cultivation of good habits. They had to get up early in the morning, perform the daily rituals, speak the truth, live simply and behave properly with everyone.
10. **Psychological System.** The Vedic education system was psychological. Two systems were encouraged in that age — verbal and meditative. The teacher and taught were both sincere. Students put forward their doubts before the teacher who tried to remove them well. Side by side, self-study and meditation was also encouraged so that the students might

realise the meaning and sense of the lesson. 'Samavartan' rituals was performed at completion of education. It was more or less like convocation of the universities.

11. **Equal Opportunity to Gain Education.** In Vedic period every one was allowed to gain higher education without distinction of caste or creed. There are some evidences in Vedic literature that some Rishis were born of Shudra mother or father.
12. **Women Education.** Women education also received proper attention in Vedic age with the result that soon women became Rishikas. They composed hymns. They used to take part in religious rituals. They were also taught practical and useful handicrafts and household duties.
13. **Physical Education.** Though the Vedic education was religious yet useful and needful subjects for general public were not neglected, people could gain the education of various arts and crafts side by side. Agriculture, animal husbandry, etc. also developed well. The Rigveda mentions about some cities where these arts were in practical use and people were aware of these sciences. The sea trade was also practised in those days. Thus in Vedic age education had its international form, as well as national form.

To conclude, the aim of Vedic education was lofty. It aimed at providing full opportunity for the development of human traits to enable students to get full opportunity to develop themselves. Thus Vedic education was fully capable of character-building, development of various branches of knowledge and leading to economic prosperity.

QUESTIONS FOR EXERCISE

1. Explain the meaning and ideals of Vedic education. Which agencies carried out Vedic education?
2. "There is no country other than India, where quest of knowledge has enrooted itself as deeply and so rapidly that the keen desire of gaining knowledge had produced so permanent and violent influence." On the basis of the above statement of Prof. F. W. Thomas, explain with suitable examples, the aims and form of education adopted in ancient India.
3. Describe the characteristics of Vedic education.

CHAPTER 2

POST-VEDIC EDUCATION

Post-Vedic period extends between 1400 B.C. and 600 B.C. or from the end of Rigvedic period to the beginning of Buddhism and Jainism. In Vedic period austerity and sacrifices had a prominent place. With the spread of Vedic culture, the sacrificial rituals dominated and the Brahman priests gained the highest position in Indian society. The priests were divided into four categories to carry out the ritual duties as follows:

1. **Hotri.** They were also called 'Hota' and they used to recite the prayers of Indra, Agni, Varuna, etc. In their invitational prayers they visualized the Gods.
2. **Udgata.** These priests recited only the 'Mantras' of some Yajna.
3. **Adhawaryu.** These priests performed different practical duties of the rituals.
4. **Brahman.** These priests looked after all the activities of the rituals.

Prominent of the rituals influenced post-Vedic education system. The general aim of Vedic education was to serve the means of 'salvation' *i.e.* 'Moksha'. Even in Brahmanic age, this very aim remained intact. But it naturally got more connected with rituals. The ritual system and activities, with their practical knowledge, took place of 'self-realisation and austeric-meditation' in the Brahmanic age. Vedic students began to lay stress on it. This new development had adverse effect on spiritual meditation, yet it led to a substantial improvement in education. It resulted in the discoveries of various new spheres of knowledge and Physical Science. Handicrafts, Geometry, Arithmetic and Astronomy, etc., were improved to a great extent. Shaping of materials, selection of place, construction of altar (Vedi) and their measurement, proportional shaping and decision of suitable time and place for the rituals were responsible for this learning. Physiology was also introduced side by side. Practical and useful subjects in post-Vedic period increased the importance of Brahmanic education. Brahmanas, Aranyakas and Upanishads were mostly developed in post-Vedic period through these sources. We can have some knowledge about the educational system of post-Vedic period as follows:

1. **Brahmanas Literature.** Brahmana books were second to Vedas. These consisted of the methods of rituals and meanings of the Mantras in prose. They dealt with the performance of various methods of different rituals called 'Vishi'. 'Atharvaveda' consists of the explanation of hymns and stories and description of chivalry of kings, etc. These may be called the books of priests.

Following are worth mentioning among the available Brahmanas:

1. 'Attreya' and 'Kaushitaki' related to 'Rigveda'.
2. 'Samaveda' related to Tandya.
3. Taittariya and Shatpath Brahman related to 'Yajurveda'.
4. Gopath related to 'Atharvaveda'.

2. **Aranyakas.** Aranyaka books are appendices of Brahmanas. They used to be at the end of each 'Brahmana', they were written for those Sanyasis who were devoted to spiritual meditation and lived in lonely forest. They deal with theoretical and philosophical aspects of the rituals in the style and language of 'Brahmanas'.
3. **Upanishads.** Indian spiritualism has reached its zenith in 'Upanishads'. The Western scholars like Schaupenhauer, Max-Mullar, MacDonald, etc., have praised the minute philosophical analysis of the 'Upanishads'. Such a minute and clear description of God and Brahman is not found in any other culture of the world. To quote Mr. Schaupenhauer, "It is destined sooner or later to become the faith of the people." In his book *'Philosophy of the Upanishads'* he said, "Its philosophical conceptions unequalled in India or perhaps any where else in the world." MacDonald said,' "'Brahma' or Absolute is grasped and definitely expressed for the first time in the history of the human thought in the Brihadaranyak Upanishad."

Scholars have given different interpretations to the word 'Upanishad'. These are as follows.

(1) Upanishads are the books that deal with the spiritual knowledge and Absolute. (2) These enable a man to realise oneness with Brahman. (3) Upanishad is that knowledge which enables one to gain the absolute knowledge (Brahma Vidya). (4) That which enables the nearness or oneness with Absolute God and destroys the illusion and its effect. (5) The study of that divine knowledge which enables one to sit near the Absolute (God, Brahman). (6) Upanishads are the books which deal with the divine or absolute knowledge ('Brahman'). (7) Literally, Upanishad means sitting down near. Thus these books were written in a particular way. They were meant for meritorious students, who after finishing their general education secretly, studied the mysteries of spiritualism.

Intellectual Trend

In *Ancient Indian Education* Dr. R. K. Mukerji said, "The expression Upanishad literally means sitting down near and indicates confidential session in which the secret or estoric doctrines were taught to the selected pupils towards the close of the studentship." The student not satisfied with general knowledge of Gurukulas and who wanted to have higher spiritual knowledge used to go to the 'Ashramas' to eminent spiritual scholars and continued the studies further. Thus the trend of Vedic education system diverted towards meditation in the 'Upanishad', propagated that the Absolute (Brahman) cannot be achieved by rituals, but by self and inward meditation. True knowledge was recognised as the means of salvation or Moksha merging of self with Absolute was called salvation or Moksha.

This intellectual trend of Uparishads resulted in the development of 'Vyakarana' 'Shiksha', 'Kalpa', 'Chhanda' and 'Jyotish'. Vedangas aimed at the actual understanding of the meaning of the Veda-mantras. 'Nirukta' by 'Yaska' is one of the most important work. It deals with the meaning of the world in simple prose. It was written about sixth century B. C. Panini's Vyakaran gave a refined shape to Sanskrit language.

AIMS OF EDUCATION

1. **Realisation of True Knowledge.** According to this ideal the education enables the realisation of true knowledge and

achievement of Absolute (Brahman). Real knowledge is the realisation of the ultimate relation of soul, Absolute and the world. This is not possible by sensuous knowledge of worldly matters which pollutes the soul and makes it forget its real form.

2. **Realisation of the Absolute.** In this period, the education was considered to be a process of inward meditation and thinking. Inquisitive students used to concentrate all their senses in inner meditation diverted from outwardly attraction and tried to realise the Absolute (Brahman).

Thus post-Vedic education was not meant only for the sake of education. It was for the sake of life. It has been rightly said in Mundkopanishad, "After achievement of real knowledge, all the doubts get destroyed and thus it enables the realisation of Absolute (Brahman), and therefore, it makes it possible to fulfil the ultimate end of human life." Self study was emphasised in post-Vedic period.

Upanishads are known as 'Para-Vidya'. They were considered to be above all the knowledge (Vidyas). This knowledge enables the unity of soul and Absolute. The knowledge of the things which does not bring about the union of the soul with Absolute has no value. It does not deserve to be called knowledge. As the subjects of study increased, a student was not expected to read all of one subject and allied literature. The student who studied three Vedas was called 'Shrotriya'. It was said that real knowledge could be gained only through the study of three 'Vedas'. The study of 'Veda' had been divided into various branches and branches into various sections. In post-Vedic period the trend of specialised study was rather common and emphasised.

Duration of Study

Though the course of study during Upanishadic period has much increased yet the period of study remained the same. It was twelve years as in the Vedic period. Svatketu had studied for twelve years with his Guru Satyakam Jabal. He had lighted Yajnagni *i.e.* sacrificial fire and served the cows of his Guru.

METHODS OF EDUCATION

(i) Shravan (learning), (ii) Manan (Meditation), and (iii) Nididhyasan (realisation and experience) were the three methods prevalent in Brihdaranayaka Upanishad in post-Vedic period.

These have been termed as three stages of education.

1. **Self Meditation and Study.** The students were given verbal lessons and guidance by the Guru and they studied and meditated over it. Thus they got them to heart. Through experience they realised their truth and utility. Thus, by selfmeditation the disciple made the knowledge as his own. He gained the realisation through self-meditation and study. While giving short outline of Absolute knowledge to his disciple Bhrigu said that he would gain extensive knowledge of Absolute by self-study and realisation. After the use of this method of meditative self-realisation, Bhrigu, was able to gain self-achieved knowledge of 'Absolute'.
2. **Question-Answer Method.** Besides this method, there also prevailed the question-answer method in those days. It was during this period that this method came in vogue. In Kenopanishad, the disciple asked the teacher that what is that guiding force that drives the heart, spirit, eye and ears to action and it is there that the Guru guided Shishya. The words of the Guru were delivered a lecture regarding Brahman or also led to encouraging and that it created an environment of study and made the mind attentive.
3. **Enigmatic Method.** The best illustration of the enigmatic method is found in the *Svetasvatar* Upanishad, where it is said that Reality is like a great circumscribing felly whose tyres are the three Gunas, whose ends are the sixteen kalas, whose spokes are the fifty Bhavas or conditions of Samkhya philosophy, whose counter-spokes are the ten senses and their ten objects, whose six sets of eight are such as the eight Dhatus, and eight-fold Prakrti and so on, whose rope is the Cosmic Person, whose three paths are the Good, the Bad and the Indifferent or yet the Moral, the Immoral and Amoral, and finally which causes the single infatuation of the ignorance of self on account of the two causes, namely good and bad works. Puzzles can also be found in *Isavasyopanishad* and other Upanishads.
4. **Aphoristic Method.** Aphoristic method of Upanishads has been widely used in the later philosophical treatises as well. In this method, much knowledge is compressed

in small aphoristic sentences, which require sufficient intelligence to understand them. It is for this reason that the same sentences have been interpreted differently, by different commentators. In the *Madukya Upanishad* it has been said,' The syllable Om is verily all that exists. Under it is included all the past, the present and future, as well as that which transcends time. Verily, all this is Brahman. The Atman is Brahman. This Atman is four-footed. The first foot is the Vaiswanar, who enjoys gross things... in the state of wakefulness. The second is the Taijasa, who enjoys exquisite things... in the state of dream. The third is the Prajna who enjoys bliss in the state of deep sleep, the fourth is the Atman who is alone, without a second, calm, holy and tranquil." This passage has been differently interpreted by different systems of Vedantic philosophy.

5. **Etymological Method.** In the etymological method, the meaning of the word is explained according to its root. In the *Brihadaranyaka Upanishad* we are told that 'purusa is really Purisaya' *i.e.* inhabiting the citadel of heart. Examples like this can be seen in other Upanishads also.
6. **Mythical Method.** Mythical method has been mostly used in the teaching in Upanishads, *e.g.* in the Kena Upanishad, the parable of the Indra and demons has been told to preach humanity. Sometimes the myth is introduced for aetiological purpose, as for example the myth of the sun coming out of the huge world egg. Sometimes one finds the transcendental myth, *e.g.* in the Aitereya Upanishad, it is said, how the Atman entered the human skull and became individualised as the human soul. Similarly, a myth is sometimes introduced for the sake of parody also.
7. **Analogical Method.** Things which cannot be explained by reasoning are explained by analogy, *e.g.* Yajnavalkya introduces the analogy of the drum of the conch in order to explain the processes of the apprehension of the self. Aruni explains the non-difference of the apprehension of the self and individual soul from the universal soul by the analogy of the juices in constituting honey or the rivers in flowing into the ocean and being merged into it.
8. **Dialectical Method.** The dialectical method is one of the most widely used methods of the Upanishads. In this method,

the philosophers assembled at some place and dramatically discussed different problems among themselves. In the Upanishads such discussions and symposiums have been mentioned at many places.

9. **Synthetic Method.** In the synthetic method, the discussion of the dialectical method is substituted by the creative synthesis of the synthetical method. In the fourth chapter of the Brihadaranyaka Upanishad, Yajnavalkya synthesise the several standpoints explained by the king Janak. Examples like this can be found in Chandogya, Prasna and other Upanishads.
10. **Monologic Method.** Though the philosophers of the Upanishads speak very seldom but when they speak, sometimes they forget the presence of others and go on talking to themselves for a long time. In the Brihadaranyaka Upanishad, Yajnavalkya, replying to the questions of the king Janak, regarding the nature of the soul, is lost in self-speech. In the Kathopanishad in the discussion of Yama and Nachiketa, Yama goes on talking to himself for a long time while replying to the third question of Nachiketa.
11. **Ad hoc or Temporising Method.** The teachers of the Upanishads taught the disciple according to his mental and psychological level. In the temporising method, as the spiritual level of the inquirer increases, the teacher not only shows him the path ahead, but tells him the whole truth at once. This method has been accepted as very much important by the modern psychology of education as well. In the famous parable of Indra and Virochana, Virochana is satisfied by the first answer of the teacher Prajapati, but Indra is not satisfied and goes on questioning. Prajapati tells him the secret of soul first in the body, then in the dream and sleeping stages and it is after that alone that he tells him the nature of soul. In this method, the inquirer himself struggles to understand the truth and the teacher only guides him. Hence this method is very much important in the spiritual evolution.
12. **Regressive Method.** The regressive method is in the form of many successive questions in which every new question carries us behind the answer to the previous one. Thus when Janak asked Yajnavalkya about the light of man,

Yajnavalkya told that it was the sun. Janak went behind answer after answer, carrying from the fire to the Atma, which exists behind them all as the light-in-itself. In the same Upanishad, the regressive method has been used in the discussion between Yajnavalkya and Gargi.

AGENCIES OF EDUCATION

1. **Branch or Shakha.** Acharya Sayana has given a commentary on the three branches of 'Veda' only, but later on this word 'Shakha' began to denote various branches of all the 'Vedas' that had grown in various 'Gurukulas' or seats of learning. Since the Vedas were prescribed orally, some changes in the original form were inevitable. Therefore, if at one place some changes took place in the pronunciation of hymns, only original hymns remained at other place. While at the third place some new hymns were added and so on. At certain places all these changes took place simultaneously. Thus different versions of 'Vedas' were preserved in various 'Gurukulas' and the expansion of these branches was not limited to Vedas. The branches of Brahmans as relating to these branches were also changed and evolved.
2. **Charnas.** Generally, branches and chamas are taken as synonyms but they differ much. According to Panini only a group of disciples who studied in one branch or Shakha was charan. In '*Malatimadhav*' of Jogdhar, Charan has been defined as such individuals, who study particular branch of Vedas and form a group. Such a group of students is called 'charan'. The number of chamas differed from time to time. In the days of Panini there were 24 stages and Panini in his 'sutras' has given their names as well.
3. **Parishad.** The word 'parishad' means all things expanded on all sides. In 'Upanishads' the word has been used for a conference of learned men assembled for deliberations upon the philosophical problems. Later on, the parishads were set up at the places where learned 'Brahmanas' lived in good numbers and gradually these institutions became permanent. They used to establish high principles of philosophy and impart knowledge.

   Indeed the member of any 'charans' might be the member of a parishad. It used to consider the high philosophical facts and lay down new theories. The 'Parishad' was not limited to any particular 'Veda', but it had a wide vision. There are precedences that the member of various 'charans' might be the member of one 'Parishad' and also the different members of one 'charan' might be members of different 'Parishad'. Therefore, modern universities might be taken as the representatives of these parishads where the students received higher education. According to Dr. R. K. Mukerji, "We may say in modern phraseology that a 'Parishad' corresponds to a university comprising students belonging to different colleges called charans."

4. **Gotra or Kula.** Gotra or Kula was based on family traditions which might be real or imaginary. Various 'Gotras' or 'Kulas' related to ancient 'Rishis' as their ancestor or forefather. Methods of education, rules and traditions of that Rishi were observed in that particular 'Gotra' or 'Kula'. Thus, the members of all the three castes Brahmanas, Kshatriyas, and Vaishyas recognised some Rishi as their original forefather. Even at present, 'Gotra', has an important place in Hindu society. It is an important consideration at the time of marriage. Actually there are eight Gotras—Jamdagni, Gautam, Bharadwaja, Vishwamitra, Vashishtha, Attri, Kashyap, and Shandilya. These were further divided, and later on again subdivided. These small sub-divisions may be called families only. Generally all the 'Brahmans' are said to be descendants of Bhrigu, Angrish, Vishwamitra, Vashishta, Kashyap, Attri, Agastya and Shandilya, etc.

VALEDICTORY FUNCTION

After completing education and at the time when the students were to leave Gurukula for their homes to enter into family life, 'Gurus' gave them final instructions and advised in order to guide them in their future life. The original form of 'Samavartan' instruction was as follows:

"Always speak the truth, fulfil your duties, never ignore self study. Do not break the ancestral and old traditions after giving Dakshina to Acharya. Never go away from truth. Never leave Dharma. Do not ignore the useful works. Do not miss the opportunity of becoming great. Never be careless in duties towards Gods and forefathers."

"Treat mother as Goddess, and father as God. Treat Acharya (Teacher) as God (Deva). Treat guest (Athithi) as God (Deva). Always perform deeds free from faults, not others. Imitate the good deeds that have been done and not others. Some Brahmans are greater than I. You would respect them by giving them suitable place. Whatever gift you give, give it with full regard and respect and with pleasure and humility. Give with fear and kindness."

"If any doubt arises in your mind regarding Religion or good conduct, then take advice from the Brahmans, who are dispassionate, noble and tender hearted and fit the purpose and follow as they do. This is my instruction to you, you follow it. You follow it in this very form."

These instructions are like the torch-light guidance for the student to make his future family life fully useful and successful and every word is full of confidence and good wishes of the Guru. It gives the light which might enlighten the social life of the Shishya. R. K. Mukerji has rightly pointed out, "These words read almost like chancellor's convocation address of modern universities."

EDUCATION FOR DIFFERENT SECTIONS

Education of Kshatriyas

In Vedic age, caste system was mostly based on occupational basis, but in post-Vedic period, it began to be established on ancestral basis and so, naturally various social groups sprang up. While on the one hand, the domination of 'Brahmans' was on the increase on the other hand 'Vaishyas' and 'Shudras' were falling down in social status. Great agricultural groups Vaishyas had begun to divide into functional groups as Chariotmakers, Blacksmiths, Carpenters, etc. They became new castes. Later on 'Shudras' began to lose their social respect till finally they were regarded as untouchables.

This system affected the education system in general. Brahmans were mainly authorised for Vedic-study and of spiritual knowledge but some Kshatriyas had also become great 'Rishi' just as learned philosophers like Janak, etc. Similarly many other Kshatriya kings had also gained spiritual knowledge and tried for salvation (Mukti), *e.g.* the prominence of spiritual knowledge of king Ajatashatru of Kashi was recognised and honoured by Gargeya, Balaki and various other Brahman Acharyas.

No Education for Lower Castes

In post-Vedic age, no reference is found about the education of 'Vaishyas' and 'Shudras'. The aim of the life of 'Vaishyas' was laid down as agriculture, trade and commerce. They used to gain their education in the art of production of grains and other useful material and arrange for their distribution. They did not take any interest in the intellectual education. The condition of shudras was even worse. They had to serve the three higher castes. They used to work in the field as labourers and plough the fields, tame the animals and do some handicrafts, etc. They also took interest in dancing, music, etc. However, Shudras were not free to get 'Vedic' knowledge now as they could in Vedic age.

Women Education

The women in post-Vedic period were not enjoying the social and educational privileges as they did in Vedic age. Neither could they freely participate in social functions, nor could they inherit the family property. However, their religious position was quite safe. They could participate with their husbands in all the rituals. They were authorised to gain higher education and spiritual knowledge. They used to participate in religious conferences. In the conference organised by Janaka, the famous discussion between Yajnavalkya and Gargi is well known. One of the two wives of Yajnavalkya was Maitreyee. She was very learned and she used to clear the doubts of her husband at times.

In Upanishadic period, women were working even as teachers. They were trained in dancing, music, fine arts, etc. To quote Dr. R. K Mukerji: "Women were taught some of the fine arts like dancing and singing, which were regarded as accomplishments unfit for men."

TYPES OF EDUCATION

1. **Practical Education.** Post-Vedic practical education had four main constituents —
    1. Bhikshatan (Alms).
    2. Keeping 'yajnagni' (sacrificial fire).
    3. Taming the animals of the Ashram.
    4. Cultivation.

    Bhikshatan (going out) for alms cultivated modesty in the disciple. Keeping 'Yajnagni' enlightened the spiritual light of his mind. Service of the land and animal maintained his health and sound character.

2. **Mental Education.** Mental education had three states: (i) *'Shravan'* (hearing), (ii) *Manan* (meditation), and (iii) *'Nididhyasan'* (realisation). Mental education was based on feelings and experiences. It has been said in Dattatreya Aranyaka that while pronouncing the 'Mahabharata (teaching) neither the Guru nor the Shishya should keep standing or walking or lying, but they should attentively sit on Kushasan. Self-study had been called 'Brahman Yajna.' The student should never be careless in self-study. Mental education aimed at self-study.
3. **Moral Education.** Moral education was related to the practice of good behaviour and pondering over useful instructions. The disciple had to lead the life of a Brahmachari. He had to observe certain special practical exercises to keep the purity of the character. He had to take very simple and pious food. Anger, amusement or recreation, jealousy, pride, etc., had to be kept away. He had to keep his mind calm and peaceful and concentrate on his studies. He had to put on simple clothes and no decoration of the body. Either he had to keep all the hairs or get them all shaved. *In Manav Dharmashastra* it has been said that the student should avoid intoxicating drinks, meat, using scented things, rich food, killing of animals, using oils or other luxurious things, intercourse with women, desire for good things, greediness and telling a lie, etc. The guru also tried to improve the character of the students.

CURRICULUM

Sarad Sanatkumar Sambad mentioned in Chhandogya Upanishad throws some light on the curriculum prescribed. Students in that period were taught the four Vedas — Rigveda, Yajurveda, Samaveda, and Atharvaveda, the Itihas-Purana, the grammar of Vedas, Shraddha, Kalp, Arithmetic, Godly knowledge, Vidhishastra, Ekayam, Demonology, Spiritualism, Chattra Vidya, Astronomy, snake charming, dancing and singing, etc. Narad knew all these things. The conversation of Yagyvalakya and Maitreyee mentions all the four Vedas and Itihas Purana Vidya, Kalpa Sutra, Mantra, etc.

MITHILA — SEAT OF LEARNING

In the Upanishadic age Mithila was a prominent seat of Brahmanical system of education. It was named as Videh. Here Janak used to hold religious conferences, wherein learned Rishis and Pandits took part in the religious discussions. Later on, this place produced devotees of Lord Krishna. Famous poet Vidyapati who had written in Hindi and Jaideo who was a prominent poet of Sanskrit literature were born here. Jagdhar had written commentaries on Shrimadbhagwagita, Devi Mahatmya, Meghdut, Geet Govind and Malatimadhava, etc.

From the 12th century to 15th century, Mithila had been an important centre of learning and culture. Besides literature and fine arts, scientific subjects were also taught there. There was also a Nyaya Vidyalaya. The Pandits of this centre gave a new shape to Nyaya Shastra, named as Navya Nyaya. Mithila was renowned throughout the whole sub-continent. Mithila was famous for its Pandits of Nyaya and Tark Shastra and their learning attracted the students from various parts of the country. The glory of Mithila remained unquestioned up to Mughal period.

The snatakas (Graduates) of Mithila were strictly examined and degrees were given to successful candidates. After the end of the study, the last examination was conducted. This examination is described like this — A needle was pierced in the book and the student was asked to explain the page where the needle stopped. It meant that the student should be well prepared throughout the whole book.

THE IMPORTANT PLACE OF THE TEACHER

During this period the teacher enjoyed a predominant place in his Gurukul and in the entire society. He showered all love and affection on his pupils and used to teach them whatever he knew. But before doing this he always tested the ability of a particular pupil. The pupils were free to discuss various points with the Guru. One finds many examples of free discussion between the teacher and his taught. For an example, Brahma gave Bhrigu the knowledge of the ultimate of Absolute in an outline form and advised him to perceive the same through thinking and meditation. Bhrigu accepted this advice and realised Absolute on the basis of the same.

Daily Routine of Students

During the post-Vedic period the Ashramas (Schools) were generally organised and run by Gurus (preceptors). It was compulsory to adhere to the rules of discipline and conduct laid down in Ashramas. No distinction was made between students in this respect. Every one was required to observe celibacy. Rules of conduct were enforced keeping in view the physical, mental and moral development of students. Strict adherence to rules of conduct and discipline was an inseparable aspect of education in those days. This is as follows:

(i) *Practical Education.* Practical education consisted of three parts: to beg alms, to prepare fire for the Yajna-kund and to look after the animals and other fellow-beings of the Ashrama (School). Beside, the students were also expected to do some agricultural work. There were varying aims of all these three aspects of practical education. Begging of alms was meant to teach politeness. Preparing of fire for the Yajna-kund signified mental development of students. Rearing up Ashrama animals and doing agricultural work were meant to make the students self-dependent. Thus to inculcate the quality of practicalness was the chief aim of practical education.

(ii) *Mental Development.* Hearing, thinking and meditation were the three parts of mental education. All these three aspects were considered necessary for full mental development. Thinking over the heard things and perception through meditation were the accepted methods of mental development.

(iii) *Moral Education.* Leading a disciplined and controlled life is the real basis of moral education. Moral education affects the conduct of the individual. Oral instruction alone cannot improve one's conduct. Observance of celibacy was considered necessary for good conduct.

The Teacher-Taught Relationship

During the post-Vedic period the teacher-taught relationship was of the ideal nature. The teacher was the protector of the student in all circumstances. He was very much respected by the student. He occupied a more dignified place than the father. The student was like a son for the teacher who consistently thought and endeavoured for his development. It was the sacred duty of the student to render service to the teacher. The student was always ready to execute any command of the teacher with all humility. During this period special attention was paid to the analysis of the essential truth. However, Yajnas still occupied a prominent place in the Ashrama, Rituals were attached less importance. To arrange for boarding and lodging for the student was the responsibility of the teacher. He used to nurse the student when he fell ill.

The Teacher's Place in Society

The teacher enjoyed a dignified place in the ancient Indian society. During the Vedic and post-Vedic periods his place was second to that of God only. He was more respected than the king in society. The Guru-Ashrama was known as the Gurukul (the family of the teacher). The Guru was regarded as a Rishi (Sage) or Acharya (the one who practises what he professes). He was given this significant place, because without him it was impossible to attain knowledge. He was the guide and could help anyone to carve out his course of action. He used to bring light wherever there was darkness. Thus the people always felt his necessity whenever there was a difficulty in solving any issue or problem. During the Upanishadic period, when self-study was considered as dignified, the place of Guru in society remained intact. No knowledge could come without the assistance from the Guru. The attainment of salvation was not possible without the help of the Guru.

Restrictions on Teachers

The teacher was expected to lead a life of penance free of worldly things. He, too, was required to follow all the rules of strict discipline, thinking and meditation which were prescribed for the students. One finds many references to such a position in the Maitrayan Upanishad. After the demise of the Guru if his son was not considered worthy of the same one of his disciples could succeed him.

Faith in the Teacher

It was compulsory for the students to have full faith in the teacher. Only those students were considered as deserving of attaining real knowledge of supreme truth who had full faith in the teacher. The student was always in search of a real Guru for attaining real knowledge. The Guru on the other hand wanted to find out a really deserving student who he could give all that he knew.

Convocation Address

After receiving education for twelve years the students used to assemble near their teacher (Acharya) for blessings before going home. On this occasion the Acharya used to give some advices for happy and smooth running of their future life. The teacher used to tell them how to lead a life of householder (Grihastha), how to take care of the society and the nation and how to serve the humanity as a whole. The teacher used to tell all these in a ceremony known as Samvartan Samaroha like the modern convocation address.

QUESTIONS FOR EXERCISE

1. "The Education system of post-Vedic period (Upanishad period) had comparatively more developing trend than Vedic education." Discuss the above statement with suitable examples.
2. What was the aim of Upanishadic education? Show the importance of the teacher in education.
3. Explain the methods and agencies of education in post-Vedic period.
4. Describe the post-Vedic education for different sections and of different types.
5. Write short note on Mithila — Seat of Learning.
6. Distinguish between the nature of education during the Rigvedic and post-Vedic periods. In what sense the system was similar in the two periods?
7. What aspects of the Vedic and post-Vedic systems of education should we incorporate in our modern system of education and why?

CHAPTER 3

BRAHMANIC EDUCATION

Vedas are divided into two parts, namely, Samhita, the collection of Mantras and Brahmanas in which these mantras have been explained. The main aim of Brahmanas was to give details of the sacrifices (Yajnas). Brahmana books have been sub-divided into three sections — Brahmanas, Aranyakas and Upanishads. The spiritual aspects of sacrifices are dealt with in Aranyakas and they are useful for Vanprastha Ashram, when people spent their lives in lonely forests. Higher spiritual study of these books was possible only in places distant from the hum-drum of life. But Brahmanas were useful for common people. Upanishads were the last part of Vedic literature. They are called 'Vedanta'.

In Vedic Samhitas — Rigveda, Samaveda, Yajurveda and Atharvaveda — were followed by Brahmanas. Some scholars have found the seeds of Vedangas in the Brahmanas.

The Brahmanas and Aranyakas vary according to the branches of every Veda. Aitereya and Kaushitaki are the two Brahmanas of Rigveda, out of which Aitereya is very prominent. In the same way Aitereya Aranyaka and Sankhyayana are the two Aranyakas of Rigveda. Samaveda has many Brahmanas and Tashandh is considered to be the best among them. It is also called Panchvinash. Taittariya Brahman and Tattariya Aranyaka are related to black Yajurveda, whereas the famous Shatpatha Brahmana is related to Shukla Yajurveda. It is considered to be the most important after Rigveda. Gopatha Brahman is related to Atharvaveda. It is considered to be a new work on Brahmanic literature.

AIM OF EDUCATION

In his book named '*History of Indian Education, Ancient and Later Times*' F. E. Keay, observes, "Not only did Brahmana education develop a system of education which survived the crumbling empires and the changes of the society, but they also through all these thousands of years, kept a glow of the torch of higher learning, and numbered amongst them many great thinkers who have left their mark not only on the learning of India, but upon the intellectual life of the world." This shows the aim of Brahmanic education. It is similar to the aim of Vedic education when the education was considered to be the means of gaining knowledge. The Acharyas of Vedic period had declared that a man without the knowledge is like an animal. Education was related with every aspect of life. Its main aim was all round development of human life, *i.e.*, the physical, mental and spiritual development of human life.

In Vedic education emphasis had been laid on the religious aspect of education, but the Brahmanic education included worldly aspect as well. The aim of education was to achieve self-reliance, self-control, formation of character, individual development, knowledge of social and civil life, and preservation of national culture with the physical development.

PRINCIPLES OF EDUCATION

The main principles of Brahmanic education were as follows:

1. **Age of Education.** Brahmanic education was very particular about the age of starting education. It started just after the 'Upanayan' ritual which was performed between four and nine years of age. After it, the boy was sent to Guru for the study.
2. **Whole Time Living in Gurukula.** The disciple lived in direct contact of the Acharya Guru in the Gurukula who treated him like his own son. The Guru's undertook all the responsibilities of their taught in regard to the boarding, lodging, etc. The disciple became a member of his family. Thus, the Guru got sufficient opportunity to study the mental capacities of the student and to develop them properly.
3. **Regulated Routine.** The daily routine of the student was regulated. As a rule the student went to bed early and got up early. The motto before him was simple living and high thinking. A sense of discipline grew up among the disciples. 'Bathing, Yajna, Poojan, Bhiksha (going out for alms), serving the Guru, reading Vedas, etc. formed the daily routine of students.

4. **Character Building.** Brahmanic education paid a good deal of attention to the formation of character of the students. Atharvaveda goes to the extent of saying that proper rearing, education and suitable environment can bring everything to the student.
5. **Strict Celibacy.** The students were supposed to maintain strict celibacy. It has been said that after Upanayan ritual, the boy is reborn as a Brahmachari and spends a new life in that form. Thus the student life was a life of austerity and strict control of the senses and the mind. This led to the proper development of the personality of the students.
6. **Specialisation.** Though Brahmanic education prepared the students for the entire life in its fullness, yet the tendency towards the specialisation had grown up.
7. **Individual Teaching.** Instead of collective teaching, individual teaching prevailed in Brahmanic education. Thus, the chances for the development of inner talents of the students were fully utilised and the education could be made useful for the life.
8. **Practical Education.** Brahmanic education was not only theoretical. It gave practical knowledge to face the struggles of life and become successful in the future career.
9. **Wide Curriculum.** In Brahmanic education, the course of study was much more vast than that of Vedic period. Besides all the four Vedas, the study of Itihas-Puranas, Vyakaran, Arithmetic, Shraddha-Kalp, Astrology, Ethics, Demonology, Yajurveda, Snake charming, etc. were undertaken.
10. **No Corporal Punishment.** In Brahmanic period education was based on psychological principles. Corporal punishment was taken to be a sin. Acharyas like Apastamb, Manu, Gautam, etc. all were opposed to the corporal punishment.
11. **Education Per Choice.** In Brahmanic period, students were free to study according to their choice and ability. To be educated was the duty of the citizens. Spiritual knowledge could be gained, mostly by Brahmans but Kshatriyas were also eligible for it.
12. **No Effect of Caste on Curricula.** Karma-siddhanta and stratification of caste system had no effect on the courses of study in Brahmanic education.

METHODS OF TEACHING

1. **Oral System.** In the Vedic period, Veda mantras were learnt by heart. The oral system of teaching enabled the handling over of vast traditional knowledge from generation to generation. The students used to sit at the feet of the teachers and acquired education. This system continued even in the Brahmanic age. The Guru used to take care of the correctness and accuracy of the pronunciations. The students were taught the meaning of the mantras while they were learning them. This enabled them to understand things well. Besides the study of Vedas, they studied the sutras and their exhaustive explanations.
2. **Subjects Composed in Verses.** In Brahmanic age, the students were taught Vyakaran, Nyaya Shastra, Smriti, Jyotish, etc. All the subjects were composed in verses to make them learn by heart. Even stiff uninteresting subjects were written in verses. The student had to remember and meditate over the lessons taught in the class. Thus, they practised self-study. Education was given through discussions and debates. Conferences and sabhas were also organised. Learned teachers threw light on the secrets of the abstract philosophical principles and topics. Great and abstract moral truths were made easy and understandable through examples and parabolas. The art of writing had not yet developed well and so the education was mostly oral.
3. **Individual System.** Due to individual system of education, the students were asked questions daily. So they used to keep the preparation of their subjects up to date. The students coming from rich families lived in the Gurukulas like ordinary students and performed the general duties such as grazing of cows, fetching wood from the forests, lighting fire and begging for alms, etc. These duties were considered useful for spiritual development.

DURATION OF EDUCATION

The students had to study in the Gurukula for 12 year After that they were allowed to go home, and the Guru gave them final instructions. This ritual was called the Samavartan Sanskar. At that time, they were specially instructed to speak the truth, to fulfil the duties and never to be careless in self-study. These teachings were to be observed in future life. The valedictory instructions used to inspire the students in future life.

CURRICULUM

In the vast courses of study of the Brahmanic education, practically all the useful subjects were included. Hence it was capable of all round development of life. Following were the chief characteristics of the curricula.

1. **Predominance of Religious Education.** Brahmanic education aimed at the inner as well as outer purities for supreme development of life. This led towards the salvation. With this aim in view the educand was made to learn Vedic mantras. The curriculum gave important place to Karmakand or Havan, Yajna, etc.
2. **Introduction of Literature, Pertaining to Havan, Yajna, etc.** In Brahmanic age, the literature concerning Karmakand was profousely produced. The Brahmacharis were taught to perform the sacrifices (Yajna) and Karmakanda.
3. **Itihas and Puranas.** Brahmanic education included "Itihas' and 'Puranas'.
4. **Variety of Subjects.** Different subjects of worldly and spiritual concerns were included in courses.
5. **Prosody and Rhetorics.** The teachers used to encourage students to the study of Pingal Shastra so that they might learn mantras correctly.

CHARACTERISTICS OF EDUCATION

1. **Religious Stamp.** Dr. R. K. Mukerji says, "Since the birth of the oldest Vedic poetry we find Indian literature for a period of more than a thousand years bearing an exclusively religious stamp. Even a thousand years after the compilation of 'Rigveda' religious ideas continued to inspire education. The main aim of education was the propagation of religious ideas and principles. The teachers employed the following methods in order to encourage the students to have religious outlook:
   (i) Every student by all means observed celibacy through mind, body, word and action, etc.
   (ii) The students had to take keen interest in religious ceremonies frequently performed in the Gurukulas.

(iii) The students had to participate in daily prayers in the morning and evening.

(iv) Every student had to observe occasional fasting in Gurukula.

2. **Character-Building.** Realising the significance of character in the life of man, the educationists of ancient India laid a good deal of emphasis on the character-building. They used the following methods to achieve the task:

3. **Proper Environment:**

(i) *Freedom from Temptations.* The teacher kept him in an environment where his ideas remained free from various temptations of worldly pleasures and amusements.

(ii) *Religious Instruction.* The teacher used to give religious education very often.

(iii) *Study of Religion.* In the early student life, the study of religious books was considered essential.

(iv) *Religious Rituals.* The students were encouraged to take part in everyday religious rituals. They realised that spiritual development is possible only through the development of the character.

4. **Full Growth of Personality.** Following methods were applied for the full development of the personality in Brahmanic age.

(i) *Self Regard.* In Gurukula-life students were inspired to utilise their moral and spiritual powers for the development of their racial culture. A learned man was respected more than the kings. The king was respected only within his kingdom. While a learned man was respected everywhere.

(ii) *Self-Reliance.* Self-reliance is the mother of self-confidence, the basic element of every kind of development. Hence Brahmanic educational system sought to develop it in various ways. Self-reliance gave the power of making the social life successful without any fear.

(iii) *Self-Control.* In Brahmanic education much emphasis was given to self-control. The students seriously practised control over their sense-organs. This was the reason why the student-life was kept simpler as a rule accompanied with the principles of high thinking and high morality.

Even the sons of kings and rich persons had to lead the same ordinary student life as the son of a common man.

5. **Beginning of Education at Appropriate Age.** In order to make a man a successful citizen, his education must start at a suitable age. The parents in that age, thought it their duty to send their wards, to the Gurukula at the suitable age. Those who failed in this duty, by any reason were called the enemy of their wards. Dr. A. S. Altekar says, "Ancient Indians were convinced that no good results would follow if education is begun late in life."
6. **Assisted All-Round Development.** The individual education system in Brahmanic age, enabled the teachers to look after the inner and outer development of the students. Thus, they educated them in such a practical way so that they may not lose courage in the future struggle of life. They prepared them for the success of whole life.
7. **Psychological System.** The Brahmanic education system was psychological. It was opposed to corporal punishments. The teachers educated the students on psychological principles.
8. **Social Ideals.** The Brahmanic education realised the social value of a man. It encouraged the social ideals in the students so that they raise themselves above the selfish motives and gave proper attention to social service and helpfulness.
9. **Well regulated life.** Their daily routine was to observe celibacy and lead a regulated student life in the Gurukula. They paid due attention to their studies. The students habituated themselves for doing every work at proper time and well. From the beginning of their lives, they had a well regulated life.
10. **Development of Justice and Capability.** Brahmanic education encouraged subject like philosophy and logic. The teachers used to give opportunity to the students to judge and decide themselves. Therefore, they improved their talent to take decisions and to be impartial.
11. **Self-Study.** The students were encouraged to take up self-study and self-experiment. They followed the 'Brahmayajna' of self-study. Realising self-study as Brahma-Yajna Shatpath

Brahman says, "One who does carry on self-study becomes the lover of self-study, and always remains independent. He fulfils his daily needs and has sound sleep at night. He does not only become the spiritual analyser but also controller of sense organs. Besides, he has intellect, wit and wisdom, and improves his Prajna Shakti and fulfils all the four Dharmas and realises the spiritual powers to fulfil the Brahman Dharma."

12. **Intimate Relation of Teacher and Taught.** Guru is one who destroys the ignorance and teaches the religion. Teacher-taught relations were so close and affectionate that in Gurukulas some students even forgot their homes and remained as permanent members of the families of the Gurus. They were called 'Antevasin'.

13. **Samavartan Upadesh (Valedictory Instructions).** The students used to spend the long period of 12 years with their Gurus in their families After that period, having completed their education, they were allowed to go home to enter the family life. At the time of departure, the Gurus used to give the final instructions as follows:

    (i) Always speak the truth and follow the Shishya's Dharma.
    (ii) Never neglect self-study.
    (iii) Occasionally present yourself to acharya and give him possible Dakshina (gift).
    (iv) Entering the family lifc, maintain the Vansh parampara.
    (v) Never neglect good deed and useful things.
    (vi) Always consider your parents, 'Guru' and 'Athithi' (Guests) as Gods (Deva).
    (vii) Always perform the good deeds and follow the good qualities of elders (Gurujans).
    (viii) Whenever some respected person comes, pay him due respect. Always maintain the feeling of regard while giving any 'dan' (gift) and this must be according to the capacity. Always think that all the things belongs to God and it would be a mistake to think it as one's own.
    (ix) In case of doubt, follow the 'Brahmins' with ideal character, good ideas, wise counsellors and followers of religious ways.

ADVANTAGES OF BRAHMANIC EDUCATION

1. **All Round Development.** Brahmanic education was fully successful in the all round development of human life. In enabled highest achievement of life *i.e.* Salvation (Moksha) through self-realisation. The educationists accepted the knowledge of spirit as divine knowledge. They gave maximum importance to inward as well as outward development. They used to realise the principle of world as a family for the last stage of life, when they would renounce the worldly affairs and walk on the path of salvation.
2. **Character Building.** The teachers paid a good deal of attention to the character building of their taught. The inmates of the Gurukula lived in beautiful surroundings of nature and achieved their physical and psychological development. The atmosphere of these 'Gurukulas' was ringing with the craze for knowledge. The educands acquired the knowledge of various useful sciences and observed the rule of internal discipline. Rules of discipline, in those Gurukulas were very strict. However, the discipline was free from fear of Gurus. There existed a spiritual relationship between the teacher and the taught and this was reflected in various activities of life.
3. **Strict Routine.** The students were given rules of life that were rather very strict. They had to get up early, go to bed early, lead a life of strict discipline and keep away from luxury. Celibacy was the central point of life. Discipline of the sense organs was the way of life. This system of education only brought about the moral, spiritual and physical development of the students. It also led to the development of their character and personality.
4. **Teacher-Centered.** Acharyas or teachers were the centre of the entire educational administration. State or rulers could not brook any interference into the affairs of Gurukulas. This system led to the preservance of old culture and literature of India.
5. **Social Prosperity.** From the point of view of social prosperity as well, the system was very successful. Although the system had the elements of religion in it, yet it did not neglect the worldly progress. Prosperity of the society and civil obligations were also the objectives of the Brahmanic system of education.

DISADVANTAGES OF BRAHMANIC EDUCATION

1. **Religion Dominated Brahmanic Education.** Education was fully dominated by religion. Like the educationists of the Medieval Europe, in India also too much of stress was laid on religion in education and even in ordinary affairs of life.
2. **Ritualism.** Since most of the teachers were 'Purohits' they laid stress on Religion and History, Philosophy, Natural Sciences, etc. Ritualism were relegated into the background.
3. **Neglect of Worldly Progress.** Since the education laid a good deal of stress on the abstract principles of philosophy, it failed to carry the general public to it and worldly prosperity received a setback.
4. **Dogmatism.** In this system of education, a good deal of importance was given to the Shastras. Everything based on them was thought to be correct and nothing else. 'Vedas' and 'Smritis' were quoted by way of examples. Since the people at large thought that only what is written in Shastras is correct, this led to blunting of the reasoning faculty.
5. **Neglect of Manual Arts.** Those who did mental labour were considered superior to those who did manual labour. Due to this feeling, the people of higher 'Vamas' did not give protection to art and crafts. Handicrafts, drawing, dance, etc. became the pursuits of the ladies and shudras. Later on, with the growth of dogmatism, shudras were degenerated into untouchables.
6. **Lack of Co-ordination.** Brahmanic system of education did not have the co-ordination in teaching of various subjects. Study of the subject in broad perspective or comprehensive study was lacking. Neglect of education of women, education of general people and the language of general people are also the defects, pointed out in regard to Brahmanic system of education.

In spite of the above mentioned disadvantages Brahmanic system of education was well planned. It did succeed in bringing about all-round development of character and personality of the educands.

QUESTIONS FOR EXERCISE

1. Discuss the aims, principles, methods and curricula of Brahmanic education in ancient India.
2. Explain the characteristics of Brahmanic education. Discuss its advantages and disadvantages.

CHAPTER 4

EDUCATION IN DHARMA SHASTRAS

According to Dharma Shastras education is the chief duty during Brahmacharya Ashram. Details of education in Dharma Shastras have been given in connection with discussion concerning Brahmacharya Ashram.

OBJECTIVES OF BRAHMACHARYA ASHRAMA

The first of the four ashramas is Brahmacharya ashrama. It starts with the Upanayana ceremony. Brahmacharya means the leading of the life according to Brahman. In this Ashram the student or Brahmachari spent 25 years with his teacher studying the Vedas and leading a life of self-control. The education and control of the Brahmacharya prepared a person for future life. Certain rules and observances are prescribed for all Brahmacharins. They are of two kinds, some are prescribed for a very short time and some have to be observed for all the years of studenthood. The first kind of observances were generally concerned with studies. The second kind of observances *i.e.* those which have to be observed throughout this period were concerned with the daily routine and general discipline of the persons in this stage of life. Of the two the latter were definitely more important. These are principally acamana, gurususrusa, vaksamyama (silence), samidadhana. The smritis have laid down detailed rules about these observances. The rules centre principally around agniparicarya (worshipping fire), bhiksa (begging for food), samdhyopasana, study of Veda and its methods and duration, avoidance of certain foods and drinks and other matters like singing, etc., gurususrusa (including honouring him and his family and other elders), and the special vratas of the Brahmachari. The rules about different aspects of the student's life also fall in the category of the rules about Brahmacharya ashram.

CLASSIFICATION OF BRAHMACHARINS

The Brahmacharins were further divided into two types: *upakurvana and naisthika*. The former meant those who offered some return to the teacher. These were celebates for a certain period. According to Yajnavalkya smriti, naisthika has been derived from nistha. Therefore, it includes Brahmacharins who were determined to lead a life of celibacy till death. The word naisthika occurs in Vishnu Dharmashastra, Yajnavalkya smriti and Mahabharata. In Chhandogya upanishad, it has been said that the third branch of Dharma is the status of a student who stays with his teacher's family and who wears out his body to the end in the family of his teacher. According to Manu smriti and Yajnavalkya smriti if the student likes so, he may stay with his teacher till his death, serves his teacher and study the Vedas. He has to perform throughout his life the duties of offering fuel sticks, Veda study, preparing food, sleeping on the ground (not on a cot), and of self-restraint. If the teacher be dead he may stay with and serve the teacher's son if he is worthy or the teacher's wife or he may worship the fire kindled by his deceased guru; he should thus wear out his body; he obtains the highest worlds of bliss and is not born again.

DUTIES OF BRAHMACHARINS

Scope of Study

The Dharma Shastras have prescribed details about the duties of the Brahmacharin. It appears from certain passages of the Upanishads that the usual duration of Brahmacharya was 12 year. The main function of the Brahmacharin was to study the Vedas. The study of the Veda means the study of the mantras and the Brahmana portion of the particular shakha or shakhas. According to Yajnavalkya smriti the student should study everyday according to his ability also Vakovakya Purana, Narasamsi Gathas, Itihasa Vidyas if he desired to please the gods and manes. Yajnavalkya smriti further enumerates 14 vidyas, Vayu Purana, Vrdha-Gautama and other works, *viz.* Four vedas, six angas, puranas, nyaya (logic), mimamsa and Dharma Shastra. Some added four more to these, *viz.* the Upavedas of Ayurveda, Dhanurveda, Gandharvaveda and Arthashastra (which were affiliated respectively to the four Vedas) and thus the vidyas are also spoken of as 18.

Duties in Guru's Ashrama

According to *Chhandogya Upanishad:* the student had to serve the teacher by tending his cattle, had to beg for food and announce it to the teacher, and to look after his sacred fires and to learn the Veda only in the time that would be left after doing work for the guru. Besides these, the rules concerning his conduct towards the teacher, the teacher's wife and son, concerning the method of salutation and showing respect, the food, drinks and actions allowed or prohibited to students are too numerous to be set out in detail. Both Manu smriti and Yajnavalkya smriti, along with some other notable Dharmasutras, lay down the following rules for the Brahmacharin. The student should speak the truth, bathe everyday, should not look at the sun; should avoid honey, flesh, perfumes, the wearing of flowers, sleeping by day, rubbing oil on the body, putting collyrium in the eyes, going in a cart, wearing shoes and holding an umbrella, love affairs, anger, covetousness, infatuation, vain discussions, playing on musical instruments, luxurious baths with hot water, meticulous cleansing of the teeth, ecstatic states of mind, dancing, singing, calumny of others, dangerous places, gazing at women or touching young women, gambling, serving a low person (or doing very low work), injury to animals, obeisance or harsh talk and wine. Manu prescribes that he should not sleep on a cot and should observe complete celibacy, but if he suffers from night emissions he should bathe, worship the sun and repeat thrice the mantra 'punar mam'. *The Apastamba Dharma Sutra* contains similar rules of conduct. According to it the student should not wash his limbs with hot water (generally), but he may do so if they are smeared with dirty and impure matter provided he does it out of the sight of the teacher and that he should not bathe in water in a sportive manner, but should bathe in it motionless like a stick. It also not only prohibits him sexual intercourse but ordains that he should speak with women only as much as is absolutely necessary. The student was not to laugh, but if he could not help laughing he should do so covering his face with his hands.

Duties Towards Teachers

According to Guatama and Baudhayana Dharma Sutra the student to serve his teacher by following after him when he goes anywhere, he should help the teacher in his toilet and bath and should shampoo his body and take food left by him (ucchista), he should be diligent in doing work that would be pleasing and beneficial to the teacher; he was to study when the teacher called him, he was not to cover his throat with a piece of cloth or was not to sit in the presence of his teacher with his feet on his lap, was not to stretch his feet, he was not to clear loudly his throat, nor to laugh, yawn or crack the knuckles; he was when called by the teacher to reply at once leaving his seat or bed and was to approach the teacher even when he called from a distance; he should always occupy a seat lower than that of his teacher and should go to sleep after his teacher and rise before him. Similar rules have been prescribed by other Dharma Shastras. According to Manu smriti a pupil should not mimic the gait, the manner of speech and the actions of the teacher. It calls upon the pupil to close his ears with his hands or fingers or to leave the place where somebody indulges in calumnies about the teacher or points out the faults in him, and states if the pupil himself finds fault with his teacher or calumniates him, the pupil in the next life is born as an ass or a dog. One of the rules for the student was that he was not to pronounce the name of his teacher even when the teacher was not present without prefixing or affixing an honorific addition such as sri, bhatta, acharya, etc. The student should not speak of his teacher, the teacher's son or wife or of a man who has been initiated for srauta sacrifice by their bare names. When it is absolutely necessary to refer to these by name the student should not pronounce the name and gotra of his teacher as they are, but by means of a synonym. According to Apastamba Dharma Sutra, even after returning home a snataka should avoid touching his former teacher with his fingers to call his attention, frequent muttering of something in his ears, laughing into his face, calling him out loudly, speaking his name, ordering him about. According to Manu smriti a man who has been initiated for a srauta sacrifice should not be addressed by his name, even though he may be younger than the person addressing, but that one should use the words bhoh and bhavat when addressing him or speaking about him and may refer to him by words like diksita, etc. Very detailed mles were laid down about pratuthana or rising from one's seat to receive a person, abhivadana or saluting a man, upasamgrahana or saluting by clasping the feet of the teacher or another one's hands, pratyabhivadana or returning a salutation, and namaskara or bowing with the word namah. According to Apastamba Dharma Sutra, the student must clasp his teacher's feet when he meets his teacher after sunrise, and also beginning the day's lesson of Vedic study and even after finishing it. This has been corroborated by Manu.

Abhivadana

According to Dharma Shastras Abhivadana is of three types, *viz.* Nitya or obligatory every day, Naimittika to be done only on certain occasion and Kamya to be done only if a person has certain rewards in view. The manner of abhivadana was as follows. A Brahmana shall salute stretching forward his right arm on a level with his ear, a kshatriya holding it on a level with the chest, a vaishya holding it on a level with the waist and a sudra holding it low up to his feet and that the salutation shall be by joining one's hands. There were other rules about honouring one's elders in the presence of one's teacher or honouring the teacher's teacher or about one's behaviour when a gentleman comes to see one's acharya and leaves him, which are here passed over for want of space. In the case of certain persons one was to show honour only by rising from his seat and not by abhivadana. The works on Dharmashastra give very interesting rules about the grounds on which respect was to be shown to a person.

Brahmacharin Dharmah

Certain rules and observances were prescribed for all Brahmacharins by the Dharma Shastras. These were known as Brahmacharindharmah. They were of two kinds. Some were prescribed for very short time and some had to be observed during the entire period of this ashram. Thus, according to the *Asv. gr. Sutra,* "For three nights, or twelve nights or a year after upanayana the Brahmachari should not eat ksara and lavana and should sleep on the ground." Milk had to be avoided for three days, along with the avoidance of ksara, of lavana and vegetables, and the duty of sleeping on the ground, of not drinking out of an earthen vessel, of not giving the remnants of his food to sudras and several other observances which he has to continue throughout the period of studenthood. These latter are briefly indicated in many offering samidha into fire, begging food, not using a cot, working for the teacher, daily bath, tarpana of gods, sages and pitrs, etc.

Observances of Studenthood

Then, there were observances that last throughout the period of studenthood. These are principally acamana, gurususrusa, vaksamyama (silence), samidadhana. These rules centre principally round agniparicarya (worshipping fire), bhiksa (begging for food), samdhyopasana, study of Veda and its methods and duration, avoidance of certain foods and drinks and other matters like singing, etc., gurususrusa (including honouring him and his family and other elders), and the special vratas of the Brahmachari. The principal constituents of samdhyopasana are these: achamana (sipping of water), pranayama, marjana or thrice (sprinkling himself with water to the accompaniment of several mantras), aghamarsana, offering of water to the sun (in the morning and generally of Varuna in the evening).

Qualifications of Student

The Dharma Shastras have laid down qualifications of the student who deserved to be taught. According to Manu 10 persons deserved to be taught *viz.* the son of the teacher, a student who serves his guru, one who gives some knowledge in exchange, one who knows Dharma or who is pure (in body and mind), who is truthful, who is able to study and retain it, who gives money (for teaching), who is well-disposed and who is one's near relative (agnate). According to Yajnavalkya smriti, besides all these, the student must be grateful, not inclined to hate or prove false to the teacher, healthy and not disposed to find fault. The student should always be dependent on and under the control of the teacher and should stay with no one but the teacher.

STATUS OF THE TEACHER

The Pivot of Education

The pivot of the whole educational system of ancient India was the teacher variously called acharya, guru, upadhyaya. In Manu and other smritis there is some divergence about the greatness of the acharya. According to Manu smriti the father (janaka) and the teacher are called father (pita) but the father who imparts the sacred Veda is superior to the father that gives birth, since the birth in spiritual learning is for a Brahmana of eternal benefit, here and hereafter. But in another place Manu says that an acharya is ten times superior to an upadhyaya, the father is superior to a hundred acharyas, while the mother is thousand-fold superior to the father. According to Gautama, the acharya is the highest among all gurus while according to some the mother is higher than the acharya.

Definition of the Teacher

The Dharma Shastras define the acharya as one who performs the upanayana of the student and imparts the whole Veda to him. The Nirukta defines acharya as follows: he makes the student understand the proper course of conduct, or collects wealth from the student or gathers together the meanings of words, or increases the intelligence of the student. According to Apastamba Dharma Sutra, "The acharya is so-called since the student gathers his duties from him." According to Manu smriti, the teacher, after performing upanayana, teaches his pupil the rules about saucha (bodily purity), acharan (rules of conduct in every day life), the offering (of fuelstick) in fire and samdhya adoration. Though the words acharya, gum and upadhyaya are very often used as synonyms ancient writers made a distinction between them. According to Manu smriti, an upadhyaya is one who teaches to a student a portion of the Veda or the Vedangas (subsidiary lores of the Veda) as a means of his own livelihood and a gum is one who performs the samskaras and who maintains the child. This latter's definition shows that gum means the father here. According to Yajnavalkya smriti, the gum is one who performs the samskaras and imparts the Veda. This corroborates the statement made above that originally the father himself taught the Veda to his son. The word gum is often used in the sense of any elderly person, male or female, who is entitled to respect. According to *Visnu Dharma Shastra* the father, the mother and the acharya are the three highest gurus of a person. According to Manu smriti whoever confers on another the benefit of knowledge, whether great or small, is the latter's guru. All these praises of guru by the Dharma Shastras show that they held knowledge as the highest value and insisted upon the sense of gratitude in everyone who gave knowledge. Faith in the teacher was a necessary qualification for the achievement of knowledge. It is undeniable that this glorification of the teacher may have led to some of them loosing their heads but in contrast to the modern western philosophy of education, making the educand rather the educator the pivot of education, it has its advantages. In fact both these extremes are unjust, the former to the educand and the latter to the educator. In a proper system of education both should be given a proper place.

Qualifications of the Teacher

The Dharma Shastras did not praise the teacher without any reason. They insisted upon very high qualifications for being a teacher. They warned about the dangers of entrusting the job of a teacher to persons not worthy of it. According to Apastamba Dharma Sutra, he whom a teacher devoid of learning, initiates enters from darkness into darkness and he also (an acharya) who is himself unlearned (enters into darkness). It further provides that one should desire a performer of one's upanayana who is endowed with learning and whose family is hereditary learned and who is serene in mind and that one should study Vedic lore under him up to the end (of Brahmacharya) as long as the teacher does not fall off from the path of dharma. Similar qualifications had been laid down by other Dharma Shastras. The teacher had to be a Brahmana, learned in Vedas, knowing Dharma, pure, coming from a good family and having an ideal character. In educational system also the Dharma Shastras insisted upon the vama hierarchy. It had been generally maintained that only a Brahmana should be the teacher. According to Vayupuran, as to the acharya in upanayana must be a Brahmana; as to the study of Veda one should ordinarily learn the Veda from a Brahmana teacher; in times of difficulty (*i.e.* when a Brahmana is not available) one may learn the Veda from a kshatriya or vaishya teacher; but in such circumstances the only service that a Brahmana student rendered to the guru would be following after the non-Brahmana teacher; he had not to render bodily service (such as shampooing or washing the feet, etc). The Mit. on Yajnavalkya smriti earmarks that a kshatriya or vaisya should teach a Brahmana only when urged by him and not at his sweet will. Manu allowed teaching only to a kshatriya, but did not allow him to make it a means of his livelihood. In fact the Indian thinkers prescribed a social structure with definite division of labour and permitted only exceptions in certain cases. They very much insisted upon keeping the social structure in tact and not violating it. This rigidity obviously resulted in so many disadvantages but it also facilitated continuity, regularity and order in social system.

Method of Instruction

In India the method of instruction of education was generally oral. The first thing that was taught to the body was the pranava and the vyahrtis and the Gayatri. Then the boy was to be taught other parts of the Veda. Detailed instructions were laid down about the method of teaching. According to Manu smriti, the student should sip water (achamana) when about to begin Vedic study, should face the north, should fold both hands together (and place them on his knee), should wear light (pure) clothes, should at the beginning and end of Vedic study clasp the feet of the teacher with crossed hands and should touch the right foot of the teacher with his own right hand and left foot with the left hand, should repeat 'om' at the beginning and at the end of Vedic study. The teacher should say to the pupil 'repeat' and should stop from teaching with the words 'let there be a pause'. The study of the Veda was the first duty of every twice born person (dvijati). According to Manu smriti, the whole Vedas together with Upanishads were to be learnt by every dvijati. According to Yajnavalkya smriti it is Veda alone that confers the highest bliss upon dvijatis by enabling them to understand and perform sacrifices, austerities and auspicious acts (like samskaras). Since the literature was very wide concessions had to be made to the shortness of human life and the weakness of the human mind. Therefore, generally it was prescribed that one should study that Shakha of the Veda which his ancestors studied and should perform religious rites according to it. As the study of the Veda was a duty enjoined upon a Brahmana, so teaching Veda to another was a duty. This exclusive glorification of the brahmanas very much led to what N. K. Dutt describes as the "pride of scholasticism" among the professed scholars. And it has been rightly pointed out by S. Cromwell Crawford, "Compounded with racial and sacerdotal pride, the pride of scholasticism elevated barriers between brahmanas and non-Brahmanas." In this way "the good effect of the strictness of Brahmacharya in specialising learning and in enforcing high moral discipline was neutralised by the increased rigidness and hauteur of caste, which is one of the many factors making India a land of contrasts."

Teacher's Duties

It should not be supposed that the Dharma Shastras, while insisting upon educands' respect towards the educator, used less strict words while insisting upon educators' duty towards the educand. In fact the educational relationship was a two way relationship. It was reciprocal. According to Apastamba Dharma Sutra, "Loving him like his own son, and full of attention, he shall teach him the sacred science, without hiding anything in the whole law. And he shall not use him for his *own* purpose to the detriment of his studies, except in times of distress. The pupil who attending to (teacher), accuses his (principal and first) teacher of ignorance, remains no (longer) a pupil. A teacher also, who neglects the instruction (of his pupil), does no (longer) remain a teacher." The purpose of education was the moral and intellectual growth of the students. These two elements were never separated. Indeed, the latter was contingent upon the former. According to the Sacred Law, only the person who is pure may be instructed in the Veda. Neither (the study of) the Vedas, nor liberality, nor sacrifices, nor any (self-imposed restraint), nor austerities, ever procure the attainment (of rewards) to a man whose heart is contaminated (by sensuality). Moral culture not only preceded intellectual culture, but was the weightier of the two: A Brahmana, who completely governs himself, though he knows the Savitri only, is better than he who knows the three Vedas, (but) does not control himself.

CRITICAL EVALUATION

Absence of Social Justice

The absence of social justice in education is particularly observed in case of partiality towards the education of all the vamas other than Brahmin and also of the women. These were given a secondary place. Literary education among women was in languishing state. Therefore there was no question of co-education. Not much material is available about the education of kshatriyas, vaishyas and sudras. The entire education system was entrusted to Brahmanas. Summing up the state of education in Dharma Shastras, P. V. Kane has written, "The salient features of the educational system outlined in the Dharma Shastras work are the high and honourable position assigned to the teacher, the close personal contact of the pupil with the teacher and individual attention, the pupil's stay with the teacher as a member of his family, oral instruction and the absence of books, stern discipline and control of emotions and the will, cheapness as no fees were stipulated for."

The institution of education as prescribed by Dharma Shastras can be favourably compared with any other system of education in the West, ancient or modern. Given the high character and scholarship of the teacher, it was the most ideal system of education. However, its defects are equally obvious.

Summarising these defects, P. V. Kane, has admitted, "The defects of the Indian system were that it was too literary, there was too much memorising, boys under it had hardly any instruction in useful manual arts and crafts, the studies were not brought in contact with practical life. The discipline was vigorous and joyless. Many of these defects were due to the exigencies of the caste system which assigned particular avocations to particular castes." Kane, however, rightly adds, "We cannot and should not compare the system with the systems of education prevalent in the 20th century, when several subjects such as literature, music and the fine arts, handicrafts, mathematics, science, history and geography are taught in the schools to all boys and when it has been recognised that education is a prime concern of the state."

QUESTIONS FOR EXERCISE

1. Describe the objectives, classification and duties of Brahmacharya ashram according to Dharma Shastras.
2. Explain the status, qualifications, methods and duties of teacher according to Dharma Shastras.
3. Write Critical note on Education in Dharma Shastras.

CHAPTER 5

THE BUDDHIST SYSTEM OF EDUCATION

The most important systems of education in medieval India were the Buddhist system of education and the Muslim system under Muslim rulers. Gautama, the Buddha, revolted against the prevalent brahmanical religion. He was against the rigid classification according to Vamas. He established equality among people. He particularly pleaded for simplification of life. It is hence that he ignored metaphysical questions and concentrated upon practical ethics. However, it has been rightly pointed out that Buddha was born, lived and died a Hindu. It is hence that one finds a covert continuation of Brahmanical tradition in the Buddhist system of education. Like the ancient Indian philosophy, Buddha also considered Dharma as the highest aim of life. What was preached was known as Dharma. The monasteries and the Buddhist sangha aimed at the preaching of Dharma.

Continuation of Brahmanical Tradition

The following may be considered as the characteristics showing continuation of the Brahmanical tradition in the Buddhist system of education.

1. **Educational Institutions.** The Buddhist sangh was parallel to the Gurkula of the Hindus. It was the centre of Buddhist system of education. As R. K. Mukerji has pointed out, "The Buddhist system is practically that of the Buddhist order or sangha. Buddhist education and learning centred round monasteries as Vedic centred round the sacrifice. The Buddhist world did not offer any educational opportunities apart from or independently of its monasteries. All education, sacred as well as secular, was in the hand of monks." The following description of Nalanda, the famous Buddhist university by the Chinese traveller Huen Tsang

may be equally taken as a description of Hindu Gurukula: "The priests, to the number of several thousands, are men of highest ability and talent. Their distinction is very great at the present time, and there are many hundreds whose fame has rapidly spread through distant regions. They follow the precept of moral law. From morning till night they engage in discussion. The old and the young mutually help one another."

2. **Going Out of Home for Education.** Both the Brahmanical tradition and the Buddhist system of education agreed in the rule that the student has to leave his home and reside with the teacher. This was known as *pabbajja* according to the Buddhist tradition. The student in ancient India was known as *antevasin* one who lives out of his home. Describing the condition that the student should leave all the marks of their family life while joining an educational institution, the Buddha laid down, "As the great streams, disciple! However many they may be Ganga, Yamuna, Achiravati, Sarabhu, Mani. When they reach the great ocean, lose their old name and their old descent and bear only one name, the great ocean, so also, my disciple, those four castes, Kshatriyas, Brahmins, Vaishyas and Sudras, when they, in accordance with the law and doctrine which the perfect one has preached, forsake their home and go into homelessness, lose their old name and whole paternity, bear only one designation, ascetics, who follow the son of the Sakyas House." One who took the path of pabbajja was known as *pabbajjit* or one had become a homeless for the cause of education.
3. **Minimum Age for Initiation.** Both the Brahmanical system and the Buddhist system of education admitted the age of eight years as the minimum age for initiation in education. Both considered the period of twelve years as the minimum period for studentship. The word Brhamchari corresponded to the Buddhist epithet *Scunners* which meant the student who has been initiated.
4. **Service of the Teacher.** Like the ancient Brahmanical system the Buddhist system also insisted upon the duty of the student to serve his teacher by all means. The teacher in both the systems admitted only as many students as he could cope with.

FUNDAMENTAL DIFFERENCES

In spite of the above similarities with the Brahmanical system of education the Buddhist system exhibited some fundamental differences, of these the most important are as follows:

1. **Federated Institutions.** While Gurukula was developed around the family of a single teacher, most of the Buddhist educational institutions were large units including thousands of students and a number of teachers. Thus Vihara or the Buddhist monastery' was a federated educational institution of the pattern of a modern university. Describing this distinction R. K. Mukerji has maintained, "While Brahmanical culture depended upon the system of individual schools and ideal succession of teachers and disciples the Buddhist culture was the product of the confederation of such schools into larger monastic institutions comprising number of teachers and students (sometimes as many as 10000 as at Nalanda) promoting a partaking of a wider, collective, academic life with its own advantages as an educational and educative agency and factor."
2. **Opposed to Caste System.** While some of the Brahmin teachers used to teach only brahmins, others also considered varna while giving admissions to the student. The Buddhist system of education, on the other hand, insisted that the student may be admitted on his personal merit and not on the basis of his family or caste. The Buddhist nuns and monks, therefore, came from all castes.
3. **Medium of Instruction.** While the Brahmanical education was given in Sanskrit, the language of the elite, the Buddhist system of education insisted upon Pali or Prakrat and other popular languages as the medium of instruction. This was another step towards democratisation of education and making it popular.
4. **Aim of Education.** The aim of education, according to Buddhist system, was to influence the younger sections of society according to the Buddhist thought. To fulfil this primary aim, its secondary aim was to train monks and nuns for the purpose. Therefore, the system had a missionary aim. However, gradually the monastic schools admitted even the lay students.

5. **Curriculum.** In concurrence with the above mentioned aim of education the Buddhist system developed a curriculum around Buddhist religion. However, gradually it also included comparative study of Hinduism and Jainism. The curriculum which initially included theology, philosophy and logic was gradually extended to Sanskrit literature, astronomy, astrology, medicine, law, polity, administration, music, art and technical education concerning so many trades. Thus the curriculum of the Buddhist universities was almost as much versatile and varied as any of the modern university. Therefore, the institution used to attract students not only from all parts of India but also from distant countries such as Korea, China and Tibet.

THE BUDDHIST SYSTEM OF EDUCATION

The history of education in Buddha period is interrelated with the history of monasteries and 'Viharas' because there were no independent educational institutions or centres, other than those religious centres. Only monks and shramanas were authorised to impart education to the people. Thus, the monasteries and 'Viharas' took the place of sacrificial altars and as a result, these places became the centres of cultural life. Thus, the methods of these monasteries and 'Viharas' were the educational methods of that time. Rules and regulations of Buddhist monasteries and 'Viharas' were not framed by Lord Buddha. They had been taken from Hinduism and the various sects of Sadhus and nuns so they resembled 'Vedic' systems.

Rules of Admission

Admissions into Buddhist monasteries were based more or less on the rules and regulations observed by Gurukula as in Vedic period. Like the students of 'Vedic' period, here also the students had to present themselves before the teacher to ask for the admission. Like the 'Upanayana', 'Pabbaja or pravrajya' is to go out. The boys went out of their families and joined the monasteries. Everyone had the opportunity to undergo 'Pabbaja' and become a 'Buddhist' monk. After admission into 'Sangh' they could remain a monk. They had to change the former caste, dress, character, etc. Though theoretically, all the castes were allowed to get admitted into the monastery but practically and mostly the people of higher classes were admitted there. However, it is also true that some of the monks were derived from the lower castes. At the time of entering into the 'Sangh' the disciple must have attained the age of eight years and during this period the new monk made his preparation for the sangh-life. Afterwards at the age of 20 years, he accepted 'Upsampada' and became full-fledged member of the 'sangh'.

The System of Pabbaja

At eight years of age, one could go to any 'Vihara' or 'Sangh' according to his own will. With head shaved and a yellow cloth in hand he went to the principal monk and requested him for admission in 'Sangh'. He thus surrendered himself fully. The monk caused him to put the yellow clothes on and surrendered to the three words of shelter in a loud voice:

I go into the shelter of Buddha.
I seek the shelter of Dharma.
I enter the shelter of Sangh.

After taking the above three vows, one became entitled to admission. No one could get admission into the 'Sangh' without the consent of his parents. Patients of infectious diseases like Leprosy, T. B., Eczema, etc. and government servants, slaves and soldiers were not allowed to be admitted into 'Sanghs'. However there was no discrimination of any kind on the basis of caste or creed.

Rules for the Students

Now the admitted student was called "Samner". He had to follow the following rules:

1. Not to kill any living being.
2. Not to accept anything given to him.
3. Live free from the impurity of character.
4. Not to tell a lie.
5. Not to use any intoxicating thing.
6. Not to take food at improper time.
7. Not to speak ill of anybody.
8. Not to take any interest in music, dance, play show, etc.
9. Not to use luxurious and scented things.
10. Not to accept the gifts of gold or silver, etc.

The ten rules were essentially observed by the new monk. The 'Upajsaya' *i.e.,* the teacher took all his responsibilities up to the age of 20 years when he became mature and capable for accepting 'Upasampada'. For the teacher, he was 'Sadvi Biharak'. Lord Buddha himself taught that teacher should recognise his taught (Sadvi Biharak) as his son and the taught (Sadvi Biharak) should recognise the teacher (Upajsaya) as his own father.

Upasampada

After completing the education for twelve years, the 'Monk' had to undergo the 'Upasampada' ritual at the age of 20 years and then he became the permanent member of the 'Sangh'. There is also evidence that only such monks who had enough of spiritual knowledge were taken in sangh. They were directly given 'Upasampada'. Their 'Pabbaja' and 'Upasampada' both the rituals were performed simultaneously.

The method of performing 'Upasampada' was slightly different from 'Pabbaja'. It was similar to Vedic 'Samavartan' ritual with some difference. After 'Samavartan' the Brahmachari entered into family life but after 'Upasampada' he became a full-fledged monk, having no concern with family life. While Pabbaja was a ritual for a limited period, 'Upasampada' was permanent. It was for the whole life. Celibacy or chastity was considered essential for Brahmanic education. While among Hindus those observing celibacy for the whole life were rare in 'Buddhistic' education it was a common feature. In this respect, Buddhistic education was more austere than Brahmanic education. In the 'Buddhistic' education, the disciple, after acquiring education would become a monk for the whole of his life and not return home.

At the time of 'Pabbaja' the new monk of 8 years would go to the teacher and say with folded hands, "You are my teacher (Guru)". Thus their relationship was established. The 'Upasampada' was performed before the entire 'Sangh'. Therefore, 'Upasampada' was given unanimously or on the decision of the majority.

Restrictions on Admission

In 'Buddhist' education also, like 'Vedic' education, the eligibility and the competence of the entrant was taken into account. A candidate could not be admitted into 'Sangh' in the following conditions:

1. Without the permission of his parents.
2. Patient of any infectious or serious disease.
3. Convict of any serious moral sin.

4. Under any legal responsibility and who was not free from legal bondage.
5. Not found generous and laborious during the probation period, which sometimes was four or five days.

Thus Buddhist sanghs did not intend to destroy the family system. No one was admitted into 'Sangh' without the due permission of his parents. Similarly those who wanted to get rid of their social, moral and economic obligations were not admitted. Moreover, only those were allowed admittance who were healthy both mentally and bodily. Hence Buddhism spread rapidly and in an organised manner, in so many countries of the world.

The Qualifications of the Teacher

In Buddhist educational system much stress was laid on the efficiency of the teachers. This has been described as follows:

(a) *High Moral Order.* The teacher himself, must have spent at least ten years as monk. He must have the purity of character, purity of thoughts and generosity, etc.

(b) *High Mental Order.* Essentially the teacher was expected to be of a high mental order, so that he might teach his disciple the religion and nobleness and he may also successfully combat the wrong religious notions.

Duties of the Teacher

In Buddhist system of education, the teacher was responsible for the proper education and upkeep of the disciple. He had to fulfil the needs of the disciple during the education period. He had to treat them affectionately. He had to supply his disciple with all the necessary materials. He was responsible for their physical and mental development. At the time of sickness he would attend to the treatment and care of his students. The teacher taught them through question-answer, explanation and such other methods, so that the student might gain full knowledge and realise 'Nirvan.'

Daily Routine of the Disciple

Regular service of the 'Guru' (teacher), was essential in the Buddhist system. In morning the student would arrange for water, duetonic, etc. for the teacher. He would also look after his meal. He would cook the food, feed the teacher and clean the utensils. He would go out for alms with the teacher. After bath the students would get ready for the education. The teacher would impart education, according to the system of the day.

Thus the disciple had to serve the teacher and keep the place tidy. His daily routine depended on the orders of the teacher. He was not bound to obey anyone else except his teacher. He could not take any service from any other person, nor could he go anywhere without the permission of the teacher. Thus the disciples used to live under the disciplinary control of their teachers.

Teacher-Taught Relationship

In Buddhist period like 'Vedic' period the relation of the teachers and the taughts was close, affectionate, pure and good. Their duties were fixed and they used to fulfil them well.

The teachers used to lead a very simpic life. They had limited needs. Being learned men of high character, knowing themselves and having self-control, they put the same ideals before their taughts. Huen Tsang wrote that the teachers living in 'Bauddh Viliams' were great and eminent scholars. They put inspiring ideals before the students. They were paid very little for their personal expenditure. Prominent teachers of even a famous university like Nalanda, were often receiving for their expenses, money equal to three times being given to an ordinary student. If any student failed in serving the teacher, he was considered inefficient and turned out of the 'Sangh'.

The duties of the disciple were settled. He was called the 'Sidh Biharak'. He gained knowledge while serving his teacher. The teacher took every care of his student. He did not let him suffer in any way. The disciples were also ready to serve teachers. If the disciple was aware of the mental troubles of the 'Guru' he used to amuse him by religious conversations and other means. While taking lessons, the disciples gained knowledge meekly. The teacher enlightened the inner sense of the students through different methods such as explanation, question-answer, lecture, etc. If the disciple had some doubts the teacher would try to remove those doubts. He could take help from other people of the 'Sangh' also if required.

In Buddhist period the position of 'Sangh' was above everything. If the teacher behaved against the honour of the sangh then the taught was duty bound to bring the defects of the teacher to the notice of the sangh. He would request for proper action against him. After the due penances, he could again request for his re-establishment. Thus the relation between teacher and the taught was based on high ideals in Buddhist period. Toquote A. S. Altekar, "The relations between the novice and his teacher were final in character, they were united together by usual reverence, confidence and affection."

School Administration

In Buddhist period generally one monk could teach a new Bhikshu but Lord Buddha had recognised that capable teachers could teach more students also. Indeed, in Buddhist period, there were no organised Gurukulas like that of Vedic period. The education was imparted through monasteries and Viharas. These monasteries and Viharas were the base of Sangh. Here the students resided as full monks or Bhikshus. Teachers and taught lived together. The ruins of the universities like Nalanda, etc. show that there was arrangement for the accommodation of thousands of students in them.

Originally the Buddhist centres of education were groups of new monks, who were being educated in Buddhism under the guardianship of teachers. But like the Shiksha Mandals of Vedic system they did not enjoy independent status. Thus, the big and extensive monasteries and Viharas were back-bone of Buddhist education where thousands of monks could live thereafter. All the educational schemes were conducted by the Sanghs situated in these monasteries and Viharas. The teachers discharged their duties under the collective control of the Sangh. Thus Buddhist educational institutions were based on federal principles, where small pathshalas worked under the control of big groups of the sanghs. Some students were occasionally allowed to live in their private residences.

The Buddhist Viharas were palatial and magnificent buildings and were very comfortable. Jetavana Vihara built by prince Anath Pindaka was famous. There were fine and well furnished separate rooms for dining, bathing, sleeping, reading, studying, shastrarth (discussions), etc. Yastivana, Venuvana and Seetvana, etc. were also famous Viharas of that time. These Viharas were used not only for religious purposes but also as the centres of arts and crafts, architecture, painting, etc.

The monks and students used to follow the principles of simple living and high thinking. Their lives were full of purity, nobleness, dutifulness, and humanity. Both the teachers and taught alike, were using Chivar (a simple dress of a mendicant). Music, dance, use of scents, etc. were prohibited to them. The teacher and taught, both used to go for the Bhiksha and spent their lives on whatever they got in it. They were not allowed to accept more than what they actually required. Sometimes they were invited to take their foods at the houses of certain householders.

Curriculum

Like Vedic education Buddhist education was mainly religious. Its aim was to attain Nirvan (Salvation). Most of the monks were carrying on the study of teachings of Buddha and Dharma Shastras. Sutta, Binaya and Dhamma Pitak, etc. were the main subjects of their studies. They educated people in spinning, weaving, painting, tailoring, writing, arithmetic and printing, etc.

Type of Education

In primary education, reading, writing and arithmetic were taught. In higher education, Religion, Philosophy, Ayurveda, Military training, etc. were included. Everyone was free to chose his subjects without any restriction.

Brahmanic education was also going on in Buddhist period. In Buddhist centres also, the subjects of Brahmanic education, such as the four Vedas, History, Puranas, Prosody, Dhvani, Poetry, Vyakaran, Jyotish, Vedanga, Sankhya, Yoga, Music, Ayurveda, Tantra, etc. were taught. The knowledge of Sanskrit was essential for higher study. The study of Vedas was very necessary. Learning the mantras of Vedas by heart was the system of that time. Bodhisatva himself had acquired the knowledge of Vedas. The general knowledge of Grammar was also considered necessary. The students were taught Sanskrit alphabets, Sandhi Samas (Compounds), etc. Thus both the worldly and spiritual aspects of education were included in education.

Jataks do not name the science, fine arts and useful arts and crafts. Milinda Panha, however, described the 18 sippons (arts) which were included in the courses of study. The study of Elephants, Horses, Chariots, Archery, Swords, Hunting, Science of palmistry, Snake charming and Ayurveda was prevalent at that time. There is also reference to surgery and its practical training.

Jeevak had conducted two serious operations after his student life.

Travelling was considered to be an important part of education. Nature study, the study of Law and Military training, etc. were also included in the courses. Thus the sphere of education was vast in the Buddhist period but the students were gaining higher education in one subject only, in which they could specialise.

Education of Monks

Education of monks started with Sutant. Due to their tender age, they could only remember those sutras. After sutant they started Binaya which was taught through question-answer method. Afterwards they were trained to preach religion. Some Buddhist monks tried to gain the highest knowledge through austerities like Hindu Sanyasies. Some had however concentrated on worldly affairs and emphasised the physical knowledge and physical strength. There was arrangement for the study of separate subjects at separate places. There was provision for their separate residences so that there may not be any disturbance in study.

METHODS OF TEACHING

Buddhist education aimed at purity of character. Like Vedic education it was training for moral character rather than psychological development of the students. One had to attain the stage of Bodhisattva. Mental and moral development was emphasised. Earlier, there was predominance of Religion. Following were the methods of teaching:

1. **Verbal Education.** Though the art of writing had been well developed up to the Buddhist period, yet, due to shortage and non-availability of writing materials, verbal education was prevalent as it was in the Vedic age. In Buddhist scripture, *Binaya Pitaka* there is description of the smallest things up to the biggest thing, yet there is no mention of writing material. Thus writing was not very common in those days. In *Mahabagga,* writing has been described as means of livelihood. In the same book there is description of orders given to a monk to go to the adjacent place to gain verbal knowledge of various things. There is reference to such family men who had invited monks to hear sutants from them and learn it by heart. The teachers used to give

lessons to the novices who learnt them by heart. The teacher used to put questions on learning the lesson by heart.

2. **Discussions.** In order to win discussion or Shastrartha and impress the general public, it was necessary to improve the power of discussion. This was also needed to satisfy the critics and opposing groups and establish ones own cult. Thus rules were framed for discussion. Yogachary's *Dasha Bhoomi Shastra* written in 400 A.D. has dealt with the rules and regulations in regard to discussions in several chapters of the 15th part of the book. It laid down that the discussion should be done on useful subjects, and should be held at the meeting places of scholars, Royal place, Minister's office and Assembly.
3. **Evidences.** To establish the disputed point the following evidences of eight kinds were required:
   1. Theory (Siddhanta)
   2. Cause (Reason)
   3. Example (Udaharan)
   4. Parallelism (Sadharmya)
   5. Contradiction (Vaidharlmya)
   6. Evidence (Pratyaksh)
   7. Argument (Anuman)
   8. Induction (Agamana).

   It was laid down that the debators must be well-versed in their subjects and fluent in speech so that they could influence the audience well.
4. **Prominence of Logic.** The importance of discussion encouraged the logic in the Buddhist period. The controversial matters could not be decided without logical arguments. Logic was also useful in the development of the mental power and knowledge. Thus in later period, logic began to be used for the sake of logic and lost its proper utility.
5. **Tours.** The main aim of Buddhist monks was to propagate Buddhism. Hence some Acharyas like Sariputta, Mahayuggalva, Aniruddha, Rahula, etc., gave importance to tours for educating people. After the completion of education, the students were encouraged to undertake long trips to gain the practical and real form of the theoretical knowledge gained by them.

6. **Conferences.** Conferences were arranged on every full moon and first day of the month (Pumima and Pratipada) in the Buddhist sanghs. The monks of different sanghs assembled and put forward their doubts freely The attendance of every monk was compulsory in such conference. If any one happened to be sick he had to inform the sangh or he had to present himself in the same condition. If the monk happened to be an accused person then he had to prove himself innocent. Generally, the conferences decided the personal guilts. Common guilts were put before the scholars of other places. An annual conference was arranged in which a well-renowned monk would challenge the whole sangh to disprove his purity. Thus Buddhist education laid great emphasis on the morality of the monks.
7. **Meditation in Solitude.** Some Buddhist monks were more interested in isolated spiritual meditation in lonely forests and caves. Only those monks were considered fit for lonely meditation who had fully renounced the worldly attraction and had spent enough time in the sanghs and had gained the efficiency for solitaiy meditations. Some old monks resigned from their responsibilities of the sanghs and went to lonely forest to spend peaceful life. Their isolation was unlike the isolation of Vedic saints as they lived near the janpadas or populated places, so that they might get the Bhiksha and also might get the chance to serve the monks who happened to get there.

Medium of Instruction

The medium of Buddhist education was the common language of the people. Lord Buddha himself gave his teachings in local languages. These replaced Sanskrit in Buddhist education. Yantra-Mantra-Tantra, etc. were prohibited in Buddhist education.

EDUCATION OF THE GENERAL PUBLIC

Only those people were admitted in Buddhist sanghs who had renounced the worldly attractions and accepted the life of a monk. They were educated in Buddhism. They were permanent members of the sangh and spent a collective life. There was no provision for the education of common man in the Buddhist sanghs. But since they were dependent on the endowment by the public and the rulers, it was necessary for them to teach Buddhism to public, during their tours. They used to allay the doubts of the public and create confidence in them. Religious education in the public was arranged under the patronage of the rulers. According to *Mahabagga* king Bimbisar had ordered 80,000 villagers to accept the teachings of Lord Buddha. But for the general education of the children of the followers of Buddhism no arrangement was made by the sangh. They had to go to other educational institutions. *The Jatakas give* description of such educational institutions.

The following facts may be mentioned in this connection:

1. Buddhist education was not limited to monasteries and Viharas. It was provided by monks in their ashrams and cottages like Brahmanic education.
2. Brahmanic and Buddhist education were not contradictory to each other but complementary.
3. The system was taught to the public also.
4. The system of presenting fees to the teacher before starting education was common in those days.

FEATURES OF THE HIGHER EDUCATION

'Milinda Panha' has given the description of the courses of study of Brahmanic and Buddhist education. The Jatak books have described the system for higher education. The following are the salient features of Buddhist higher education:

1. **Centres of Education.** In Buddhist period, there were many centres, where foreign students used to come for higher studies. Among such centres was 'Takshshila' the spiritual capital of India of the time. In all the centres, students came for higher studies after completing their primary and some times secondary education.
2. **Minimum Age of Education.** In 'Takshshila University' the minimum age for admission was 16 years, since the students were admitted only for higher studies. This was almost like the modern universities.
3. **Education Fee.** Education fee was about 1,000 coins charged in the beginning. The students who could not pay in cash could pay as manual labourers or after completing their studies. Those who were unable to pay the fees, in any form, were given education as a charity. Actually, fee was

not charged for the pay of the teachers, but it was realised to meet the expenditure of the centre. Expenditure consisted of boarding and lodging charges of the students and maintenance of the centre. The centre was more or less like the universities of modern times.

4. **Scholarships.** The meritorious students who did not have means to support themselves were given scholarships by the government.
5. **Residence of Students.** Generally, the students lived in the centres with their teacher. However, some married people and students residing in private lodges, were also allowed education. Sometimes, teachers married their daughters to suitable matches from amongst their students. They also lived outside the institution, but continued their farther studies.
6. **Teaching Arrangements.** One Head teacher, with the help of his assistants called 'Vidwacharyas' arranged for the education of about 500 students. More students could not be put under him. Efficient and experienced students were appointed as assistant teachers. Meritorious students used to teach the students of lower classes.
7. **Teaching Honrs.** The teaching work was done during day time as well as night hours according to convenience. The students who paid fees were taught during the day. Those who worked to pay the fees were taught during the night hours. Similarly, the students residing outside the campus were also taught during the night hours.
8. **Syllabi.** Students were given Literary, Scientific and Vocational education. Only specialised education was imparted. Religious teachings were also included in literary education. Except Atharvaveda, all the Vedas formed the foundation of this education. Buddhism was also taught there. In Jatakas the following subjects have been mentioned constituting syllabi of higher education:

   (i) Medicine
   (ii) Vashikaran Kama-tantra.
   (iii) Tantra-Mantra.
   (iv) Archery (Dhanur Vidya)
   (v) Elephant taming (Hathi Sutra)

(vi) Hunting (Akhet-Vidya)
(vii) Giving life to the dead
(viii) The knowledge of the voices of various animals.

9. **Examination.** The students had to prove their practical ability in the above arts before Royal audience and at prominent places.
10. **Means of Education.** Books were taught and there was art of writing. These were essential means of education.
11. **Equality in Education.** There was no favouritism on the basis of caste and creed in the centres. All the students had to lead almost similar simple life. No students could have any personal money. All used to have similar food, clothes and mode of living, etc.
12. **Spiritual Knowledge.** Some students, who could not be satisfied even through higher studies used to go to the isolated places of ascetic monks and spent their lives in search of truth and Nirvan. Gradually gaining spiritual knowledge they became ascetics in their future life. These ascetics lived in lonely places of Himalayas. Sometimes more than one ascetic lived together in a cottage. Beside these lonely places, some of them resided near the populated places in some forests as well.
13. **Commercial and Occupational Education.** Buddhist education was basically religious, yet, occupational education was not neglected altogether. Mahabagga mentions arts of spinning, weaving and tailoring, etc. Even monks in the monasteries were allowed to learn these arts, 19 sippons (arts and crafts) have been mentioned. Among the other useful arts taught were Architecture, Arithmetic, Painting, Agriculture and Animal Husbandry, etc.

MEDICAL EDUCATION

References to medical sciences are found in good deal in Buddhist scriptures. This shows that even before 500 B. C. Medical Science had developed to a great extent. Medical men were well versed in medical treatments as well as in Surgery. Jirak was an eminent specialist in Medicine and Surgery. He had studied this science for seven years in 'Takshshila'. Then he undertook many journeys and gained the knowledge of innumerable 'Jaris and Booties' (herbal and medical plants). He treated innumerable patients.

There is also mention of serious but successful operation of stomach of the son of a prominent businessman of Kashi, and of the brain of the son of a businessman of Rajgriha. Charak had also flourished during that very period. *'Millinda Panha'* mentions the name of many Chikitsa Shastries, as Narad, Dhanvantari, Angarik, Kapil, Atula and Pubba Kachhayan, etc. The development of the treatment of snake-bite had taken place. Snakes were called with the help of Mantra and caused to suck up the poison. Thus the following facts may be noted about the Medical education of Buddhists:

1. **Expertise.** Emphasis was laid on the development of the Medical Science. There were many medical experts during that period.
2. **Surgery.** Chikitsaks (Medical men) were not only experts in the examination and treatment of most serious diseases but they were also efficient in serious surgical operations of brain, stomach, etc.
3. **Practitioners.** The important cities of the time had many medical practitioners.
4. **Takshshila.** Takshshila was the main centsre of Medical education where the complete course of the science was completed in 7 year. In the end, the students were examined in the knowledge of different types of medical plants. After completing the education, the teacher ordered the novice to go to his home and practice medicine and surgery.
5. **Journeys.** In spite of difficulty of means of transport the Chikitsaks used to undertake long journeys for treatment of the patients.
6. **Remuneration.** Although the remuneration of the doctors w as not fixed yet they received sufficient payments.
7. **Snake Bites.** There were easy treatments for snake-bites.

EDUCATION OF WOMEN

Though Buddha had first refused admission to women in Sanghs but later on at the request of his disciple Anand he agreed to give admission to women in the Sangh. Even then, women were kept under stricter rules and their places were lower than that of male monks in the Sanghs. Beside this the rules of admission of women in Sangh were stricter. Two years of probation was fixed for women monks before their permanent membership. The assent of the whole Sangh was also essential. Moreover, they had to live separately. They were instructed by a special monk only twice in a month. They could not live alone with the teacher. To Quote K. M. Panikkar. "In the fifth year of Buddha's ministry, the widowed queen of Suddhodhan asked to be allowed to leave the world under the doctrine of the Tathagat. Buddha refused the request three times, but the lady cut off her hair, put on mendicant clothes and followed the group. Finding the queen and other women, who were with her weeping at one of halts, Ananda, the disciple took pity and made request to the master. This also was refused three times. Then Ananda asked him the straight question, "Is a woman, who has gone forth from a house to a houseless life in the doctrine and discipline declared by Tathagat, capable of realising the spiritual truth?" "She is capable" Buddha answered. Ananda pressed home the advantage and Buddha agreed to the ordination of women."

Buddhist Sangh had given attention to the cultural development and social uplift of the women. There are many examples, which show that Buddhist Sanghs gave high spiritual training to women. Even among Lord Buddha's disciples there were Theri Shishyas prominent among them was Dhamma Dinna.

Generally women entered the Sangh out of keen interest and deep religious feelings. Some had also joined in to get rid of the troubles of the worldly affairs. As the Bhikshunis did not like to maintain inferior position, so they were more interested in the studies leading pious life. Though Buddhist literature does not speak much of the system of education of Bhikshunis, yet, there are some references of new-comer Bhikshunis taking charge of their education. There were Bhikshunis whose spiritual knowledge was very high and they could influence a good number of people. There is a story of a Bhikshuni named Sumka whose lectures influenced the audience very much. Many Bhikshunis took the duties of social services also. They served the sick, orphans, etc. and considered it to be their prime duty. Some of them had studied philosophy deeply and had become poetess and writers. Some of them had even gone to foreign countries to preach Buddhism. Sheel Bhattarika, Prabhudevi and Viyanka were famous in those days as poetess and writers. Sister of Emperor Ashoka Sanghmitra was a very famous Bhikshuni who had done remarkable services to Buddhism. Some Bhikshunis had studied even politics and took active part in politics of the day. Dr. R. K. Mukerji says, "The Buddhist convent opened out to women opportunities for education and culture and varied spheres of social service in which they made themselves the equal of men supplementing their work in the spread of their faith."

MERITS OF BUDDHIST EDUCATION

1. **Well Organised Centres.** Buddhist education was imparted in well-organised centres, Monasteries and Viharas which were fit places for the purpose.
2. **Cosmopolitan.** Buddhist education was free from communal narrowness.
3. **Simple and Austere.** Bhikshus led a life of austerity and simplicity.
4. **Total Development.** Buddhist education laid much emphasis on the physical, mental and spiritual developments of the novies.
5. **Disciplined Life.** Both the teachers and the taught led disciplined life. Contact with women was strictly prohibited.
6. **No Politics.** Politics was not allowed in Monasteries and Viharas. These were fully controlled only by Upadhyayas and Gurus.
7. **Ideal Teacher-Taught Relationship.** The relation between the teacher and the taught was ideal. The teacher considered the novice as his son and the novice considered him as his father.
8. **No Corporal Punishment.** Corporal punishment was absolutely forbidden.
9. **Both Sanskrit and Local Language.** Though higher education was given through the medium of Sanskrit, but general subjects were taught in local languages.
10. **International Impact.** Buddhist education helped India to gain international importance. It also developed cultural exchange between India and other countries of the world.

DEMERITS OF BUDDHIST EDUCATION

1. **One-sided.** Being mainly religious, Buddhist system could not give proper attention to the occupational, industrial and technical education so it may be called one-sided.
2. **Blow to Family.** It gave severe blow to the social development because it derided family ties. Leaving their

family life Buddhist Bhikshus devoted their whole lives to Sangh and Buddhism.

3. **Neglect of Military Training.** Non-violent Buddhist education neglected the military training and use of weapons. Acharyas did not give any attention towards the essential type of education.
4. **Loose Atmosphere.** The control and discipline of the monasteries began to vanish in the name of democracy. As a result the places of religion turned into the centres of recreation for the Bhikshus and Bhikshunis.
5. **Escapism.** Buddhist education neglected the physical development. Struggle for life was substituted by spiritual meditation and so its all round progress was barred. People began to escape from worldly duties.
6. **Degeneration.** Useless people violating social orders and even culprits were given shelter in Buddhist Sangh and so it was natural for monasteries to degenerate into the places of wickedness.

Looking at Buddhistic system of education from various points of view, it may be concluded that the system began to face downfall due to its own shortcomings and demerits, which developed in the monasteries and Viharas. In the later period, however, Buddhist system of education had more qualities than its demerits. It laid the foundation of a high culture and inspired people to lead pure, simple and ideal life.

GURUKULA

The study of education system in Vedic period and Brahmanical education system, makes it clear that in those days, the residence of the Teachers (Gurus) were the educational institutions, called Gurukulas. Here, the teacher and the taught lived together as the members of a single family. The main emphasis was laid on inner and spiritual uplift for the spiritual and philosophical development of taught. It had the highest importance in the educational system of the day. Well-organised educational institutions like that of modern age had not come into being in Vedic and Buddhist periods. In the Vedic period Sanghs, Monasteries and Gurukulas had been established. Vedic and Upanishadic literatures describe Sanghsand Parishads. The learned persons from different places used to assemble there and debates and discussions took place.

Mainly collective study was practised in Gurukulas situated in villages and woods. In Gurukulas, with the spread of Buddhism, a good deal of attention was given to the development of the organised educational institutions. Inspired by the Buddhist system the educational institutions were started. Special effort in Hindu temples and monasteries too, was encouraged for establishing the educational institutions of different types in different localities.

These educational institutions came into being in the Buddhist period. Lord Buddha realised the necessity of education for devotees at large. So he established the monasteries and Viharas, where education was also imparted. Gradually, these monasteries were turned into full-fledged centres of education where Bhikshus, Bhikshunis and even common people were given chance to acquire education. The foreigners also started coming to these places to study the Buddhist religion. As a consequence, Nalanda and Takshshila developed into universities of international importance.

The educational institutions of the Buddhist period were managed on the basis of democratic principles. Widely renowned scholars were appointed Kulpati or the highest authority of the institution. Various heads were appointed for different subjects taught in the university. Appointments were made on the basis of learning and qualification. Favouritism on the basis of caste, creed or religion had no place.

TAKSHSHILA

Historical Review

Takshshila was the most important educational centre of ancient India. It had widespread reputation in India and in foreign countries. It attracted hundreds of scholars from various countries of the world. Situated at the distance of 20 miles in the west of Rawalpindi Takshshila was the capital of Gandhar Kingdom. According to Valmiki Ramayana, Prince Bharat had founded this city and appointed his son Taksha as the ruler of the territory. The city was named after him. It is said that the Nagyagya of Janmejaya was performed in this very city. It had been the main centre of learning and education of Brahmanic system as well. Up to the 7th century B. C. it was considered to be the centre of learning and culture. Scholars, from distant places like Rajgrih,

Kashi and Mithila, etc., used to go there. It was very famous for its philosophers and scholars in the time of Alexander.

Due to geographical situation and prosperity, Takshshila had to suffer the disasters of foreign invasions. It saw many ups and downs. It was invaded and conquered by the Persians in the 6th century B. C., by Greeks, in 2nd century B. C. by Sakas, in 1st century B. C. by Kushans and by Huns in 5th century A. D. The ruins of the city prove that it was destroyed and rebuilt many a time. Nevertheless, the invaders maintained their capital in this very city and also preserved its prosperity. Thus, the educational system of the Takshshila was influenced by the contact of different cultures.

Salient Features

1. **Organisation.** There was no organised institution or university at Takshshila. Education was imparted on family system. Thousands of learned teachers privately taught their disciples. The fame of Gurukula due to these eminent scholars had spread far and wide. This made it an international institution. These teachers were unparalleled scholars of their subjects. They imparted specialised training in their subject at their own residence independently. There were many Gurukulas being run privately. They imparted special education in various subjects. They were independently managed with no direction or recognition from any outside institution. Students were admitted according to the decision of the teacher. They were taught the subject of their own choice. They completed their education according to their sweet will. There was no examination system. No degree or diploma was awarded to the students after completion of their education.
2. **Tuition Fee.** Only higher studies were conducted in Takshshila. So the students of more than 16 years of age were admitted. Perhaps the fee was about 1,000 coins current at the time. Those students who were not able to pay the fees had to pay it in the form of manual labour. Sometimes the students were allowed to pay the fees even after finishing their education. Those students who were unable to pay the fees in any form were educated out of charity. Some meritorious students without proper resources were

awarded the government scholarships. In Takshshila all kinds of students, poor and rich, were given opportunity to study.

3. **Number of Students.** Jatakas mention that eminent teachers had to teach up to 500 students. A. S. Altekar has accepted the presence of 103 students under a teacher of good reputation. So it is possible that some eminent teachers may be having near about 500 students. As only one teacher could not manage for the proper education of such a large number of students, therefore, it is possible that one great teacher would be keeping some assistants and probably, they would have been selected from the well versed students, who would have been given chances to work as teachers.

4. **Boarding and Lodging.** The students in Takshshila resided with their teachers in boarding houses, but some lived outside too.

   For example, Prince Janhu of Kashi (Banaras) lived in a private lodge. Teaching work was carried on in the day and night. Those who paid fees in terms of money were taught during the day hours. Those who worked instead of payment of fees were taught during the night hours. The students, residing outside the boarding houses were taught during the night hours.

5. **Curriculum.** At Takshshila the education system was divided in two categories—Literary or General and Scientific or Industrial education. In Literary or Art departments, all the religious literatures were included. Besides Atharvaveda other three Vedas—Rigveda, Yajurveda and Samveda were the foundation-stone of education. Learning of Vedas by heart was the order of literary education. Besides the Vedas, Vyakaran, Philosophy, Literature, Jyotish, etc., Buddhist literature were also taught at this centre.

   Eighteen handicrafts and technical subjects like Greek architecture and arts were taught in scientific and industrial education. Eighteen Arts were—Ayurveda, Surgery, Archery, Warfare, Jyotish, Prophecy, Book-keeping, Trade and Commerce, Agriculture, Chariot-driving, Mesmerism, Snake-charming, Hidden treasure investigation, Music, Dancing and Painting. Practical experiments were also conducted in scientific and industrial education. Some of the university scholars gave public demonstration of their skill going from one place to other.

6. **Education Based on Equality.** There was no difference between the rich and the poor in the university of Takshshila. Those who paid their fees in cash and those who paid in the form of manual labour were treated equally. There were no differences in standard of living of the students, all of them led a simple life. The princes were not provided with any personal cash which might enable them to have the luxuries of life. According to Jatakas the Prince of Banaras entered the university with a pair of chappals and ordinary clothes and an umbrella of leaves. Prince Janhu did not have money even to purchase the Kamandala he had broken unknowingly in the darkness of the night. Every group of the society was given equal opportunity to develop its abilities. There was no discrimination on the basis of caste or creed. The Kshatriyas were studying Vedas along with the Brahmanas. Similarly, the Brahmanas were joining the Kshatriyas in the study of archery and warcraft. A Brahman Rajpurohita had sent his son to Takshshila to study the Archery' instead of Vedas. The students were also taught Greek language and the art of Greek warfare. The medical course in the university was completed in seven year Jeevaka became a medical graduate only after completing the seven years course.

NALANDA UNIVERSITY

Historical Review. Nalanda was situated in the state of Bihar at a distance of seven miles in the north of Rajgrih and in south-east of Patna at a distance of 43 miles. In the beginning it was a small village. Later on it flourished as a centre of Buddhist religion and learning. Lord Buddha delivered many lectures while staying in Pravarik forest of Nalanda. His prominent disciple Sariputta was born in Nalanda. In Nalanda the Vihara was established by Emperor Ashoka. He built a Sangharam (residence for Buddhist nuns). However, it did not flourish as an university before the 3rd century A. D. Nagarjuna came to study here at about 300 or 330 A.D. from far south. The history of Nalanda as a centre of learning begins from 450 A. D. Fahyan visited the place in 410 A. D. Some scholars think that at that time it might have been the centre of Brahmanical learning instead of Buddhist. Whatever the case but the glory of this centre was beyond doubt in and after 5th century A. D. At the time of the Chinese pilgrim Huen Tsang (629-845), it was a most important seat of learning.

Salient Features

1. **Central Place.** Nalanda had been the central place o Buddhism and Jainism alike. Lord Buddha delivered his many leactures there. His prominent disciple Sariputta was born there. Vardhaman Mahabira, the founder of Jainism also spent his 14 rainy season in Nalanda.
2. **Development.** Huen Tsang says that 500 businessmen had purchased the land worth 10 crores of gold coins and endowed it to Lord Buddha for this centre. Though followers of Brahmanism Gupta emperors assisted the centre. Kumar Gupta, Buddha Gupta, Tahagat Gupta, Baladitya, Bajra and Harsh had built one Sangharam each at this place. In the 9th century, King Balputra Deva of Swarnadeep had also endowed six villages to Nalanda Vihara.
3. **Buildings.** Starting with one or two monasteries, Nalanda had become the centre of religion and learning in a short period. It attracted scholars not only from the different parts of India, but also from other countries of Asia, namely China, Korea, Java, etc. With the increase of students, the residences were expanded. It became a network of monasteries with big rooms for sleeping and lectures, libraries and observatories surrounded by a wall. There was a massive gate at the entrance. In front of it was the college building. Apart from this there were eight other buildings in the middle of the Sangharam.
4. **Ashoka the Founder.** Emperor Ashoka is said to be the first founder of Nalanda Vihara. He had built a Vihara at the birth-place of Sariputta, the prominent disciple of Lord Buddha.
5. **Famous Seat of Learning.** Great teachers were imparting education at Nalanda. Scholars used to flock there from far and distant places to acquire knowledge of different branches of learning.

6. **Admission.** The admittance examination in Nalanda was not easy. According to Huen Tsang only about 20 per cent of the students succeeded in this examination. Sometimes even foreigners could not secure their admission and returned home. There were not less than 10,000 students in the university.

   The minimum age limit for admission was 20 year According to the general rules of Buddhist Sanghs those students whose standard may be called equivalent to the Higher Secondary of modern education were also taught. They did not have to appear in Admission examinations. According to the religious rules of the Sangh they were admitted after the trial of their characters. Non-receptive and uncultured students were not admitted.

7. **Boarding and Lodging.** Boarding and Lodging were provided to the students free of cost by the university. The students devoted their full attention to their studies. Huen Tsang has attributed freedom from economic worries as the real cause of success of the students. At the time of Itsing three thousand students were fed by the university. According to A. S. Altekar, the number of students in the university was about five thousand in the middle of 7th century.

8. **Teachers.** The number of teachers in Nalanda University was 1,510 at the time of Huen Tsang. They were categorised into three classes according to their efficiency. Best 10 teachers could explain 50 books on Sutras and Shastras. There were 500 teachers of second grade who could explain 30 books. 1,000 teachers were in the third grade who could explain only 20 books.

   The Kulpati or Chancellor of the university was Shilabhadra. He had studied all the Sutras and Shatras books and could explain them fully well. He was the most honoured by every one. Besides him, there were hundreds of scholars in the university. Notable among them were Jitsmitra, Chandrapal Sthirmitra, Dharampal, Nagaijuna, Gyanmati, etc. The fame of the university was mainly due to these learned teachers, whose name made the glory of the university spread throughout the world.

9. **Courses of Study.** Besides the study of Buddhism and Buddhist literature all other subjects of the time were also included in the course of study. Though the Vihara belonged to Mahayana school of Buddhism, yet Hinayana scriptures were also taught there. The prominent supporter of Hinayana school Itsing had also studied there for 10 years and found the teaching useful. Vedas, Vedanta, Sankhya, Dharmashastra, Purana, Jyotish, Ayurveda, etc. were the subject of study along with physical education. Students were given practical training in many subjects. Huen Tsang studied Yogashastra, Nyaya, Hetuvidya, Shabda-Vidya, Vyakaran, Jyotish and various philosophies, etc. There were arrangements for 100 lectures daily in various subjects in which the attendance of students was compulsory. They themselves did not want to miss them.

10. **Methods of Teaching.** There were three methods of teaching:

    (i) *Verbal and Explanatory.* According to verbal method, the students were given lessons from the book and they studied them with explanation. The students were given opportunity to clear out their doubts.

    (ii) *Lecture Method.* The specialist teachers of different subjects, delivered their lectures separately. The students were given chance to put questions at the end of the lectures and thus they got their doubts removed.

    (iii) *Discussion.* In Shastrarth *i.e.,* discussion method well-versed scholars discussed the important questions on fixed dates and days. Generally, the discussions continued till night and cleared every kind of doubts.

11. **Management.** The management of Nalanda University was carried on democratic lines. Manager-in-Chief was called Bhikshu Mahasthavir. He was a kind of Kulapati or the President. He was elected by all the Bhikshus. The election was held on the basis of experience, purity of character and learning. The Kulapati used to be the most reputed scholar of Buddhism.

    The Sangh appointed two committees to advise the Kulapati in various matters of importance. The first committee was like the Academic Council, which used to advise the Kulapati on the questions of education and teaching. Academic Council gave its advice to Kulapati in admittance in the university, setting the course of study, routine of the teachers, etc. This council managed the library too. It was assisted by other teachers and students according to its requirements.

The other committee was responsible for the general administration, construction of new buildings, maintenance and management of the existing buildings, proper arrangement of residence of the students in boarding houses, food and clothing for all the Bhikshus and also the general matters concerning the Sangh. This committee had to manage 200 villages attached to the university.

In order to facilitate the daily working of the university, the Sangh had appointed heads of the departments under whose directions the daily working took place. Boarding houses were managed by the students under the directions of the departmental heads. In the boarding house, the rooms were allotted according to the age and older students had more privilege than the new ones. The students themselves decided the punishment for every kind of offence or sin. Therefore, it seldom occurred. Thus, the working of the university went on with full co-operation and sympathetic coordination of the teacher and taught. The students had full regard and respect for their teachers and the teachers provided encouragements to their students.

12. Library. To quote A. S. Altekar, "The authorities of the Nalanda University had felt that the Vihara without the Library is similar to a fort without weapon." The university had a very big library corresponding to its reputation. This library was placed in three big buildings—known as Ratnasagar, Ratnoradhi and Ratnarantak. Rare and valuable books were kept in Ratnasagar from where the foreigners might copy them to take to their countries. Itsing had copied four hundred Sanskrit books consisting of about five lakhs of slokas.

At the end of 12th century Bakhtiyar Khilji invaded Nalanda, destroyed the university and put the library to fire.

QUESTIONS FOR EXERCISE

1. Show the continuation of a Brahmanical tradition in Buddhist system of education. Point out fundamental differences.
2. Describe the salient features of Buddhist higher education.
3. Write short note on — (a) Buddhist Medical Education, (b) Buddhist Women Education.
4. Assess the merits and demerits of Buddhist Education.
5. Write short note on Takshshila.
6. Write short note on Nalanda University.

CHAPTER 6

THE ISLAMIC EDUCATION

After the defeat of Prithviraj Chauhan, Mohammad Gori laid the foundation of Muslim rule in Northern India. Many kings ruled over India during the Muslim period. The sultans of Slave dynasty were the first Muslim rulers in Northern India.

THE SLAVE DYNASTY (1206-1286)

1. **Qutubuddin (1206 A. D. to 1210 A.D.)**—Qutubuddin was the first Sultan to rule India. He belonged to the Slave dynasty. Though he loved education, but was a begot in religious matters. He hated Hindus. During his four years' rule he demolished many Hindu temples and constructed mosques in their places. Maktabs (primary schools) were established in these mosques. Muslim religion was principally taught in these Maktabs.
2. **Iltutmish (1211 A.D. to 1236 A.D.)**—Iltutmish was a lover of education and an able administrator, however, as his major portion of the time was absorbed in consolidating his position education was completely ignored during his time.
3. **Razia (1236 A.D. to 1242 A.D.)**—Razia was an able administrator. She loved education. Learned persons were greatly honoured in her court. During her short tenure education was encouraged and expanded. A big educational institution known as Muijji Madarasa was established at Delhi.
4. **Nasiruddin (1246 A.D. to 1265 A.D.)**—Of all the sultans Nasiruddin was the greatest lover of education. He used to copy down the Holy Quran and prepare caps for earning his livelihood. He was himself a learned man. So he encouraged education. He honoured learned persons who adorned his court. During his tenure Persian was developed further.

Many good books were written during his rule including Tabkati Nasiri, the famous historical document.

5. **Balban (1266 A.D. to 1286 A.D.)**—Balban was the strongest Sultan of the Slave dynasty. An ardent lover of literature, he encouraged education and patronised a number of scholars in his court. Because of the oppression by Changez Khan a number of learned persons fled from the Central Asia and sought and found protection and patronage in Balban's court. Balban used to reward scholars on their great works. Amir Khusro was the most influential and bright scholar of his court. During Balban's 20 years rule culture and literature were greatly encouraged.

THE KHILZI DYNASTY (1290-1316)

1. **Jalaluddin Khilzi (1290 AD. to 1296 A.D.)**—Jalaluddin, the founder of the Khilzi dynasty, was a lover of education. Like Balban he encouraged and honoured learned persons. He established a library at Kiluguri near Delhi whose head was Amir Khusro.
2. **Alauddin Khilzi (1296 to 1316)**—Alauddin Khilzi was a cruel despot and had no respect for education. The cause of education got a set-back during his days. He seized the lands attached to Maktabs and Madarsas and harmed educational institutions a great deal.

THE TUGHLAQ DYNASTY (1320-1389)

1. **Ghayasuddin Tughlaq (1320 to 1325)**—There have been three sultans under the Tughlaq dynasty and all the three were great lovers of education. Literature developed during this period unprecedentedly. Ghayasuddin Tughlaq was a great lover of education. He respected scholars. He established a cultural society and rewarded a number of scholars for their literary works. He extended many facilities to learned persons.
2. **Mohammad Bin Tughlaq (1325 to 1351)**—After the death of Ghayasuddin his son Juna Khan sat on the throne under the name of Mohammad Bin Tughlaq. He was a great writer and scholar. His court principally consisted of learned persons, writers, artists and philosophers. Such a big assembly of learned persons was not found earlier in any Sultan's

court. Being himself a great writer, Mohammad Tughlaq encouraged scholars to create literary works. Scholars from distant places came to him. He built a number of Maktabs and Madarsas. Maulana Moinuddin was a great literary figure of his times.

3. **Firoz Shah Tughlaq (1351 to 1389)**—Firoz Tughlaq was a peace-loving and libral ruler who loved education. He was a conservative Muslim. During his 38 years' rule he opened a number of Maktabs and Madarsas. He used to grant stipends to poor students and reward literary persons. He established a great Makatab in Firozabad.

SAYYAD DYNASTY (1414-1451)

The Sayyad dynasty ruled over the country for 37 year. It did not do anything worth mentioning in the field of education.

THE LODI DYNASTY (1451-1526)

1. **Bahlol Lodi (1451 to 1481)**—The first ruler of the Lodi dynasty Bahlol Lodi was an able ruler interested in education. Literary works were encouraged during his times because of his libral policy. He started a few Madarsas also.
2. **Sikandar Lodi (1481 to 1517)**—Sikandar Lodi was a great writer and a lover of arts. He respected scholars and rewarded them for new writings. Many foreign scholars visited his court. Sikandar was a poet and prepared a Diwan (Collection of poems) of 9000 poems. He was a disciple of Shekh Sultan Jamal. He used to compose verse under the pen-name Gulrukh. He got translated into Persian a book on Ayurveda under the title Tibbat-e-Sikandari.
3. **Ibrahim Lodi (1517 to 1526)**—Ibrahim Lodi was the last ruler of the Lodi dynasty. He loved arts. But due to wars and other difficulties he could not pay any attention to education and development of literature.

After Ibrahim Lodi the Mughuls established their rule in the country. Thus ensued a new era in the history of India.

EDUCATION DURING THE MUGHAL PERIOD

1. **Zaheeruddin Mohammad Babur (1526 to 1530).** Babur, the founder of the Mughal empire in India, gave a new turn to

Indian history. He was a great scholar of Turkish and Persian literature. He had established his reputation as a scholar by writing his autobiography Twzuk-a-Babure'. He was also a poet of excellence. He opened a department 'Shuhrat-a-Aam' for producing literary works. He opened some new Maktabs and Madarsas.

2. **Humayun (1530 to 1539; 1554 to 1555).** Like his father Humayun was greatly interested in the development of literature. He was a lover of books. During his life time he opened many Maktabs, Madarsas and libraries. Tazkirat-ul-Wakiyat a great book was written during his days. When he regained his kingdom after defeating Shershah Suri he converted the 'Shermandal' into a library.

3. **Akbar (1556 to 1605).** The greatness of Akbar lay in his great contributions in the field of art, literature, culture and civilization. He himself was illiterate but he was greatly interested in education. He gave place to learned persons in his court and himself participated in their learned discussions. The nine jewels of his court were distinguished scholars. Abul Fazl, his brother Abul Farjeez Faizi, Abdul Rahim Khankhana, Abul Qadir, Balavusu, Birbal, Tansen, MansinghandTodarmal were authorities in their fields. Akbar tried to reorganise education and place it on a stronger footing. He wanted to make education enable the students to earn their livelihood after being educated. The teacher was required to work as a guide. The student was encouraged to depend upon self-study. Akbar tried to simplify the alphabets. The student was required to memorise some poems. Akbar was very liberal in religious matters. He wanted that Muslims and Hindus should receive education in their own religions. Mathematics, physiology, medicine, agriculture and other traditional subjects were the essential parts of the curriculum for Madarsa.

   Akbar's rule is regarded as the golden age for promotion of new literature. All the Indian languages were developed during his days. Many original works were produced. Many translations of great classical works were prepared. Abul Fazl wrote Akbarnama. In addition to cash rewards Akbar used to grant Jagirs to literary persons. Literary discussions were usually organised in the 'Ebadat Khana' at Fatehpur

Sikri near Agra. Many foreign scholars from countries visited Akbar's court. His palace library consisted of many precious foreign books. Faizi was the head of this library.

4. **Jahangir (1605 to 1627).** Jahangir was himself a scholar and lover of arts and literary works. Following his father's policy he opened many Maktabs and Madarsas. He gave grants also to the existing ones. He wrote a book named 'Jahangirnama'. The poets Surdas, Tulsidas and Keshavadas flourished during his rule.
5. **Shahjahan (1627 to 1653).** Of all the Mughal emperors Shahjahan was the greatest lover of arts. He got constructed Taj Mahal which is one of the wonders of the world. He was more interested in arts than in education. He continued the educational policy initiated by his father and grandfather. He helped the existing Maktabs and Madarsas although he did not open any new ones. Literature, art, education and culture were well developed during his days. Shahjahan used to patronise learned persons and artists.
6. **Aurangzeb (1657 to 1707).** Notorious for his bigotry and cruelty Aurangzeb was narrow-minded in religious matters. He put an end to the liberal policy initiated by Akbar, though he helped Muslim institutions. He obstructed the growth of Hindu educational institutions, culture and civilization.

SALIENT FEATURES OF EDUCATION

1. **Aim of Education.** The aim of education during the period was the extension of knowledge and the propagation of Islamic principles, laws and social conventions. Education was based on religion. Its aim was to make persons religious-minded. The Muslim education also aimed at the achievement of material prosperity.
2. **Organisation of Education.** Education was organised in 'Maktabs' and 'Madarsas'. Primary education was given in 'Maktabs' and higher education was given in Madarsas.
   (i) ***Maktabs.*** In 'Maktabs' children were made to remember the 'Ayats' of 'Quran'. They were also imparted the education of reading, writing and primary arithmetic. When the children had learnt the Arabic script, they were given the education in Persian language and script. The stories of Prophets and Muslim 'Fakirs' were also told to

the children. Children were imparted the knowledge of art of writing letters and conversation.

(ii) *Madarsas.* After completing the primary education, the children were sent to 'madarsas' to receive higher education. Hence there were separate teachers for different subjects. Special emphasis was given to the education of religious as well as secular subjects. The religious education included the study of 'Quran', Mohammad Saheb and his preachings, Islamic laws and Islamic history, etc. The secular education included the study of Arabic literature, Grammar, History, Philosophy, Mathematics, Geography, Politics, Economics, Greek language, Astrology and Agriculture, etc.

3. **State Patronage.** During the Muslim period education received a great patronage of state. The Muslim rulers established many Maktabs, Madarsas, libraries, etc., and patronised many scholars. They also granted scholarships to many students.
4. **No University.** There was no university in Muslim education. Education imparted in 'Maktabs' and 'Madarsas' had the stamp of religious orthodoxy. Hence Hindus could not get much benefit out of it. The provision of education was only for higher and middle classes. There were no means for imparting education to the children of common people.
5. **Neglect of Vernaculars.** Arabic and Persian languages had been adopted and the vernacular languages had been altogether neglected.
6. **Teacher-Pupil Relationship.** Due to the changing viewpoint towards the education, great ideal of teacher-pupil relationship which existed in the ancient India declined in the Muslim period.
7. **Discipline and Punishment.** In the Muslim period, the teachers did not receive that much respect. Hence in order to ensure the maintenance of discipline, the teachers were empowered to give different types of physical punishments.
8. **Examination.** The system of examination was not prevalent in the Muslim period. It depended upon the will of the teacher to send the pupil to the higher class or not.

9. **Degrees.** There was also the system of giving degrees after the completion of education. The students, who acquired special knowledge in religion, were given the degree of 'Alim'. The students completing the education of logic were conferred the degree of 'Fazil'.
10. **Education of Women.** Although there was 'Pardah' system during the Muslim period, yet Islam did not oppose the education of women. These two contrary factors influenced the education of women in two ways. The girls were entitled to receive education equal to that of the boys up to a definite age but thereafter their education was stopped. However, the girls of higher classes used to continue their studies at home.
11. **Military Education.** In order to establish their supremacy over the Hindu kings, Muslim rulers had to wage constant wars. Keeping this situation in view provision of military education was made compulsory.

MERITS OF MUSLIM EDUCATION

1. **Compulsory.** Education was compulsory, specially for boys.
2. **Co-ordination.** There was proper co-ordination between religious values and material or worldly needs and well-being.
3. **Character.** Great stress was laid on character building.
4. **Personal Touch.** There was a personal touch between the teacher and the taught.
5. **Curriculum.** Curriculum included arrangement for the teaching of various subjects.
6. **Practical.** Great stress was laid on practical utility.
7. **Incentives.** There was arrangement for rewards and scholarships for meritorious and intelligent students. This provided an incentive to learning and education.
8. **Literature.** Under Muslim rulers, through educational system, a good deal of development of literature took place.
9. **Free.** The education during the Muslim rule was mostly free.
10. **Writing of History.** During this period, the tendency to write history was developed. This tendency was different from the tendency of the ancient India. It helped preservation of record.

11. **Institutions.** During this period, great attention was paid towards establishment of educational institutions. Prosperous people w ere encouraged to establish institutions.
12. **Special Centres.** There were centres of specialized education.

DEMERITS OF MUSLIM EDUCATION

1. **Unsuitable.** Unsuitability was characteristic of the institution of education.
2. **Disbalanced.** Education of the Hindus was neglected. This brought about a disbalanced development of education.
3. **Material.** There was predominance of material considerations.
4. **No Universal Education.** There was no provision for universal education.
5. **One-sided Curricula.** There w as too much emphasis on teaching of Arabic and Persian. This led to neglect of other subjects.
6. **Lack of Co-ordination.** There was no co-ordination between reading and writing.
7. **Lack of Psychological Basis.** Muslim education lacked psychological incentives.
8. **Evil Effects of Corporal Punishment.**
9. **Defective Curriculum.** Curriculum was defective.
10. **Indifference Towards Women Education.**
11. **Low Status of Teachers.** The teacher-taught relationship was not ideal. The teacher did not occupy that position that he occupied during the Vedic period.
12. **Wrong Methods of Teaching.** Oral or verbal method of teaching did not help the consolidation of the knowledge.
13. **One-sided Personality.** In Muslim education there w as no place for allround development of the personality.
14. **Lack of Individual Attention.**
15. **No Development of Reasoning.** No encouragement to students to develop their power of reasoning.

ORGANISATION OF EDUCATION

The Muslim prophets had urged their followers to preach and expand their religion. Education in its religious philosophy was necessary for preaching Islam. Therefore, the primary form of Muslim education was religious. For this purpose Maktabs (primary schools) were also started and attached to mosques. In these Maktabs small children were given education in Islamic religion. Gradually Muslim rulers adopted more liberal policy in education. Besides Islamic religion other subjects began to be taught in Maktabs and Madarsas.

MAKTABS

In the Maktab children of all people were given primary education. Along with religious education they were also taught reading, writing and arithmetic. The children of rich people generally did not attend Maktabs. Their parents used to make private arrangement at their homes for their education.

The Ceremony at the Time of Admission

The child was taken to the Maktab on the first day in new clothes. At first he was required to repeat some verses of the Koran. If he was not able to do this, his education was started by pronouncing the word 'Bismillah', that is, his education was begun on the name of Allah (God). After this Bismillah ceremony the child was required to write something after a few days. On this occasion his close relations were also invited. The child was required to go to a Maktab regularly for receiving education.

The Maktab Curriculum

At first reading and writing were taught in the Maktab. Then the child was taught arithmetic and a certain portion of Koran. He was not expected to know the meaning of Koran, it was enough for him to memorise it. When the child was fully acquainted with the Persian script, he was taught its grammar. Then he was taught some love literature of Persian, *e.g.*, Laila-Majanu and Yusuf-Julekha, etc. General practical education was also given in Maktabs. Letter-writing, writing applications and accountancy were taught. Hindu boys could also be admitted in Maktabs.

The children of royal families were taught in palaces under the strict control of Maulavis. The princesses were taught Arabic and Persian and Islamic religion. Besides, they were also taught political science, law jurisprudence and military science in order that they could be able administrators. It was compulsory for princes to receive military training. Thus the children of the higher class people were given both theoretical and practical education.

MADARSAS

After completing the education in a Maktab, one could go to a Madarsa for higher education. During the Muslim period Madarsas were centres of higher learning. Madarsas were granted Jagirs (land and villages) by the kings for their maintenance. They used to receive other financial grants as well. Some learned scholar was appointed as head of the Madarsa and he used to carry on the teaching work with the assistance of other teachers appointed for the purpose. The king never interfered in the administration of a Madarsa. The rich people also used to give financial assistance to Madarsas. There was no official person or department for supervising the work of Madarsas. Akbar himself accepted the State responsibility of promoting education. Other rulers used to take interest in it either for their personal prestige or for expansion of Islam. Some hostels were also constructed along with Madarsas for providing residential accommodation to students.

CENTRES OF HIGHER EDUCATION

1. **Delhi.** Early Muslim rulers made Delhi their capital. Hence it became a centre of Muslim Education. Nasiruddin established, 'Madarsa-i-Nasiria' in Delhi under the chairmanship of 'Shiraz'. Other rulers of Slave dynasty also developed Delhi as an important seat of Muslim education. Allauddin Khilji established many 'Madarsas' in Delhi and appointed renowned teachers therein. These institutions had more than 40 learned Muslim theologists and teachers of Muslim Law. Delhi had become a centre of literature and art during the days of Allauddin Khilj i. During the reign of Mohammad Tughlaq and his successor Firoz Tughlaq Delhi continued to enjoy the status of an important seat of Muslim education.

   During the reign of the Mughuls, Delhi maintained its original status and also improved itself. It now became the most important seat of Muslim education in Northern India. Humayun established an institution for the study of Astronomy, Geography, Persian, Grammar, Philosophy and Astronomy. Akbar's 'Aaya' had established a big institution in Delhi in 1561, and the famous scholar Badayuni received education in this very institution. Jahangir and Shahjehan also maintained the status of Delhi and contributed to its educational importance. Aurangzeb tried to transform Delhi into a city of orthodox Muslim education. He established many new educational institutions and gave financial aid to the existing ones.

2. **Agra.** Sikandar Lodi made Agra an important centre of Muslim education. He established many 'Maktabs' and 'Madarsas' in the city where students from foreign countries came to study. It was characterised by a rich efflorescence of learning and literature. It became a radiant centre of Islamic culture and philosophy. After Sikander Lodi, Babur and Humayun also established certain 'Madarsas' in Agra. Akbar made Agra a centre of learning, education and culture, craft and fine arts. During his reign, Agra became a huge university where scholars and learned men came from far and wide. In his book '*Muslim Education in India*' Mr. Jaflfar described this situation as following: "Men of learning and erudition from Arabia, Persia, and Bokhara poured into it in ever increasing numbers at the prospect of receiving better patronage from the rulers of India, who were remarkable for their munificence.... The result was that, in course of time, Agra grew into a great literary city, containing several schools and colleges where people flocked from far and wide for higher education."

   Akbar built many schools at Fatehpur Sikri. After his death, Jehangir and Shahjahan added certain 'Madarsas' and educational institutions to the existing ones and also gave financial aid to them. During the reign of Aurangzeb, Agra assumed a very important place as a seat of Islamic education. With the downfall of Mughul empire Agra also declined in its reputation.

3. **Jaunpur.** During the reign of Turks, Afghans and Moghuls, Jaunpur enjoyed the status of an important seat of Muslim education. Sher Shah Suri received his education in one of the schools of the city. It had institutions of various and varied types. Here students from far and wide received education and acquired knowledge of History, Political Science, Philosophy and War-crafts as well. Ibrahim Sharki established many 'Madarsas' in Jaunpur and arranged for

their finance. Mughul rulers from Humayun to Shahjehan tried to maintain it as a seat of learning. During the rule of Mohammad Shah 20 institutions were established in this city. With the downfall of the Moghul empire the importance of this city as a seat of learning started fading.

4. **Bidar.** Bidar, a city in the south under Bahmani rulers, was a famous seat of learning. Mohammad Gawan established many 'Maktabs' and a big 'Madarsa' over here. In this 'Madarsa' very learned 'Maulvis' were appointed. Attached to this 'Madarsa' there was a big library which housed about 3,000 books on Islamic theology, culture, philosophy, medical science, astronomy, history, agriculture, etc. There were 'Maktabs' in the rural areas as well. Through them Arabic and Persian were spread. There was not a single village under Bahmani rule, which did not have at least one educational institution. It was, therefore, quite natural for Bidar to be a very important seat of Islamic education in south India.

CURRICULUM

Maktabs used to fulfil religious objective of education. But in the Madarsas, practical affairs of life were also attended to along with religious objective of education. Akbar tried to give a practical shape to education in an unprecedented manner. But education remained religious in spirit and form in spite of his efforts.

After completing Maktab education one could go for higher education in a Madarsa. Islamic religion was compulsorily taught to all the students though Akbar stopped this tradition of compulsory Islamic education to all. He provided study of Hindu religion and philosophy also in many Madarsas. He provided books for the same in some Madarsas of his days. But the Muslim students were compulsorily taught Muslim religion, Sufi philosophy and sermons ascribed to Muslim prophets. A Hindu was also free to study Muslim religion and philosophy. Akbar introduced the study of medicine, history, geography, economics, political science, philosophy, astrology, law and mathematics, etc. He made the study of Vedant. Jurisprudence and Patanjali compulsory for Sanskrit students. In his famous book "Aine-a-Akbari" Abul Fazl has described the educational system introduced by Akbar. Aurangzeb understood the importance of practical education. He regarded as futile education purely in language. But his ideas remained confined only within the four walls of his palace and the general public was never benefited by the same.

Some persons were appointed in the Muslim courts to record historical events from time to time. Because of this tradition many Muslim rulers have themselves written their autobiographies which are still preserved as precious historical documents. Law in those days was based on religious practices. So the study of religious principles was in a way education in law. As some Muslim rulers were interested in music also, so provision was made for education in music as well.

The Method of Teaching

Oral education and memorization of the assigned lessons were the chief methods of teaching during the Muslim period. The Muslim students were required to memorise certain portions of Holy Koran. Writing and Arithmetic were also taught in some Maktabs. There was no scientific method of teaching inthe Maktabs. So most of the students used to memorise Koran and prayers for most of the time. Realising the futility of this method Akbar encouraged writing and tried to reform the scripts. He ordered that the work should be written down first before memorizing. Thus Akbar tried to give a scientific basis to education so that the students might be trained in practical affairs of life as well. To make educational procedure systematic Akbar urged that the student should be first given the knowledge of alphabets, then word-knowledge and afterwards sentence-knowledge.

As the method of teaching was oral, the main task of the teacher was to give lectures and students used to listen to them passively. Then the students were advised to read some relevant books. They were required to prepare their lessons individually. This method made them active.

Co-operation of students was sought in maintenance of discipline during the Muslim period. Like the Buddhist system some senior students were appointed monitor for guiding and controlling junior students. In the absence of a teacher, a senior student of higher class used to teach junior ones. The students of medicine, music and crafts were given practical training also. Thus started practical education during this period.

Examination System

There was no formal examination system during the Muslim period. The teacher used to decide as to when a student was competent to receive education of a higher standard. So he had his own personal method to assess the capacity of a student and to advise him for receiving education of higher standard. The purpose of education was not to prepare a person for earning his living but to develop his personality. There was no prescribed standard for declaring a student failed or passed. This does not mean that all the students were considered alike. The abler student was given recognition by awarding stipends and prizes. There was no half-yearly or annual examination fixed for students. The students were examined from time to time in practical situations of life. In courts, debates and groups of poets, the knowledge and achievement of a student was assessed at times. On such occasions kings and great scholars used to come to participate. The ability of a student was carefully evaluated on such occasions. The really deserving one was rewarded by money and praise.

Pupil-Teacher Relationship

The pupil-teacher relationship during the Muslim period was as cordial as during the ancient days. As the people believed that no knowledge was possible without a teacher, hence the student used to respect and serve the teacher with all devotion. The society also respected him. There were hostels attached to many Madarsas. The teachers also resided in them with their students. This situation helped the teacher and students to understand each other. The teacher loved his students and tried his best for their development. As there were no hostels with Maktabs, so no personal relationship existed there between the teacher and his students. When the students left a Maktab after completing their education they had little impact of their teacher on them. The students of Maktabs were young children, there was no problem of indiscipline in them. Consequently there was no feeling of disrespect in the students for their teacher.

Indiscipline and Punishment

During the Vedic and Buddhist periods a student used to be expelled from the Ashram or Vihar on a charge of indiscipline. But during the Muslim period the student was given severe corporal punishment on the charge of indiscipline. Usually most of the students were obedient. The unruly one, if located, was severely punished. The teacher was the sole judge of the indisciplined behaviour as well as the nature of punishment to be given for the same. Nobody questioned his authority. Caning, making the student to stand or run for a long time and distance or to hang him up side down were some of the types of punishments usually given. The students were usually terrified by such a servere punishment. It is difficult to say if this had a healthy effect on the teacher.

Rewarding

Brilliant and industrious students were greatly respected. They were given praise and rewards. Sometimes they were awarded good government jobs also. In Madarsas the teacher used to reward good students. The rich people took pride in rewarding good students.

Hostels

In the Vedic days the student was to live in the Ashrama in a natural environment. He was required to lead a life of hardship and penance. Physical comforts were tabooed for them. During the Buddhist period the life of the student was comparatively easier in the sense that physical comforts were not tabooed for them. But during the Muslim period the student enjoyed greater physical comforts and facilities. In the hostels attached with Madarsa various types of living facilities, clothes, food and necessary books and other things were provided to the students by the State. During his travels in India Ibn Batuta has described the working of some Madarsas. Because of the good arrangements in their hostels, he preferred to live with students for some time. In his book he has written that the students were given by the State good non-vegetarian diet, good clothes, beds, fruits and milk. Perfumed oil was also given to students. Thus the State took great care for the comforts of the students of Madarsas. However, as Ibn Batuta could not visit all the Madarsas, he has given his views about a particular Madarsa which was especially looked after by the emperor. Some books of that period have mentioned that some hospital was also attached with some Madarsas. Some Madarsas had swimming pools also for the students.

Subjects of Education

1. **Military Training.** Muslim rulers established their empire in India because of their superior skill in warfare and higher military organisation. They were conscious of the fact that they could win because of their superior skill and organisation of the armed forces. Therefore, they paid especial attention to military education of their children. The princes were given especial military training besides education in practical affairs of life and state affairs. The young princes were also taken to battle-fields for practical experiences. The Mughal emperors paid especial attention to military education, because they knew that they could hold up their empires only through superior forces.
2. **Fine Arts.** Development of fine arts had reached its peak during the Mughal period. The Mughal emperors believed that along with strengthening of military powers it was also necessary to maintain pomp and show in the court. They encouraged education in fine arts so that great artists might develop their art for contributing to the glory of the court. Music and painting developed very much during this period. One of the great courtiers of Akbar Tansen, the great musician, developed many musical tunes 'Rag and Raginis'. Dancing was also developed during this period, Anarkali, the great dancer belonged to Akbar's times. Painting was also encouraged. Jahangir, himself was a great painter. Sir Thomas Row, the British Ambassador, who visited the royal court has praised Jahangir's love of painting.
3. **Crafts.** Crafts developed during the Mughal period, as it received the royal patronage. Embroidery, ivory work, exquisite ornaments were regarded as symbolic of the excellence attained by handicrafts during the Mughal period. Because at that time there was no institution for technical education training in crafts was given in the traditional manner in families.

   Preparation of war goods also encouraged handicrafts. Boats, ships and chariots were manufactured on a large scale. This helped the artisians to be busy in their work and earn their livelihood. Taj Mahal of Agra, Red Fort of Delhi and Buland Darwaza of Fatehpur Sikri are excellent examples of the development of architecture during the Muslim period.

4. **Women Education.** Purdah system has been a part of Muslim culture since long. This system was observed strictly during the Muslim rule in India. Girls were not allowed to go to a Madarsa for receiving higher education. However, they were allowed to go to a Maktab for primary' education. The girls could learn only reading, writing and arithmetic. But even during the Muslim period there have been some very learned women who made unique contributions to the development of literature. The empress Nurjahan was a learned woman. She very well carried on state administration. Arrangements for education of princesses were made in the palace. Similarly, rich people used to arrange for education of their girls in their own homes. Music was taught to princess in the palace by carefully selected Ustads (teachers).

   Sultana Razia, Princess Gul Badan, daughter of Babur, Aurangzeb's daughter Zebunnisa are examples of learned royal ladies. Gul Badan wrote the famous 'Humayun Nama' Zebunnisa was a scholar of Arabic and Persian. Sultana Suleema, Mumtaz Mahal, Jahan Ara were highly educated in art and literature. However, as only the royal princesses and ladies and daughters of very rich people could receive education during the Muslim period, education of common Muslim women was completely ignored.

DEVELOPMENT OF LITERATURE

Muslim literature made great progress during the Muslim period. The Muslim rulers were very conscious of their glory. They used to appoint able persons to write the history of their period. Hence we find the written history of the Muslim period. Muslim rulers were conscious of the fact that they had come from foreign lands. So they wanted to preach their religion. At the same time some of them also wanted to become acquainted with the Indian culture. Therefore, they encouraged able persons to write a number of books in the field of literature and culture.

In the reign of every ruler some historical book was written. In this context one may mention Ziauddin Barauni's Tawarikhe Firoz Sah' and Yahia Abdulla's 'Tarikhe Mubarakshahi', Babur's autobiography 'Babur Nama', Abul Fazl's 'Aine Akbari' and 'Akbar Nama', 'Dandi Tarikhe Alfi' and Badayuni's 'Muntkabut Tawarikh'.

Muslim rulers were lovers of art. Although many earlier rulers did not hesitate in destroying many beautiful specimens of arts and architectures built by many Hindu rulers, however, they bestowed great honour to Persian literary figures and Muslim artists in their royal courts. Amir Khusro was a great scholar during the Tughlaq's and Khiljfs periods. In the days of Muhammad Bin Tughlaq Mir Hasan Dehalawi composed his Diwan (collection of poems). Babur himself was a writer and poet of repute. He had his own style which was famous as Baburi. Abul Fazl and Abul Faizi were great literary figures of Akbar's days. Famous musician Tansen and Ram Das lived during Akbar's times.

QUESTIONS FOR EXERCISE

1. Describe the efforts of the rulers of the Tughlaq dynasty for the development of education.
2. How was Indian education discouraged under the Sultanate rule? Explain briefly with some examples.
3. Describe the efforts of the Mughal to encourage education and literary works.
4. Describe the salient features of educational centres of Muslim education under Islamic rule.
5. Explain the organisation of education during the Muslim period in India.
6. Discuss the merits and demerits of education during the Muslim period in India.
7. What were the Madarsas during the Muslim period? Explain their organisation, curriculum and methods of education. To what extent are they prototypes of our modern universities?
8. What similarities and dissimilarities do you find in education of the ancient and medieval periods in India?

CHAPTER 7

EDUCATION UNDER THE EAST INDIA COMPANY

East India Company came to India for exploring business possibilities but it ultimately thought to establish its own empire in the country. Towards the achievement of this goal, they mingled with the Bengal politics. They obtained the Diwani powers in Bengal and acquired full control over the Nawab. After acquiring the Diwani powers and the political grip over Bengal they showed that they were progressive and that they wanted the welfare of the people. They wanted to prove that they could control the affairs of the government much better than the Nawab. They paid attention to education in order to show that they were really interested in the public welfare. They continued the government grants to educational institutions, though they did not think it wise to introduce any change in the educational set up. Able scholars, both Hindus and Muslims, continued to receive financial supports which they were already enjoying. The Directors of the Company thought that they should win the support of influential people for consolidating their position. Hence they provided for higher education and better government services for such people. Towards this end a college was started each at Calcutta, Madras and Benares (Varanasi).

The Calcutta Madarsa

The English people wanted to win the sympathy and support of influential Hindu and Muslim people. The higher class section of the Muslim population demanded the establishment of a Madarsa for higher education. The English people accepted this demand at once. Warren Hastings laid the foundation stone of the Calcutta Madarsa in October, 1780. Its main purpose was to educate the higher class Muslim gentry and to make them faithful supporters of the English government by providing good government services.

Based on Muslim religious principles a seven-year curriculum was instituted in the Calcutta Madarsa. Law, philosophy, logic mathematics, astronomy and grammar, etc. were included in this curriculum along with Islamic theology. Arabic and Persian were accepted as the chief media of instruction. The Madarsa soon attracted students from all the corners of the country. It received full financial support from the Company. The whole affair was very well organised and efficiently run.

Through the Calcutta Madarsa the company succeeded immensely in winning over the Muslim gentry in its favour. As it was also necessary to influence the Hindu section of the population, so the political resident of Benares, Jonathan Duncan founded the Benares Sanskrit College in 1791. Hindu religious principles, jurisprudence and other subjects were taught here through the Sanskrit medium. The Calcutta Madarsa was given a much higher financial grant in comparison to the Benares Sanskrit College.

At first Maulavis were made incharge of the Calcutta Madarsa and Pandits for the Benares College. But when they failed to control affairs, an English officer was also appointed at each place for keeping things into order. But no changes were made in the curriculum. They were run according to the respective religious principles as before. The East India Company was not yet hilly prepared to undertake the total responsibility for education. There were following causes for its reluctance to shoulder the entire responsibility:

1. At that time the government was not responsible for running educational affairs in England. Hence, desiring to follow the British policy as at home the Company, too, did not want to shoulder the educational responsibility.
2. The Company also feared that the people might ultimately rise against the British rule and would demand independence after having obtained higher education. This would endanger the British interests in the country.
3. The Company wanted to educate only a few people which it needed to run the affairs of the government.
4. The Company thought that the Indians themselves were not keen to receive education. Therefore, it thought that education must not be imposed on them.

5. The major interest of the Company was to accumulate money as much as possible for sending it to England and not to spend it on education of the people.
6. During this period the policy of the Company was narrow and it was centred round its own selfish interests. When the government in England was compelled to shoulder the responsibility of education under the public pressure, the Company, too, had to change its policy of indifference and began to take greater interest in the same.

Role of Charles Grant

Charles Grant was an ordinary officer of the company. He had come to India in 1773. He played an important role in education of the period. He studied the problems of education in India very closely. After his return to England he wrote an essay entitled 'Observation'. It contained a description of the conditions of the Indian people. It pointed out the deplorable affairs in the educational field. The description given in the 'Observation' influenced the British Parliament and it took upon itself the responsibility for education in India. Some people criticised Grant for drawing a very uncharitable picture of the Indian people in his essay. Grant has observed that "light must be brought through education in India. Then the people will learn to behave rightly. So far they have not been told about the right things. So education should be given to them for understanding things in the right perspective." However, Grant's real purpose was to help the Indian people.

He was of the view that medium of instruction should be the Indian language along with English as well. Special importance should be given to English in the education of Indian people, because it was through English that they could catch up the latest trends in literature, science, philosophy, religion and other subjects. English alone would revolutionise the thoughts of the Indian people for enabling them to hold their own uniqueness ultimately. At first English teachers should be appointed and later they might be replaced as able Indians were available.

The British Parliament gradually accepted the suggestions given by Grant and the same were implemented. But this process took 40 years when in 1813 a Charter was published.

The Charter of 1813 A.D.

The Charter of 1813 was published due to efforts of Charles Grant. Wilberforce helped Grant immensely in getting his ideas accepted. This Charter gave a new direction to education. Therefore, Charles Grant regarded as the father of modern education in India.

The Charter of 1813 revolutionised the enlightened opinion in India. Now it became a responsibility of the Company to make arrangement for education of the Indian people. The British Parliament advised the Company that it should spend at least one lakh rupees per year on education. The Christian missionaries were made free to spread education in the country on their own lines. The Charter had a good impact on the Indian people. Many enlightened Indian groups opened their own educational institutions to protect their civilisation and culture. Thus there was expansion of education in the country before the next Charter was published after 20 years in 1833. During these 20 years both the modern and indigenous system of education expanded.

PROGRESS OF EDUCATION (1813-1833)

During the period from 1813 to 1833 education was expanded. The responsibility for expanding education fell on the Company. It was asked to spend at least one lakh rupees per year on education. The Company had not been given any specific instruction on this issue. Consequently, the direction of education remained uncertain during these 30 years due to the following:

1. **The Medium of Instruction.** It could not be decided whether the medium of instruction should be English or Indian languages. There were many developed languages in the country such as, Hindi, Urdu, Sanskrit, Arabic, Persian, Gujarati, Marathi, Bengali, Tamil, Telugu, Kannad and many others. So the question arose as to which language should be taken up as the medium of instruction. Many groups with divergent views on this issue came up on the surface.
2. **System of Education.** Allied to former question was another issue was to how to expand English education in the country.
3. **Aim of Education.** This was the third problem to solve. Should education be made available to all, or should it be given to only a selected few?

4. **Measures.** What measures should be adopted for reforms of the prevailing system of education? This was a controversial issue. Should education be within the strict control of the government or should it be run by some forthcoming private enterprises?
5. **Role of Missionaries.** Another problem before the Company pertained to the Christian missionaries who were trying to preach and spread Christianity in the *garb* of educational *expansion*. Therefore, the company was to decide whether the missionaries should be given a free hand in their educational practices or should the Company itself shoulder the total responsibility.

Educational Policy

In order to carve out a path to be followed by the Company, one group wanted to make Indian languages as the medium of instruction. It included suchbig English officers as Munroe, the Governor of Madras and Mount Elphinstome, the Governor of Bombay. The second group included such important figures as Warren Hastings and Minto. This group wanted Sanskrit, Arabic and Persian as medium of instruction. The third group consisted of some young Englishmen and Raja Ram Mohan Roy who wanted to make English as the medium of instruction. This group believed that education through the English medium alone could equip Indian youth with Western literature, science and other types of knowledge which alone could make the native literature and culture richer. The Christian missionaries were in favour of English as the medium of instruction. There were some influential Englishmen and Indians in all the three groups. Ultimately English was accepted as the medium of instruction. This was what a few English officers, missionaries and Raja Ram Mohan Roy wanted. English was made the medium of instruction because of the support in Bengal and in some other company provinces. This decision gave a great set-back to the development of Indian languages and their literatures.

The evil results of English as the medium of instruction soon came upon the surface. It created such a group of persons who were Indians in birth and complexion, but mentally regarding themselves as Englishmen. These Indians became the connecting link between the English rulers and the general public to be ruled over. They became more interested in safeguarding the interests of the English people at the cost of the interest of Indians. The missionaries also got a good opportunity to preach and convert in the garb of spreading education. They gave incentives of good services and good education for converting Indians to their own faith.

Expansion of Education by the Company

The company was given sanction of spending annually one lakh rupees on education, but no instructions were given by the British Parliament as how to spend this amount. So the Company approached its Board of Directors for instructions. The Directors showered praise on the Indian system of education and advised that learned Indians should be suitably rewarded and great Indian books must be well preserved. The Directors further advised to help Indian teachers who are in financial difficulties, to give adequate financial assistance to old schools lying in bad shape.

The above instructions were mainly directed towards strengthening the roots of the British empire in the country so these helped only a limited group of the Indian people. Realising this situation Lord Muir asked for an additional sum of one lakh rupees for opening new educational institutions and for regenerating the old ones. Metcalf, too, supported this policy and observed that a liberal policy was ultimately in the interest of the British empire. In England, too, there was a wave in favour of a more liberal policy. So another Charter was published in 1833.

QUESTIONS FOR EXERCISE

1. What were the major difficulties before the East India Company in the first quarter of the nineteenth century with regard to framing an educational policy?
2. Discuss the importance of the Charter of 1813. What were the problems of education before the East India Company at this time and how were they solved?

CHAPTER 8

ANGLICIST-OCCULTIST CONTROVERSY: MACAULAY'S MINUTE

CHARTER ACT, 1813

In 1813 the East India Company was compelled to accept responsibility for the education of the Indians. Charter Act of 1813 made a provision for an annual grant of a sum of not less than one lakh rupees for the promotion of learning in India. Clause 43 of the Act stated, "It shall be lawful for the Governor-General-in-Council to direct that out of any surplus which may remain of the rents, revenues and profits arising from the said territorial acquisitions, after defraying the expenses of the military, civil and commercial establishment and paying the interest of the debt, in manner hereinafter provided, a sum of not less than one lakh rupees in each year shall be set apart and applied to the revival and improvement of literature and the encouragement of the learned natives of India and for the introduction and promotion of a knowledge of the sciences among the inhabitants of the British territories in India."

CHARTER OF 1833

The territorial boundary of East India Company was gradually expanding, so it became essential for her to issue another notification. In 1833 was issued the notification concerning education in India. Following facts were notable in the notification:

1. The missionaries of all the countries were given the facility of preaching their religion in India.
2. The Governor of Bengal was made superior to the Governors of other provinces and his policies were to be followed by others.

3. Any Indian or natural citizen of the emperor territory was not to be appointed to any service or post on the basis of caste, creed or some other consideration.
4. Education grant was raised to ₹ 1,00,000 from 10,000.
5. In the Council of the Governor-General a fourth member *i.e.* Law Member was added.
6. In due course of time, the provision of this Charter influenced the education in India to a very great extent. This Charter of 1833 occupies a very important place in the history of Indian education.

ANGLICIST-OCCULTIST CONTROVERSY

The Charter Act of 1813 did not specify the methods to secure the objects of, 'revival and improvement of literature', 'the encouragement of learned natives of India' and 'the introduction and promotion of a knowledge of sciences among the inhabitants of the British territories in India'. The vagueness of its Clause 43 intensified the Anglicist Occultist controversy in India. Since the dawn of 19th century, there emerged two groups among the officials of the company, one group was that of the Orientalists or Classicists who wanted to promote Indian education through the medium of Sanskrit, Arabic and Persian. The developing Western education in India was carried on through the medium of English.

During this violent controversy Lord T.B. Macaulay came to India as a Law member of the Governor-General's Executive Council. Lord Macaulay was appointed President of the General Committee on Public Instruction by Lord William Bentinck, the Governor-General of India. The government wanted the advice of Macaulay on the implications of the Clause 43 of the Charter Act of 1813. Macaulay presented his lengthy minute to Lord Bentinck in 1835. In the minute he advocated education of the classes in India and made a vigorous plea for spreading Western learning through the medium of English. He thought that it was possible only through English education to bring about a class of persons, Indian in blood and colour, but English in tastes, in opinions, in morals and intellect. This minute was accepted by Bentinck and it opened a new chapter in the educational history of India. Princep, the leader of the Orientalist part, was asked to express his view on medium issue. In his letter of February 15,1835, Princep dealt with all the arguments of Macaulay and advanced suggestions for improvement of oriental literature and education. However, Lord Bentinck rejected it. This ended the controversy between Anglicists and Orientalists.

LORD MACAULAY'S MINUTE ON INDIAN EDUCATION

Lord Macaulay came in India as a Law member of the Council of Governor-General on June 13,1834 during the violent Oriental and Occidental controversy. According to the Charter of 1833, he was appointed Law Member of the Governor-General's Council. He was a learned scholar of English literature and a very fluent orator. He was appointed the Chairman of the Society of Public Instructions of Bengal by Lord William Bentinck. The Government demanded his advice on the following two issues as a Law Member:

1. Could the granted money of ₹ one lakh be spent in any other way also besides the oriental education?
2. What was the actual meaning of articles of the Order of 1813?

Macaulay did not take part in any of the policy laying of the Government of India. Nor did he ever participate in the meetings of the society. He had avoided all these things with a view to avoid objection on his appointment as Law Member. The Minutes put by him on February 2,1835 were his scheme of education. In this minute he supported Western education through English medium in India. The main features of his Minutes were as follows:

1. **Meaning of the Word 'Literature'.** In the Order of 1813 the word 'Literature' meant English literature and not Sanskrit or Arabic or Persian literature.
2. **Indian Scholar.** As used in the Order of 1813 'Indian Scholar' meant 'a scholar' who is learned in the Locke's Philosophy, Milton's Poetry *i.e.* English Literature. Hence Indians should gain thorough knowledge of English literature and Western philosophy.
3. **Repudiations of Orientalist's Ideas.** Opposing the Orientalists, Lord Macaulay wanted to continue the Oriental Educational Institutions. He said, "The admirers of Oriental system of education have used another argument, which, if we admit to be valid, is decisive against all changes." He concluded that to assist the oriental system of education means to put a deadlock in the way of future progress.

4. **Medium of Instruction.** Criticising the native literature and languages, Lord Macaulay advocated English to be made the medium of instruction in India. He said, "A single shelf of a good European library was worth the whole native literature of India and Arabia." He maintained that current Indian languages are mostly incomplete, inefficient and lacking in scientific vocabulary. Hence, important books may not even be translated in those languages. Therefore, Macaulay discarded the local languages and degraded these literatures. He cracked many malicious jokes on Sanskrit literature, which proved his ignorance of it.
5. **Support to English.** Lord Macaulay flourished in an age when English nation and English language were progressing throughout the whole world by leaps and bounds. British had taken their own culture and literature as the best in the whole world. They were trying to gain political and cultural supremacy throughout the world. In support of English Lord Macaulay said, "It stands pre-eminent even among the languages of the West...whoever knows had ready access to all the vast intellectual wealth which all the wisest nations of the earth have created and hoarded in the course of ninety generations. It may also be said that the literature now extent in that language is of greater value than all the literature which three hundred years ago was extent in all the languages of the world together."

   Macaulay advanced the following facts for proving English to be the most useful language for Indians.
   1. It is the language of the Rulers and highly placed Indians use it.
   2. It is possible that it might be the language of trade and commerce in the Eastern Waters.
   3. The progressive Europeans of Australia and Africa use it and their relations with India are increasing day by day.
   4. Latin and Greek had brought resurrection in England, similarly these will do it in India.
   5. Indians themselves are in favour of studying English more than Arabic or Sanskrit or Persian.
   6. Indians might be made learned in English literature and it is the duly of the Government to make efforts for it.

7. The students of Oriental Institutions want the financial help whereas the students reading in English schools are ready to pay fees, etc.

6. **Proposal for Preparing Code in English.** Macaulay was not in favour of the study of Hindu and Islamic law through Sanskrit, Arabic and Persian. He called it a foolishness to continue the Oriental institutions for the knowledge of laws. He proposed to get all the Law books of Sanskrit and Arabic and Persian translated into English and prepare the Code of Law.

7. **Religious Concept.** Macaulay was strictly secular minded. He did not like to interfere with the religions of Indians in any way. He said, "If the medium of instruction happened to be Sanskrit and Arabic or Persian, then we shall have to teach incorrect history, Jyotish and Medical Science, because they are related to a false religion. We are neutral and remain always neutral in religious matters and shall never encourage open religious conversion. With such behaviour we shall never allow the people at the cost of money given from the Government purse to..., their youth in learning the method of purifying the body after touching a donkey or perform some ritual to clear the skin of killing goat."

   Thus, Lord Macaulay advocated Western education and English medium for education in India. He proposed to stop the grants of Oriental institutions and save the unnecessary expenditure. He wanted to utilize the money properly in opening English schools and developing the Western system of education in India.

8. **Ways of Grant Utilisation.** Macaulay made a declaration stating the ways of expenditure of the money granted for education in India. Following points are worth mentioning in this regard:
   1. British government's main aim is to spread European literature and Science among Indians and so all the money granted for education will be spent for that purpose.
   2. Oriental institutions will not be closed and their teachers and students shall continue to receive their pay and scholarships as usual.
   3. Oriental literature will not be published in future as sufficient money had been spent on this item.

4. The money, thus saved, will be spent in the spread of English literature and Science among Indians through English medium.

This declaration decided the policy, medium, means and aims of education in India as adopted by the British government. Governor-General himself was admirer of English education. Therefore, assisted by Lord Macaulay, he got the opportunity of enforcing his thoughts. He thought that many social evils will end with the development of English education.

CONTRIBUTION OF LORD MACAULAY

Lord Macaulay's Minutes ended the controversy going on, about the education system in India, for about 20 year. An education policy was laid down. Following are the statements enabling the student to evaluate Macaulay's contribution to Indian education.

1. **Ending Anglicist Orientalist Controversy.** In their book *"A Student's History of Education in India"* Nurullah and Naik say, "To call Macaulay a torch bearer in the path of progress, gives an exaggerated account of the role that he actually played." Lord Macaulay was not the first person who pleaded the cause of Western education. He was not the founder of Occidentalist group, as these elements were working before his arrival in the country. These were started many years earlier by Christian missionaries and men like Raja Ram Mohan Roy. Macaulay, however, ended the Oriental-Occidental controversy and laid the foundation-stone of modern education system in India.
2. **Cause of Political Disorder.** Some critics have called Macaulay responsible for Indian slavery. This is also not reasonable. Political disturbances could take place in the absence of his education policy also, as many Indian students were studying in mission schools. The Indian rulers, whose powers had been snatched away by the English rulers had also assisted the political disorder to a great extent. Therefore Macaulay was not the cause of political disorder in India.
3. **Denigration of Indian Languages.** Some scholars had criticised Macaulay for denigrating Indian languages with malicious remarks, like calling them rustic, undeveloped and inefficient. Thus he had given a great blow to the development of these languages. However, as the Chairman

of the Society of Public Instructions, Macaulay said in his report of 1836, "We have much interest in the development of Indian languages. We do not see any reason that the order of 7th March checks us in our efforts and we had already paid attention to its improvement... the development of native languages is our final aim and our all the efforts should be utilised in its cause." Hence, Macaulay cannot be blamed for denigrating native languages.

4. **Ignorance.** A learned scholar like Macaulay could not recall even the European scholars, who had praised Sanskrit grammar, philosophy and literature. He cracked jokes on it though he himself was ignorant about it. This charge of ignorance is irrefutable.
5. **Religious Motive.** Through English education Macaulay wanted to create, "a class of persons, Indian in blood and colour, but English in taste, in opinions, in morals, and in the intellect." Of course, his policy succeeded to a great extent. He did create a group of WOGS (Western Oriented Gentlemen) who would always co-operate with British rulers in exploitation of Indians. In a letter to his father in 1836, Macaulay wrote, "Our English schools are increasing with leaps and bounds and now the condition has reached to a position that it has become difficult to accommodate the students. Hindus are much influenced with education. There is no Hindu, who may keep real faith in his religion after studying English. I have full confidence that if our education policy succeeds then no idolator will be left in Bengal. All this will be done naturally without any religious preaching and interference." This statement clearly unravels the sinister motives of Lord Macaulay.

RESOLUTION OF MARCH 1835

Lord William Bentinck accepted the arguments advanced by Macaulay in support of his educational policy. He observed, "I give my entire concurrence to the sentiments expressed in this minute." The Resolution of March 1835 was the first declaration of the British Government in the sphere of education in India. It determined the aim, content and the medium of Instruction in India. Promotion of Western sciences and arts was acknowledged as the avowed object.

William Bentinck passed the following orders in resolution:

First. His Lordship-in-Council is of the opinion that the great object of the British Government ought to be the promotion of European literature and science among the natives of India; and that all the funds appropriated for the purpose of education would be best employed on English education alone.

Second. But it is not the intention of his Lordship-in-Council to abolish any college or school of native learning, while the native population shall appear to be inclined to avail themselves of the advantages which it affords, and his Lordship-in-Council directs that all the existing professors and students at all institutions under the superintendence of the Committee shall continue to receive their stipends...no stipend shall be given to any student that may hereafter enter at any of these institutions; and that when any professor of Oriental learning shall vacate his situation, the Committee shall report to the Government the number and state of the class in order the Government may be able to decide upon the expediency of appointing a successor.

Third. It has come to the knowledge of the Governor-General-in-Council that a large sum has been expended by the Committee on the printing of oriental works; His Lordship-in-Council directs that no portion of the funds shall hereafter be so employed.

Fourth. His Lordship-in-Council directs that all the funds which these reforms will leave at the disposal of the Committee be henceforth employed in imparting to the native population a knowledge of English literature and science through the medium of the English language; and His Lordship-in-Council requests the Committee to submit to government with all expedition, a plan for the accomplishment of this purpose.

Changes Enforced in Indian Education

As is clear by the text of the resolution of March 7,1835, the following changes were enforced in Indian education by it:

1. European literature and science will be propagated among the Indians.
2. Funds will be employed only for encouraging English education.
3. Future allocation of funds to oriental students and teachers will be stopped.
4. No funds will be available for printing of oriental works.
5. The medium of education will be English.

DOWNWARD FILTRATION THEORY

In India Christian missionaries calculated that lower classes of the people generally follow the ideas of higher classes. Hence, if some people of higher classes could be converted to Christianity, the people of lower classes will follow them. Therefore, efforts were made for spreading English education through mission schools. In the beginning of 19th century the British rulers thought that in order to run the British rule in India peacefully, it is essential to make higher classes the blind followers of the Governor's Council of Bombay. Macaulay said in his Minute, "It would be more suitable to provide higher education to higher classes than to give elementary education to the mass." In their despatches dated September 29,1830, the Director of the Company had written to Madras Government, "The improvement of education, however, which most effectually contribute to elevate the moral and intellectual condition of a people are those, which concern the education of the higher classes of the persons possessing leisure and natural influence over minds of their countrymen. By raising the standard of education among these classes you would eventually produce a much greater and more beneficial change in the ideas and feelings of the community than you can hope to produce by acting directly on the more numerous class."

Lord Macaulay had similar ideas. In his Minute of 1835, he said, "At present we should create such a group of people who may work as a mediator between us and the common people, a class of persons, Indian in blood and colour, but English in tastes and opinions, in morals and in intellect. It will be their duty to develop the native languages and enable it to convey the knowledge to the common people." Again on July 31,1837 he said, "At present we don't aim at educating directly the common people. We aim at creating a class of persons, who among their countrymen distribute some of the knowledge we gave." The Society of Public Instructions in Bengal had also approved the same ideal and expressed its ideas in 1839 in these words, "Our efforts should be concentrated first on the education of higher and middle class of people." Declaring it as government policy, Sir Auckland said, "The government should educate the higher class of the people so that the filtered culture reach to the public." Therefore, this policy was followed up to 1870 and emphasis was laid on the education of the people of higher classes in the society.

Meaning of Filtration Theory

Filtration theory means "Education is to be filtered to the common people. Drop by drop, the education should go to the common public so that at due time it may take the form of a vast stream which remained watering desert of the society for long times and high class of people should be educated and common people gain influence from them."

Causes of Filtration Theory

The following were the causes which led to make the Filtration Theory the Government policy:

1. **Need of Government Servants.** The company government needed various types of workers to run the business of government. They wanted to have cheap servants who may work in different capacities. This aim could be fulfilled only by an educated higher class of people of India. So the government started the policy of education of higher class.
2. **No Money for Mass Education.** The Government did not have enough money to take the responsibility of educating the masses.
3. **British Belief.** British rulers concluded that if the standard of living and ideas of the people of higher classes in society could be changed through English education then the people of the lower classes will also be influenced and they shall be loyal to the British Government.
4. **Loyal Indians.** If some people from higher classes in society, educated on English lines, could be given higher posts in Government services, then naturally they will use their influence for controlling the masses from going against the government rule.
5. **Further Expansion.** After educating some people, the responsibility of educating other people could be left to them.

Thus, Filtration theory fulfilled the aim of Lord Macaulay and the directors of the Company. It decided the education policy of India supported by the higher authorities. The higher education began to progress rapidly. The declaration of Lord Hardinge of 1844 gave preference to people educated in English schools for the Government service. So, the main aim of education was securing Government job for which a large number of Indians started reading in English schools. After getting Government service the educated persons were cut off from the common people. Thus education created a false vanity among the educated persons. They became more self-centred. They started thinking themselves higher than an ordinary Indian. They maintained very little touch with common people. They became Anglicised to such an extent that even their daily routine and behaviour became westernised. Sometimes it used to be worse than that of the European officers. The higher and rich class went on progressing and common people went on degenerating. 'Filtration Theory' continued to cast its shadow up to 1870 after which it faded from Indian soil.

Causes of Failure

Thus Filtration Theory failed as a government policy in India due to following reasons:

1. **Expansion of Mass Education.** The Government began to increase the number of English schools. It was, however, unable to provide jobs to all the educated Indians. Naturally many of them started new schools to get themselves employed. This began to create more job seekers.
2. **Awakening.** As the number of schools increased a lot, this system only fulfilled the need of education of the common people. Educated on Western lines some people were of wide vision and without caring for Government services and self interest they started schools for educating general public. Thus, an awakening took place. People became conscious of their real status. Later on led by Mahatma Gandhi they played leading roles in the National Movement and the British rulers had to leave India.

QUESTIONS FOR EXERCISE

1. Explain the Anglicist-Occultist Controversy started by Charter Act, 1813.
2. Give a critical evaluation of Macaulay's Minute on Indian education.

   Trace the influence of Macaulay's Minute over the Commission of 1882 on the system of Indian education.
3. "The credit or discredit of introducing English education into India is not exclusively Macaulay's." Comment on

this statement and state with reasons your approval or disapproval of Macaulay's education policy in India.

4. Write a short note on the contribution of Lord Macaulay to Indian education.
5. Explain clearly that in history of Indian education the year 1833 tookatum towards a new direction. Discuss those changes which were enforced in Indian education since 1835.

CHAPTER 9

PROGRESS OF EDUCATION DURING 1835-1853

Britishers started their attempts to improve Indian educational life on the basis of the indigenous system of education. When British rule was being established in this country in the beginning of the 19th century they appointed a committee to survey the real position of education in India. This survey was conducted in Madras, Bombay and Bengal only.

EDUCATION IN MADRAS

Sir Thomas Munroe, the Governor of Madras, ordered all the collectors of the Province of Madras to survey the educational condition of the province and report to them. On the basis of these references he (Sir Munroe) prepared his own report as follows:

1. **Schools and the Number of Students.** Historian Mill had said that each village of Madras had a primary school, but the number of the students per school was very little. Sir Munroe accepted that in the population of 1,25,00,000 only 1,88,000 people were reading. It means that out of each 67 persons only one boy was going to school. In the districts of Bellary and Kanara the average number of students per school was about 12. Some people used to educate their children at their homes. Generally they did not go to schools. Sir Munroe accepts that 26,903 students were being educated at their homes in Madras city. This number was five times the number of the students going to schools.

   Most of the students were Hindus. Very few of the girls entered the schools. In Bellary district the data show that out of 9,941 students, there were only 91 girls.

2. **Medium of Instruction and the Courses of Study.** The general condition of the schools was unsatisfactory. Most

of them were giving ordinary education in provincial language. Twenty-three schools were teaching Sanskrit and only one English. There was no uniformity in the courses of study. Some schools were giving education in Persian and Marathi. Nevertheless, primary schools were, in general, teaching ordinary arithmetic, reading of manuscripts and documents. Students were made to learn by heart beautiful poems and fine stories and also good instructions.

3. **Period of Education.** According to the Collector of Bellary a celebration was made at the time of starting the education to which the kith and kin of the boy were invited. They performed 'Havan' and 'Ganesh Pujan' and afterwards the 'Guru' made the boy recite the prayer of 'Ganeshji'. He also made the boy write the name of 'Ganeshji' on rice. The parents of the boy gave the 'Dakshina' (Gift) to 'Guru'. Now the boy started reading. At his admission in school on the first day, the name of the goddess of learning (Saraswati Devi) was written on the hand of the boy and then he started reading. The boys of well-to-do persons continued their study up to 14 to 15 years but poor students had to leave the education after some time.
4. **Time Table.** The time table for all the students was almost the same. The school used to start at about 6 A.M. When the majority of the students were present teaching started after "Saraswati Vandana" *i.e.* prayer of the goddess of learning.
5. **Punishment.** The punishment in the schools was harsh. The students, who were found guilty were severely caned. Sometimes some of the guilty students were hung from the roof. Sometimes they had to practise sitting up for a long time. Late comers also had to do some exercises as physical punishment. This system was rather too harsh for common students.
6. **Method of Teaching.** In primary schools there were four classes from beginning to the end. In the first class small children were made to write the alphabets on sand or ground with their fingers. When they grew acquainted with the alphabets then they started writing on small wooden planks. *i.e.* 'Patti' with chalk and pen of wood (Sentha). Thus they learnt the 'Matras' and joint letters. Afterwards they were made to write the names of men, places and animals,

etc. In the evening, the boys of lower classes were made to remember the number up to hundred and 'Pahara' "Pauna", 'Add ha', etc. A monitor controlled the whole class. The good students of higher classes were given chances to teach the students of lower classes. The teacher himself used to teach the students of higher classes. The whole system was almost a domestic one.

7. **Condition of the Teachers.** The teachers in primary' schools were ill-educated and ill-paid. Hence ambitious men did not join this job. To quote Sir Munroe, "The teachers in general do not earn more than seven or eight rupees monthly, which is not an allowance sufficient to influence men properly qualified to follow the profession. It may also be said that general ignorance of the teachers themselves is one cause, why none of them drew a large body of scholars together; but the main causes of the low state of education are the little encouragement which it receives from there being but little demand for it, and the poverty of the people."

EDUCATION IN BOMBAY

On March 10, 1824 the Governor of Bombay province asked the collectors of all the districts to send report prepared after the survey of education in their districts. It was received in the year 1824-25, but due to its incompleteness another report was asked for in 1829. The report contained the following references:

1. **Condition of Schools.** In Bombay province there were no separate school buildings. The work of education was carried on in temples, houses of the teachers and residences of respectable persons. All the villages in the province had at least one school in each village. The number of schools were increasing in big villages and towns. Those schools were giving cheap education in three ₹. By way of fee they were paid 'Sidha' (grain worth satisfying a man for one time) or a rupee per month by the guardians of the students.
2. **Number of Students.** While population of the whole province was 46,81,735 there were only 2,705 schools and 35,135 students were receiving education. The highest number of students in a school was 150. The average of the students per school was 15 only. This number does not include the number of the students reading at homes

of the teachers of respectable persons. Only boys were taught in these schools. The Harijans were not admitted in these schools. Among the students about 30 per cent were Brahmans.

3. **Courses of Study.** The students were taught to read, write and do ordinary and practical arithmetic. They were made to learn by heart, the 'Pahara and Ginti' (counting of numbers, etc. also).
4. **Period of Education.** The period of education was six year Generally they read up to the age of 14 year. In Gujarat the period was only two to three years.
5. **Methods of Teaching.** In general, education was given verbally as there were no printed books. The new student was put under the charge of a good and somewhat elder student, who used to look after the ordinary education of the new comer. He reported about the particulars of his younger ward to the teacher. Thus the teacher got sufficient time to look after the school in general. He used to teach the group of the students, who had already learnt something. The classes were composed by group of students having approximately similar standard. The system was very cheap. A single teacher could manage a large number of students and look after their education. Economic status of the schools was not good. Proper education was rather impossible under the circumstances.
6. **Muslim Madarsas.** In Bombay province, at some places, Muslim students read separately under some Muslim teacher (Maulvi) but in many places they read with Hindu students.
7. **Punishment and Discipline.** At school the discipline was strictly maintained. Hard punishment was given to the students for not maintaining discipline and failing to learn lessons.
8. **Condition of the Teachers.** Generally, teachers were 'brahmans', but some Marathas 'Bhandaris' and 'Vaishyas' were also working as teachers. Their essential qualification was the thorough knowledge of 'Pahara' and ordinary arithmetic and the hand writing had to be fine and legible. As a tradition they got only three to five rupees per month as pay. They were generally invited at festivals and some gifts

and presents were given to the teacher on these occasions. The report considered the teachers inefficient. But according to Shri Parulekar "Knowledge of multiplication and other tables in their long and complicated array was essential to every teacher, but beyond that a tolerably good hand writing and ability to teach simple writing formed the minimum attainments of a common school-master."

EDUCATION IN BENGAL

Unlike Madras and Bombay, the educational survey in Bengal was made by Sir William Adam, and enthusiastic missionary. He had keen interest in Sanskrit and Bengali languages and had studied them well. He became interested in Indian education after coming in contact with Raja Ram Mohan Roy. He secured the permission of Lord William Bentinck for the educational survey and put up the report of his work done during the period of 1835 to 1838.

Given below is a summary of the three reports of Sir Adam:

1. **First Report.** No village in Bengal was without a primary school. There were about a lakh of schools scattered in all the villages.
2. **Second Report.** This extensive report gives full details of education in Thana Natur of District Rajshahi. The population of the Police Station Natur was 1,95,297 and there were 485 villages, with only 17 primary schools, having 562 students. Among these schools 10 were teaching Bengali, 11 Arabic and four Persian, two schools taught Bengali and Persian both. The custom of personal education was more prevalent. In 238 villages, there were 1,588 such families who had arranged for the education of their children at homes. The students started education at the age of eight and read up to the age of 14 year Teachers were paid ₹ five per month only per student.
3. **Third Report.** This deals with details of education in Murshidabad, Burdwan, Birbhum, Tirhut and south portion of Bihar and gives the data in regard to the condition of education. In these districts there were 2,567 schools, in which Bengali, Hindi, Sanskrit, Arabic and Persian were taught. Side by side there were eight schools of English education and six for the education of girls, 242 boys and 214 girls were studying. The Hindus were generally reading Bengali

and Sanskrit and Muslims were reading Arabic and Persian. Urdu was not included in the course of study. According to Adam, these schools did not have any source of income and the teachers were provided their livelihood by rich citizens, landlords and 'talukedars'. Some rich people had opened a pathshala at their residence. Education of women was considered against Muslim religion. Hindus thought that educated girls would become widows. Even then, some well-to-do families had arranged for the education of their girls.

HIGHER EDUCATION

Higher Education in Bengal

1. **Sanskrit Vidyalayas.** Adam's report says that there were 190 Sanskrit 'Vidyalayas' where higher education in Sanskrit was given. In these 'Vidyalayas' there were 2,358 students. This was the condition at the beginning of the 12th century. Among these 'Vidyalayas', two enjoyed the patronage of the Maharaja of Burdwan' and the rest were run by the private teachers. There was only one teacher in each 'Vidyalaya'. Some of the 'Pathshalas' were put up at the residences of the teachers and others were run in the buildings erected by some rich landlord or through collective efforts. The teachers were given a pay of about 64 rupees yearly and their economic condition was not satisfactory.

   The courses of study were very vast having the subjects 'Vyakaran' (Grammar), Literature, Lexicography, Alankars, Medical Sciences, Logic, Laws, Purans, Jyotish and 'Vedant' for study.
2. **Muslim Madarsas.** There were 'Madarsas' for the higher education of Muslims in Arabic and Persian. In South Bihar there were 219 schools with 1,438 students out of which 867 were Hindus and the rest were Muslims. In Muslim institutions, only 12 gave Arabic education and the rest taught Persian. Institutions were located at the residences of the teachers or in the 'Verandah' of some well-to-do landlords. Almost all the teachers of these institutions were highly qualified and each school had only one teacher. In one institution only there was a Hindu teacher. In all other institutions, there were Muslim teachers. These teachers had an average income of ₹ five per month.

Higher Education in Bombay

In Bombay, there were 164 and 16 'Vidyalayas' in Poona and Ahmadnagar, respectively. There were institutions in other cities also. In Surat, there was the famous 'Madarsa' for higher education of the Muslims. It had an annual donation of ₹ 32,000. It was established for 'Bohara' students. It had 125 Bohara students and the rest were other students. Students had come from different parts of the country'. Arabic was mainly taught in this school.

Higher Education in Madras

In Madras the institutions for higher education used to admit the students, who had already completed a particular standard. They taught Literature, Rhetorics, Philosophy, Religion, Astronomy, etc. Only 'Brahman' and people of higher castes were authorised to seek education in these institutions. Teachers generally worked with the idea of social and religious services, with very little consideration for economic gain. Some 'Vidyalayas' were helped by landlords and big traders, who used to arrange for the livelihood of the teachers in the form of donations and gifts.

About the educational conditions of India in the beginning of the nineteenth century Sir Munroe has said, "The state of education here exhibited low as it is compared with that of our own country, is higher than it was in most European countries at not very distant period." However, the condition was not encouraging in any way. The standard was gradually falling. Some of the 'Pathshalas' were losing their existence after suffering bad lot for sometimes. The teachers were ill-Paid.

EDUCATION BY MISSIONARIES

Europeans from different countries had started visiting India in connection with their trade since the last quarter of 15th century. Vasco-De-Gama, a Portuguese sailor came to India in 1498. Afterwards, Dutch, French, Spanish, Danes and English people came and started their business through trading companies. Gradually they began to convert their 'Kothies' into fortresses and page boys into soldiers. They began to acquire land through different means. They started to spread their religion Christianity and influence the political field. They took the cause of primary education among Indians. Mr. Allen has put forward two reasons to why missionaries spread education: Firstly, that they could make Indians understand their religious theories and principles better if they got their education on the Western lines. The second aim was to gain contact with Indians through these institutions. Therefore, they started educational institutions, almost in all the towns of India, through their own method of education. East India Company also made education as a means to spread Christianity but it had to give it up due to political and administrative reasons. Infact, the credit for present form of education has to be given to the Christian missionaries.

1. **The Portuguese.** Portuguese were the first Europeans who came to India and they were the people who started modern system of education here. The follower of Jesuit religious sect St. Francis Xavier came to India in 1542 A. D. He used to walk on foot from village to village with a bell in hand preaching Christianity. He distributed small books, related to Christianity in the villages. He started a university at Kochin. Even today his name is associated with many institutions.

   The main centres of Portuguese activities were Bombay, Goa, Daman, Diu, Ceylon, Chittagong and Hugli. They started primary schools in those places. There they used to teach the children of Portuguese Europeans. Those who followed Christianity, their children were given free education. These schools were giving education in Portuguese, Christianity, Arithmetic, local languages and some handicrafts. The children of the poor people were also given food, books, etc. If they agreed to be the followers of Christianity.

   They started the first degree college in Goa in 1575, where 300 students were studying. St. Anne College was started in Bandra. Some other colleges were also started at other places. Christianity, Logic, Grammar and Music, etc., were taught in these colleges. According to Barnier being influenced by Jesuit Bishops, Emperor Akbar started a Jesuit College at Agra where the students from 30 families were taught.

   Later on with the downfall of Portuguese their educational institutions became limited to Goa, Daman and Diu.

2. **The Dutch.** In the 17th century Dutch came to India to carry on trade in the same way as other European races. Factories were set up at Chinsura and Hugli in Bengal

and at Nagapattam on the coast of Madras. Schools were started where the children of workers of the company and some Indian children were taught. They did not make their educational institutions the centres of religious propaganda. They started a college in Ceylon. Due to enmity with Britishers they could not stay in India for long. With them, their educational attempts were also finished.

3. **The French.** The French established a trading company in 1664. They established their Kothies in Pondicherry, Mahi, Yaman and Karikal. In those places, they started primary schools. They opened their institutions for all the Indians. Education was given by Indian teachers through local languages. The teaching of Christianity was compulsory. They started higher secondary schools where French language was taught like other Europeans. They also had to face the opposition of the British. Most of their land possession were captured by the East India Company and the schools were also taken over by them.
4. **The Danes.** Some inhabitants of Denmark came to India in 17th century and started factories in Travancore and Serampore. They never tried to establish their kingdom and political influence. They limited their activities up to education and religious expansion. In 1845, they sold their colonies to the Britishers and left India with bag and baggages. Till then they had converted about 50,000 Indian people to Christianity.

   Two German Bishops named Ziegenbalg and Plustscham came to India. Due to financial assistance from Denmark, they took the help of society for promoting Christian knowledge. They used local languages as medium of education to facilitate the spread of Christianity in India. They distributed a large number of Tamil translations of Bible among the people. They prepared a Tamil Grammar and Dictionary. They started schools for those boys who adopted Christianity and they were taught through Tamil. Danish religious preachers gave preference to Muslims and started separate schools for them. They started a training college for teachers in Travancore. Teachers trained here were appointed in primary schools. Schools were started in Madras Fort, St. David, Trichnapalli and Tanjore, where besides other subjects, English was taught.

5. **The British.** In 1600 A.D. British East India Company was established. It started trade with India and spread its influence in political field also. Several missionaries came to India and they established institutions for spreading education. East India Company established institutions for imparting instructions in English. Gradually, it also established Sanskrit colleges at Madras and Banaras.

   Propagation of Christianity was stopped by East India Company. However, they did not completely ban the activities of the missionaries from England. Missionaries made a good deal of attempt for the propagation of education in India with the object of spreading Christianity. Due to their efforts, several institutions were established. These institutions imparted European education as well as Indian education.

Government Efforts

On June 3,1814 East India Company came out with an announcement to spend about a lakh rupees for Indian system of education, especially Hindu system of education. Following efforts were made in this direction:

(i) ***Bengal*** In 1823 a committee was appointed to make arrangement for education. It tried its best to propagate education in all possible ways.

(ii) ***Bombay.*** In this State, East India Company Government tried to give encouragement to Indian as well as European system of education. It also started the grant-in-aid system in order to control the working of the Indian system of education.

(iii) ***Madras.*** The condition of education in Madras was not satisfactory in primary, secondary and higher secondary education.

Non-Missionary Effort

As a reaction to the attempts of the missionaries to spread Christianity, several non-missionaries established organisations like Brahmo Samaj had made attempts for the spreading of European system of education. These bodies established institutions in Bombay, Bengal, Madras, Delhi, U. P., etc.

Charter of 1833

In 1833 a new Charter was issued which aimed at the spread of Indian as well as foreign system of education. Thus in the early years of nineteenth century, notable attempts were made to establish institutions on European lines.

GOVERNMENT EFFORTS

According to the Order of 1813 the East India Company Government had to handle her educational responsibility in India.

On June, 1814 the Directors of East India Company issued a notification with an intention to encourage Hindu system of education. On October 1 and 2,1915, Lord Hastings issued certain orders in which he talked about spending the amount of one lakh in a way as to enable the general public to get proper education. Lord Hastings thought of strengthening company's administration by educating Indians. Therefore, he proposed to set up one school for Hindus and one for Muslims for making education popular in each district. Sir Charles Metcalf expressed his liberal ideas in his Revenue Notification of Delhi province. Since a revolutionary change was taking place in the English society, India could not remain uneffected.

The Directors of the Company were cautious about their duties concerning education in India. They started their attempts on the governmental level since 1823. Following was done by the Company Government in different provinces:

1. **Bengal.** Central Committee of Public Instruction was appointed on July 17, 1823. It was authorised to spend one lakh of rupees. Some members of this committee were strong admirers of Oriental literature. Among them H. H. Wilson and H. J. Prinseva were notable. The committee did the following work during 1823 A.D.:
   - (i) Sanskrit colleges at Calcutta, Madras and Banaras were reorganised.
   - (ii) Institutions were started for Western education in Calcutta, Agra and Delhi in 1824 A.D.
   - (iii) In 1824 Calcutta Education Press was established.
   - (iv) Many books were published in Sanskrit, Arabic and Persian.
   - (v) To give scientific education to Indians some European scientific books were translated into Indian languages.

(vi) Those books were recommended as text-books.

(vii) Scholarships were given to Sanskrit, Arabic and Persian students of various institutions.

In his letter dated December 11, 1823 Raja Ram Mohan Roy appealed the Calcutta, Madras and Sanskrit College, Banaras and emphasized the education of Mathematics, Philosophy, Science and Chemistry, etc. It was not heeded and the scheme of Sanskrit College was fulfilled. The Company itself was not satisfied with orientalised policy of the committee. So it imposed restriction on it and ordered to encourage Western education in India. It arranged for Western education in Calcutta, Madras, Sanskrit College, Banaras and Agra College, Agra. English schools were started at Delhi and Banaras.

2. **Bombay.** In 1821 Poona Sanskrit College was started. On the demand of grant by The Bombay Native Education Society', Lord Elphinstone issued a notification putting forward the following conditions for Government grants:

(i) Improvement in education methods of Indian institutions and the increase in the number of schools.

(ii) Issue of books to the students.

(iii) To encourage the people of the lower classes in society to secure education.

(iv) To open schools for development of European sciences and Western higher education.

(v) To pay attention towards the publications and writings of moral and scientific books in Indian languages.

(vi) To set up an institution for higher study of English language and gaining knowledge of European researches for the desirous students.

(vii) To encourage Indians to study the higher branches of knowledge.

Lord Elphinstone supported public education and put up the suggestions for:

(a) Opening Government schools; and

(b) Giving grants to education committees.

Thus grant system started and education came under the control of Government. The notification of the Governor was, however, severely criticised by his Council of

Members. A controversy started between Anglo-Vernacular languages. It lasted till Macaulay's report. The Directors of the Company did not appreciate all the suggestions of Governor. They gave a grant of ₹ 600 per month to Bombay Native Education Society.

3. **Madras.** While surveying the education system in Madras Sir Munroe pointed out three main defects: inefficiency of the teachers, poverty of the people and negligence of the Government, for the decline in the standards of education. In his notification of May 10. 1826 he suggested that two institutions of high standard should be established in each of the 20 districts: one for Hindus and one for Muslims. One Vernacular school should be opened in each 300 tahsils and one Teacher's training school in each tahsil. Emphasis was laid on the payment of better pay to the teachers and publication of Oriental books. Munroc put up a demand of ₹ 48,000 to carry out his schemes. This was granted in 1828. But meanwhile Munroe was expired in 1827. Thus the completion of the scheme fell to Public Education Committee. The Committee had no foresight of Munroe and so the result was not satisfactory. Therefore, up to 1830 only 61 Vernacular schools in tahsils, nine district schools and one Teacher's training school could be started and their success was also not satisfactory. Thus no satisfactory progress could be made in Madras up to 1833.

EFFORTS OF MISSIONARIES

The Order of 1813 A.D. had given the right to the missionaries to complete their mission. Hence a network of missionaries was set up throughout the whole country to popularise Christianity and convert people. They made the education of institutions their instrument for the purpose. They made local languages the medium of instruction and prepared course books, grammars and dictionaries, etc. Their efforts in various provinces may be described as follows:

1. **Bengal.** In Bengal Baptist Mission started its work in 1815. About 15 schools were opened. In 1818, they started the publication of *'Samachar Darpan'*. They started a college where the Indian and Anglo-Indian boys were taught to preach religion also.

'London Missionary Society' and 'Church Missionary Society' worked much for the expansion of education. The former started 30 primary schools near Chinsura, in which 3,000 students were studying. These societies worked during 1814 to 1818. The latter started 10 Vernacular schools in Burdwan and near about with 100 students. In Behrampur and Bhavanipur also several schools were opened. By 1824 these societies had opened about 27 schools for girls, in which about 500 girls were receiving education. In 1920 Bishop College was established in Shrirampur.

In 1830 a Scottish youth named Mr. Duff landed on the Indian soil and started the work of education, with a slogan, that Indians can only gain salvation (Moksha) through 'West and Bible'. He established the Scottish Church College in Calcutta in 1830. Here the medium of education was English and the teaching of Bible was essential.

2. **Bombay.** As compared to Bengal the educational work of missionaries in Bombay was very limited. The American Mission had opened one school in Bombay in 1817. During the period of 1824-1826 nine schools were opened for girls. Two girls schools were opened in Ahmadnagar in 1831. Dr. Wilson had opened six girls schools and one boys' school in Bombay in 1829 and 1832, respectively. Church Missionary Society also started some schools for boys and girls in Bombay. In Bassein and Nasik, Irish Presbeterian Missionary Society had opened English and Vernacular schools in Kathiawar.
3. **Madras.** Church Missionary Society opened a large number of schools in Madras. There were 107 schools with 2,882 students in Tinneveli. Mr. Gough opened nine schools in Madras with the help of Religion Preaching Society of England with 283 students. Welshian Mission started two schools each in Nagapattam and Madras. Besides, many schools were opened in Chittoor, Salem, Coimbatore, Visakhapatnam, Kudappa and Bellary also.
4. **Other Places.** In Ajmer four schools were started in 1823 on Lankastrian system where 100 students were studying. After four years all were united into one school. Many schools were started in Burdwan, Agra, Meerut, Banaras, Jaunpur, Azamgarh, Mathura and Ludhiana, etc.

CHARACTERISTICS OF MISSION SCHOOLS

During the period 1813 to 1833 a large number of primary schools were started by missionaries due to which the education in India got re-organised. Modern schools were organised on the lines of the missionary schools. Their characteristics were as follows:

1. **Religious.** The aims of these mission schools were religious propaganda so the teaching of Bible was essential.
2. **Regular.** All the schools were running regularly with a set course of study. School hours were fixed and Sunday was a closed day.
3. **Vast-Curriculum.** The curriculum of these schools was vast. It included Grammar, History, Geography, etc.
4. **Publication of Text Books.** These missionaries had arranged for the publication of text books. Due to their efforts dearth of text books was removed.
5. **Many Teachers.** Previously, one teacher used to teach all the classes, but these missionaries arranged for more teachers. They started teaching through different teachers on the modern lines.
6. **Mother Tongue as Medium.** The medium of education in these schools was local languages.

EFFORTS OF NON-MISSIONARIES

Inspired by these missionaries, many non-missionaries made personal efforts to propagate education. These were as follows:

1. **Bengal.** The founder of 'Brahmo Samaj' Raja Ram Mohan Roy, David Hare, Radha Kant Deva and Sir Edward Hide East made notable efforts for development of modern education. Raja Ram, Mohan Roy was the first Indian to plead for the expansion of Western education, with its subjects and methods. He did not condemn Western literature and culture but tried for the synthesis of East and West. Mr. David Hare was also of the same opinion. He had experienced that most of the Indian boys wanted to read English. Thus, on March 14,1816 a public meeting was arranged at the residence of Sir Edward Hide East. The proposal for starting 'A Hindu College' for respected Hindu students, was passed and a subscription of 60,000 rupees was raised. The foundation stone of the college was laid on January 20,1817. The college started getting grant since 1824. It was the first secular type

of colleges, where Politics, Grammar, Bengali, Hindustani, Mathematics, History, Geography, Astronomy, etc. were the subjects of study. Within three years the number of students increased from 169 to 437. As Sanskrit and Persian were not included in the syllabus, so the chances for combination of eastern and western cultures were lost.

A 'Calcutta School Book Committee' was established which distributed free or on nominal cost about 1,25,446 copies of school books from 1817 to 1821. Calcutta Vidyalaya Samaj was organised to open Anglo-Bengali School in Bengal in 1819. By 1821, this Samaj opened 115 schools. Both these societies continued to function till 1833.

2. **Bombay.** Members of 'Church of England' set up a 'Bombay Education Society' to open the schools for educating the children of Europeans and Anglo-Indians. This society started schools at Bombay, Surat and Thana. Many Hindus, Muslims and Parsis also joined these schools. This society also started four other schools for Indian Students — two in Bombay, one in Girgaon, and one in Majhgaon. An 'Indian School and Course Book Committee' was appointed under this committee. It inspected the educational arrangement in Bombay. It reported that there is dearth of course books, proper teaching methods, efficient teachers and money. It asked the parent Committee to appoint six Indian learned persons as inspectors, after getting them trained in Marathi, Gujarati, Kannad and Urdu for the inspection of these schools. The society was given a grant of ₹ 600 per month. The work of publishing books was taken up by the Government through the efforts of Lord Elphinstone. In 1826, the Committee appointed 24 trained teachers for Government schools for Kannar and Gujarati and started engineering classes in 1826. It started many schools and published about 50,000 books at a cost of about ₹ 2,00,000 by 1883.
3. **Madras.** Maharaja of Mysore gave ₹ 350 per year to English schools. 'Banglore and Madras Schools Society', was given a grant of 6,000 rupees yearly. A rich person named Pachyappa Mudaliar had given a gift of ₹ 4,00,000. This could be utilised for starting schools for poor students to give free educationin 1842.

4. **Delhi and U. P.** In Delhi, Wm. Frazer opened a school for the children of landlords and peasants. In 1829, Nawablslamud-daula encouraged higher education with a donation of ₹ 1,70,000. In Banaras, Jai Narain Ghosal donated 20,000 rupees and opened 'Jai Narain School' where students were allowed to study the subjects on Western line. Moreover, poor students were given fooding, lodging and clothing too. In 1825, his son gave 30,000 rupees to the school. Pt. Gangadhar Shastri had given his property worth ₹ 1,50,000 to Sanskrit College, Agra which generated an income of ₹ 20,000 annually. Now it is known as Agra College, Agra.

EDUCATION IN NORTH-WEST PROVINCE (U.P.)

By this time the schools opened by Lord Auckland at Delhi, Agra and Banaras were in good shape and were imparting English education. James Thomson was the Lieutenant Governor of this new province. He w as a farlighted administrator. For winning the heart of the people education should be given through the medium of mother tongue. The newly organised province was educationally backward in comparison to other provinces. Thomson made following plan for educational expansion:

1. ***To Encourage Rural Schools.*** To donate books to students. To encourage poor and brilliant students by giving prizes and clothes. To give financial help to teachers from time to time in order to boost up their morale. To inspect the working of the schools. To make provision for training of teachers.
2. ***Opening New Schools.*** To levy local taxes for expansion of education and to encourage rich people to donate at least five acres of land for opening new schools and for helping teachers to earn their living.
3. ***Education Department.*** To establish a department of education in the province for running educational affairs in an organised manner.

In 1845, Thomson issued instruction to each district magistrate of his province to look after the schools within his jurisdiction. He ordered that the old schools should be renovated and put on stronger roots. He advised the district magistrates to expand education and encourage the local public to participate in the same.

In 1846, Thomson placed an educational plan before the Governor-General in which he proposed that a new school should be opened in each village consisting of 200 families and each school should be given at least five acres of land for the sustenance of the school teachers. This proposal was accepted in 1848 and the scheme was put into operation. As a result, a large number of schools in each subdivision (Tahsil) sprang up and their financial position, too, was not bad.

Thomson respected the feelings of the people. He tried his best to accommodate the same in expansion of education. Lord Dalhousie liked his scheme and instead of implementing it in eight districts he proposed before the company to include 23 districts in the scheme. He also advised that the scheme should be implemented in Bihar and Bengal also. The other provinces, too, accepted the lead given by Thomson and established departments of education.

Two schools were opened for expansion of higher education. In 1852 a normal school and St. Johns College were opened at Agra. The Bareilly School was started in Bareilly. In 1853 the Jai Narain Ghoshal School was raised to the status of a college. In 1854 there were 3920 schools in Agra division with 53,000 students in them. There were 976 students in the college established at Delhi, Banaras and Agra. In 1854 a proposal was made to give stipends to students and to introduce the North-Western Province scheme of education in other provinces also.

QUESTIONS FOR EXERCISE

1. Describe the condition of Primary Education in Madras, Bombay and Bengal provinces in the beginning of 19th century under British Government.
2. Write a short note on Higher Education in British provinces in 19th Century.
3. "Modern Indian education was started by the schools established by the missionaries." Discuss this statement.
4. Discuss the efforts made by the early Europeans for spreading education in India.
5. "The beginning of present system of education in India can be traced to the efforts of the Christian missionaries." Discuss.

6. Give a short account of educational efforts made by British government and missionaries in India.
7. What were the characteristics of Mission schools? Describe the efforts of non-missionaries for propagation of education in 19th century in India.
8. What were the special features of educational expansion in Bombay during 1835 and 1853?
9. Give an assessment of James Thomson's educational efforts in the North-Western Province.
10. Write a note on the expansion of education in Bengal during 1835 and 1853.

CHAPTER 10

THE WOOD'S DESPATCH (1854)

East India Company had to take orders from the British Parliament after every 20 years and in each order something was written about the education in India. In the order of 1763, Charles Grant wanted to add some articles about the education in India. In the order obtained in 1813, a sum of one lakh was sanctioned for the development of education in India. Again, in the order of 1833 the sanctioned sum of ₹ one lakh was increased to ₹ one million yearly. Therefore, when time for the order of 1853 came, the Directors of the Company decided to lay down a definite policy in regard to educational matters of India. A Parliamentary committee was appointed to survey the educational progress in India. The committee studied the issue thoroughly. It heard the ideas of the persons like Traivelian Pairy, Marshaman, Wilson, Halide, Cameron, and Duff, etc. who had thorough knowledge of Indian education. The committee reported that the question of Indian education would not be ignored any longer and its development will not be in any case harmful to British Empire. The suggestions of the committee were favourably considered by the board of Directors. As Charles Wood was the Chairman of the Board of Control, so the declaration was Christianed as 'Wood's Educational Despatch' though it was written by John Stuart. It decided the educational policy of the company government. 'Wood's Educational Despatch' has a very important place in die History of Education in India.

THE RECOMMENDATIONS OF WOOD'S DESPATCH

Wood's Despatch is a long report consisting of 100 paragraphs. In it all the important educational points have been dealt in detail. The main recommendations of the Despatch are as follows:

1. **Acceptance of Educational Responsibility.** For the first time the Despatch clearly accepted the responsibility of British Government for education in India.
2. **The Aim of Education.** The aim of education was to raise intellectual fitness and moral character of the educands.
3. **Courses of Study.** Mr. Wood recognised the usefulness of Sanskrit, Arabic and Persian, and recommended them as subjects of study in regular institutions. Like Macaulay, he also recognised the usefulness of Western knowledge for Indians.
4. **Medium of Instruction.** The Despatch pointed out that due to dearth of course books in Indian languages, the medium of education should be English. But this should be used by those people who have proper knowledge of English and are able to understand the European knowledge through this language.
5. **Department of Public Instruction.** The Despatch recommended that Department of Public Instruction should be set up in all the provinces. Its highest official should be designated as the Director of Public Instruction. He should be assisted by Deputy Educational Director, Inspectors and Deputy Inspectors of Schools.
6. **Establishment of Universities.** The Despatch suggested for the setting up of the universities at Calcutta, Bombay and Madras and if necessary at other places too.
7. **Establishment of Regular Institutions.** The Despatch emphasised establishment of the graded schools as follows:
   (i) Universities
   (ii) Colleges
   (iii) High Schools
   (iv) Middle Schools
   (v) Primary Schools.
8. **Extension of Public Education.** As 'Filtration Theory' failed, Wood emphasised useful education for the public. As the public itself was unable to get such an education, so increase in the number of Primary, Middle and High Schools was emphasised. In order to co-ordinate education at these various levels it was suggested to implement scholarships and other schemes.

9. **Grant-in-aid System.** Wood's Despatch suggested Grant-in-aid system for the institutions which fulfilled certain qualifications. He also suggested that the rules and regulations for Grant-in-aid should be framed on the lines practised in England.
10. **Training of Teachers.** Despatch expressed the desire of opening schools in every provinces of India, as they are in England so that teaching work may be conducted properly and efficiently.
11. **Education of Women.** Despatch threw light on women education and praised the persons engaged in this pious work. It suggested for its further encouragement through Grant-in-aid and other measures. It also approved the declaration of Governor-General that the Government should favourably assist the female education in India. It said, "The importance of female education in India cannot be over-rated. We cannot repair from repressing cordial sympathy with the efforts which are being made in this direction."
12. **Muslim Education.** About Muslim education, Mr. Wood said that Muslims are too backward in education. He suggested that they should be encouraged to gain more education and efforts should be made in this direction.
13. **Vocational Education.** The Despatch paid attention to the vocational education. It suggested that schools and colleges should be set up at suitable places for vocational education so that people may get such education.
14. **Encouragement to the Oriental Education.** The Despatch supported Western education through English medium for the Indians. However, it recommended for the development of Indian literature. It suggested that the books of Western literature and science should be translated in these languages. Also original books should be written, and the writers should be rewarded and encouraged.
15. **Employment.** About employment Mr. Wood laid down the following principles:
    (i) While selecting the candidates for Government services their academic qualifications should be considered well.
    (ii) Academically, highly qualified persons should be preferred than the others for Government services.

MERITS OF WOOD'S DESPATCH

1. **Decision of Educational Policy.** Due to the Wood's Despatch, British Parliament for the first time made an attempt to decide the educational policy in India and give it a legal form. The directors of the East India Company had not decided the policy about the Indian education. Through this Despatch they decided it for the first time.
2. **Aim.** Wood's Despatch clearly laid down the aim of education in India.
3. **Government Responsibility.** Through this Despatch, it was recognised to be the duty and responsibility of the British Government to educate the common people of India.
4. **Rejection of Downward Filtration Theory.** Wood's Despatch rejected the Downward Filtration Theory. It was considered totally useless for Indian education. The Despatch took active steps for the encouragement of public education.
5. **Scheme of Education.** This Despatch, for the first time, put up a scheme of education from primary standard to the university level. It gave practical suggestions based on the lines functioning in England.
6. **Literature and Culture.** The Despatch recognised the importance and value of Indian literature and culture.
7. **Indigenous Language.** The Despatch recommended Indian languages and literature for inclusion in the courses of study. Unlike Lord Macaulay it appreciated Indian literature.
8. **Books in Indian Languages.** Wood arranged to get books written in Indian languages.
9. **Translation.** The Despatch laid stress on the translation of books of Western knowledge into Indian languages. It recommended encouragement to the authors for this purpose.
10. **Deptt.** of Public Instruction. Wood suggested for settingup a Department of Public Instruction in each province with a Director of Public Instruction, a Deputy Director, Inspectors and Deputy Inspectors so that educational institutions could be properly inspected and standards could be maintained.
11. **Native Institutions.** The Despatch attracted the attention of the Government towards the improvement of native educational institutions.

12. **Indian Languages.** Wood recognised Indian languages as the media of education along with English.
13. **Universities.** The Despatch ordered for establishing universities at Calcutta, Madras and Bombay and, if necessary, at other places also.
14. **High Schools and Colleges.** The Despatch suggested for increasing the number of high schools and colleges.
15. **Providing Employment.** The Despatch paid attention to solving the problem of unemployment by encouraging the vocational education.
16. **Women Education.** The Despatch recognised the need for development of women education as the duty' and responsibility of the Government.
17. **Grant-in-Aid.** The Despatch suggested that the Grant-in-aid system as functioning in England should apply to various educational institutions in India as well.
18. **Scholarships.** The Despatch provided for the facility of scholarships to the poor and meritorious students to enable them to gain education.
19. **Meritorious Teachers.** In order to encourage general people towards education system the Despatch suggested for preference to highly educated persons in Government services.
20. **Better Pay Scales.** The Despatch recommended for better pay scales to the teachers to attract a large number of efficient persons to teaching profession.

DEMERITS OF WOOD'S DESPATCH

1. **Nominations.** All the members of Senate of the universities were to be nominated by the Government. Hence sometimes the persons ignorant about educational problems, became the members of the Senate.
2. **Government Control.** This Despatch put the education under the direct control of the Government. This Government control ended the traditional free teaching work in this country.
3. **Foreign Model.** The Despatch adopted the model of London University for Indian universities. Thus the ancient Indian university system was neglected.

4. **Education for Bread Earning.** The education has a very vast aim, but the preference of high education in Government services, as laid down by the Despatch, limited the aim of education and it became only the means of bread earning.
5. **Blow to Old Institutions.** According to the Despatch, the persons educated on Western lines and languages were to be given priority in services. Therefore, the old educational institutions began to lose their existence.
6. **Westernisation.** Wood's Despatch concentrated the attention of the people on the Western knowledge. Hence Indian literature and knowledge was neglected. A time came when people educated on Western lines began to think that everything indigenous was bad, while anything Western was good. Improvement of Indian languages was planned by filling them with translations of the Western books.
7. **Neglect of Indian Religions.** Indian education gave prominent place to Indian religion. The Western education system gave prominence to Christianity. Thus, Indian religions were neglected by educated people. They were very much influenced by Western religions.
8. **Neglect of Spiritualism.** The neglect of religion caused educated Indians forget the Indian spiritualism and disciplined way of life.
9. **Denigration of Indian Languages.** Though Wood had recognised the usefulness of Sanskrit, Arabic and Persian, yet as the aim of education was declared as the extension and development of Western knowledge, science and literature the value of Indian languages was brought down indirectly.
10. **Lack of Flexibility.** According to this Despatch, an Education Department was set up in each province and education went under the direct control of the Government. The institutions were only to obey the departmental order. So they lost their own inspiration resulting in the lack of flexibility in the educational system.
11. **Neglect of Orientalism.** The Despatch resulted in the neglect of native education system by the people. It was left without any attraction.
12. **Subservience.** Education was proposed not in the interest of Indians, but to create faithfulness towards British

Government. Its aim was to make Indians loyal to the British Government.

13. **Mercenary Aim.** Educational institutions were established to prepare persons fit for government services. Therefore, the aim of education was livelihood only.
14. **Lack of Support to Indigenous Institutions.** The Government was spending the major portion of money allotted for education in the development and extension of English schools. The indigenous educational institutions had to suffer a step-motherly treatment from the Government as well as from the higher classes of the society. Poor people were unable to support them due to want of resources. The grant-in-aid was given to those institutions where the public could be at 50 per cent of the expenditure. Therefore, it was also not much helpful for the oriental education.
15. **Ills of Foreign Medium.** As the medium of instruction was English, so the students were bound to study English in order to understand other subjects like History, Geography, Mathematics, etc. Thus, they had to spend a larger period for the study. Still the majority of the students could not gain the success that they might have gained through the media of Indian languages.
16. **Examination Centred Education.** This system of education destroyed the system of self-study and meditation. The main aim of the students was to pass the examination. They did not care to study the whole course and depended on selected reading. Examination assumed a very important place and so the whole study became examination minded.
17. **No Secularism.** The Despatch had said that government would follow a policy of secularism. It would not be partial to any religion but it did show favour to Christianity.

EVALUATION OF WOOD'S DESPATCH

1. **A. N. Basu.** "So short-cuts were devised. Unintelligent memory' work and cramming became the order of the day, and notes flooded in the education Bazar and intellectual market."
2. **H. R James.** "The Despatch of 1854 is a climax in the History' of Indian Education... . What goes before leads up to it — What follows flows from it."

3. **H. V. Hampton.** "The Despatch of 1854 marks the end of era — the age of great educational pioneers."
4. **Lord Dalhousie's Minute.** "A scheme of education far wider and more comprehensive than the local or supreme Government could have even ventured to suggest."
5. **A. N. Basu.** "The Despatch is said to be the corner-stone of Indian education. It is said to have laid functions of our present system of education."

Thus the ultimate purpose of the Despatch was just another well-guarded attempt to impose Western knowledge and learning and English language on the Indian people. However, the Despatch, in itself, was an important historical document in as much as it began a new era in Indian education by streaming it on a definite track. As a result of this Despatch, three new universities were opened in the country and the grant-in-aid system was introduced in all tie provinces. These two features had a salutary effect on the then existing conditions Many other provisions of the Despatch could not be implemented because of the Revolt of 1857 which put the British Empire in the country in danger.

QUESTIONS FOR EXERCISE

1. "Wood's educational Despatch is the *Magna Carta* of Indian education." Examine the statement. What were its principal recommendations?
2. "It points out the event past and the future event sprang of it," James Adam. Elucidate.
3. 'The Despatch of Wood might have had some significance in 1854, at present it is rather too funny to call it educational Despatch." How far do you agree with the above statement of Paranjape.

CHAPTER 11

PROGRESS OF EDUCATION DURING 1854 TO 1882

PRIMARY EDUCATION

At the time of Wood's Despatch, primary education in the country was in a very bad shape due to the reason that the company's attention was primarily diverted towards university education. So primary education remained neglected. Wood's Despatch had urged to give adequate attention to primary education and suggested certain reforms. It made the company responsible for primary education. Even then the situation could not improve, because the rules of grant-in-aid system were impracticable. Most of the primary schools were not able to fulfil the condition of arranging for at least 50 per cent of the expenditure. So they could not be benefited by the grant-in-aid system. Therefore, institutions of higher learning received the major portion of the grant and the primary education continued to be neglected.

On the basis of the declaration of 1859 it was suggested that the responsibility of primary education should rest on administrative officers. However, this policy could not be helpful. The administration had to decide about the policy concerning indigenous schools. They were to decide as to how these schools could be given Government grants. Instead of giving any grant to them they were also thinking to levy some local taxes for education. These issues could not be decided and became controversial. Therefore, each province was given the freedom to adopt its own policy for primary education. Hence each province followed its own policy. There was no uniformity in them in this respect. Each province paid attention to primary education in its own way. The progress made in various provinces has been indicated in the table at next page.

PRIMARY EDUCATION IN 1882

Province	Schools on Grant	Schools Run by Department of Education	Schools Not Getting any Grant
1. Bombay	73	3,954	3,954
2. Madras	13,323	1,263	2,828
3. Bengal	47,374	28	3,265
4. Assam	1,256	7	497
5. Berar	209	467	258
6. Punjab	278	17,549	13,109
7. North-Western Province	243	5,561	6,712
8. Central Provinces	364	894	

1. **Bombay.** The condition of primary education has been deplorable during the period. In 1870 Peile had made a plan of giving grants which could not improve the position. Only 73 could get the financial grant out of 3,954 schools.
2. **Madras.** The policy of giving grant on the basis of results of examination was adopted in Madras in 1868. This policy proved very useful. Within 10 years, that is, up to 1878 the number of schools receiving grant rose to 13,323 from 3,358.
3. **Bengal.** Halkabandi system was in vogue here. The primary school teachers were getting financial assistance. After some time in this province also the system to give financial help to teachers on the basis of examination result was adopted. The schools were given matching grant on the basis of their income. Some Pandits were required to inspect some schools. Some normal schools were opened in Bengal for training of teachers. Some Inspectors of Schools were sent abroad for higher education.
4. **Assam.** Assam was a part of Bengal up to 1874. So the primary schools were run as in Bengal and their condition was just like that of Bengal. Local taxes were levied in Assam for primary education. However, this tax policy could not improve the condition of primary schools and they remained in a bad shape.

5. **Berar.** Berar followed the Bombay policy about primary education. Many of the schools were getting Government grants. During 1880-82 number of schools were 467. Out of these 258 schools were not getting Government help. Indigenous schools were encouraged in this province.
6. **Punjab.** The education in Punjab was influenced by the policy followed in North-Western Province. There were 13,109 indigenous schools out of which only 278 were getting financial assistance.
7. **North-Western Province.** During 1881-82 there were 6,712 schools here out of which only 243 were getting Government assistance. The Halkabandi system was current here.
8. **Central Provinces.** There were 894 schools here out of which only 364 were getting grants. The Bengal policy was followed here but with little success.
9. **Coorg.** Here primary education was completely under the department of education. Indigenous schools were not encouraged here. The Bombay policy was followed here.

SECONDARY EDUCATION

Wood's Despatch

Secondary education was in a better position than primary education during this period. Many people in the country were attracted towards the Western literature and sciences. Hence there was a favourable atmosphere for the development of secondary education. The government also adopted the policy of encouraging and helping English schools. Hence good progress was achieved in secondary education during this period of 28 year Wood's Despatch had encouraged secondary schools, because the cause of the recommendations of the Despatch was that education departments were established in various provinces and Government schools were opened. Private enterprises working for promotion of secondary education were also given Government grants. The number of Government schools rose to 1363 from 169 during the period.

Role of Missionaries

Christian missionaries played a remarkable role in the development of secondary education. They were the main figure in the field of secondary education up to 1854. But the revolt of 1857 changed the British attitude. The Government became more interested in the development of secondary education. Indians, also, became more interested in learning English with a view to improve their future prospects. Hence private enterprises began to take more active interest in secondary education. Secondary education got a good stride. By 1882 the number of secondary schools rose to 2,098. Out of this number 757 schools were run by the missionaries and the remaining 1,341 were run by the Indians. During the British regime Madras had 698 schools, the highest number of schools. Bengal was in the second place with 582 schools. The number of schools was increasing in other provinces also.

The missionaries were playing the major role in spreading secondary education in the country. They were running 418 secondary schools in Madras alone. In other provinces also they have been quite active in this field. They established 118 secondary schools in Punjab, 104 in the North-Western Province and 40 in Bengal. Indians had worked harder in Bengal for spreading secondary education.

Defects in Secondary Education

It is clear that during the period from 1854 to 1888, secondary education made satisfactory progress. But the system had developed following defects which became a problem later on:

1. The neglect of the mother tongue as the medium of instruction.
2. Dearth of trained teachers.
3. Want of vocational education.
4. Predominance of bookish knowledge.

1. **The Medium of Instruction.** Wood's Despatch had urged to make the mother tongue as the medium of instruction at the secondary stage, but its recommendation was not followed. Hence the mother tongue remained neglected. English was made the medium of instruction and it got firmly established in the country. So the people began to realise that the British regime was strongly entrenched. They considered it more practicable to learn English for procuring good jobs. Up to 1862 students were technically free to choose mother tongue as the medium, but nobody

chose it for the obvious reason. The mother tongue got a blow when the University of Calcutta made it compulsory that the answers in examination should be written in English. This step resulted into adoption of English even in middle schools. Thus English was firmly taken up as the medium of instruction. It became difficult to remove this defect in future.

2. **The Dearth of Trained Teachers.** Wood's Despatch had suggested for making provisionfor training of teachers. But this suggestion was ignored. Trained teachers were not available for the secondary schools which were growing in number every year. During the period under review there were only two training schools in the country. The seats in these schools were limited and no practising school was attached with any one of them for practical work. These schools were at two corners of the country', one at Lahore and another at Madras. Naturally there was a distressing lack of trained teachers.
3. **Lack of Vocational Education.** During the British rule in the country vocational education was deplorably ignored. The British government thought that vocational education to Indians would ultimately adversely affect their trade prospects. So it was profitable for it to neglect it. Moreover, vocational education entailed heavy expenditure which the government was not prepared to incur. The Indian people, too, did not show enough enthusiasm for it. As their major attention was directed to receiving higher education for procuring good government service, they could not rightly assess the utility of vocational education. Only one agriculture college was being run in Bombay in 1882 and there was no other vocational institution in the country. The students were given four rupees as the monthly stipend for receiving education in this agriculture school.
4. **Bookish Knowledge.** Secondary education was principally limited to bookish knowledge and it gave no practical experience to students. It had a harmful impact on the youths of the land.

LORD STANLEY'S DESPATCH OF 1859

Lord Stanley was the Secretary of State for India. This post was created when the power was transferred to the Crown from the

East India Company after the revolt of 1857. Lord Stanley was a supporter of Wood's Despatch. He was keen to find out to what extent education was responsible for the outbreak of the revolt. He issued a Despatch in which he emphasised the importance of primary education neglected till then. He did not attach any importance to the grant-in-aid system which, in his opinion, was responsible for the neglect of primary education. So he urged in his Despatch that the government itself should take the responsibility of primary education and levy local taxes to meet a part of its expenditure. He was influenced by Wood's ideas and also by the educational policy then in force in Great Britain. At that time the public school system in Great Britain was being developed with the help of local taxes for education. Stanley desired that the same policy should be adopted in India as well. He also emphasised the necessity of training of teachers.

Due to Stanley's Despatch the provincial Government were made responsible for primary education. By 1871 the department of education came under the direct control of the provincial Government. During the regime of Lord Mayo the provincial Governments were authorised to make expenditure on education themselves. Lord Lyton increased this power further. Now the provincial Governments were empowered to spend on education a part of the revenue they received from law courts and irrigation departments. These developments could not make much difference to the shape of education as the same was governed by the educational policy of the Central Government which enjoyed this power up to 1882.

HIGHER AND UNIVERSITY EDUCATION

In 1845 a demand was raised for establishment of universities in India. Dr. F. J. Mouat, the then secretary of the education committee of Bengal had raised his voice for a university at Calcutta in October, 1845. After some time the same type of demand was raised in Madras also. Again in 1852 Hon. Mr. C. H. Cameron, an ex-president of education committee of Bengal raised his voice in the British Parliament for opening universities at Agra and in the three presidencies of Bengal, Madras and Bombay when the question of renewal of the Charter for East India Company was being considered. Though these efforts did not succeed but they convinced the British Government that the opening of universities in India should not be delayed. It was at this time that Wood's Despatch was realised in which establishment of universities had been recommended. By 1857 the necessary rules and regulations for the universities were framed and the universities in the three presidencies came into existence. Thus the establishment of universities was the result of Wood's Despatch.

Administration of Universities

A Senate was established for each university for looking after its general administration. The Chancellor was the President of the Senate. The Governor was the Chancellor who used to nominate a Vice-Chancellor for two year The Vice-Chancellor was the real administrator of the university. He used to perform his duties with the help of the Senate. The Senate consisted of *ex-officio* and ordinary fellows. The Principals of colleges, Judge, Bishop and Director of Public Instruction and members of the Executive Council of the Governor used to be the *ex-officio* fellows of the senate. The ordinary fellows were chosen from distinguished citizens and educationists. A syndicate, was established for every day's working. The Vice-Chancellor used to perform his duties with its help.

The Function of Calcutta University

The persons who passed matriculation examination were admitted to a University for higher studies in sciences, humanities, commerce, medicine, law and engineering. The students successful in examination were awarded degrees in their respective fields.

For the first time in 1857 entrance examination was scheduled in the Calcutta University. In 1858 only 13 candidates appeared for the B.A. and B.Sc. examinations. Out of these 13 only two could pass. These two successful candidates Bankim Chandra Chattopadhyaya and Yadunath Basu were immediately appointed as deputy-collectors. In the beginning there were no intermediate classes in the University. It was after passing entrance examination that one could appear in B.A. and B.Sc. classes. Intermediate classes were started after some time and their standard was kept quite high. Calcutta University produced 3,667 successful students during die first 14 years of its establishment. Out of these 2,666 were in F.A., 850 in B.A. and 151 in M.A. Thus on an average 262 students passed every year.

In 1865 the Premachand Roy Scholarship was instituted at the Calcutta University. In 1876 Dr. Mahendra Lal Sirkar established the Indian Association for Science for encouraging research in sciences.

An Evaluation of University Education

1. In 1857 a provision was made for forming a senate for each university, but the number of its members was not prescribed. These members were nominated for life time. Hence there was no scope for making any desirable change in the senate.
2. The senate was just a show-piece, because its members were not chosen on the basis of ability and scholarship. The government used to nominate its flatterers on the senate. These flatterers could seldom think of opposing any Government policy. In fact, they had no opinion of their own.
3. Uptill now the university was only an examining body. Wood's Despatch had desired that the university should also do the teaching work, but this could not be done.
4. The senate used to form the syndicate. It had no legal status.
5. The education in the university was limited to bookish knowledge only. It had no relationship with the actual life situation. There was no provision for vocational education in any university.
6. The main purpose of the university education was to award degrees to some successful candidates so that they could assist the British administration in the country. Such graduates were just to obey the Government of the day.
7. As university was totally under the Government control no independent educational system could prosper in it. The University teachers never felt themselves strong to voice their opinion on any matter.
8. As the teachers had no representation on the senate, the University was deprived of the benefits from teacher's experiences.
9. As English was the medium of instruction at the University, Indian languages were neglected and their development was obstructed.

The Punjab University

In addition to Universities at Calcutta, Madras and Bombay the Punjab University was established at Lahore. The demand for a university at Lahore was made in 1865. A University College was established there in 1869. This college was converted into Punjab University at a later stage. In comparison to other universities in the country the University was nearer to the Indian needs. The mother tongue was the medium of instruction. It was more imbued with the Indian ideas and ideals. Indian classical languages were taught at this University. The Western literature and sciences were taught through the mother tongue.

During the period 1854-1882 University education developed well within 28 years because the number of matriculation passed students was increasing day by day. The number of candidates at the Calcutta Entrance Examination was doubled. This situation drew the attention of the Government. So Presidency colleges were established at Calcutta and Madras for higher education.

Colleges in North-Western Province

Uptill then there was no university in the North-Western Province (U.P.). So Lord Mayo placed a proposal for the same before the Government. As a result the Central College was opened in 1872 in a rented building. The Talukdars of Awadh opened a college at Lucknow which was named after his name. It forms the basic structure of the present Lucknow University even today. In the Canning College a department of oriental learning was also opened. In 1921 the Canning College was converted into Lucknow University. Sir Syed Ahmad Khan opened the Muslim Anglo-Oriental College in 1875 at Aligarh under the patronage of the Government. This college was raised to a University later on under the name of Aligarh Muslim University.

Other Colleges

During this period several colleges were established in the country for developing higher education. Of which Rajkot College (1870), Mayo College, Ajmer (1872), Dally College, Indore (1876), of the Bengal Presidency the Metropolitan College (1878), City College (1879) and Albert College (1881) are worthy of mention. At the time of establishment these institutions were only schools, but soon they were raised to the status of colleges. In Madras

Panchyappa and Visakhapatnam schools were raised to colleges. In 1861 a college was opened at Tinnevally.

Thus except for opening a few new colleges during this period, there was no other development in the field of University education. All the universities so far established were only examining bodies and none of them were teaching centre. So only a few colleges were affiliated to each. However, higher education was developed up to some extent through these affiliated colleges.

There were only 23 colleges in the country at the time of Wood's Despatch in 1854. Out of these nine were run by the missionaries and 14 by the Company. Besides, there were three Medical colleges and one Engineering College run by the Company. By 1857 the number of Colleges became 27. By 1872 the number was raised to 78. The Elphinstone College, Agra College and Delhi College were established by 1857 because of the private Indian enterprises through raising of subscriptions. All these 78 colleges were affiliated to Universities according to territorial jurisdiction defined by the Government when Universities at Calcutta, Madras and Bombay were established.

QUESTIONS FOR EXERCISE

1. What were the causes of the slow progress of primary education during the period between 1854 and 1882?
2. Describe briefly the progress of secondary education during the period between 1854 and 1882.
3. Trace the development of higher education between 1854 and 1882.

CHAPTER 12

THE INDIAN EDUCATION COMMISSION (1882)

Historical Background

The revolt of 1857 shook the very foundation of British empire in India. The administration was taken away from the Company and transferred to the Crown. The normalisation of conditions took some time. By 1882 it was considered necessary to assess the development of education in the country and to remove the defects which had creeped into it. For this purpose Lord Ripon appointed the Indian Education Commission on February 3, 1882 under the Chairmanship of William Hunter, a member of the executive council of the Viceroy. The Commission, popularly known as Hunter Commission after the name of its Chairman, had twenty members, some of whom were Indians. Among these were Syed Mohmud, Anand Mohan Basu, P. Ranganada Mudaliar, Hazi Gulam, K.T. Talang, Maharaj Jitendra MohanTagore and Bhudeo Mukherji. Dr. Miller was its member as a representative of the missionaries, B.L. Rice, the D.P.I. of Mysore, was the secretary of the Commission.

The Aims of the Commission

1. To assess the position of primary education and to give suggestions for its reforms.
2. To evaluate the work of the missionaries in the field of education.
3. To find out if the Government institutions should be allowed to continue.
4. To assess the utility of the grant-in-aid system. To find out the attitude of the Government towards the private Indian enterprises in the field of education. To find out if they received encouragement from the Government.

5. To study the problem of primary education and to suggest measures for its reforms. But the Commission also chose to look into the affairs relating to secondary and higher education.

Within ten months the Commission produced a report of about 700 pages after hard labour. This report is of historical importance. The Commission made several sittings for the first two months in Calcutta, then for the next eight months it toured round the whole country. The Commission elicited opinion from provincial Governments. It formed a number of committees in various provinces to study the problem of primary education. It obtained more than 300 suggestions from various groups of persons. Although the Commission worked very hard for lull ten months, but it could not give any original suggestion or educational ideas. Its report was a revised and enlarged version of Charles Wood's Report of 1854.

RECOMMENDATIONS OF THE COMMISSION

Primary Education

After studying the problems of primary education from every angle the Hunter Commission gave elaborate suggestions for its reforms. The education policy, the financing system, training of teachers, organisation and curriculum, etc. etc., were studied by the Commission. Following major recommendations were made:

1. **Policy.** The Commission observed that primary education should be related to life. It should be practical and useful. Its purpose should be to make students self-dependent. Its curriculum should consist of such subjects which may further these goals. The students should be given primary education through the medium of their mother tongue. Persons who have received primary education should be given preference in services suitable for them. Primary education should be encouraged. Steps should be taken to develop primary education. The backward and tribal people should be encouraged to receive primary education.
2. **Management.** The Hunter Commission placed the responsibility of primary education on District Boards, Municipal Boards and Town Areas. Thus it made the Government free from its responsibility.

3. **Training Schools.** The Commission urged the necessity of opening training schools for training of teachers. It rightly found training of teachers necessary for development of primary education. It gave the following suggestions in this connection.
    1. Training schools should be established at such places from where trained teachers may be made available for the areas where there are no trained teachers. There should be at least one normal school within the jurisidiction of each inspector of schools.
    2. Inspectors of schools should take personal interest in the organisation and maintenance of normal schools.
    3. Normal schools should also get reasonable share of the grant sanctioned for primary education.
4. **Curriculum.** The Commission left the organisation of the curriculum on provincial Governments with the suggestion that they should organise the same in their respective areas according to the needs of the locality concerned. At the same time the Commission also suggested that subjects useful for life should be incorporated in the curriculum. It opined that agriculture, physics, trignometry, geography, medicine and accountancy should be included in the curriculum as these subjects are closely related to life.

The Impact of the Recommendations on Primary Education

By bringing it under the local boards the Hunter Commission changed the shape of primary education. This measure made the Government free of any responsibility for the same and gave an opportunity to the local boards to serve the people. Luckily, the local boards performed their task well and the condition of primary education improved. As the local boards were required to run primary schools, the provincial Government had to release the grants sanction in their favour and they could not divert it to other purposes. This eased the financial difficulty of primary schools up to some extent.

At the time of Hunter Commission there were many indigenous institutions imparting education to people on the old traditional Indian pattern. The Commission regarded these schools as very useful for imparting primary education. So it recommended financial grants for them.

SECONDARY EDUCATION

Although appointed only for primary education the Hunter Commission examined the condition of secondary and higher education as well. The Commission gave the following three important suggestions for secondary education:

1. The Government should entrust the responsibility of secondary education wholly to the Indians. It should only give financial grants for removing certain difficulties.
2. The Commission indirectly pleaded for English as the medium of instruction. It ignored the claim of the mother tongue for the same. For the middle schools the managers of schools were made responsible to organise education according to the local needs.
3. The secondary school curriculum should be divided into two parts. In the first part literary and science subjects should be grouped and in the second part there should be such vocational subjects which might be useful to life.

Training of Graduate Teachers

The Commission emphasised the necessity of teachers' training for raising the standard of secondary education. At the time of Hunter Commission there were only two training schools in the country, one at Lahore and the other at Madras. The Commission recommended that the duration of training for graduates should be shorter than for those who are not graduates. The trainees should be examined both in theory and practice of teaching.

Grant-in-Aid

The Grant-in-aid system was started in England in 1861. It was started in India in 1865. There was no uniformity in this system in India. In Madras it was based on teachers' salary, in Bombay on examination result, in Central Provinces and North-Western (U.P.) Provinces it was only for a fixed period. The Commission urged that there should be a uniformity in this system and the same policy should be followed throughout the whole country.

EDUCATION DEPARTMENT

Hunter Commission realised that the efficiency of Education Department had gone down. It was not helping the development of education. So the Commission gave the following suggestions for the reorganisation of education department:

1. For inspecting primary schools such local persons should be appointed who are conversant with the local environment.
2. The number of inspectors should be increased.
3. The emoluments of assistant inspectors should be increased.
4. Mostly Indians should be appointed as inspectors.

HIGHER EDUCATION

Hunter Commission gave some important suggestions for improvement of higher education. It observed that at the time of giving grant it should be checked that the educational institution well utilises the given grant. The grant should be determined keeping in view the strength of the teachers and students, need and capacity of the institution. The colleges engaged in higher education should be given sufficient grants for Experimental laboratories, reading rooms, libraries, equipments, science rooms, building and furniture, etc.

INDIANISATION OF RESOURCES

Hunter Commission was required to consider whether the Government schools should remain under the control of the Government or should they be transferred to Indian hands. This problem arose because most of the schools and colleges were opened by the Government according to the recommendation of Wood's Despatch. Missionaries were also influenced by this measure as they found the Government as their rival in the field of education. Consequently, missionaries also opened a number of schools. So the Government thought over the problem of retaining its schools or handing them over to Indians. Some people were of the view that the Government should withdraw itself completely from the field of education. The other group of persons wanted that the Government should wholly control education. The Commission studied this issue and recommended that the Government should withdraw itself completely from the field of education.

RELIGIOUS EDUCATION

Hunter Commission was required to give its opinion regarding the policy that the Government should adopt for religious education. The Commission recommended as follows:

1. The government should have no hand in the religious education in schools.

2. The managers of the non-government schools should be free to give or not to give a place to religious education in their schools. The Government should place no restriction in this respect.
3. While giving grants special attention should be paid to the standard of the schools which give religious education.

WOMEN'S EDUCATION

Hunter Commission made the following recommendations with regard to women education:

1. **Education in Special Subjects.** The Commission maintained that, because of the different nature of their life duties, the curriculum for girls should be different from that for boys. Subjects useful in their life should be included in their curriculum. The Commission observed that literary subjects would not be useful for girls. Therefore, they should be given education in subjects useful in their life.
2. **Education by Local Boards.** The local boards should be made responsible for women's education. In the absence of such a local board in some areas the government should shoulder the responsibility for women education.
3. **Women Teachers.** Only lady teachers should be appointed in girls schools.
4. **Inspectress.** Inspectress for girls' schools should be appointed. This policy would encourage women education also.

MUSLIM EDUCATION

After studying the problems of Muslim education Hunter Commission gave the following suggestions to improve it:

1. Local bodies should be made responsible for Muslim education.
2. The indigenous Muslim schools should be encouraged.
3. The medium of Muslim schools should be Hindustani except in those schools where the people do not want this medium.
4. Muslims should be given greater assistance in the field of higher English education.
5. Special provisions should be made for scholarship for Muslim students.

6. The number of freeships for Muslim students should be fixed.
7. Normal schools should be opened for training of Muslim teachers.
8. The existing Muslim schools should be recognised and encouraged.
9. Muslim inspectors should be appointed for Muslim schools.

EDUCATION OF THE BACKWARD CLASSES

Hunter Commission recommended that in Government schools special facilities should be provided for backward classes. It further suggested that some Government schools should be opened for children of backward classes. The suggestions of the Commission led to the progress of education of backward classes.

EDUCATION OF ABORIGINES

Hunter Commission suggested that special provision should be made for education of aborigines. Keeping in view the geographical and social conditions and traditions of the people. Special types of schools should be opened in their areas.

THE MISSIONARIES

Missionaries had become rivals to the Government in the field of education. On the appointment of the Hunter Commission they had hoped that they would be given special facilities and consideration in the field of education with permission to open as many new schools as they wanted. They had also hoped that they would be recognised as supreme in the field of education. But these hopes of the missionaries were belied. They did not mind when primary education was entrusted to local boards, because they had no interest in this area. They were glad when it was suggested that the Government should withdraw itself from the field of secondary education. But they were annoyed when the Commission suggested that the Government should be entrusted to private enterprises and it did not include missionaries in 'private enterprises'. Against the missionaries, the Commission observed that "They (missionaries) should never be given full control in the field of education as they can never win the sympathy and respect of the Indian people". Hence the missionaries were very much discouraged. Thus the recommendations of the Commission encouraged Indian private enterprises a great deal.

SPECIAL EDUCATION PLAN

Hunter Commission recommended that special schools should be opened for the children of Rajas, Maharajas, Nawabs and Talukdars.

CRITICAL EVALUATION

The recommendations of the Hunter Commission have a special place in the history of Indian education. Hunter Commission tried to give a direction to Indian education which was in a bad shape. It drew the attention of the Government towards the neglect of vocational education and to overemphasis on bookish education. It encouraged private enterprises in the field of education. It helped the development of education in the country. However, following recommendations of the Commission have been very harmful:

1. The Commission neglected the claim of the mother tongue and supported English as the medium of instruction. Consequently the Indian languages were neglected.
2. The Commission suggested to charge lower fee in private institutions. This led to the opening of schools of lower standard.
3. Since education was entrusted to private enterprises, the Government became indifferent to education of the people. This attitude ultimately harmed the cause of education.
4. According to the suggestion of the Commission the Government was to control the inspection department. Hence the Governmental control over education was tightened leading to loss of flexibility in education. Through its inspectorate the government used to interfere in the working of institutions without any resultant responsibility for their improvement.

QUESTIONS FOR EXERCISE

1. Examine the recommendations of the Hunter Commission for reforms of primary education.
2. What is the importance of Hunter Commission in the history of Indian education?

CHAPTER 13

PROGRESS OF EDUCATION DURING 1882-1900

The Hunter Commission, though appointed only for primary education, studied the problems relating to secondary and higher education as well. The Government attached great importance to the suggestions given by the Commission and tried to implement the same as far as possible. This was done as follows.

PRIMARY EDUCATION

According to the recommendations of the Hunter Commission the responsibility for primary education was entrusted to the local bodies which were established in the country during the days of Lord Ripon. County Councils were established in Great Britain at this time and the local bodies in India were formed on the same pattern. As the progress appears to be very slow in the beginning of any new scheme, so the progress of primary education under the local bodies appeared to be very slow in the beginning. The indigenous schools were also brought under the control of the local boards due to which they got a great set-back and began to fade away from the scene. At places where they were added to the Government schools they lost their identity. In 1882, only ₹ 24 lakh and in 1902 ₹ 46 lakh were spent on primary education. Although the Hunter Commission had recommended full Government financial assistance for primary education, but this assistance was almost negligible. During a period of 20 years the Government help was increased only by ₹ 22 lakh. As the local boards were not rich, primary education did not progress satisfactorily.

SECONDARY EDUCATION

Secondary education was benefited by the recommendations of the Hunter Commission. The commission had recommended for total governmental withdrawal from the field of secondary education. But the education departments continued their control over secondary education. This situation helped the development of secondary education, because the education departments worked for its expansion in order to make their own position stronger. Formerly, the department had not taken so much interest in the development of secondary education. The financial position of Government schools was quite sound and the standard of education in them was better than that in the aided schools. The aided schools were facing financial stringency.

The Hunter Commission had recommended for diversification of the secondary curriculum into two separate parts — 1. Literary and science, and 2. Vocational. The first was meant to prepare students for university classes while the second was meant for imparting vocational education useful in practical affairs of life. Those days the students were more interested in procuring services. They had little interest in vocational education. So vocational education could not be encouraged, although some arrangement for vocational education was made after 1882.

UNIVERSITY AND HIGHER EDUCATION

Secondary education prepared students for higher education. Therefore, its progress had its impact on university education. As secondary education progressed between 1882 and 1902, the university education also progressed during this period. Youths began to come to universities to obtain good services. As the Commission had recommended for encouraging private enterprises in the field of education, so many colleges were opened by voluntary organisations. Their number was larger than the colleges started by missionaries. By 1882 there were 37 colleges run by missionaries, whereas the number of colleges run by voluntary organisations at this time was 42. By 1902 there were 191 colleges in the whole country. Out of these 145 were art colleges, 30 law, four engineering, five training, four medical and three agricultural colleges. Besides, there were 12 women's colleges for higher education in the country by 1902.

The Indian National Congress was established in 1885. It created a feeling of nationalism and patriotism. Youths educated in colleges were greatly influenced by the revolutionary ideas of Rousseau, Byron, Burk, Bacon, Milton, Locke, Wordsworth and others. The educated Indians were imbued with the ideals of sacrifice, national morality and independence. They were perturbed over the foreign rule in the country and they began to dream for national freedom. This situation led to the generation of nationalism in education. The Indians intensely realised the necessity of education. They thought that education would be a good tool for obtaining freedom. Therefore, the task of expansion of education was accelerated by private enterprises under the control of Indians. It was at this time that several great personalities were born who took the vow of national service with the ultimate objective of winning national freedom. High Schools began to be developed into colleges and a number of new colleges were also established. Great persons like R.P. Paranjape, Bal Gangadhar Tilak, Triplankar, Ayanger took the work of education in their hands. The Fergusan College was established at Poona in 1870. Sir Surendra Nath Banerji controlled the management of Ripon College at Calcutta.

The name of Maharshi Dayanand Saraswati will remain immortal in the field of education in India. He stood for ancient ideals of education and established a number of D. A. V. colleges in the northern part of the country. He tried to remove the evils of Hindu society and religion through his educational ideals. The Arya Samaj took up his work and tried to propagate his ideals of life throughout the whole country.

In the city of Banaias (now Varanasi) Mrs. Annie Besant established the Central Hindu College in 1898 on the basis of Hindu ideals. Later on, this college became the nucleus for the Banaras Hindu University established by Mahamana Pandit Madan Mohan Malviya.

CRITICAL EVALUATION

Education in India was developed with a greater stride during the 20 years that followed the appointment of Hunter Commission.

The number of schools and colleges increased. But the standard of education fell down due to paucity of funds. The educational institutions did not have proper buildings, libraries and other necessary equipments. There were no trained teachers for schools. Bookish knowledge was overemphasised, the students were not given practical experiences useful in actual life situations. Thus the education given to youths was one-sided. The sole purpose before the students was to pass the examinations with good marks. In fact, nothing useful in practical life was taught to them. In its report the University Education Commission of 1902 has remarked that, "the purpose of education in India is not to receive education but to pass examination." The Indian public was not unaware of this defect. However, two groups of people were thinking differently about education. One group was keen for expansion of education and the other group was perturbed over the fall of standard of education. Gopal Krishna Gokhale was the advocate of the first group. He insisted on expansion of education. He believed that the Indian youths should be educated on the Western pattern as the same would do good whether it was of poor standard or high. Thus Gokhale emphasised quantity instead of quality. In a way he was very right because it was from the quantity that quality could also come out. In view of the things as existing then this appeared to be the right measure also because of the very few people educated in English.

QUESTIONS FOR EXERCISE

1. Trace the development of education during the period of 20 years that followed the appointment of Hunter Commission.
2. What were the chief weaknesses of education in India during the period from 1882 to 1902? Give reasons for the same.

CHAPTER 14

PROGRESS OF EDUCATION DURING 1900-1920

LORD CURZON'S EDUCATIONAL POLICY

In 1899 Lord Curzon was appointed Governor General of India. He toured Asia from 1882 to February 1885 prior to the appointment and got ample opportunity to study geographical conditions and the importance of India. Therefore when he became Governor General, it was natural for him to make certain fundamental reforms in the Indian administrative set up. The work that he accomplished in his seven years' rule, would have taken decades for others to perform. Within this short period Curzon paid his attention to each and every aspect of administration. There was scarcely a day when some commission was not sitting or some reform was not being done in respect of administration. He paid his attention towards the reforms of Indian education. At this time, the wave of nationalism was flowing fast. Some able and sacrificing social reformers were demanding 'National Education'. They thought that only national education could safeguard the culture, civilization, literature and language of India. The educational institutions supporting the national education were Dayanand Anglo College of Lahore and Gumkula Kangri institution established by Swami Shraddhanand at Haridwar, the central Hindu College of Banaras, etc.

Indian National Congress was established in 1885. It was the most popular national institution of the country. Later it brought freedom to India. The period from 1897 to 1902 was the period of silence in Indian history. The number of students was meagre. Schools were very few. Two dreadful famines and ravaging plagues had shaken India. Thus, it was natural for Lord Curzon to pay attention towards Indian education.

Shimla Education Conference (1901)

Lord Curzon convened a conference with himself in the chair with the view to reform Indian education. Education Directors from every province of India and the representatives of Christian missionaries were invited in this conference. It continued for 15 days and considered every aspect of Indian education from Primary to University. Here, for the first time, Curzon declared his educational policy as follows:

1. British government will continue to control every item of the education and also direct Indian education.
2. Public institutions will be established as and when needed. They shall serve as models for the private institutions.
3. The Central Government will have complete control over Indian education. Their educational policy shall also be conducted and directed.
4. British Government will spend more money on education.

All the proceedings of Shimla Conference were not disclosed. It did not have any Indian representative in it. Hence Indians took it to be a conspiracy against themselves and felt annoyed. They thought that probably the Government wanted to abolish the national feeling through discarding Indians from educational field and handing it over to European and Christian missionaries.

INDIAN UNIVERSITY COMMISSION (1902)

In accordance with his education policy declared at Shimla Conference, Lord Curzon appointed 'Indian University Commission' in 1902. The main reason for an appointment of this Commission was that Curzon himself thought that an ideal university should have two aspects. Firstly, it should aim at expanding and encouraging knowledge and education. Secondly, it should build the character of the students. From this viewpoint, Calcutta, Madras, Bombay, Punjab and Allahabad universities had certain shortcomings which were responsible for lowering the standard of education. Thus, it was necessary to enquire into the present condition of the universities. British Government also considered Indian universities as Indian counterparts of London University. Since London University had been reorganized in 1898, Indian universities also needed to be amended.

(i) ***Terms of Reference.*** Following were the terms of reference of Indian University Commission:

1. To survey future prospects and the conditions of the universities in India established by the British Government.
2. To suggest ways and means for the organisation and working of Indian universities.
3. To lay down the procedures by which the standards of Higher Education may go up at the earliest.

(ii) ***Suggestions.*** The Commission visited various universities. It put forward the report containing following recommendations in regard to Higher education:

1. The Senate and Syndicate should be re-organised. The members of the Senate and Syndicate should be reduced to nine and 15 respectively and their term should be of five years.
2. Certain facilities for teaching should be given after amending the constitution of the universities.
3. There should be a suitable representation of the teachers and the scholars of the affiliated colleges in the University Senate.
4. There should be a suitable arrangement for teaching in the colleges affiliated to the universities. The rules for recognition should be strictly observed and enforced.
5. Affiliated colleges should be strictly supervised by the universities.
6. Universities should appoint teachers to impart higher education.
7. Suitable amendments should be made in the curriculum and the examination system of the universities.
8. Hostels should be built for the students.
9. Arrangement for scholarships should take place according to the position of the students.
10. The standard of the Matric examination should be high, while abolishing the Inter-Examination, the curriculum of B.A. should be three years.
11. There should be a managing committee for every college. Besides managing the colleges concerned it should also appoint competent teachers. It should pay attention towards the discipline of the students and the construction of buildings and hostels, etc.

(iii) *Evaluation.* The Commission did not aim at introducing any revolutionary change in the system of university education. It sought to recognise the existing pattern, though its recommendations did not find favour with the Indian public. There was no representation of any Indian in the Commission though later on, Dr. Gurdas Banerjee and Syed Hasan Bilgrami were made members. Even then Indians did not feel happy. They were suspicious of the intentions of Curzon. They thought that Government wanted to suppress nationalism. By recommending the abolition of second-rate degree colleges the Commission created a wave of anger among the Indian educationists.

INDIAN UNIVERSITY ACT (1904)

On the basis of Indian University Commission (1902) Lord Curzon decided to frame the educational policy of state. An Education Act was put forward on March 11,1904. This later on became a law in 1904. It highlighted the defects of Indian education in the following manner:

A. Defects

1. As the only aim for acquiring higher education is to get an employment, the scope of education has become narrower. The persons who are not selected for Government jobs are unable to get into other jobs as well.
2. Undue importance is attached to the examination system. Therefore, the students only aim at passing the examination.
3. The courses are absolutely bookish. Very little attention is paid towards intellectual development. Instead of attaining real knowledge students try to get through the examination by cramming the material.
4. The development of Indian languages has been stunted due to the importance given to English.
5. Industrial and technological education is neglected. The persons who acquire this education do so only to get Government jobs. Vocational education is not properly attended to.

B. Suggestions

While pointing out the above mentioned defects. Curzon advanced a number of suggestions in the Indian University Act for the improvement of higher education. These were as follows:

1. Universities were given the right of teaching along with the right of conducting examinations. Universities had the right to appoint teachers to conduct teaching. It inspired them to carry on research, to manage libraries and laboratories and to make out plans to bring about discipline among the students.
2. So far the number of the seats in the Senate of the universities were not fixed and the Government used to make life-long nominations. According to this Act the number was fixed at 50 as the minimum while the maximum number was hundred. Their term was determined for five years.
3. According to the Indian Universities Act, the members of the Senate got the right to elect members. Such elected members were not to be more than twenty for the universities of Calcutta, Bombay and Madras and 15 for other universities.
4. Legal status was given to the syndicates of the universities. Proper representations of professors was made compulsory in these syndicates.
5. The Government secured the right to make amendments and reforms and give approval to rules framed by the Senates of the University. The Government also had the right to make laws in this regard by themselves.
6. Rules in regard to granting of recognition were made strict. In order to raise the standard of education, the syndicate could make the inspection of the college imparting higher education.
7. The territorial jurisdiction of universities was not fixed, with the result that in some places some colleges had secured recognition from two universities. In the 27th Article of this Act, it was made clear that the Governor General shall by his ordinary or extraordinary orders, fix the territorial jurisdiction of each university. Relations between the University and the colleges shall be established and maintained according to this provision.

GOKHALE'S BILLS (1910-1912)

Gokhale's Bill 1910

Gopal Krishna Gokhale was very much concerned towards primary education in India. With the policy of the Government of India, enunciated in 1904, primary education was gaining a good ground. However, it was not in proportion to the growing population of India. Only 2.38 per cent boys and 2.07 per cent girls were able to get education. At this time the Maharaja Sayaji Rao Gaikwad of Baroda had made primary education free and compulsory within the territories of his State in 1906. This attempt inspired Gokhale.

As a member of the Imperial Legislative Council, he moved the following resolution on March 19, 1910.

"That this council recommends that a beginning should be made in the direction of making elementary education free and compulsory throughout the country, and that a mixed commission of officials and non-officials be appointed at an early date to frame definite proposal."

Following were the important suggestions contained in this resolution:

(i) Elementary education should be made free and compulsory in the area where 35 per cent boys were receiving education. This provision should apply to the age group of 6 to 10 years.

(ii) The cost of primary education should be shared by the provincial Government and the local bodies in the ratio of 2:1.

(iii) A secretary should be appointed to organise, supervise and look after the primary education.

(iv) There should be a separate department in the Central Government to draw up a scheme for the expansion of primary education. In the budget statement there should be a portion describing the progress of primary education at the primary stage.

The Government assured Shri Gokhale that it would seriously consider the matter and so he withdrew his resolution. Later on, the Government accepted only last three recommendations of Shri Gokhale. In 1940 a Department of Education was organised in the Central Government and the Secretary was appointed. The record of the progress of primary education also started to be published by Government. But the Government did not make the primary school education free and compulsory, while this was the main plank of Gakhale's Bill.

Gokhale's Bill 1911

Gokhale was not discouraged. He made further attempt to draw the attention of the people in India as well as in England towards the condition of education. He waged a stronger fight against the Government and presented a Bill on March 16, 1911 in the Legislative Council. The object of the Bill was to provide for gradual introduction of principle of compulsion into the elementary education system of the country. The following were main suggestions contained in the Bill:

(i) Compulsory primary education should be introduced in the areas where a certain percentage was fixed by the Governor General-in-Council.

(ii) After securing the sanction of the Government, the local bodies shall enforce the rule. Local bodies shall have the right to introduce compulsion in the whole or part of the area under their jurisdiction.

(iii) Local bodies were also given the right to levy cess to meet the cost of free and compulsory primary education.

(iv) Expenditure on education was to be shared by the local bodies and the provincial Government in the ratio of 1:2.

(v) Primary education should be made compulsory for the boys of the age group of 6 to 10. The defaulting guardians should be penalised for non- compliance of the provisions of sending their wards to recognised primary schools.

(vi) The primary education shall be made compulsory for girls.

(vii) Guardians whose income is less than ₹ 10 should not be asked to pay any fee for their wards.

Although Gokhale's Bill was rejected, but it focused the attention of the entire country on education. The Government reconsidered its policy on education and a new educational policy was launched in 1913.

GOVERNMENT RESOLUTION ON EDUCATIONAL POLICY (1913)

While rejecting Gokhale's Bill, the Government promised to extend recurring and non-recurring grants to primary education, as it could not ignore the growing popular demand for the spread of mass education. Gokhale's Bill created a flutter in the British Parliament also. In the course of the discussion on the Indian budget, the Under-Secretary of State for India admitted the need for paying more attention to Indian education. As a result, the Government of India passed a resolution on Educational Policy on February 21, 1913. The outbreak of the First World War, however, delayed the development planned in the resolution. Many important items were postponed owing to financial stringency.

Introduction to the Resolution

The Government of India have refused to recognize the principle of compulsory education for financial and administrative reasons of decisive weight but they desired the widest possible extension of primary education on a voluntary basis. The time has not yet arrived to dispense wholly with fees. The fees derived from those pupils who can pay them are now devoted to the maintenance and expansion of primary education. A total remission of fees would involve to a certain extent a more prolonged postponement of a provision of schools in villages without them. In some provinces elementary education is already free. In the majority of provinces liberal provision is already made for giving free elementary instruction to those boys whose parents cannot afford to pay fees. Local governments have been requested to extend the application of the principle of free elementary education amongst the poorer and more backward sections of the population.

It is the desire and hope of the Government of India to see in the not distant future some 91,000 primary public schools added to the 100,000 which already exist for boys and to double the 4½ millions of the pupils who now receive instruction, in them.

Major Provisions of the Resolution

(i) There should be sufficient expansion of lower primary schools, where along with instruction in the three R's, children should be taught drawing, knowledge of the village map, nature study and physical exercises.

(ii) Simultaneously upper primary schools should be opened at the proper places and if need be, the lower primary schools should be raised to the status of upper primary schools.

(iii) Local boards' schools should be established in place of private aided schools.

(iv) Maktabs and Pathshalas should be adequately subsidised.

(v) The inspection and management of private schools should be made more efficient.

(vi) In most of the parts of India, it may not be practicable to prescribe a separate curiculla for rural and urban, but in the urban schools there is sufficient scope for teaching Geography and organising school excursions, etc.

(vii) The teachers should have passed vernacular middle examination and received one year's training.

(viii) Provision be made for refresher courses for the teachers of primary education during vacations.

(ix) A trained teacher should get a salary not less than ₹ 12 p.m. Again, there should be provision for his increment in salary, pension and provident fund.

(x) The number of students under one teacher should generally range between 30 and 40.

(xi) Improvement should be made in the condition of middle and secondary vernacular schools and their number should be increased.

(xii) Schools should be housed in sanitary, spacious but inexpensive buildings.

(xiii) Emphasis was laid on the education of women too. Suggestions were put forth concerning special curriculum of practical utility for girls. It was clearly stated in the resolution that too much importance should not be attached to examination in the education of girls.

(xiv) Number of women teachers and inspectors should also be increased.

(xv) The State should not completely withdraw from the sphere of secondary education.

(xvi) Further establishment of State institutions was proposed to be stopped.

(xvii) Existing institutions should continue to serve as models and proper grants-in-aid should be sanctioned to private institutions.

(xviii) An improvement in the mode of examination and curriculum was also recommended.

(xix) The Resolution provided for the expansion in University education. The existence of five universities and 185 colleges was considered to be insufficient in view of the vast needs and demands of the country.

(xx) The Resolution suggested that universities and high schools should be assigned distinct spheres of activities.

(xxi) The universities should be relieved of the responsibility of granting recognition to high schools and they should be kept under provincial governments.

(xxii) The establishment of teaching universities was suggested by emphasizing the separation of the two functions of the universities teaching and examining.

(xxiii) Recommendations were made concerning the inclusion of subjects of industrial importance in the curriculum and provision of facilities to the students desirous of prosecuting research work.

(xxiv) The Resolution put forth certain valuable suggestions pertaining to the character formation of students and hostel life.

THE CALCUTTA UNIVERSITY COMMISSION, 1917-1919

Historical Background

The appointment of this Commission was proposed in 1914, but due to the outbreak of the World War I, it could not be possible. Because of the World War I, the proposed Chairman of the Commission, Lord Haildon had refused to head it. The Government, too, concentrated its attention and energy over the war. However, the Government had become keen to find out the defects in the educational system. It felt the necessity to do something for education in order to pacify the public opinion. So the Calcutta University Commission was appointed in 1917 under the Chairmanship of Sir M.E. Sadler. The Commission was named after, Calcutta University as it was principally required to look into the affairs of this University and suggest measures for its reforms. Sir Asutosh Mukherji, Dr. Ziaddin Ahmad, Dr. Gregory, Sir Hartog and Prof. Ramsay Muir were some of the more important members of the Commission. Sir Asutosh Mukherji was the most influential member of the Commission. Most of the recommendations of the Commission were patterned on his views.

The Aims of the Commission

The Commission was required to examine the condition and workings of the Calcutta University and suggest measures for its reforms. It was authorised to study the condition of other universities in the country. After the name of its chairman, this Commission is also popularly known as Sadler Commission.

Functions of the Commission

In March, 1919 the Commission submitted its report to the Government. This report was in 13 parts and it had elaborate suggestions for reforms of Calcutta University. The suggestions, though for Calcutta University, could be equally applicable to other universities in the country.

The Commission started its report with the examination of secondary education, as it considered it as the basis of University education. The Commission studied the various problems of University very carefully and gave constructive suggestions for the reforms of both secondary and university education. The Commission examined the organisation, nature and working method of the University and gave suggestions for their improvement.

Defects of Secondary Education

The Commission drew attention to the following defects of secondary education:

1. The secondary schools are suffering from lack of useful educational tools and equipments.
2. Secondary education had become narrow because of being over in fluenced by public examination.
3. The standard of secondary education has fallen down to a deplorable degree.
4. The secondary schools are not inspected periodically and they are not given useful suggestions for their improvement.
5. Suitable subjects for intermediate classes are not included in the curriculum. The Commission was of the opinion that the study of subjects to be taught at the intermediate stage should be begun at the secondary level also.

The Commission opined that secondary education at the time neither prepared students for university education nor did it create self-dependence in youths. So the secondary' education should be put on the right track for giving a desirable direction to university education.

Suggestions for Reforms of Secondary Education

1. Only intermediate passed candidates should be admitted to universities. The intermediate classes should be separated from universities. The B.A. studies should be of three years' duration.
2. Intermediate colleges should be established as a necessity. Intermediate classes should be run independently or they should be attached with high school classes.
3. Subjects useful for practical life should be compulsorily taught in intermediate classes. Science, art, agriculture, medicine, engineering and teachers' training should be included for intermediate classes.
4. A board of High School and Intermediate Education should be established in each province. It should be made independent of the existing education department. Its management should consist of representations of high schools, intermediate colleges, universities and the government.
5. Mother tongue should be the medium of instruction in the intermediate colleges.

The Commission sought to make the universities free of the burden of intermediate colleges. It desired that the universities should concentrate their attention on higher education and research work alone.

University Education

The Commission opined that the Calcutta University had assumed a huge dimension in the form of its various affiliated educational institutions. So it was not possible for the University to perform its task successfully. Therefore, the Commission gave the following suggestions:

1. Another university should be established at Dacca.
2. The various colleges within the urban area should be organised into one university which should take up teaching work.
3. The colleges in the rural areas should be grouped into one organised college university.

For administration, functions and organisation of the university the Commission gave the following suggestions:

1. The university should be given enough freedom for the performance of its duties. Its rules and regulations should be liberal and flexible.

2. The powers of the university teachers should be widened.
3. The B.A. course should be of three years duration. The honours course should also be instituted.
4. Outside experts should serve on selection committees for appointing readers and professors.
5. The Vice-chancellor should be a salaried officer.
6. Teaching facilities should be provided for various subjects.
7. Special attention should be paid on health of university students. For this a director of health education should be appointed.
8. In place of senate a court of representatives should be appointed. This court should look after the internal affairs of the university. An executive council should be formed in place of the syndicate.
9. There should be a board and an academic council in the university. The board will prescribe the curriculum, conduct examination, organise research work, hold convocation and confer degrees. The academic council will deal with problem relating to education.
10. Muslims should be provided especial educational facilities in order that their backwardness may be removed.

Women Education

The Commission gave the following suggestions for encouraging women education:

1. Under the Calcutta University control a board for women education should be constituted for preparing useful curriculum for women education. Women should be given education in medicine and teachers' training.
2. Co-education should be started in universities and women should be encouraged to benefit themselves by the same.
3. For young girls purdah schools should be opened.

Teachers' Training

The Commission rightly realised the necessity of teachers' training without which it was not possible to improve standard of secondary education. So the Commission gave the following suggestions for teachers' training:

1. Education should be taught as an independent subject both in intermediate and B.A. classes.

2. Education departments should be opened in Calcutta and Dacca Universities for teaching education as an independent subject.

Vocational Education

The Commission observed that the students in India were especially interested in literary subjects due to two reasons: Firstly, the students in universities came from rich homes and they were not interested in any particular vocation of life, except in obtaining higher education for procuring good services. Secondly, there was no provision for vocational education and it was not possible for youths to understand its importance. Remarking that without some sort of vocational education the development of the individual would be narrow, the Commission gave the following suggestions:

1. Vocational education should be started at the intermediate stage. This would facilitiate the beginning of vocational education at the university stage.
2. Provision for higher vocational education should be made in universities at earliest.

CRITICAL EVALUATION

1. **Guideline for all Universities.** The recommendations of the Commission, though meant for only Calcutta University, served as a guideline for the entire university education in the country. Accordingly, the various universities in the country began to re-organise themselves. Thus the Commission gave a new life to universities.
2. **Benefit to Calcutta University.** Calcutta University was benefited immensely. Its working capacity was increased and it no more remained only an examining body. It was now engaged in teaching and doing research. Consequently, the student community was greatly helped to receive better higher education.
3. **Education Useful to Life.** To make education useful to life, the Commission recommended for women education, vocational education and teachers' training.
4. **Emphasis on Mother Tongue.** By declaring the mother tongue as the medium of instruction the Commission fulfilled a great need of the country.

Criticism of the Commission

1. The Commission has been criticised on the ground that it proposed many new things much before time and they were not suitable in view of the circumstances then prevailing.
2. It is said that the Commission tried to pattern the Calcutta University on the lines of Oxford and Cambridge Universities. This attempt was not appropriate as the condition in India was different from that in England.
3. Creating a separate board of high school and intermediate education was also considered as much ahead the time.

Utility of Recommendations

1. Due to the suggestions, of this Commission a number of new universities were opened in the country. Of these the Universities at Patna, Lucknow, Aligarh, Agra, Dacca, Delhi, Nagpur, Hyderabad and Mysore may be mentioned.
2. The recommendations of the Commission revolutionised the shape of secondary education. The recommendations of the Commission have been much more important than those of anyprevious Commission or Committee on education.

EDUCATIONAL PROGRESS DURING 1905-1920
PRIMARY EDUCATION

Expansion of Education

Lord Curzon had been the most magnificent Viceroy of India. His personality and policy left its inevitable impact on each and every aspect of administration. He was a lover of education and influenced all the aspects of education in the country from primary to university. Because of his particular interest, primary education progressed rapidly during the period from 1905 to 1912. He tried both for quantitative and qualitative development of education. The number of schools and students at the primary stage increased during his days. In 1912 the attention was particularly given on qualitative development. Consequently, the development of primary education was slower. The qualitative development could not be useful, as illiteracy had to be wiped out first.

Free and Compulsory Education

The Indian people consistently and persistently demanded for making primary education compulsory and free. But the Government was in no mood to accept this demand. The example of Baroda in the development of primary education was before the country. The Maharaja of Baroda made primary education free and compulsory in his State. At this time Gopal Krishna Gokhale again raised his voice for making primary education free and compulsory. He introduced a Bill on March 19, 1910 in the Central Legislative Council for making secondary education also compulsory. But he withdrew the Bill on the assurance from the Government.

Gokhale's Efforts

Gokhale persistently tried for making primary education compulsory. It was because of his efforts that the Indian National Congress at Allahabad and the Muslim League at Nagpur passed resolutions in 1910 for making primary education compulsory and free. The Secretary of State for India in England declared that new departments had been opened for propagating literacy programmes. In spite of all these efforts Gokhale could not succeed in this objective, however, he continued his demand and did not deviate from his objective of making primary education compulsory and free. On March 16,1911. Gokhale placed his Bill in the Central Legislative Council for making primary education compulsory and free, but because of the opposition of the Government officers the Bill could not be passed.

But the outlook of the British Government changed in 1912. Because of the persistent efforts of Gokhale, enough progress of primary education was made between 1912 and 1917. In 1911, the Emperor George V declared a grant of one lakh rupees for primary education and in his address to the Calcutta University he accepted the demand for development of education. On the basis of the resolution of 1913 board schools were established in all the provinces except in Madras, Orissa and Bengal, where there were many private schools which could not be converted into board schools. In Bengal in place of board schools, panchayati primary schools were opened. The purpose of this plan was to open at least one primary school within 10.4 sq miles.

In 1917 it was declared in the British Parliament that it wanted to establish responsible Governments in India in the form of autonomous administrative units. For this it was necessary to educate the Indian people. Hence governmental and private efforts were made for the spread of literacy. The district and municipal boards were authorised to enact laws for development of education in their areas.

Patel Act of 1918. Vitthal Bhai Patel introduced a Bill in the Legislative Council in Bombay in order to declare primary education compulsory'. This Bill was passed. It speeded up the development of primary education. Other provinces in the country were also encouraged by it. The Government of India accepted in principle the necessity of compulsory primary education. By 1921 the various provinces passed their compulsory primary education.

Compulsory Primary Education in Provinces

1. **Bihar and Orissa.** Primary Education Act of 1919 both for rural and urban areas was passed in these provinces in order to make primary education compulsory. Children within 6 and 10 years of age were to be educated under the orders of local bodies.
2. **United Provinces.** Compulsory Education Act was passed in 1919 which included both boys and girls within its jurisdiction. But this Act was not applicable for rural areas. It was meant only for municipal limits.
3. **Punjab.** Compulsory Education Act was passed, but it was meant only for boys of rural and urban areas.
4. **Bengal.** Compulsory Education Act was passed in 1919 only for boys of the municipal areas. In 1922 girls were also included.
5. **Madras.** In 1920 the Compulsory Education Act was passed both for boys and girls. This Act helped the development of primary education.
6. **Central Provinces.** In 1920 the Compulsory Education Act was passed for the whole province. Both the boys and girls were included within this Act.

Thus by 1920 compulsory primary education was accepted as the general policy throughout the whole country.

SECONDARY EDUCATION

During this period there was satisfactory development of secondary education, because it led to university degree which was considered to be a good passport for procuring some good service. The number of high schools and students increased. This led to fall of educational standard as schools lacked in the necessary equipments corresponding to rise of number of students. This resulted into slow progress for some time. Lord Curzon's policy of qualitative development also arrested the progress of secondary education to some extent. Rules for recognition were made stricter under the qualitative policy. But on the public demand several new high schools were opened by 1922. There were 7530 high schools with 11,06,803 students in them in the country. In 1905 these figures were only 5,124 and 5,90,129 respectively. Thus the number of schools increased one and halftimes and that of students increased twice.

Vocational Education

According to the recommendations of the Hunter Commission some sort of vocational education was also started in high schools.

Medium of Instruction

English remained the medium of instruction at the secondary level. Its foundation became stronger and stronger day by day. Efforts were made to make the teaching of English more effective. For this purpose some teachers were trained and some equipments were organised. Mother tongue remained the medium of instruction only up to the middle stage.

Teachers' Training

Lord Curzon paid special attention to training of teachers. So some new training schools were opened. In 1912 there were only 15 training schools with 1400 pupil teachers in them. By 1921-22 there were 13 training schools to train teachers for teaching of English alone.

HIGHER AND UNIVERSITY EDUCATION

After the establishment of Allahabad University in 1887 no new university was opened for the next 30 years, but the number of colleges increased. In 1917 there were 185 colleges for higher education with 61,200 students in them. These colleges were affiliated to Calcutta, Bombay, Madras, Allahabad and Punjab Universities according to the territorial jurisdiction defined for each university. The following table indicates the development of higher education up to 1917:

S.N.	University	Affiliated Colleges	Number of Students
1.	Calcutta	58	28,618
2.	Madras	53	10,216
3.	Allahabad	33	7,807
4.	Punjab	24	6,558
5.	Bombay	17	8,001
	Total	185	61,200

New Universities

The number of colleges was beyond the control of the various universities within their territorial limits. The Sadler Commission had emphasised the necessity of opening new universities in view of too many existing colleges. Hence efforts were made to open some new universities during the period under review.

1. **Mysore University.** Established in 1916, it eased the situation in the Madras University.
2. **Patna University.** Started in 1917 for higher education in Bihar and Orissa, this university was different from other existing universities in the sense that the Government was not empowered to interfere affiliation of any new college with it.
3. **Banaras Hindu University.** Although the Government had agreed for its opening in October, 1915, this University was established on February 4, 1916. Teaching was started in 1916. The first final examination was held in 1918. Mahamana Madan Mohan Malviya did admirable work for the organisation of this University.
4. **Aligarh Muslim University.** It was started with the name of Anglo-Mohammedan School. Sir Syed Ahmad Khan established this University. This University is centrally controlled like the Banaras Hindu University.
5. **Lucknow University.** Started in 1921 by Sir Harcourt Butler and the Talukdars of Avadh, this is a developed form of the Canning College.
6. **Dacca University.** It was established in 1920 as a result of the recommendation of the Sadler Commission. After the partition of India in 1947 it became a part of Pakistan, but now it is in Bangladesh since 1971.

7. **Osmania University.** Established in 1918 at Hyderabad by the Nizam, Urdu has been the medium of instruction in this University since its very inception.
8. **Allahabad University.** This was reorganised in 1921. It was made purely residential.
9. **Lady Hardinge College.** It was started at Delhi in 1916 for imparting medical education to women.
10. **S.N.D.T. School.** It was opened at Poona during the period under review.
11. **Bhandarkar Oriental Research Institute.** It was opened in 1913.
12. **The Institute of Philosophy.** It was started in 1916.

Teaching in Universities

By 1921 there were 12 universities in India. Out of these six were affiliating universities, five were teaching and one was both teaching and affiliating. The universities used to organise the teaching work in the affiliated colleges.

Honours and Post-Graduate Education

These courses were taught by the universities. The universities taught those subjects also which were not taken up by colleges. The universities used to invite scholars from abroad for giving lectures.

NATIONAL SPIRIT IN EDUCATION

During the first quarter of the twentieth century an attempt was made to infuse education with a national spirit. This was considered necessary for weakening the foundation of British Empire and for winning freedom. The national movement also accelerated the development of this spirit. A demand for nationalisation of education arose. Mrs. Annie Besant vehemently criticised the existing educational set-up and regarded it as a sure path to national degradation and lack of national morality and honour. Mahatma Gandhi criticised the educational system and considered it unsuitable to Indian needs. He pointed out the following three major defects of the prevailing education system:

1. The Indian education is fully based on foreign culture and civilization. It was an insult to Indians to give them education devoid of their culture.
2. The existing education system is narrow', one-sided and unphysiological. It educates neither the heart nor the hand.

3. To have a foreign language as the medium of instruction is an insult to the entire nation and a deliberate attempt to weaken the Indian people. Real education cannot be given through the medium of foreign language. Mother tongue alone can be a medium of real and practical education.

National Education

At this time the leaders of the country felt very much agitated about the real nature of national education. Gradually, its shape came up on the surface.

1. **Education Under Indian Control.** Education should be fully controlled by Indians. It should be entrusted to Indians from the British hands. This demand was made in order to base education on Indian culture and to keep it above communal considerations.
2. **The Spirit of Love for the Nation.** Education should generate a love of the nation in the students in order that they might appreciate the greatness of the Indian culture and traditions. For this the curriculum should include the study of Indian history, literature, geography, arts and sciences.
3. **Banishing the Feeling of Inferiority.** Students should adopt Indian ideals and culture and not consider the same inferior to the foreign ones. As Indian ideals and culture were much superior to the Western ones, the people should accept them in preference to any other. Indian knowledge and sciences should be developed as the same were to benefit them.
4. **Education in Western Knowledge and Science.** People in India should learn the good things from all countries. They should learn various things through the medium of mother tongue. One should not feel shy of learning things from others, as this was the only way to make the country developed and progressive.
5. **English Language to be Regarded as a General Subject.** English is an ordinary subject of study. Its study should not be overemphasised in preference to that of Indian languages. The students should not consider English as superior to Indian languages, The mother tongue should be given the supreme position. English language could be learnt for the sake of acquiring knowledge but not for procuring any service.

6. **Meeting Inadequacy of Vocational Education.** Education useful to life is an essential aspect of national education. In the absence of vocational education national education will be meaningless. The individual can be happy only when he receives vocational education. Education given to the students at the time was devoid of any vocational bias. It was bookish and theoretical. Vocational education was encouraged.

It was organised firstly, for those youths who were expelled from educational institutions for taking part in national movements. For this purpose Gurudas Banerjee founded the Society for the Promotion of National Education in Bengal, The second proposal was made in the Calcutta Congress of 1906 for such a type of education which could fulfil national needs. However, this movement could not catch up because of the partition of Bengal. Still, the idea of education for fulfilling national needs continued to live.

QUESTIONS FOR EXERCISE

1. Discuss Lord Curzon's Education policy.
2. Describe Gokhale's efforts to further the cause of education in India.
3. Enumerate the major provisions of Government Resolution on Educational Policy (1913).
4. "The Report of the Calcutta University Commission had far reaching consequences upon the development of University Education in India as a whole." Justify the statement giving the chief recommendations of the report.
5. Give a brief account of the recommendations of the Sadler Commission.
6. Trace the development of compulsory primary education between 1905 and 1922.
7. Describe the development of secondary education between 1905 and 1922.
8. What were the principal ideas behind the national system of education and why?
9. Examine the recommendations of the Sadler Commission.
10. What has been the impact of the recommendations of Sadler Commission on the nature of higher education in India?

CHAPTER 15

EDUCATION UNDER DYARCHY (1921-1937)

MONTFORD REFORMS

The Montford reforms introduced dyarchy in the field of education as well. While some subjects were under the Centre some others were under the provincial governments. These were called reserved and transferred respectively.

The Montford reforms prevented the Central Government to introduce any educational reforms as it used to do previously. All the educational powers were transferred to the education ministers of the various provincial Governments. However, the Central Government enjoyed all powers as before in North Frontier Province, Delhi, Ajmer, Marwada, Bangalore, Secunderabad and Bilochistan. The Central Government controlled the Delhi, Banaras and Aligarh Universities also. The schools and colleges run for education of Indian princes also remained under the Central control. The Indian national leaders looked with suspicion at the provisions of Montford Reforms. Therefore, the public, in general, also considered Montford Reforms as a great illusion. These 'Reforms' did not help the development of education in the country, in spite of the fact that they had increased the powers of the provincial Governments with regard to education.

HARTOG COMMITTEE

Simon Commission was appointed to report on the condition of India with regard to its demands for political independence. It was authorised to appoint a committee to help it in preparing a report on education. It appointed the Hartog Committee for this purpose. The Hartog Committee studied the various aspects of education and submitted its report before the Commission in 1929. It applauded the progress of education between the period

1918 and 1927. In its opinion the progress was both quantitative and qualitative and the people in India had shown commendable interest in primary, secondary and university education. The women and the backward classes, too, were not behind. There was noteworthy increase in the number of schools and students.

Hinting at the defects of the existing system of education, Hartog Committee opined that education was not effective particularly at the primary stage. The Committee recommended that the relationship between the Government and the local bodies should be clearly defined. It emphasised qualitative improvement of education, while the people were urging for quantitative development. Thus it once again created the controversy between qualitative and quantitative development.

PROGRESS OF EDUCATION DURING 1921-1937

PRIMARY EDUCATION

By 1921 primary education was declared compulsory in most of the provinces, due to the efforts of Gopal Krishan Gokhale. Laws were enacted for the same everywhere. Its progress continued till 1937.

1. **Bombay.** The compulsory education law was enacted in 1923. Primary education was made compulsory for all boys and girls in the province, but the city of Bombay was excluded by this law.
2. **United Provinces (U.P.).** In 1926 primary education was made compulsory in the rural areas. For this purpose the district boards passed their laws.
3. **Assam.** In 1926 the primary education law was passed in Assam. It was applicable for all the boys and girls both in urban and rural areas.
4. **Bengal.** In 1930 in Bengal "The Primary Education Act" was passed with a view to reorganise primary education. Both the government and the public in this province were keen for development of primary education. By this Act primary education was made compulsory for all the boys and girls in the province. But this Act was not applicable for the city of Calcutta. The district boards in the province were not empowered to levy education taxes for primary education.
5. **Punjab.** This province made much more progress in primary education than any other province in the country. The compulsory primary education Act was implemented in a wider area. Hence, primary education developed rapidly.

The Hartog Committee

In its report, the Hartog Committee emphasised the importance of primary education. After Lord Curzon none else had given attention to primary education, because during the first quarter of the twentieth century greater importance was attached to secondary and university education. As a result, primary education remained almost neglected. Progress of primary education has not been satisfactory in spite of laws passed for compulsory primary education in various provinces.

The Hartog Committee blamed the provincial Governments for poor progress of primary education. It observed that primary education had become meaningless and ineffective. So it argued for its qualitative improvement. But the people in the country were rightly asking for quantitative development of primary education. Therefore, the recommendations of the committee aroused sharp reactions. In fact, first of all it was necessary to spread literacy. For this quantitative development of primary education was necessary. But unfortunately little was done up to 1937 to develop primary education.

PROGRESS OF PRIMARY EDUCATION (1926-1937)

Year	No. of Schools	No. of Students
1926-27	1,84,829	80,17,923
1931-32	1,96,708	91,62,450
1936-37	1,92,244	1,02,24,288

The progress of compulsory primary education was also very slow in various provinces. Only 3,034 villages and 167 towns could be benefited by the compulsory primary education scheme.

SECONDARY EDUCATION

Hartog Committee studied the condition of secondary education also. In its opinion its condition was better than that of primary education. The Committee praised the work of secondary school teachers but it also hinted at some of its shortcomings. It said that the greatest weakness of secondary education was that the sole purpose of secondary school students was to receive further education in universities. It also pointed out that there was great wastage at the secondary stage because of a huge number of students who foiled every year at the Matriculation examination. It remarked that this situation was due to premature promotion of students in high school classes and also because of lack of innate capacity on the part of many students for benefiting themselves from secondary education.

Curriculum

The Hartog Committee criticised the secondary school curriculum. In its opinion it was narrow. It did not prepare students to stand on their own legs after passing the Matriculation examination. As a result, a student wanted to go for university education after matriculation. This entailed wastage of both time and money. Therefore the Committee recommended that the secondary school curriculum should enable the students to stand on their own legs for a living. This would check their rush to higher education for which they might not have the aptitude and capacity. The committee recommended for increasing the number of optional subjects in order to cater to the varying interests of different students. The purpose of the Committee was to solve the problems of students, to make them self-dependent and to improve the lot of the people in villages. The Committee envisaged that the implementation of these suggestions would ultimately make the rural environment healthier and various schemes for village upliftment would also succeed.

Scale of Pay

The Hartog Committee also recommended for improving the scale of pay of teachers. It rightly realised that unless the teachers were satisfied, they would not do their job well. But the Government did not choose to implement the recommendations. The teachers in Bengal and Bihar were much less paid than the teachers in other parts of the country, but no attempt was made to raise their salaries. The teachers' salaries were not raised in any part of the country. The Committee remarked that the qualitative improvement of education was not possible, unless the condition of teachers was improved.

SECONDARY EDUCATION DURING 1921-1937

Year	No. of Schools	No. of Students
1921-22	7,530	11,06,803
1936-37	13,056	22,87,872

During this period the number of schools and students was doubled. But the real cause of this improvement had been the efforts of private enterprises and awakening of national spirit. A spirit and love for education was developed in all the sections of the people. There was a healthy competition in the people for opening new schools. Many teachers opened their own schools by being dissatisfied with the existing state of educational affairs.

HIGHER EDUCATION

A number of new universities and colleges were opened during this period. A love for higher education was developed in the students because they realised that secondary education could not fulfil their aspirations. As the university educated persons were getting preference over Matriculation passed individuals, therefore there was a rush towards higher education. The importance of secondary education for obtaining service had ended and its place was taken up by higher education. New universities were opened at Delhi (1922), Nagpur (1923), Agra (1927), Waltair (1926) and Annamalai (1929).

THE NUMBER OF AFFILIATED COLLEGES (1921-37)

Year	No. of Teaching Departments in Universities and Colleges	No. of Students
1921-22	207	66,258
1936-37		1,26,228

Besides some special institutions were also established. Of these the Visva Bharati founded by Rabindra Nath Tagore has been most distinguished. At a distance of about 160 Km from Calcutta this institution was established in Bolpur also known as Shanti Niketan. Here ancient languages, Vedant, Indian languages, philosophies and various sciences are taught. It is a research centre for science and various Western and Eastern philosophies. There are many distinguished departments in this institution. It has now been made as a Central University.

Suggestions by Hartog Committee

The Hartog Committee gave some important suggestions for this stage as well. It praised the growth in number of affiliated colleges. It also hinted at the fall of standard in university education due to the worsening of its environment because of growth of affiliated colleges. It criticised the introduction of Honours courses in some universities and pointed out that they were outmoded. The Indian public opinion also felt that the universities had failed to meet the needs of the people. The country was undergoing political upheavals. It needed youngmen with a spirit of sacrifice and hard work. The universities were unable to contribute anything in this sphere. Hence a discontent against them spread in the people.

Although the teaching and research work had already been started in some universities. Most universities were conducting only examinations. There were no good libraries in any university. It was the duty of universities to produce individuals who were tolerant, liberal and suitable to undertake great responsibilities. The universities in India were not equal to this task. The Hartog Committee gave the following suggestions for their reforms:

1. It recommended the establishment of some affiliating universities keeping in view the great demand for higher education. It admitted that the standard of education in the affiliated colleges of these universities would be poorer than in teaching universities, but under the circumstances affiliated colleges alone could meet the demand for higher education of the people.
2. The teachers for affiliated colleges should be appointed by universities.
3. The admission in universities should be controlled on the basis of abilities and aptitudes of students.
4. The Honours course should be of more advanced nature than the pass courses and these courses should be instituted only at the universities.
5. Provision should be made for technical education by the universities. The universities have to control the problem of unemployment by opening opportunities.

QUESTIONS FOR EXERCISE

1. Evaluate the recommendations of Hartog Committee for reforms of education.
2. Give an account of educational development during 1921 and 1937.

CHAPTER 16

THE BASIC EDUCATION

Mahatma Gandhi had been writing in *Harijan* since long his views in regard to education. Later on these articles formed the basis of 'Basic Scheme of Education'. In one of his articles appeared in the *Harijan* of July 31, 1937, Mahatma Gandhi has clarified his view in regard to education in the following words: "As a nation we are so backward in education that we cannot hope to fulfil our obligations in this respect in a given time during this generation, if this programme is to depend on money. I have, therefore, made bold, even at the risk of losing reputation for constructive policy, to suggest that education should be self-supporting. By education, I mean an all-round drawing out of the best in the child and man—body, mind and spirit. Literacy is not the end of education nor even the beginning. It is only one of the means w here by men and women can be educated. Literacy in itself is no education. I would, therefore, begin the child's education by teaching it a useful handicraft, enabling it to produce from the moment it begins its training. Thus, every school can be made self-supporting, condition being that state "takes over the manufacture of these schools."

Wardha Conference

The same year, in October, a conference of national workers was called at Wardha under the presidentship of Mahatma Gandhi and, after considering his ideas, passed the following resolution:

1. That in the opinion of this conference free and compulsory education be provided for seven years on a nation-wide scale;
2. That the medium of instruction be the mother tongue;
3. That the conference endorses the proposal, made by Mahatma Gandhi, that the process of education through

some form of manual work, and that all other abilities to be developed or training to be given should, as far as possible, be integrally related to the central handicraft chosen with due regard to the environment of the child;

4. That the conference expects that the system of education will be gradually able to cover the remuneration of the teacher.

This conference appointed a Committee of distinguished educationists under the chairmanship of Dr. Zakir Hussain to prepare a detailed syllabus. Among others who served on the Committee Prof. K. G. Saiyidain's name is prominent. The report of the Committee published in March 1938, has come to be known as the Wardha Scheme of Education. It was approved by Mahatma Gandhi and was placed before the Indian National Congress at its Haripura Session held in March 1938. The Congress accepted the scheme and passed the following resolutions:

1. Free and compulsory education should be provided for seven years on a nation-wide scale.
2. The medium of instructions must be the mother tongue.
3. Throughout this period education should centre round some form of manual and productive work and all other activities to be developed or training to be given should, as far as possible, be integrally related to the central handicraft with due regard to the environment of the child.

ZAKIR HUSSAIN COMMITTEE

Besides Dr. Zakir Hussain as Chairman, this Committee consisted of nine more members. They include Arya Nayakam, Vinoba Bhave, Kaka Kalelkar, J. C. Kumarappa, Kishori Lal Mashroowala, Prof. K. T. Shah, etc. The Committee had the right to co-opt certain other members also.

Zakir Hussain Committee submitted two reports, one in December 1937 and the other in April 1938. In the first report were included the basic principles of Wardha Scheme of Education, its aims, teachers and their training, organisation of the schools, administration, inspection and other important handicrafts like spinning and weaving, etc. The second report dealt with Agriculture, Metal work, Wood craft and other basic handicrafts. An attempt was made to present an elaborate curriculum of all these subjects and to suggest ways and means to establish their co-relation with the other subjects.

What is Basic Education?

Although Wardha Scheme of Education has been called, "Nai Talim" as well as basic education, but it is popularly known as 'Basic Education'. Basic stands for fundamentals. It means that this scheme of education was based on the national culture and civilisation of India. It shall have close relationship with the basic needs and interests of the educands. It shall also try to impart such a knowledge to him which will help him to have a reasonable relationship with the environment and to use his knowledge in this task. The central pivot of this scheme of education shall be some handicrafts whose teaching shall enable the student to be able to solve the problem of his livelihood.

AIMS AND IDEALS OF BASIC EDUCATION

1. **Drawing out the Basic.** Elaborating his views about the aims of education, Gandhiji has said, "By education I mean an all round drawing out of the best in child and man, body, mind and spirit. Literacy is not the end of education, not even the beginning. It is one of the means whereby man and woman can be educated. Literacy in itself is no education."
2. **Livelihood.** Gandhiji was highly critical of the educational policy implemented by British Government. In his opinion the aim of education is self-dependence, and education must enable every girl and boy to develop the ability to depend upon himself or herself. The ability to earn one's livelihood is part of this independence or self-reliance. As he himself put it, "This education ought to be for them a kind of insurance against unemployment." That is why Gandhiji placed so much emphasis upon industrial training in his own plan for basic education which was intended to acquaint the child with real life. He wanted the education to become the means of producing ideal citizens. Seeing the endemic poverty of the nation, he suggested that education in India should be based on industrial training and the development of manual skill and handicrafts.
3. **Character Formation.** Like Rousseau Gandhiji also believed in paidocentric education, that is, education which centers around the child. He impressed upon people that the cultural aspect of education was far more important than its literary aspect, because it is through the cultural aspect

that the child learns conduct and ideas and develops his character and ideals. As he puts it, "True education is that which draws out and stimulates the spiritual, intellectual and physical faculties of the children." Hence, the aim of education is the complete development of the child, its physical, mental and spiritual aspects. For him character formation was more important than literacy. He was once asked what his education would aim at after the country won its independence. He answered without hesitation that it would be designed to develop the character of the people. And, in character, Gandhiji addressed the importance of thought, word and deed, non-violence and truth. He, like many before him, felt that abstinence was an essential weapon for the educand. He was a supporter of the ancient Indian ideals of education. He in fact felt that the words educand and Brahmachari should be treated as synonymous. And for him, abstinence meant a persistent effort to reach God in the least possible time.

4. **Complete Development.** It is clear from the foregoing account that Gandhiji viewed education from a comprehensive or broadminded standpoint. Any education that develops only one aspect of a child's personality can be dubbed narrow and onesided. And it is just such an education which has been the bane of our culture. Education must aim at developing the child's personality instead of limiting itself to providing the child with bits and pieces of information. Not only must education guide the individual towards self-knowledge, it must instil in him all those qualities which go to the making up of a good and responsible citizen. Gandhiji has made a distinction between the immediate and long term aims of education, suggesting that such aims as getting certificates of merits or degrees or obtaining education for livelihood should be considered the immediate aims. But the final aim of education can only be self-knowledge. Thus, Gandhiji states that education must make the individual to live and earn his daily bread, to be the means of his sustenance. As he himself puts it, 'I value individual freedom, but you must not forget that man is essentially a social being. He has risen to his present status by learning to adjust his individuality to the requirements of social progress." His faith in religion is

at the base of his liberal attitude to education. Realization of God is, in fact, the end or the goal of all human activity and service to humanity its finest means. It is only natural that such a faith should lead him to stress the social objectives of education more than the personal or individual ones.

5. **Synthesis of Individual and Social Aims.** In this way Gandhiji synthesised the individual and social aims of education. He did not restrict education to the achievement of any one single aim. He looked to the process of education from various perspectives. Therefore, he assigned different aims to education at different times, so much so that sometimes they looked mutually contradictory and even self defeating. A closer examination of all these statements of Gandhiji, however, shows that these aims of education are complementary to each other.
6. **All Round Growth.** In the history of education different educationists have defined the ideals of education in different ways. Most educationists have, however, felt that the aim of education is integral development of human personality. Such was also the ideal of education formulated by Gandhiji. Like Vivekananda, Gandhiji maintained that character formation and manual skill were equally important. On the one hand, he wanted the child to earn while he learns. On the other hand, he also wanted the child to develop his character. According to him the criterion of an individual's cultural development is not the width of his knowledge but his inner growth. Culture, according to him, is not an adjunct of the mind but a characteristic of the soul. The aim of education is the development of such a culture. Gandhiji's plan of education laid stress upon all types of education — physical, mental, moral, aesthetic and religious.
7. **Self-Reliance.** As has been already pointed out, Gandhiji aimed at self-reliance through education. Therefore, he visualised a craft-centred education. Explaining his scheme of Basic education as an insurance against unemployment in India, Gandhiji said, "The child at the age of 14, that is, after finishing a seven years course should be discharged as an earning unit. Even now the poor people's children automatically lend a helping hand to their parents—the

feeling at the back of their minds being what shall they give men to eat, if I do not work with them? That is an education in itself. Even so the State takes charge of the child at seven and returns it to the family as an earning unit. You impart education and simultaneously cut at the root of unemployment.'' Recommending this scheme of education in the report on national education the Kothari Commission declared, ''We recommend that work experience should be introduced as an integral part of all education, general or vocational. We define work-experience as participation in productive work in school, in the home, in a workshop, on a farm, in a factory or in any other productive situation."

8. **Democratic Ideals.** Like his contemporary Indian educationists Gandhiji aimed at the evolution of democratic ideals through education. His basic plan of education amply demonstrates this fact. He aimed at an education for ideal citizenship. Education, according to him, should make children ideal members of a democratic society. The school, according to Gandhiji is itself a small democratic society in which such democratic values are imparted to the children as wide outlook, tolerance and good neighbourhood. In the miniature society of the school the child learns the virtues of sympathy, service, love, brotherhood, equality and liberty, etc. These qualities are transferred from one generation to another through education. The welfare of the individual and the nation are complementary to each other. Therefore, if the country has to progress, the future generation should develop the virtues of democratic citizenship. As Gandhiji said, "A nation cannot advance without the units of which it is composed advancing, and conversely, no individual can advance without the nation of which it is a part also advancing."
9. **Good Character.** All knowledge is useless without a good character. In his speeches to the students at various institutions Gandhiji laid emphasis upon the moral and spiritual aims of education. Emphasising the moral aim of education Gandhiji said, "The end of all knowledge must be the building up of character.'' Character building is the moral ideal of education. According to Gandhiji that is most important in a man's life. His ideals in this connection were as

much in agreement with the ancient Indian thinkers as with contemporary Western thinkers like Emerson, Ruskin, etc. Gandhiji very much admired the Indian Gurukula system of education and the ideal of Brahmacharya. According to ancient Indian ideal, education aims at liberation. This was also the aim of Gujarat Vidyapeeth established by Gandhiji in 1929. Gandhiji, however, defined liberation in a very wide sense, including political, social and economic liberation of all the members of society. Real freedom is spiritual freedom. To attain this freedom is the task of education. Again, education equally aims at intellectual, economic and political uplift, though its chief aim is moral and spiritual. Condemning the widespread indiscipline among the students Gandhiji asked them to follow the Ideal of Brahmacharya.

10. **God Realisation.** According to Indian philosophy the ultimate end of all knowledge is God realisation. This God realisation, again, is the meaning of self-realisation which has been considered to be the ideal of education by most of the educational philosophers in East and West. Agreeing with this line of thinking Gandhiji maintained that a student should live a life of Sanyasi. God realisation and self-realisation are mutually complementary, the one leads to the other. This spiritual ideal of education does not negate mundane or immediate ideals but fulfils them. In the words of Gandhiji "Self-realisation is in itself an all comprehensive ideal." This ideal includes other ideals of education. With Sri Aurobindo, Gandhiji believed that the ultimate aim of education is spiritual. He also agreed that spiritual growth includes physical and mental, individual and social development. Thus, he synthesised different ideals of education. In this scheme of Basic education, he planned for an education suitable to present-day Indian society. He pondered over the difficulties of the present-day Indian society and tried to find out their solution through education. His educational philosophy is based upon ancient Indian idealism. While he did not restrict the scope of physical education his attention was mainly directed towards spiritual growth.

THE BASIC EDUCATION SCHEME

Education for Sarvodaya

Gandhiji was very much aware of the needs of the country and considered basic education as the only type of education which may lead to success. His chief aim in planning for education in India was to fulfil the needs of the country. India is a country of villages. Most of the villagers in India cannot afford to pay for their children's education. In addition to it they require their children's assistance in their occupations. Therefore, Gandhiji planned for basic education which may not be a burden upon the parents and through which the children may be able to earn to meet the expenses of education themselves. He laid stress upon the importance of dignity of labour and manual skill. He was convinced that an education which prepares the young men for white collar jobs can hardly be suitable for an agriculture community. It is hence that he so much emphasised the learning of craft in his plan of basic education. In spite of all this idealism Gandhiji's approach everywhere was pragmatic. He was an experimenter in every field of life. Before devising his plan of basic education he experimented upon its different aspects. For him all human truths were relative. God was the only absolute. Therefore he tested everything before suggesting it for the education of the child. He postulated that the child should himself gather knowledge from the environment and put it in actual use in life. Like the pragmatists and instrumentalists Gandhiji stressed the importance of interest and activity and the need for variety in the subjects taught to the educand.

Sarvodaya Society

The social philosophy of M. K. Gandhi may be termed as 'Sarvodaya'. This was the foundation of his philosophy of education. Sarvodaya aims at all round development of all, without distinction of caste, creed, sex and nationality. Gandhiji wanted to establish a welfare state in India which he called 'Ram Rajya'. The ideal of Sarvodaya does not aim at the maximum number but maximum good of all without exceptions. While Karl Marx aimed at the welfare of the proletariat, Gandhiji aimed even at the welfare of the capitalist. According to Vinoba Bhave tire important characteristics of the Sarvodaya society are the abolition of all monopoly, emphasis on social welfare and equal moral, social and economic importance of honest work. There is no place for any type of exploitation in Sarvodaya society. No one may be forced to do certain type of work, so much so that even the wealth of the capitalist, cannot be forcibly snatched away. Centralisation, according to Gandhiji is the chief source of social evils. Sarvodaya requires decentralisation. Gandhiji aimed at political, economic, social and all other types of decentralisation. In the political field decentralisation requires establishment of village panchayats. In the economic field it requires that wealth and money should not be allowed to be concentrated in few hands but should be distributed among all the people. Social decentralisation means the abolition of all types of untouchability and social distinctions.

Nai Talim

In order to achieve the above mentioned aims of Sarvodva in India, Gandhiji presented his plan of basic education. He called it *Wai Talim* (New education) because it sought to build up a new society in the country. He realised that what the country needs today is not so much higher education as the education of the masses. Therefore, he did not lay so much emphasis upon higher education.

The basic education sought to fulfil the needs of the education in a Sarvodaya society. It is hence that Gandhi planned for craft centred education with mother tongue as the medium. Literacy, according to him, is not an end but only a means of education. Education ultimately aims at the development of both mind and body and the capacity of earning one's livelihood. The syllabi for the new education were framed in such a way so as to eliminate harrow nationalism and emphasize the ideal of Sarvodaya. World history was taught along with Indian history. Similarly, the syllabus included the study of fundamental universal ethics. The cost of education was brought down by compulsory manual labour and education was tried to be made self-sufficient as far as possible.

Social Revolution

Pointing out the value of basic education for bringing about a silent social revolution in the country Gandhiji said, "It will provide a healthy and moral basis of relationship between the city and the village and thus go a long way towards eradicating some of the worst evils of the present social insecurity and poisoned relationship between the classes. It will check the progressive decay of our villages and lay the foundation of a social order in which there is no unnatural division between the 'haves' and the 'have-nots' and everybody is assured of a living wage and the right of freedom. And all this would be accomplished without the horrors of a bloody class war or a social capital expenditure such as would be involved in the mechanisation of a vast continent like India. Nor would it entail a helpless dependence on foreign imported machinery or technical skill. Lastly, by obviating the necessity for highly specialised talent, it would place the destiny of the masses, as it were in their own hands.

Non-Violent Education

As has been already pointed out, Gandhiji emphasised the principle of nonviolence in every field of life. He considered non-violence as the characteristic human quality. He said, "Non-violence is the law of our species as violence is the law of brutes." Even truth was subordinate to non-violence. Gandhiji said, "One had better not speak it (truth) if one cannot do so in a gentle way." To those who doubted the value of non-violence to be the principle of human social organisation, Gandhiji pointed out, "The fact that there are so many men still alive in the world shows that it is based not on force of arms but on the force of truth and love." This principle of non-violence, Gandhiji used in every aspect of education, so much so that his theory of education may be called non-violent-education. Explaining his idea he wrote, "If India has resolved to eschew violence, this system of education becomes an integral part of the discipline she has to go through. We are told that English spend millions on education. America also does so. But we forget that all wealth is obtained through exploitation. They have reduced the art of exploitation to a science, and might well give their boys the costly education they do. We cannot, will not think in terms of exploitation, and we have no alternative but this plan of education which is based on non-violence." Thus, according to Gandhiji India can play her role in the community of nations only by adopting the gospel of non-violence. To quote Gandhiji again, "If India also tried to build up the new society based on cooperationby means of violence.... Good brought about through force destroyed individuality. Only when the change was effected through the persuasive power of non-violent non-co-operation (*i.e.* love), could the foundation of individuality be preserved and real, abiding progress be assured for the world."

Wardha Scheme

This principle of non-violence was the basis of Gandhiji's scheme of basic education. Through this scheme he wanted to develop those qualities in future citizens of India which he considered necessary for building a non-violent society. His system of education wanted to root out exploitation and centralization in society and create a non-violent social order. In 1937 Gandhiji evolved a scheme popularly known as the Wardha Scheme of Basic National Education. This Wardha scheme was based on same principles of education which were listed by Gandhiji in a paper in 1932 in Yervada Jail. These postulates were as follows:

1. Boys and girls should be taught together.
2. Their time should be mostly spent on manual work under the supervision of the teacher. Manual work should be considered as part of education.
3. Work should be entrusted to each boy and girl after ascertaining his or her inclinations.
4. The child should know the why and the wherefore of every process.
5. General knowledge should be imparted to the child as soon as it is able to understand things. This knowledge should precede literary education.
6. The hand of the child should be trained to draw geometrical figures before he learns to write, that is good handwriting should be taught from the beginning.
7. The child should learn to read before he is able to write, *i.e.* he should learn to recognise letters as if they were pictures and then draw their figures.
8. By this method and by word of mouth, the child should acquire much knowledge before he is eight years old.
9. Children should not be compelled to learn anything.
10. The child should be interested in whatever he learns.
11. The process of teaching should be conducted in a play-way, for play is an essential part of education.
12. All education should be imparted through the mother tongue of the child.
13. Every Indian child should learn Hindi-Urdu, *i.e.* Hindustani as a national language before his literary training commences.

14. The second stage of the child's education begins when he is eleven and lasts up to sixteen.
15. Manual labour has a place in education during this period also. The lime for literary training should be increased according to need.
16. The child should learn some vocation as preparation for his future life.
17. He should acquire a general knowledge of World History, Geography, Botany, Astronomy, Arithmetic, Geometry and Algebra.
18. A boy or a girl of sixteen years should know sewing and cooking.
19. In the third stage which begins at 16 and end sat 25, a young man or woman should receive education according to his or her desires and circumstances.
20. The education commencing at the age of nine should be self-supporting. The student, while he is learning, should be engaged in such a vocation that its produce may meet the expense of the school.
21. Production should, no doubt, begin right from the start. But it may not be enough to meet the expenses during the initial years.
22. Teachers cannot possibly have big salaries, but they must get enough to maintain themselves. They should be animated by a spirit of service. They must have a good character.
23. Huge and costly buildings are not necessary for education.
24. English can and should have a place in the syllabus only as a language. Just as Hindi is our *lingua franco,* English is a language of international intercourse and commerce.

On October 23,1937, a conference was organised at Wardha to finalise the basic system of education. This conference resolved that the children should be provided free education for seven year Mother tongue should be the medium of education. Every educand must be taught some basic craft. The expenses of education should be met by the sale of the production in the school. In order to implement these recommendations a committee was formed under the chairmanship of Dr. Zakir Hussain. This Committee highlighted the basic principles, aims and organization of basic education in its first report on December 2,1937. In its second report in 1940 this Committee reviewed the curriculum of basic education. Its recommendations were accepted by Indian National Congress in its session at Haripura. After Zakir Hussain Committee, another Committee was formed under the chairmanship of B.G. Kher to review basic education. This Committee connected it to Sargeant scheme. In the final form, the basic principles of Gandhi's scheme of primary education were: compulsory free education, education through craft, education through mother tongue, self-reliance, education connected with the life of the educand and finally inculcation of the ideals of democratic citizenship. A booklet was published by Government of India to popularise Gandhian system of education entitled *Understanding of Basic Education.* This booklet thus summarised the scheme of basic education, "Activities involving personal and community cleanliness are the foremost in a basic school. Education for the young is not stuffing impractical ideas into the minds of children. It is essentially training them in good habits, the daily experiences that every child has to undergo as regular morning evacuation, cleaning the teeth, nose and eyes, bathing, physical exercise, washing clothes and other daily activities can be exploited for teaching as well as the inculcation of good habits."

Means of Education

The scheme of basic education clarifies the means of education. According to M. K. Gandhi, the most important means of education in basic scheme was craft. About this means of education Gandhiji said, "The principal idea is to impart the whole education of body and the mind and the soul through the handicraft that is taught to the children. You have to draw out all that is in the child through teaching all the processes of the handicraft, and all your lessons in History, Geography, Arithmetic will be related to the craft." Thus some handicraft was necessary to be the centre of the child's education. Besides, other crafts recommended were: weaving, carpentry, agriculture, gardening and other handicrafts and rural crafts. It was pointed out that the following criteria should be followed in deciding about the basic craft:

1. Craft fulfilling individual and social means.
2. Craft based upon local requirements.
3. Craft in tune with the local conditions.

4. Craft favourable to the interest, aptitude and ability of the child.
5. Less expensive and simple craft.
6. Craft leading to all round development of personality.

Education through Activity

At the back of craft as the means of education were the psychological principles of education through activity as is visible in the Western play-way of education, project methods, etc. Besides, this means of education was economically useful as the basic craft could be utilised by the educand to earn his livelihood. It was also supported to create a tendency for physical labour in the educands. According to Gandhiji "Labour is the source of all wealth. All higher castes live on exploitation of the lower castes. Wealth is inevitably reduced and large scale poverty occasioned." Thus, craft was a means to inculcate the lesson of physical labour.

Principle of Synthesis

Another important element in the means of education in the basic scheme was synthesis between the actual problems of life and education, between different subjects of the curriculum and finally between theoretical education and practical ability. In order to implement the principle of synthesis in basic education it was insisted that the teachers and educands should together formulate yearly projects divided into quarterly, monthly, weekly and daily projects. After this planning, the means such as raw material and necessary tools should be gathered. Efforts should be made to fulfil the schedule of the projects. Each project must be evaluated monthly or quarterly as the case may be. In the end the teachers should note their experiences in order to profit by them in future.

Adult Education

Our discussion of the Gandhian scheme of education so far shows his emphasis upon primary education and the education of the child. He, however, equally devoted his thought to the adult education also known as social education. He realised that in order to bring about a Sarvodaya society in India, the views of the adults should be changed. Therefore, he made adult education programme a vital element of his political movement. Thousands of volunteers were trained in adult education at Sabarmati and

Sevagram Ashrams. They spread in thousands of villages and hundreds of urban centres to educate the adult males and females in night schools. The help of thousands of regular teachers in so many educational institutions was also utilised for this purpose.

An important characteristic of Gandhian philosophy is the aim of Sarvodaya. Therefore, he planned different types of education for the country. Besides basic education and social education he thought seriously over rural education and education of women.

Medium of Instruction

A staunch votary of mother tongue as the medium of instmclion, Gandhiji said, "I must cling to my mother tongue as to my mother's breast, in spite of its shortcomings. It alone can give me the life giving milk." He was vehemently against English as the medium of education in this country. He said, "To inflict English on children is to stunt their natural growth and perhaps to kill originality in them." He pointed out to many modern Western countries including U.S.S.R. who have made tremendous scientific progress without any help of English language. He maintained that our insistence on English is a remnant of our long slavery to the British. He was never prepared to accept this submission to foreign yoke. He maintained that the national language alone can be the vehicle of creating a common culture and rich literature. He was very much conversant with the language problem in India. He wanted to keep the country united particularly from the point of view of language. Therefore, he devised a common national language Hindustani which may be written in both Devanagari and Persian script. According to him there is no difference in Hindustani and Urdu.

SEVEN YEARS' COURSE

1. **Basic Crafts.** The following may be chosen as basic crafts in various schools:
   (i) Spinning and weaving.
   (ii) Carpentry.
   (iii) Agriculture.
   (iv) Fruit and vegetable gardening.
   (v) Leather work.
   (vi) Any other craft for which local and geographical conditions are favourable and which satisfies the conditions mentioned above.

Even where an industry other than spinning and weaving or agriculture is the basic craft, the pupils will be expected to attain a minimum knowledge of spinning with the takli, and a practical acquaintance of elementary agricultural work in the local area.

2. **Mother Tongue.** The proper teaching of the mother tongue is the foundation of all education. Without the capacity to speak effectively and to read and write correctly and lucidly, no one can develop precision of thought or clarity of ideas. Moreover, it is a means of introducing the child to the rich heritage of his people's ideas, emotions and aspirations, and can therefore be made a valuable means of social education whilst also instilling right ethical and moral values. Also, it is a natural outlet for the expression of the child's aesthetic sense and appreciation, and if the proper approach is adopted, the study of literature becomes a source of joy and creative appreciation.
3. **Mathematics.** The objective is to develop in the pupil the capacity to solve speedily the ordinary numerical and geometrical problems arising in connection with his craft and with his home and community life. Pupils should also gain a knowledge of business practice and book keeping.
4. **Social Studies.** The objectives are:
   (i) To develop abroad human interest in the progress of mankind in general and of India in particular.
   (ii) To develop in the pupil a proper understanding of his social and geographical environment, and to awaken the urge to improve it.
   (iii) To inculcate the love of the motherland, reverence for its past, and a belief in its future destiny as the home of a united cooperative society based on love, truth and justice.
   (iv) To develop a sense of the rights and responsibilities of citizenship.
   (v) To develop the individual and social virtues which make a man a reliable associate and trusted neighbour.
   (vi) To develop mutual respect for the world religions.

   A course in history, in geography, in civics and in current events, combined with a reverential study of the different religions of the world showing how in essentials they meet in perfect harmony, will help to achieve these objectives. The study should begin with the child's own environment and its problems. His interest should be awakened in the manifold ways in which men supply their different wants. This should be made a starting point to arouse their curiosity about the life and work of men and women.

5. **General Science.** The objectives are:
   (i) To give pupils an intelligent and appreciative outlook on nature.
   (ii) To form in the pupils habits of accurate observation and of testing experience by experiment.
   (iii) To enable them to understand the important scientific principles exemplified in:
      (a) The natural phenomena around, and
      (b) The application of science to the sendee of man.
   (iv) To introduce them to the more important incidents in the lives of the great scientists whose sacrifices in the cause of truth make a powerful appeal to the growing mind.
6. **Drawing.** The objectives are:
   (i) To train the eye in the observation and discrimination of forms and colors.
   (ii) To develop the memory for forms.
   (iii) To cultivate a knowledge of and appreciation for the beautiful things in nature and in art.
   (iv) To draw out the capacity for tasteful design and decoration.
   (v) To develop the capacity to make working drawings of objects to be constructed.

   These objectives can be obtained by:
      (a) Drawing made by children to illustrate read or observed material.
      (b) Object and memory drawings, *e.g.*, drawings of plants and of animal and human form (correlated with working general science, handicraft, etc.)
   (vi) Designing.
   (vii) Scale drawing, graphs and pictorial graphs.

The work in drawing during the first four years should be correlated chiefly with work in reading and pictorial representation in nature study and the craft. During the last three years emphasis may be laid on design and decoration and mechanical drawing, so as to enable pupils to make correct working drawings.

7. **Music.** The objective is to teach the pupils a number of beautiful music. The child's natural sense for rhythm should be developed by teaching him to keep his own time by beating with the hand. Walking in time to a fixed rhythm can be a great aid in achieving this.

   Care should be taken to select only the best and most inspiring songs, the artistic interpretation of some healthy and elevating theme. Special emphasis should be placed on group or choral singing.

8. **Hindustani.** The object of including Hindustani as a compulsory subject in the school curriculum is to ensure that all the children educated in these national schools may have a reasonable acquaintance with a common *lingua franca.* As adult citizens they should be able to cooperate with their fellow-countrymen belonging to any part of the country. In teaching the language the teacher should in various ways quicken in the students the realisation that this language is the most important product of the cultural contact of the Hindus and Muslims in India. It is the repository—in its more advanced forms—of their best thoughts and aspirations. They should learn to take pride in its richness and vitality and should feel the desire to serve it devotedly.

In Hindustani speaking areas this language will be the mother-tongue, but the students as well as the teachers will be required to learn both the scripts, so that they may read books written in Urdu as well as in Hindi. In non-Hindustani speaking areas, where the provincial language will be the mother-tongue, the study of Hindustani will be compulsory during the fifth and sixth years of school life, but the children will have the choice of learning either one or the other script. However, in the case of teachers who have to deal with children of both kinds, knowledge of both the scripts is desirable.

At any rate, every public school must make adequate provision for the teaching of both scripts.

Same Syllabus for Boys and Girls

In general outlines, the syllabus of studies will be the same for boys and girls up to the fifth grade of the school. In grades fourth and fifth the syllabus in general science should be so modified as to include domestic science for girls. In grades sixth and seventh, the girls will be allowed to take an advanced course in domestic science in place of the basic craft.

DISTRIBUTION OF WORK IN THE CURRICULUM

The Basic craft	3 hours 20 minutes
Music, drawing and arithmetic	40 minutes
The mother tongue	40 minutes
Social studies and general science	30 minutes
Physical training	10 minutes
Recess	10 minutes
Total	5 hours 30 minutes

In making this estimate, spinning and weaving has been taken as basic craft. The distribution might vary from craft to craft, but in no case should the time allotted to the basic craft exceed the above estimate.

The schools were expected to work for 288 days in a year, average of 24 days in a month.

In view of the diversity of pupils' interests it was recommended that as far as possible a variety of crafts should be provided for, at least during the last two vesurs of the school course.

Every school should have attached to it a plot of land big enough for a school garden and a playground.

TEACHERS' TRAINING

It was considered desirable to give preference to local persons in appointment as teachers It was considered necessary to appoint only trained teachers. Two types of curricula as enumerated below were provided for the training of the teachers:

(a) **Long-term Training.** This required a person to undergo study in an institution for three years.

(b) **Short-term Training.** For this the teachers had to devote only one year.

The method of teaching employed under the basic scheme of education is different from the normal method of teaching. Education is imparted through activities. The students are given knowledge of various and varied subjects in a short period of time.

The boy is given oral teaching of the mother tongue. In the elementary class gradually he is also taught to read and write. As soon as he learns to read and write, he is also given the education of some basic art.

As the boy progresses further and reaches higher classes, he is given knowledge of different subjects. He is not given independent education of these various subjects. These subjects are taught through the medium of some basic craft, failing which it is taught through some other method. While teaching all subjects, all the subjects taught should be inter-related. After completing the duration of seven years, the child is able to acquire knowledge of different subjects. He also acquires the knowledge of the basic crafts so that he is able to solve the problems of employment in his future life successfully.

MERITS OF BASIC EDUCATION

(i) ***Compulsory Free Education.*** This scheme aimed at imparting compulsory and free education to the children of 7-14 year Education was also free from the economic poverty of the parents because they did not have to pay for the education of their children. The educands themselves earned the cost of their education.

(ii) ***No Wastage.*** There is no wastage involved in this scheme of education.

(iii) ***Citizenship Traits.*** Children acquire traits of citizenship and learn to solve the problems of their future life.

(iv) ***Close to Life.*** Basic education has close relationship with life. It creates responsibilities among the children.

(v) ***Productive.*** This education shall be imparted through some handicraft or productive activity. This handicraft or productive activity shall be the means as well as the end. Other subjects taught shall be related to it.

(vi) ***Mother Tongue.*** The medium of instruction shall be the mother tongue instead of English.

(vii) ***Progress of Indian Languages.*** Ample opportunity has been given for the progress of Hindi as well as regional languages.

(viii) ***Paidocentric.*** Basic scheme of education treats the child as the centre of education. He is imparted knowledge through some activity of self-aspiration. He acquires knowledge more or less independently. It lays great stress on the individual interest of the child.

(ix) ***Ideals.*** The scheme rings with the ideals of nationalism, patriotism, secularism, etc.

(x) ***In Consonance with Environment.*** The education is in perfect consonance with the geographical, economic and social conditions of the country. This scheme of education is started in the rural atmosphere which forms the basis of this education.

(xi) ***High Principles.*** Basic scheme of education is influenced and inspired by the high principle of the truth and non-violence.

(xii) ***Trained Teachers.*** Only trained teachers are appointed under this scheme of education and they have more freedom in their job.

DEMERITS OF BASIC EDUCATION

(i) ***Not Good for Urban People.*** It is said that this scheme of education is useful only for the villages. It cannot do any good to urban population.

(ii) ***Industrialisation of Education.*** Due to emphasise on productivity, apprehensions were expressed that the basic schools are likely to degenerate into centres of cottage industries. Teachers may treat the schools as factory and children as means of earning money.

(iii) ***No Co-Relation between Basic Craft and General Education.*** It is not possible to impart education of all subjects through the medium of some basic craft. Such co-relation may not lead to overall development of the students. They may not be able to acquire general education.

(iv) ***Insufficient for Preserving Cultural Heritage.*** Basic scheme of education has no place for religious education. This scheme may be like a religion divorced from spirit or soul. It may not succeed in preserving the cultural heritage of India.

(v) ***Defects in the Time-Table.*** Too much time (3 hours and 20 minutes) were given to the basic craft, while very little time had been given to other subjects. The basic education provided for 288 working days would put a heavy burden of work on the children of tender age.

(vi) ***Costly.*** As it would take a long time, this scheme of education would also be costly and not cheap.

(vii) ***Neglect of Secondary and Higher Education.*** Too much emphasis has been laid on primary education and no importance has been attached to secondary education and higher education.

(viii) Industrial Retardation. In this age of technological advancement and scientific development emphasis on spinning and weaving would retard the industrial growth of the country.

(ix) Utopian. This scheme is only utopian and far away from practical utility. It lacks a definite philosophy of education. It is based more on sentimentalism.

(x) ***Unpsychological.*** It was unpsychological on the part of Gandhiji to assume that children's products will be easily sold and that its sale proceeds will be sufficient to meet the salary of teachers and other expenses of the basic schools.

QUESTIONS FOR EXERCISE

1. Write an essay on Basic Education. Is psychological foundation a critic of Basic Education?
2. Discuss the fundamental principles of Basic Education (Wardha Scheme of Education). How far are they workable?
3. "Basic Education should not only be looked at as a revolution in the field of education, but as a means of bringing about the revolution in the social, economic and psychological structure of the Indian Society itself."
   To what extent has Basic Education helped in the realisation of this objective?
4. What are the fundamental principles of Basic Education? Attempt an estimate of its progress in the country.
5. "There is nothing new in Basic Education." Do you agree or disagree with this statement? Give reasons.

CHAPTER 17

SARGEANT REPORT ON EDUCATION (1944)

Historical Review

After the Second World War in the post-war period the attention of the Government of India was drawn towards the plan for development of the Indian life in its various phases. To meet these requirements, the Reconstruction Committee of the officers of the Executive Council deputed John Sargeant, the Education Advisor to the government of India to draw up a memorandum for the development of Indian education in the post-war reconstruction period. He submitted his memorandum before the Central Advisory Board of Education in 1944. The board accepted it *in toto* and recommended its enforcement.

The scheme was known as 'Sargeant Scheme of Education' since the memorandum was prepared by Sir John Sargeant. It is also known as 'Report by the Central Advisory Board of Education, 1944' and also a scheme of 'Post-War Education Development in India'.

Sargeant Scheme of Education has a historical importance from the point of view of development of national education system. It is a comprehensive treatise on the problems and future organization of Primary to University education in India. This was the first report that presented a comprehensive picture of education in India.

SUGGESTIONS

A. Pre-Primary Education

In regard to pre-primary education, the scheme contains the following suggestions:

(i) Nursery schools should be started for the success of National Scheme of Education. Children from 3-6 years of age should be admitted in these schools.

(ii) These nurseries may be attached to junior basic schools in rural areas. In the urban areas where there are sufficient number of children these nursery schools should have separate existence.

(iii) Pre-primary education should be free. The basic aim of it should be to impart social experience and education of general behaviour of the infants. It should not burden them with general education.

B. Primary or Basic Education

The Committee recommended, free and compulsory primary or basic education should be provided to children of the age group 6-14. This education should be based on some fundamental craft. In this regard the Committee agreed with the scheme of basic education. But it did not agree with the idea that the things manufactured by the students should meet the expenses of the education.

1. **Categories.** Basic schools were divided into two categories:
   (i) Junior Basic Schools, and
   (ii) Senior Basic Schools.
   (a) *Junior Basic Schools.* In these shall study the boys from 6-11 years of age. Education in these schools shall be compulsory for all.
   (b) *Senior Basic Schools.* In these shall study children of 11-14 years of age. Only such boys should be sent to Senior Basic School who cannot continue their studies for High Schools.
2. **English.** Teaching of English has not been given any place in Junior Basic Schools. The Education Departments of the provincial Governments were authorised to take final decision in regard to Senior Basic Schools.
3. **Ratio of Teachers and Students.** In the Junior Basic Schools, there should be one teacher for every 30 students. In Senior Basic Schools, there should be one teacher for every 25 students.
4. **Examination.** Instead of external examination there should be internal examinations. Certificates should be issued after the completion of the studies.

C. Secondary Education

1. Recommendation:

(i) Those students who have exceptional aptitude for higher studies should be sent to secondary schools of education. This education should be for the age group of 11-16 years.

(ii) Students below the age of 11 should not be allowed to enter these schools. Their abilities and aptitudes, interests, etc. should be borne in mind while giving them admission.

(iii) Students shall have to study at least up to the age of 14 year In these schools they should not be allowed to leave schools before this age.

(iv) Fee shall be charged from the students for receiving education at this stage, but 50 per cent of the students shall be free. It has also been recommended to give scholarships to the poor students so that they may not be deprived of this stage of education.

2. Categories. There should be the following division of the schools on the basis of the curriculum:

(a) Academic
(b) Technical.

3. Courses. Both these schools shall have certain subjects in common such as:

(i) Mother Tongue
(ii) English
(iii) Modern language
(iv) History
(v) Geography
(vi) Mathematics
(vii) Science
(viii) Economics
(ix) Agriculture
(x) Art
(xi) Music
(xii) Physical Education.

(A) Academic. In the 'Academic High Schools', classical languages and Civics shall also be taught along with other subjects. For the girls there should be provision for Home Science.

(B) *Technical.* In the 'Technical High Schools' there shall be provision for the girls for Home Science:

(a) Wood Craft
(b) Metal Craft
(c) Elementary Engineering
(d) Drawing
(e) Commerce
(f) Shorthand
(g) Typewriting
(h) Accountancy
(i) Book-Keeping
(j) Business Method, etc.

4. **Medium of Instruction.** Mother tongue should be the medium of instruction. English should be taught as a second compulsory subject.
5. **Aim of Education.** The aim of education should be to make the boys self-dependent and able to stand on their own legs.

D. University Education

(i) Three-Year Degree Course. Sargeant Scheme of Education has suggested a three-year Degree course. It was suggested that the Intermediate classes should be done away with 11th class should be added to the High School while the 12th class should be added to university education. University education shall run for three years.

(ii) Rules of Admission. There should be strict rules for admission to university. Out of 15 students completing Secondary Education, only one should be allowed to pursue university education.

(iii) Standard. In order to raise the standard of university, the scheme has recommended the appointment of competent teachers, improvement in salary scales, and reforms in the condition of service. There should be closer contact between the teachers and the taught.

(iv) UGC and other Schemes. The scheme has suggested for the appointment of University Grants Commission, introduction of tutorial system and improvement of the methods of research.

E. Technical, Industrial, Vocational and Craft Education

Sargeant report laid a good deal of stress on industrial and vocational education. It suggested for the full time and part time instructions in order to fulfil the requirement of all the different categories of the skilled hands:

1. **Higher Category of Workers.** According to Sargeant report there was need for higher category of workers for the industrial and vocational fields. This category included Chief Executive, Research Workers, etc. The students desirous of acquiring education of this category should join the Technological Department of some university or some other full time technological institute, after completing their education at some Technical High School. The rules for admission to this category of education should be strict. Very few students shall join this scheme of education.
2. **Lower Category of Workers.** This category shall include foremen, charge- hand and other ordinary executive and administrative officers. They should be given training in the Technical High School. They should also be given facilities for training in higher classes.
3. **Skilled Craftsmen.** Skilled craftsmen are very much needed for successful execution of industrial and occupational schemes. Students should have passed the curriculum of some Technical High School. In order to achieve training of this category of works, students who have finished their education at some senior basic school, may be given training in some Junior Technical Education as fall time students and then they may be put in for this task.
4. **Semi-skilled and Un-skilled Workers.** Students who have studied in Senior Basic Middle schools with some basic craft, shall be admitted to this category of the workers.

F. Education of the Adults

Sargeant Report made recommendations in regard to the education of uneducated adults from 10-40 year It said that Adult education is very much essential for the success of the ideal of democratic way of life. It would facilitate the primary education.

Two Types of Education. This scheme envisaged two types of education for the adults:

(a) General Education, and

(b) Technical or Vocational Education.

It also suggested for the establishment of separate institutions for children, old men, ladies, etc. Curriculum should include Geography, History, Civics, Economics, Hygiene, etc. along with three R's. There should be circulating libraries. There should be pictures, magic lanterns, film shows, gramophone records, radio, folk- dance, music drama, etc. to make adult education more interesting. If these means are employed, the task of educator of the adults will be lighter and easy. The teachers will be trained for the task. No class of adult education should have more than 25 educand.

G. Training of the Teachers

There should be an army of trained teachers for the rapid progress of education and the successful execution of the plans of education. There should be 22,17,033 trained teachers in all, including about 20 lakhs of undergraduate trained teachers and 1,8,1,320 trained graduate teachers. For the training of the graduate teachers, it was suggested to impart education to them by training colleges.

For the training of the under-graduate teachers, there should be following three types of training institutions:

(i) Pre-Primary.
(ii) Basic.
(iii) High School.

Teachers for technical and industrial education maybe taken in institutions for the purpose and other industrial courses. Refresher courses should be started for all the categories of the teachers. The salary scales of the teachers should be improved. Free training should be provided in the Training Colleges and Schools. Scholarships should be given to the poor and deserving boys so that they may not be deprived of this part of education.

H. Education of the Physically Handicapped

Special institutions should be started for the education of the students physically or psychologically handicapped. Here the educands may engage themselves in such productive activities, that may be of use to them in the future life.

1. **Core of Health.** Stress was laid on the health of the boys. It was suggested to provide physical education and due medical check-up and treatment for the students of 6-11 and 14 years of age. Complete medical record of the students should be maintained which would enable to find out the

physical condition of every student while going from one institution to the other. Physical record should be sent along with the academic record of the boy. Every teacher, if he found any sign of ailment in any student shall bring it to the notice of the Health officer who shall arrange for the free treatment of the boy. Physical training should be made compulsory. Boys should be provided with mid-day meals.

2. **Recreational and Social Activities.** Recreational and social activities must be organised in the institutions. These should be in accordance with the requirements of the age of the students. They may be any one of the following:
   (i) Gardening.
   (ii) Debating and education tests.
   (iii) Folk-dance.
   (iv) Junior Red Cross.
   (v) Scouting.
   (vi) Accounting.
   (vii) Inter-College debates, etc.
3. **Employment Bureaus.** The scheme made the following recommendations, in this regard in order to provide the students with requisite employment.
   (i) Under the control of the Education Department a number of employment bureaus should be established.
   (ii) Universities should have their own employment bureaus.
   (iii) These bureaus should discharge the following functions:
      (a) Contact with all educational institutions.
      (b) Advise the outgoing students about the openings for employment available to them.
      (c) Contact with employers and arrangement for trade apprentices.
4. **Administration of Education.** The scheme made the following suggestions in regard to administration of the educational institutions and other aspects of education:
   (i) The province should remain the main unit of educational administration.
   (ii) The activities of the university and higher technical educational bodies should be co-ordinated on all-India basis.

(iii) Close co-operation should be maintained in regard to education between the Central and the provincial Government.

(iv) The provincial administration should take over all the educational powers from the local bodies, except where they were discharging their functions properly and nicely.

(v) In every province there should be an Education Advisory Board.

Merits of the Scheme

This scheme of education presented a comprehensive picture of the problems and requirements of Indian education. Thorough and minute study of the conditions of education in India was made before making recommendations:

1. **First Comprehensive Scheme.** In the words of Prof. K. G. Saiyadain, "It does not start with the assumption that India was destined to occupy a position of educational importance in community of nations. It is based on the conviction that all other countries have achieved in the field of education as well than the competence of this country. It was the first Government attainment to make a commendable attempt for framing a national scheme of education."
2. **Criticisms and Suggestions.** This existing scheme of education was severely criticised without any fear of favour and valuable suggestions put forward. It contained a thorough study of the Indian education and suggestions for its reforms.
3. **Importance to Teachers.** Due importance was given to the teaching profession. Recommendations were made for the improvement of the salary scales and the conditions of service.
4. **Equal Opportunities to Students.** It recommended provision of equal opportunities to all the students at various stages of education.
5. **Education of Handicapped.** For the first time the attention of the Government was drawn towards the education of the handicapped.

Demerits of the Scheme

To quote Nurullah and Naik, "The only ideal held up by the report is that of education system of England, while as a matter of fact England is a country, which cannot serve as a model of India, because the social, political and economic conditions in the two countries are so vastly different."

In short, the following are the demerits of the report:

(i) ***Not-Original.*** It was not an original report. It was only a patchwork of the recommendations of different Committees and Commissions on education. About primary education it only contained gist of Wardha Scheme of Education.

(ii) ***Ideals not Means.*** It laid down only the ideals to be achieved, but not the means to achieve those ideals.

(iii) ***Copy of British System.*** It shall be wrong to call it a National Scheme of Education. It was only a copy of the pattern practised in England.

QUESTIONS FOR EXERCISE

1. Outline the main recommendations of the Sargeant Scheme of the Government of India. In what respect does it differ from the Wardha Scheme so far as Primary Education is concerned?
2. Analyse the main recommendations in respect of Secondary Education made in the report of the Central Advisory Committee on post-war educational institutions.
3. Outline the main features of Sargeant Plan and show how far the plan provides us with the scheme of national system of education.
4. What were the recommendations of the Scheme of Central Advisory Board of Education (Sargeant Report) with regard to the Primary and High School Education? On what grounds has the scheme been criticised?
5. Describe and discuss the proposals made by Sargeant Report on the organisation of Secondary Education in India.

CHAPTER 18

PROGRESS OF EDUCATION 1921-1947

PRIMARY EDUCATION

Almost all the provinces passed the Acts in regard to compulsory primary education by the year 1930. According to these Acts the responsibility of primary education was entrusted to the local institutions. These institutions were empowered to impose education cess in order to meet the expenditure to be incurred on education. The provincial Government promised financial help to meet the expenditure of the education. Only those boys and girls could take benefit of the provision of compulsory education who were ordinarily between the age of six and seven years.

As a result of Compulsory Education Acts and the sense of nationalism, the expansion of compulsory education received an impetus. Under the guidance of Mahatma Gandhi, the father of the nation, women also demanded their rights. They organised All India Women Education Conference in 1927. They demanded the right of receiving education equal to those of men. The efforts of Mahatma Gandhi and B. R. Ambedkar brought about consciousness among the Harijans. They also went a long way to expand education. Due to the efforts of these great leaders, the people started taking interest in primary education. Fortunately for India, the organisation of the provincial education came into the hands of Indian ministers and the Government contributed much for the expansion of primary education.

The progress of compulsory primary education continued till 1930. From 1931 to 1937 the development of compulsory education received a set back. There were two main reasons for this. Firstly, the world-wide economic depression influenced India. Hence, the expensive schemes of compulsory education were postponed. Secondly, the Hartog Committee appointed in 1927, emphasised that instead of aiming the quantitative increase in primary education special attention should be given to the qualitative progress of primary education and the policy of consolidation of education should be followed. In spite of opposition of the people, the Government implemented the suggestions of this Committee, which brought about a set back in the expansion of compulsory education.

In 1937, Congress ministries were formed in six out of 11 provinces at the time of provincial autonomy. They made vigorous efforts to provide compulsory primary education in their provinces. They established primary schools in those villages, where there were none. Local institutions were given additional grants so that they could meet the expenditure of compulsory primary education. Girls schools were opened at the places where people demanded it. These efforts of the Congress ministries led to a great expansion of primary education. By 1947 compulsory primary education was available for boys in 229 cities and 10,017 villages and for girls in 10 cities and 1404 villages.

SECONDARY EDUCATION

The Calcutta University Commission appointed in 1917 made study of the defects of the secondary education. It arrived at the conclusion that unless and until the secondary education is reorganised, it would not be possible to make any reform in the university education. It recommended the establishment of a Board of Secondary and Intermediate Education in each province.

In 1929, Hartog Committee accepted that as compared to the education of common people, secondary education had made more progress. However, the Committee added that because of large number of failures in Matriculation examination, the rate of wastage in secondary education was very high. Abbott and Wood suggested in their report in 1936-37 that up to the stage of high school, Indian language should be made the medium of education and the teaching of English should not be given in literary form. The Sargeant Report of 1944 also made many important suggestions in regard to secondary education. It laid down that high school course should be made of six year. No student below the age of 11 years should be admitted in high school.

No restrictions were imposed on secondary education in spite of the suggestions made by the above mentioned Committees and

Commissions. It continued to expand in an unrestricted manner. The number of secondary schools, which was 2,953 in 1916-17 increased to 4,883 in 1947-48.

After pointing out the defects, wastage and stagnation in the field of primary education Hartog Committee put forward its recommendations.

Defects of Primary Education

Hartog Committee made a thorough study of the primary education in India. It realised that the progress of primary education has not been satisfactory. Proper attention had not been given to the expansion and progress of primary education.

1. **Difficulties in the Path of Progress.** The following difficulties were discovered by the Committee in the path of progress of primary education:
   (a) ***Rural Problems.*** The committee realised that the majority of the Indian population resides in villages. Hence primary education is more a rural problem than an urban one. The Committee also felt that primary education can easily be organised in two, but it presents a number of problems in villages.
   (b) ***Poverty, Illiteracy and Conservatism.*** The Committee found that the villagers are poor, illiterate and conservative. They do not appreciate the advantage of education. They are unwilling to send their children to schools due to conservatism and economic reason. Children help their parents in agriculture and if they send their children to schools, their work suffers resulting in economic loss, which they are unable to bear.
2. **Unfavourable Circumstances.** For the convenience of the villagers it is necessary to have at least one primary school in every village. But it was not so when Hartog Committee explored the problem. There were no good means of transport. During winter and rainy season it became difficult for children to go to distant places to study in schools. Hence the Committee noted that there are many backward areas where primary education has not been encouraged.
3. **Ill-Health.** As villages did not have hygienic conditions, epidemic often broke out. Due to unhygienic conditions, seasonal illness detained the boys from going to schools.

Then, agriculture work was also there. All these factors created difficulties in regular attendance of the children in the schools. The Committee also found very serious barriers of caste, religion and communal feelings making the expansion of primary education complicated.

4. **Wastage and Stagnation.** According to the Committee "Wastage meant the premature withdrawal of children from schools at any stage before the completion of the primary course."

By stagnation, the Committee meant "retention in lower class of a child for a period more than what was needed for that class". The Committee found a good deal of wastage and stagnation in the field of primary education. The Committee also drew the attention of the society and the authorities towards the causes and the factors responsible for wastage and stagnation. These factors were as follows:

(i) ***Illiteracy and Poverty.*** After leaving primary schools, children do not find suitable environments to retain their literacy since most of the parents are illiterate. On the other hand, while they are at school, their poverty poses a difficulty in buying books and other suitable material for study. Due to these factors, children normally relapse into illiteracy.

(ii) ***Lack of Trained Teachers and Insufficiency of Inspecting Staff.*** The Committee found that 60 per cent of the primary schools were single teacher schools, where ail the subjects to all the classes were taught by one teacher who had no training and qualifications. As there was insufficient inspecting staff, schools could not be inspected regularly and their standards went on degenerating.

(iii) ***Method of Teaching.*** The method of teaching employed by the teachers was unscientific and stereo typed. Schools did not have enough educational material and equipment. The curriculum was not scientific and up-to-date. All these things resulted into a good deal of wastage and stagnation.

(iv) ***Lack of Regularity.*** The Committee found that there was lack of regularity in the schools. There were certain schools that did not hold their sessions regularly and it was not proper to call them as schools even.

(v) *Defects of Education Act.* The Committee found that the primary education Act was also defective. According to this Act, the responsibility for compulsory primary education had been left over to the local bodies, who were not very efficient and competent.

(vi) *Unsatisfactory Distribution of Schools.* The distribution of schools is unsatisfactory. There are large areas without a school, while in others are many schools indulging in cut-throat competition for children.

(vii) *Poverty.* Due to poverty many of the villagers employed their children in the work of agriculture at a very early and tender age.

Recommendations of the Hartog Committee

1. **Planning to Make Primary Education Compulsory.** The Committee recommended that primary education should be made compulsory but there should be no hurry about it. First of all, study of the environment and the circumstances of the locality should be made in which the primary education is to be made compulsory and a plan drawn accordingly. A good deal of thought should be put into the plan and then only a step should be taken.
2. **Govt. Inspection and Control.** The Government should themselves undertake the responsibility of inspection and control of the primary schools. The present system of giving it over to the local bodies has not worked successfully.
3. **Qualitative Development.** Qualitative development should be made instead of increasing the number of primary schools. A policy for the consolidation of the primary education should be taken up. Solid steps should be taken in this direction.
4. **Four Years Duration.** At least four years should be devoted to primary education. Every effort should be made to raise the standard of the primary education.
5. **Time Table.** The time table of the schools should be drawn up in accordance with the environment and the circumstances of the schools.
6. **Elimination of Bad Schools.** Such institutions should be done away with where the number of students is very small and there is no provision for good education.

7. **Curriculum.** Curriculum of the primary schools should be made more liberal and scientific in accordance with the circumstances and environment. Due attention should also be paid to the fact that education should be of practical value to the students in life.
8. **Reduction of Wastage and Stagnation.** Special attention should be paid to the lowest class in the primary schools and efforts should be made to reduce wastage and stagnation prevailing therein.
9. **Centres for Rural Welfare.** Primary schools should serve as centres for rural uplift works, medical relief, adult education, mass literacy, sanitation, recreation, etc.
10. **Standard of Teachers.** The standard of the teachers in the primary schools should be improved. Training institutions should have better equipment and more efficient staff. Refresher courses should also be arranged from time to time. Salary and conditions of service should be made attractive. Inspection staff should also be increased so as to keep an eye on the efficiency and working of these schools.

PROGRESS OF PRIMARY EDUCATION 1937-1947

Year	No. of Schools	No. of Students
1936-37	1,92,244	1,02,24,288
1945-46	1,67,700	1,30,27,313

The above table indicates that primary education could not be developed during this period. The number of schools was reduced by 24,544, although the number of students increased by 28,03,025.

During their short tenure of about two years the Congress ministries in various provinces tried their best to develop primary education. However, they could not achieve the committed objective. During 1937-38 compulsory education could be introduced only in 146 cities and 3,995 villages for boys and for both boys and girls combined in 135 cities and 6,710 villages.

During this period the Bombay Government tried to effect qualitative improvement of primary education according to the recommendations of the Hartog Committee. It enacted two laws for limiting the powers to local bodies with regard to facilities for primary education. This obstructed the growth of primary education in the province.

During this period some efforts were made to improve the financial condition of teachers. But due to the World War II, the prices had soared so high that these efforts became useless. The teachers resorted to strikes in many provinces for getting their salaries improved. Consequently, the salaries were raised a little. This nominal increasement, however, could not improve the financial condition of teachers.

SECONDARY EDUCATION

Slow Progress

During this period the progress of secondary education had become slow. After the partition of the country there were only 11907 schools in India. Out of this number 1,733 schools were for girls. The available statistics indicate that there were 33,53,856 boys and 3,56,125 girls in these schools.

Causes of Slow Progress

1. **Soaring Prices.** There have been many causes of slow progress of secondary education during this period. But the most formidable cause was the soaring prices which gave a great set-back to the people who felt difficult to send their children to schools for secondary education. Tuition fees were enhanced, the stationery' and books cost more, the cost of living in cities touched a new high index and the expenses in hostels also became heavier correspondingly. Under the circumstances the children from middle class families were deprived of educational opportunities. The secondary education was within the reach of rich families only. Numerous poor but deserving children could not enter high schools.
2. **Lack of Enthusiasm in Primary Education.** Another reason for the poor progress of secondary education was the lack of enthusiasm in the field of primary education from where came students for secondary schools. Since many deserving students could not come for secondary education, the high schools became flooded with undeserving students.

After the achievement of Independence both the public and the Government began to take keen interest in the development of secondary education. The mother tongue was made the medium of instruction at the secondary stage. The curriculum was made more comprehensive by including a number of optionals and vocational and technical subjects. Many separate schools were established for vocational and technical education. Though much work could not be done due to financial stringency, however, the efforts made were indicative of the enthusiasm on the part of the government and public for development of secondary education. Some efforts were made to remove the dearth of trained teachers. There were about 2,110 male pupil-teachers and 1,307 lady pupil-teachers in training colleges during this period.

New Problems of Secondary Education

Due to soaring prices of daily necessities it became difficult for many teachers to have both the ends meet. So many of them left their teaching jobs for more lucrative professions. Even trained teachers began to leave schools if they got opportunities for better emoluments elsewhere. Hence, secondary education was adversely affected because numerous untrained hands had to be employed to teach in schools. As these untrained hands were always on the look-out to leave schools for more remunerative jobs, so they took little interest in teaching. This situation led to fall of the standard of education. The enrolment in training colleges also fell down.

Indiscipline in students was also spreading due to many causes:

1. Political parties entered educational institutions indirectly through undeserving students whose main job was to disturb the educational atmosphere.
2. Due to financial difficulties the teachers were very much hard-pressed and they failed to place high ideals before students. Many of them presented deplorable specimens of unworthy behaviour and attitudes towards life.
3. It became difficult for teachers to remove indiscipline from amongst students. The problem of indiscipline became more acute day-by-day.

HIGHER AND UNIVERSITY EDUCATION

Four new universities were opened during this period. In Travancore in 1937, in Utkal in 1943, in Sagar in 1946 and in Rajasthan in 1947 new universities were established. By 1947 there were in all 19 universities in the country. The table indicates the position of development of university education in the country till 1947.

DEVELOPMENT OF HIGHER AND UNIVERSITY EDUCATION TILL 1947

Universities	Kinds	No. of Students	
		In 1940	In 1947
1. Calcutta	Affiliating and Teaching	35,357	48,008
2. Bombay	" " "	17,575	43,090
3. Madras	" " "	17,454	28,888
4. Punjab	" " "	19,841	Not available
5. Allahabad	Teaching	2,056	3,502
6. Banaras	" " "	3,385	5,083
7. Mysore	Affiliating and Teaching	2,725	9,350
8. Patna	" " "	5,898	5,471
9. Osmania	Teaching	1,723	4,862
10. Lucknow	" " "	2,340	3,893
11. Aligarh	" " "	1,822	4,009
12. Dacca	" " "	1,268	Not available
13. Delhi	Teaching and Federative	2,120	4,311
14. Nagpur	Affiliating and Teaching	3,767	5,734
15. Andhra	" " "	3,599	9,445
16. Agra	Affiliating	4,132	9,936
17. Annamalai	Teaching	741	1,981
18. Travancore	Affiliating and Teaching	Not established then	5,715
19. Utkal		" "	3,662
20. Sagar	" " "	" "	1,828
21. Rajputana	Affiliating	" "	Not available

The data are based on informations received from various universities. It indicates that in 1947 there were more students in each University than in 1937. In European countries there were many universities and India stood nowhere in comparison to any one of them. According to the Sargeant Report in 1944 in England for a population of 41 lakhs there were 12 Universities, in Canada 13 for 8.5 lakhs, in Australia 6 for 5.5 lakhs, in U.S. A. 1710 colleges for 130 lakhs and in India there were only 18 Universities in

1943-44. The Sargeant Report was published in 1944. At that time there were only 18 universities in India for a population of about 40 crores. Evidently, the educational structure in India was laid on weak foundations and it was standing only because the load of higher education was very light. Therefore, the need was to make the foundations very strong, to make primary and secondary education more well organised on stronger footings. These two stages of education could be based on firmer ground only when they were properly expanded for the people and the people were awakened to realise the necessity of being educated. Even after about five decades of independence, India has not yet been able to base these two stages of education on firmer grounds.

THE ABBOTT-WOOD REPORT, 1937

The absence of adequate and proper vocational education was being felt in India. The public was raising its demand for it since long. Therefore, in 1936-37 the Government of India invited two British experts, A. Abbott and S.H. Wood, to come India and prepare a plan for vocational education in the country. These two persons toured Punjab, Delhi and U.P. Within four months they prepared a report on vocational education. This report was neither comprehensive nor successful. The Sargeant Report of 1944 was published on the basis of this report. It presented a more detailed plan of vocational education than the Abbott Report. However, the latter one cannot be ignored, as it has its own importance.

Reasons for Appointment

(i) Since 1931 there had been a slump in the economic field in India resulting into much unemployment. Wood-Abbott Committee was appointed to look into this problem and suggest ways and means for its eradication through education. In its introduction the report has very clearly stated its views in regard to this problem.

(ii) Another reason for instituting this inquiry is the fact that a large number of University graduates are not securing employment of a kind for which their education qualified them. It would not affect the unemployment, considered as a quantitative problem to divert students from universities into other educational institutions. Such a policy would offer jobs according to the educational qualifications of the unemployed without decreasing their number. By encouraging education a quick solution of the problem on unemployment was to be found in the reconstruction of educational system.

Terms of Reference

(a) "Whether any vocational or practical training should be imparted in primary, secondary and higher secondary schools and if so, what should be its nature and extent?"

(b) "Whether the technical or vocational institutions already in existence can be improved, and if so, in what manner, and if institutions for vocational and technical training be required, to suggest:

  (i) What type of institution or institutions are required for the purpose.

  (ii) What shall be the stage at which the students should be directed from ordinary lower or higher secondary schools to such institutions imparting vocational or technical education.

  (iii) What means should be adopted in order to affect this diversion successfully.

(c) The Committee was also expected to advice in regard to "the requirements of special arrangement needed to meet the special requirements of the rural areas, specially in view of the desirability of remedying the trend of the present education system to draw many boys and girls from rural areas to towns where they receive purely literary form of education, and by so doing not only congest still further the high schools but also become very largely lost to the service of the country side."

Recommendations: General Education

(i) ***Primary Education.*** The education of the infants should be properly, thoroughly and scientifically organised. It should be put into the hands of the trained women teachers. This will require a good deal of attention to be paid to the education of girls and women. Primary education should be based more upon the natural interest and activities of young children, rather than on book learning.

(ii) ***Secondary Education and University Education.*** Primary education and lower secondary education should be of

four years duration each. Higher secondary education and Degree education should take three years each.

(iii) ***Curriculum.*** The Committee recommended reorganization of the curriculum on the scientific basis. In the curriculum of rural education middle schools should be related to the environment of the educand.

(iv) ***Teaching of English and Vernacular.*** The Committee felt that it was not at all healthy to lay too much emphasis on the teaching of English. About the rural middle schools the Committee suggested that if the children were taught English, emphasis should not be laid on the linguistic studies. The medium of instruction throughout High School should be some Hindustani language. However, English should be a compulsory language for all the pupils in these schools. The Committee also suggested that, "Average students should devote less attention to the study of English prose and poetry. Arrangement should be made for those boys who want to pursue more advanced English studies. Teaching of English should be made domestic."

(v) ***Creative Manual Works.*** The Committee suggested that 'manual work should be subject of study in every school.'

(vi) ***Training of the Teachers.*** The Committee suggested that the training of the teachers should consist of two stages. In the first there should be preemployment preparation in a normal school or a training college. In the second, there should be systematic short course of training for teachers, who have had some experience of their profession. The pre-employment course of training for teachers of primary and middle schools should be a three-year course, followed just after the completion of the middle school course."

(vii) ***Teaching of Art.*** The Committee recommended that greater attention should be paid to the teaching of art. It suggested that steps should be taken to secure qualified and trained teachers for the teaching of Art in High Schools.

(viii) ***Physical Education.*** The Committee was of the opinion that physical education should not end with the physical training and games only. Better use of playground should be made by young children for purely creative purposes. Such steps would not only improve their creative faculties, but also bring about physical health.

(ix) ***Inspection and Control Over the Institutions.*** The Committee recommended for greater control over the institutions and stricter inspection. It suggested:

(a) "Government should have a greater control over those local bodies, which are in charge of education."

(b) The tenure of the office of the administrative head of the Department of Education should be more permanent. This is necessary for the formulation and execution of long range policies in education.

(c) "Inspectors should not be under the control of two masters as this interferes with proper discharge of their duties. Their scale of travelling allowances should be raised."

(x) ***Greater Equipment of the Teachers and Inspecting Staff.*** The Committee felt that there was need of more equipped and efficient teaching and inspecting staff. It therefore recommended that "if funds permit, inspectors and selected teachers should be offered facilities for studying abroad."

Vocational Education

The Committee looked at vocational education from the point of view of the problem of unemployment. For studying the problem of unemployment, it suggested not only the reorganisation of the general education but also vocational education. Wood and Abbott found that there was a problem of unemployment in India, which needed solution in a scientific manner. They, therefore, recommended reconstruction of educational system. The problem of unemployment in India could be solved only through 'industrial development of the country'. The Committee therefore wrote, "The development of the industry which will offer employment, depends upon the natural resources of the country, climate, conditions and upon actions in the fields of economics and politics, which do not come within our terms of references."

(a) ***Purpose of Vocational Education:***

(i) Abbott and Wood Committee said that "the immediate purpose of education in relation to industry is to secure to the industry the services of better qualified men and achievement, which does not by itself and at once result in more employment."

(ii) According to the Committee the second aim of the vocational education was, "an improvement in the contents and method of education will make... for steadily increasing efficiency in industry and will contribute towards its expansion."

(b) ***Importance of Vocational Education.*** The Committee felt that vocational education was important as general education. Neither of them could be called more important and more useful. They said, "If general education brings about the development of the non-material culture of a country vocational education does the same thing for material culture." Hence, both are necessary for the progress of the country.

(c) ***Recommendations regarding Vocational Education:***

(i) The vocational education should expand in accordance with the industrial requirements of the country.

(ii) The type and the form of vocational education in a province should be decided upon only after having a thorough inquiry of the trade, industry and commerce of that province.

(iii) Vocational education should in no way be considered inferior to general education and it should be treated at par with the general education.

(iv) General and vocational education should not be regarded as different branches, but as the earlier and later phases of continuous process.

(v) Separate institutions should be established for vocational education.

(vi) People engaged in cottage industries should be given proper training of their trade and occupation so that heavy industries may not harm them.

(vii) An Advisory Council for Vocational Education should be established in each province. In order to establish close and proper co-ordination between the industry and the commerce, industry and education, industrialists should encourage vocational education by making arrangement of buildings, equipment, finances, etc.

(viii) Trade schools should be established in order to make proper arrangement for vocational education. Keeping in view the requirements of the country these trade schools may be of two types:

(a) The Junior Vocational Schools should admit pupils after class VIII and provide for a three years course.

(b) The Senior Vocational Schools should admit pupils after class XI and provide for two years course.

(ix) Part-time vocational schools should be started for men already in service. Those desirous of training in these schools should be relieved by their employers by 2½ days in a week.

(x) As agriculture is the main industry in villages and therefore, in the junior high schools and senior high schools of the rural areas arrangement for the teaching of agriculture should be made.

(xi) Students who complete their courses in vocational schools should be awarded School Leaving Certificates.

(xii) Such vocational institutions should be given encouragement that have provision for the teaching of arts and crafts.

(xiii) "Junior and Senior Technical Schools should be established in industrial zones only. They should not be established in areas with a population less than 50,000."

(xiv) Students should be given vocational guidance. This would help them to choose a vocation or occupation to fit in with their aptitudes. The Government should also publish such information from time to time as may be favourable for the institutions imparting vocational education.

(xv) "The Government of India should establish on one side the vocational training colleges, junior technical schools and technical schools attended by part-time as well as full-time industrial and commercial students; and on the other side, the schools of arts and crafts."

EVALUATION OF THE COMMITTEE'S REPORT

1. **Hurriedly Written:** Wood and Abbott were educationists of eminence, but they did not get ample time to make a thorough survey of the conditions of education in India. They wrote out the Report hurriedly.

2. **Valuable Suggestions:** In spite of its being hurriedly written, the Report contains very valuable suggestions. Had these suggestions been enforced, certain tangible results would have come out. As the Second Word War broke out and the Congress ministers had to resign, the report remained only a valuable piece of document.

QUESTIONS FOR EXERCISE

1. Trace the growth of Primary and Secondary education since 1921 to 1947 in India.
2. Examine critically the main recommendations of Hartog Committee regarding improvements necessary in primary education.

CHAPTER 19

EDUCATION IN FREE INDIA: CONSTITUTIONAL PROVISIONS

Compulsory Primary Education

Free India needed expansion of education at all stages and specially at the stage of primary education. The national Government took active and sincere steps to make the primary education free, universal and compulsory. The principle of compulsory education was declared through Article 45 of the Constitution of India. It was also recommended that this education would be of basic type. Board of National Education was established on this basis. Government made vigorous efforts to expand compulsory primary education in all comers of the country.

Secondary Education

Several committees and commissions were appointed in the post-independent era. The prominent among them were the following:

1. **Tara Chand Committee, 1948.** The Committee suggested that secondary school should be multi-lateral but unilateral schools should also be encouraged keeping in view the local conditions and circumstances. A Commission should be appointed in order to investigate the problems of secondary education.
2. **University Education Commission, 1948-49.** The chief aim of this Commission was to investigate and make suggestions in regard to University education. But it also considered different aspects of the secondary education and made many important suggestions. In its opinion, the secondary education was the weakest link in the whole structure of education. It recommended that students should be admitted in the university only after completing 12 years of study in school or intermediate college.

3. **Secondary Education Commission, 1952-53.** As a result of the suggestions of Tara Chand Committee and Central Education Advisory Board, a Secondary Education Commission was appointed to study in detail the different aspects of secondary education and to make different suggestions to reform it.

Development of Secondary Education

Secondary education received an impetus after the attainment of independence. At present it is free in Andhra Pradesh, Gujarat, Karnataka, Kerala, Taminadu, Andaman and Nicobar Islands, Arunachal Pradesh and Lakshadweep and in Government institutions in Jammu and Kashmir, Nagaland, Dadra and Nagar Haveli and Pondicherry. It is free only for girls in Madhya Pradesh, Manipur, Orissa, Rajasthan, Tripura and Uttar Pradesh.

Higher and University Education

At present higher and university education is imparted through arts, science and commerce and professional colleges, research institutions and institutions deemed to be universities. There are at present 136 universities in India.

In addition to these, there are 20 other institutions which are regarded as universities.

The universities are of following three types:

1. Affiliating universities.
2. Affiliating and teaching universities.
3. Residential and teaching universities.

Generally, the policy of the Government has been to increase the number of institutions of higher education rather than to aim at the qualitative progress of higher education. Besides this there are multilateral problems of higher education, which have not attracted the proper attention of the Government and hence special efforts have not been made so far to remove the defects of higher education.

CONSTITUTIONAL PROVISIONS FOR EDUCATION (1950)

The Constitution of India came into force on January 26,1950. As it embodies our hopes and aspirations, it is but natural that education should find its place in this great document. A number of important provisions which have a direct or indirect bearing on education have been included in the Constitution. The outline of the philosophy which should govern all our institutions, educational as well as others, are indicated in the preamble to the Constitution.

Preamble

We, the people of India, having solemnly resolved to constitute India into a Sovereign Socialist Secular Democratic Republic and to secure to all its citizens:

Justice, social, economic and political;

Liberty of thought, expression, belief, faith and worship;

Equality of status and of opportunity;

and to promote among them all;

Fraternity assuring the dignity of the individual and the unity of the Nation;

In Our Constituent Assembly this twenty-sixth day of November, 1949, do hereby adopt, enact and give to ourselves this Constitution.

Article 14. Equality before Law. The State shall not deny to any person equality before the law or the equal protection of the laws within the territory of India.

Article 15. Prohibition of Discrimination on Grounds of Religion, Race, Caste, Sex or Place of Birth. 1. The State shall not discriminate against any citizen on grounds only of religion, race, caste, sex, place of birth or any of them.

2. No citizen shall, on grounds only of religion, race, caste, sex, place of birth or any of them, be subject to any disability, liability, restriction or condition with

(a) access to shops, public restaurants, hotels and places of public entertainment; or

(b) the use of wells, tanks, bathing ghats, roads and places of public resort maintained wholly or partly out of State funds or dedicated to the use of the general public.

3. Nothing in this Article shall prevent the State from making any special provision for women and children.

4. Nothing in this Article or in clause (2) or Article 29 shall prevent the State from making any special provision for the advancement of any socially and educationally backward classes of citizens or for the Scheduled Castes and the Scheduled Tribes.

Article 16. Equality of Opportunity in Matters of Public Employment 1. There shall be equality of opportunity for all citizens in matters relating to employment or appointment to any office under the State.

2. No citizen shall, on grounds only of religion, race, caste, sex, descent, place of birth, residence or any of them, be ineligible for, or discriminated against in respect of, any employment or office under the State.

3. Nothing in this Article shall prevent Parliament from making any law prescribing, in regard to a class or classes of employment or appointment to an office (under the Government of, or any local or other authority within, a State or Union Territory, any requirement as to residence within that State or Union Territory) prior to such employment or appointment.

4. Nothing in this Article shall prevent, the State from making any provision for the reservation of appointments or posts in favour of any backward class of citizens which, in the opinion of the State, is not adequately represented in the services under the State.

5. Nothing in this Article shall affect the operation of any law which provides that the incumbent of an office in connection with the affairs of any religious or denominational institution or any member of the governing body shall be a person professing a particular religion or belonging to a particular denomination.

Article 17. Abolition of Untouchability. 'Untouchability' is abolished and its practice in any form is forbidden. The enforcement of any disability arising out of 'Untouchability' shall be an offence punishable in accordance with law.

Article 24. Prohibition of Employment of Children in Factories, etc. No child below the age of 14 years shall be employed to work in any factory or mine or engaged in any other hazardous employment.

Article 25. Freedom to Manage Religious Affairs. Subject to public order, morality and health, every religious denomination or any section thereof shall have the right:

(a) to establish and maintain institution for religious and charitable purposes;
(b) to manage its own affairs in matters of religion;
(c) to own and acquire movable and immovable property; and
(d) to administer such property in accordance with law.

Article 28. Freedom as to Attendance at Religious Instruction or Religious Worship in Certain Educational Institutions. 1. No religious instruction shall be provided in any educational institution wholly maintained out of the State funds.

2. Nothing in clause (1) shall apply to an educational institution which is administered by the State but has been established under any endowment or trust which requires that religious instruction shall be imparted in such institution.

3. No person attending any educational institution recognised by the State or receiving any aid out of State funds shall be required to take part in any religious instruction that may be imparted in such institution or to attend any religious worship that may be conducted in such institution or in any premises attached thereto unless such person or, if such person is a minor, his guardian has given his consent thereto.

Article 29. Protection of Interests of Minorities. 1. Any section of the citizens residing in the territory of India or any part thereof having a distinct language, script or culture of its own shall have the right to conserve the same.

2. No citizen shall be denied admission into any educational institution maintained by the State or receiving aid out of State hinds on grounds only of religion, race, caste, language or any of them.

Article 30. Right of Minorities to Establish and Administer Educational Institutions. 1. All minorities, whether based on religion or language, shall have the right to establish and administer educational institutions of their choice.

2. The State shall not, in granting aid to educational institutions, discriminate against any educational institution on the ground that it is under the management of a minority, whether based on religion or language.

Article 41. Right to Work, to Education and to Public Assistance in Certain Cases. The State shall, within the limits of its economic capacity and development, make effective provision for securing the right to work, to education and to public assistance in cases of unemployment, old age, sickness and disablement, and in other cases of undeserved want.

Article 45. Provision for Free and Compulsory Education for Children. The State shall endeavour to provide, within a period of ten years from the commencement of this Constitution, for free and compulsory education for all children until they complete the age of 14 years.

Article 46. Promotion of Educational and Economic Interests of Scheduled Castes, Scheduled Tribes and other Weaker Sections. The State shall promote with special care the educational and economic interests of the weaker sections of the people, and, in particular, of the scheduled castes and the scheduled tribes, and shall protect them from social injustice and all forms of exploitation.

Article 246. Subject Matter of Laws Made by Parliament and by the Legislatures of States. 1. Notwithstanding anything in clauses (2) and (3) Parliament has exclusive power to make laws with respect to any of the matters enumerated in List 1 in the Seventh Schedule (in this Constitution referred to as the 'Union List').

2. Notwithstanding anything in clause (3), Parliament, and, subject to clause (1), the Legislature of any State also, have power to make laws with respect to any of the matters enumerated in the List III in the Seventh Schedule (in this Constitution referred to as the 'Concurrent List').

3. Subject to clauses (1) and (2), the Legislature of any State has exclusive power to make laws for such State or any part thereof with respect to any of the matters enumerated in List II in the Seventh Schedule (in this Constitution referred to as the 'State List').

4. Parliament has the power to make laws with respect to any matter for any part of the territory of India not included in a State, notwithstanding that such matter is a matter enumerated in the State List.

Article 337. Special Provision with Respect to Educational Grants for the Benefit of Anglo-Indian Community. During the first three financial years after the commencement of this Constitution, the same grants, if any, shall be made by the Union and by each State for the benefit of the Anglo-Indian community in respect of education as were made in the financial year ending on the thirty-first day of March, 1948.

During every succeeding period of three years the grants may be less by ten per cent than those for the immediately preceding period of three years:

Provided that at the end of ten years from the commencement of this Constitution such grants, to the extent to which they are a special concession, to the Anglo-Indian community, shall cease:

Provided further that no educational institution shall be entitled to receive any grant under this article unless at least 40 per cent of the annual admissions therein are made available to members of communities other than the Anglo-Indian community.

Article 343. Official Language of the Union. (1) The official language of the Union shall be the international form of Indian numerals.

(2) Notwithstanding anything in clause (1), for a period of 15 years from the commencement of this Constitution, the English language shall continue to be used for all the official purposes of the Union for which it was being used immediately before such commencement:

Provided that the President may, during the said period, by order authorise the use of the Hindi language in addition to the English language and of the Devanagari form of numerals in addition to the international form of Indian numerals for any of the official purposes of the Union.

(3) Notwithstanding anything in this article, Parliament may by law provide for the use, after the said period of 15 years, of

(a) the English language, or

(b) the Devanagari form of numerals,

for such purposes as may be specified in the law.

Article 345. Official Language or Languages of a State. Subject to the provision of Articles 346 and 347, the Legislature of a State may by law adopt any one or more of the languages in use in the State or Hindi as the language or languages to be used for all or any of the official purposes of that State:

Provided that, until the Legislature of the State otherwise provides by law, the English language shall continue to be used for these official purposes within the State for which it was being used immediately before the commencement of this Constitution.

Article 346. Official Languagefor Communication between one State and another or between a State and the Union. The language for the time being authorised for use in the Union for official purposes shall be the official language for communication between one State and another State and between a State and the Union:

Provided that if two or more States agree that the Hindi language should be the official language for communication between such States that language may be used for such communication.

Article 347. Special Provision Relating to Language Spoken by a Section of the Population of a State. On a demand being made in that behalf the President may, if he is satisfied that a substantial proportion of the population of a State desire the use of any language spoken by them to be recognised by that State, direct that such language shall also be officially recognised throughout that State or any part there of for such purpose as he may specify.

Article 350-A. Facilities for Instruction in Mother-Tongue at Primary Stage. It shall be the endeavour of every State and of every local authority within the State to provide adequate facilities for instruction in the mother-tongue at the primary stage of education to children belonging to linguistic minority groups; and the President may issue such directions to any State as he considers necessary or proper for securing the provision of such facilities.

Article 351. Directive for Development of the Hindi Language. It shall be the duty of the Union to promote the spread of the Hindi language, to develop it so that it may serve as a medium of expression for all the elements of the composite culture of India and to secure its enrichment by assimilating without interfering with its genius, the forms, style and expressions used in Hindustani and in the other languages of India specified in the Eighth Schedule, and by drawing, wherever necessary or desirable, for its vocabulary, primarily on Sanskrit and secondarily on other languages.

SEVENTH SCHEDULE
(Article 246)

List 1 — Union List

62. The institutions known at the commencement of this Constitution as the National Library, the Indian Museum, the Imperial War Museum, the Victoria Memorial and the Indian War Memorial, and any other like institution financed by the government of India wholly or in part and declared by the Parliament by law to be an institution of national importance.

63. The institutions known at the commencement of this Constitution as the Banaras Hindu University, the Aligarh Muslim University and the Delhi University, and any other institution declared by Parliament by law to be an institution of national importance.

64. Institutions for scientific or technical education financed by the Government of India wholly or in part and declared by Parliament by law to be institutions of national importance.

65. Union agencies and institutions for:

(a) professional, vocational or technical training including the training of police officers; or

(b) the promotion of special studies of research; or

(c) scientific or technical assistance in the investigation or detection of crime.

66. Coordination and determination of standards in institutions for higher education or research and scientific and technical institutions.

67. Ancient and historical monuments and records, and archaeological sites and remains, declared by or under a law made by Parliament to be of national importance.

List II — State List

32. Incorporation, regulation and winding up of corporations, other than those specified in List I, and universities; unincorporated trading, literary, scientific, religious and other societies and associations; cooperative societies.

List III — Concurrent List

20. Economic and social planning.

25. Education, including technical education, medical education and universities, subject to the provision of entries 63, 64, 65 and 66 of List 1: Vocational and technical training of labour.

EIGHTH SCHEDULE

[Articles 344 (1) and 351]

Languages

1. Assamese.
2. Bengali.

9. Oriya.
10. Punjabi.

3. Gujarati.
4. Hindi.
5. Kannada.
6. Kashmiri.
7. Malayalam.
8. Marathi
11. Sanskrit.
12. Sindhi.
13. Tamil.
14. Telugu.
15. Urdu.

QUESTIONS FOR EXERCISE

1. Discuss the growth and development of Primary, Secondary and Higher education in Free India.
2. Describe the provisions for education in Indian Constitution.

CHAPTER 20

NATIONAL POLICY ON EDUCATION

REASONS FOR THE FORMULATION OF THE NATIONAL POLICY

Since the adoption of the policy on education in 1968 there had been considerable expansion in educational facilities all over the country at all levels. However, the general formulations incorporated in the 1968 policy were not translated into a detailed study of implementation. Problems of access, quality, quantity, utility and financial outlay, accumulated over the years, assumed such massive proportions that they must be talked with the utmost urgency. Therefore, in January 1985, the Government of India announced that a New Education Policy would be formulated in the country. A Status Paper *Challenge of Education—A Policy Perspective* was issued by the Ministry of Education, Government of India. This document included a comprehensive appraisal of the existing system of education. There was a country-wide debate on educational reforms in the country. Finally, the New National Policy on Education, 1986, was approved by the Parliament in May 1986.

Provisions of the National Policy of Education

1. **The Essence and Role of Education.** Education is the key to our all-round development, material and spiritual.
2. **National System of Education.** The national system of education envisages common educational structure.
3. **A Meaningful Partnership.** There will be a meaningful partnership between the Centre and the States.
4. **Education for Equality.** All possible efforts will be made on the removal of disparities and to equalise educational opportunity by attending to the specific needs of the women,

scheduled castes and scheduled tribes, the minorities and the handicapped.

I. Education for Women's Equality

1. **Basic Change.** Education will be used as an agent of basic change in the status of women. It will foster the development of new values through residential curricula, text-books, the training and orientation of teachers, decision-makers and administrators, and the active involvement of the educational institutions.
2. **Literacy.** The removal of woman's illiteracy will receive overriding priority through provision of special support services.
3. **Participation.** Major emphasis will be laid on women's participation in vocational, technical and professional education at different levels.

II. The Education of the Scheduled Castes

The Central focus in the SC's educational development in their equalisation with the non-SC population will be at all stages and levels of education, in all areas and in all the four dimensions — rural male, rural female, urban male and urban female.

III. The Education of Scheduled Tribes

Many urgent measures will be taken to bring the Scheduled Tribes at par with others. These include: (i) Opening of primary school, (ii) opening of residential schools including Ashram Schools, (iii) construction of school buildings, (iv) promotion of Tribal languages, (v) promotion of Tribal culture, (vi) incentive schemes like scholarship, (vii) special remedial courses and other programmes, (viii) encouraging educated and promising members of the Scheduled Tribes to take up teaching in tribal areas, and (ix) opening of Anganwadies, Non-formal Education Centres and Adult Education Centres on priority basis.

IV. Education of the Minorities

Greater attention will be paid to the education of minority groups in the interests of equality and social justice.

V. Education of the Handicapped

The objective will be to integrate the physically and mentally handicapped with the general community as equal partners, to prepare them for normal growth and to enable them to face life with courage and confidence.

A. Adult Education. A vast programme of adult and continuing education will be implemented through various ways and channels.

B. Re-Organisation of Education at Different Stages

1. **Early Childhood Care and Education.** A full integration of child care and pre-primary education will be brought about, both as a feeder and a strengthening factor for primary education and to human resource development in general.

2. Elementary Education

(i) There will be the policy of non-detention at the primary stage.

(ii) Corporal punishment will be firmly excluded.

(iii) School timings as well as vacations will be adjusted to the convenience of children.

(iv) A phased drive, symbolically called 'Operation Black Board' will be undertaken to improve primary schools all over the country.

(v) Every primary school will be provided at least two reasonably large rooms that are usable in all weather.

(vi) As early as possible at least two teachers will be provided.

(vii) Necessary learning materials like toys, blackboards, maps, charts will be made available.

(viii) Highest priority will be given to solving the problem of children dropping out of school.

(ix) Non-Formal Education. A large and systematic programme of non-formal education will be launched for school drop-outs, for children from habitations without schools, working children and girls, who cannot attend day-schools.

(x) Resolve Regarding Primary Education. It shall be ensured that all children who attain the age of about 11 years by 1990 will have had five years of schooling or its equivalent through the non-formal stream. Likewise, by 1995, all children will be provided free and compulsory education up to 14 years of age.

3. Secondary Education

(i) ***Curriculum.*** Conscious internationalism of healthy work ethos and of the values of a human and composite culture will be brought about through appropriately formulated curriculum.

(ii) ***Pace Setting Schools.*** Navodaya Vidyalayas which will be residential and free of charge will be established in various parts of the country. These will have scope for innovation and experimentation. These schools are meant for talented children largely rural. They are envisaged to become catalysts of a nation-wide programme of school improvement.

(iii) ***Vocationalisation.*** The introduction of systematic, well planned and vigorously implemented programmes of vocational education is crucial in the proposed educational reorganisation. Vocational courses will be provided after the secondary stage. It is proposed that vocational courses cover 10 per cent of higher secondary students by 1990 and 25 per cent by 1995. Steps will be taken to see that a substantial majority of the products of vocational courses are employed or become self-employed.

4. Higher Education

(i) The main emphasis will be on the consolidation of, and expansion of facilities in the existing institutions.

(ii) Admission will be regulated according to capacity.

(iii) Teacher's performance will be assessed systematically.

(iv) All posts will be filled entirely on the basis of merit.

VI. Open University and Distance Learning

The open university and distance learning will have to be developed with care.

VII. Delinking Degrees from Jobs

A beginning will be made in delinking degrees from jobs in selected areas.

VIII. National Testing Service

Concommitant with delinking, an appropriate machinery such as National Testing Service will be established in the appropriate phase.

IX. Technical and Management Education

The reorganisation of Technical and Management Education should take into account the anticipated scenario by the turn of the century.

X. Promoting Efficiency and Effectiveness at all Levels

(1) The process of maintaining discipline in the system must be strengthened.
(2) Modernization will be undertaken to enchance functional efficiency.
(3) More effective procedures will be adopted in the recruitments of staff. Institutions will be encouraged to generate resources.
(4) Staff development programmes will be integrated and made mandatory.
(5) Excellence in performance of institutions and individuals will be recognized.
(6) Select institutions will be awarded autonomy.
(7) Net working systems will have to be established between education and industry.

XI. Re-Orienting the Content of Education

1. **Cultural Perspective.** Education and its curriculum must bring about the fine synthesis between change-oriented technologies and the country's continuity or cultural traditions. Due attention will be paid to Fine Arts, Musicology, Folklore, etc.
2. **Value Education.** Value education should have a universal appeal and should be oriented towards the unity and integration of our people. It must be based on our heritage, national and universal goals and perception.
3. **Languages.** Language policy of 1968 must be implemented energetically and purposefully.
4. **Work Experience.** Work experience, and essential component at all stages of education must be provided through well structured and graded programmes.
5. **Environmental Education.** The aspect of environmental consciousness should be integrated in the entire educational process.

6. **Mathematics Teaching.** The teaching of mathematics will be suitably redesigned to bring it in line with modern technological devices like computers.
7. **Science Education.** Science education programmes will be designed to enable the learner to acquire problem solving and decision-making skills and to discover the relationship of science with health, agriculture, industry and other aspects of daily life.
8. **Sports and Physical Education.** A nation-wide infrastructure for physical education, sports and games will be built into the educational edifice. Appropriate encouragement will be given to those talented in sports and games. Due stress will be laid on indigenous traditional games. Yoga will receive special attention.

XII. Re-Orientantion of the Process of Education

(1) Special attention will be paid to the production of quality books for children including text-books and work books.

(2) Provision will be made in all educational institutions for library facilities.

XIII. Media and Educational Technology

(1) Educational technology willbe employed in the spread of useful information, the training and retraining of teachers to improve quality, sharpen awareness or art and culture, inculcate abiding values, etc., both in the formal and non-formal sectors.

(2) Radio and T. V. programmes which clearly militate against proper educational objectives will be prevented.

(3) An active programme will be started to promote the production of children's film of high quality and usefulness.

XIV. The Evaluation Process and Examination Reform

Assessment of performance is an integral part of any process of learning and teaching. As a part of sound educational strategy, examinations should be employed to bring about qualitative improvement in education. The examination system will be recast so as to ensure a method of assessment that is a valid and reliable measure of student development and a powerful instrument for improving teaching and learning. Following measures will be taken in this regard:

1. The elimination of excessive element of chance and subjectivity.
2. The de-emphasis on memorisation.
3. Continuous and comprehensive evaluation that incorporates both scholastic and non-scholastic aspects of education, spread over the total span of instructional time.
4. Effective use of the evaluation process by teachers, students and parents.
5. Improvement in the conduct of examinations.
6. The introduction of concommitant changes in instructional material and methodology.
7. The use of grades in place of marks.
8. The predominance of external examinations will be reduced.

XV. The Teacher

1. **Status of the Teacher.** The status of the teacher reflect the socio-cultural ethos of a society. The pupils cannot rise above the levels of their teachers. The Government and the community should endeavour to create conditions which will help motivate and inspire teachers on constructive and creative lines. Teachers will continue to play a crucial role in the formulation and implementation of educational programmes.
2. **Freedom to Teacher.** Teachers should have the freedom to innovate, to devise appropriate methods of communications and activities relevant to the needs and capabilities of and the concerns of the community.
3. **Pay and Service Conditions**
   (i) The pay and service conditions of teachers have to be commensurate with their social and professional responsibilities and with the need to attract talent to the profession.
   (ii) Efforts will be made to reach the desirable objectives of uniform emoluments, service conditions and grievance—removal mechanisms for teachers throughout the country.
   (iii) The methods of recruiting teachers will be recognized to ensure merit, objectivity and conformity with spatial and functional requirements.

(iv) Guidelines will be formulated to ensure objectivity in the postings and transfers of teachers.

(v) A system of teacher evaluation will be created.

(vi) Reasonable opportunities of promotion to higher grades will be provided.

(vii) Norms of accountability will be laid down with incentives for good performance and disincentives for non-performance.

4. **Teacher's Organisations.** Teacher's organisations must play a significant role in upholding professional integrity and enhancing the dignity of teacher. They should help in curbing professional misconduct. National level associations of teachers will prepare a National Code of Professional Ethics for Teachers and see to its observance in cooperation with Government.

5. **Teacher Education.** The system of teacher education will be overhauled by taking the following steps:

   (i) District Institutes of Education and Training (DIET) will be established to organize pre-service and in-service courses for elementary school teachers and for the personnel working in non-formal and adult education.

   (ii) Selected Secondary Teacher Training Colleges will be upgraded.

   (iii) The National Council of Teacher Education will be provided the necessary resources and capability to accredite institutions of teacher education and provide guidance regarding curricula and methods.

   (iv) A network arrangement will be created between institutions of teacher education and university departments of education.

XVI. The Management of Education

1. **Decentralisation.** More stress will be laid on the decentralisation of educational institutions.
2. **Central Advisory Board of Education.** It will play a pivotal role in reviewing educational development.
3. **Indian Education Service.** A proper management structure in education will entail the establishment of the Indian Education Service as an All India Service.

4. **State Advisory Boards of Education.** State Governments may establish State Advisory Boards of Education on the lines of Central Advisory Board of Education.
5. **District Boards of Education.** District Boards of Education will be created to manage education up to the higher secondary level.

XVII. Important Role of the Head of an Institution

An important role must be assigned to the head of an educational institution. Heads will be specially selected and trained.

XVIII. School Complexes

School complexes will be promoted so as to serve as networks of institutions and synergistic alliance to encourage professionalism among teachers, to ensure observance of norms of conduct and to enable the sharing of experiences and facilities.

XIX. Local Committees

They will be assigned a major role in programmes of school improvement.

XX. Voluntary Agencies and Aided Institutions

Non-government and voluntary efforts including social activist groups will be encouraged, subject to proper arrangements.

XXI. Resources

(1) Resources to the extent possible will be raised by mobilizing donations, asking the beneficiary communities to maintain school buildings and supplies of some consumables.
(2) Fees at the higher levels of education will be raised.
(3) Effecting some savings by efficient use of facilities.
(4) Institutions involved with research and the development of technical and scientific manpower will be asked to mobilize some funds by levying a cess or charge on the user agencies.

XXII. Review

The implementation and parameters of the New Policy must be reviewed every five years.

EDUCATIONAL PHILOSOPHY OF NEW POLICY

1. **New Acculturating role of Education.** One of the most important contributions of New Policy of Education is that

it has provided a comprehensive educational philosophy covering the new acculturating role of education by way of refining sensitiveness, building scientific temper and cultivating independence of mind and spirit.

2. **Natural Perspective.** Manpower planning and its educational investment has brought in a national perspective to our development needs. A unifying policy in the development of human resources provides a social dimension to an area of personal perception. The pooling of resources in the area of personnel and research at the national level with the provision for interregional mobility with equal access for every Indian of requisite merit is a most welcome and a timely policy statement.
3. **Universalisation.** The universalisation of education up to a given level with access of education of a comparable quality is another positive aspect of the policy.
4. **Equalisation.** The special emphasis laid on the removal of disparities and equalization of opportunity by attending to the specific needs of different groups of distressed people including women, scheduled castes, minorities and the handicapped, should enhance the sense of social responsibility and a fair distribution of justice to all concerned.
5. **Efficiency.** The policy determination to promote efficiency and effectiveness at all levels (though easier said that done) brings in new dimension in the performance of teachers, students, administrators. Government officials and institutions.
6. **Beneficial.** The realisation the education needs to be managed in an atmosphere of utmost intellectual rigour, seriousness of purposes with adequate freedom for innovation and creativity should bear beneficial fruits.
7. **Cultural Perspective.** Another special feature of the policy is the concept of providing a cultural perspective to the formal system of education.
8. **Value Education.** The focus on value education and work experience as an integral part of the learning process will enable us to uphold human values necessary for raising the quality of life for all. The document speaks about combating certain negative values and promoting positive ones from

our heritage. It mentions social, ethical and moral values which have to be cultivated.

The Essence and Role of Education

The policy has envisaged the role of education as follows:

1. Education is fundamental to our all round development, material and spiritual.
2. Education is the highway to derive the maximum benefit from the areas already created by the economic and technical development and a means to ensure that the funds must reach all sections.
3. Education needs to be planned meticulously and developed with great sensitivity so as to make the best use of the human being who is a positive asset and precious national resource.
4. Education must prevent the erosion of long-cherished values.
5. Education should assist in the realisation of goals of secularism, socialism and professional ethics.
6. Education should be an effective instrument of reducing rural urban disparities.
7. Spread of literacy and education among women is the largest single factor in bringing down the growth of population in India.
8. Education should develop the activity of the coming generation to internalize new ideas constantly and creatively.
9. Education should imbibe the coming generations with a strong commitment of human values and to social justice.
10. Education has an acculturating role. It refines sensitivity and perceptions that contribute to national cohesion, a scientific temper and independence of mind and spirit.
11. Education develops manpower for different levels of the economy.
12. Education is a unique investment in the present and the future.

THE NATIONAL SYSTEM OF EDUCATION

The National Policy on Education, 1986 has envisaged the following main features of the National Systems of Education.

1. **Based on Constitutional Principles.** It derives its inspiration from the ideals and values of democracy, secularism and socialism enshrined in our Constitution.
2. **Access to Education.** It implies that up to a given level all students, irrespective of caste, creed, location, sex, have access to education of a comparable quality. To achieve this, the Government will initiate appropriately funded programmes. Effective measures will be taken in the direction of the Common School System recommended in the 1968 policy.
3. **Common Educational Structure.** It envisages a common educational structure. The 10 + 2 + 3 structure has now been accepted in all parts of the country. Regarding the further break-up of the first 10 years efforts will be made to move towards an elementary system comprising five years of primary education and three years of upper primary, followed by two years of High School.
4. **National Curricular Framework with a Common Core.** It will be based on a national curricular framework which contains a common core along with other components that are flexible. The common core will include the history of India's freedom movement, the constitutional obligations and other contents essential to nurture national identity. These elements cut across subject areas and will be designed to promote values such as India's common cultural heritage, egalitarianism, democracy and secularism, equality of the sexes, protection of the environment, removal of social barriers, observance of the small family norms and inculcation of the scientific temper. All educational programmes will be carried on in strict conformity with secular values.
5. **Education for International Understanding.** India has always worked for peace and understanding between nations, treating the whole world as one family. True to this hoary tradition, education has to strengthen this world view and motivate the younger generations for international co-operation and peaceful coexistence. This aspect cannot be neglected.
6. **Equality of Opportunity in Education.** To promote equality it will be necessary to provide for equal opportunity to all

not only in access, but also in the conditions for success. Besides, awareness of the inherent equality of all will be created through the core curriculum. The purpose is to remove prejudices and complexes transmitted through the social environment and accident of birth.

7. **Minimum Levels of Learning.** Minimum levels of learning will be laid down for each stage of education. Steps will also be taken to foster among students an understanding of the diverse cultural and social systems of the people living in different parts of the country.
8. **Promotion of Languages.** Besides the promotion of the link language, programmes will also be launched to increase substantially the translation of books from glossaries. The young will be encouraged to undertake the rediscovery of India each in his own image and perception.
9. **Universal Character of Higher Education.** In higher education in general and technical education in particular, steps will be taken to facilitate interregional mobility by providing equal access to every Indian of requisite merit, regardless of his origins. The universal character of universities and other institutions of higher education is to be understood.
10. **Priorities in Educational Reform.** The Nation as a whole will assume the responsibility of providing resource support for implementing programmes of educational transformation, reducing disparities, universalisation of elementary education, adult literacy, scientific and technical research, etc.
11. **Open and Distance Learning.** Life-long education is a cherished goal of the education process. This presupposes universal literacy. Opportunities will be provided to the youth, house-wives, agricultural and industrial workers and professionals to continue the education of their choice, and the pace suited to them. The further thrust will be in the direction of open and distance learning.
12. **Strengthening of National Institutions.** National institutions which will be strengthened to play an important role in giving shape to the National System of Education, are the University Grants Commission. The All India Council of Technical Education, the Indian Council of Agricultural

Research and the Indian Medical Council. Integrated Planning will be instituted among all these bodies so as to establish functional linkages and reinforce programmes of research and postgraduate education. These, together with the National Council of Education Research and Training, the National Institute of Educational Planning and Administration and the International Institute of Science and Technology Education will be involved in implementing the Education Policy.

13. **Meaningful Partnership.** Concurrence signifies a partnership which is at once meaningful and challenging. The Centre and the State shall give effect to it in letter and spirit.

MERITS OF THE NEW POLICY ON EDUCATION

The 1986 policy laid down under the 12 heads containing 156 paragraphs is a comprehensive statement. It includes all the important ideas and ideals to reform and transform education in India to meet the needs of our fast developing technological society. Sincere efforts of a great magnitude will have to be made by all concerned in the implementation of the educational reforms. Important merits of the New Policy on Education are as under:

1. **Basic Values.** The New Education Policy is based on the basic and essential values underlying the Preamble of our Constitution.
2. **The Total Man.** The New Educational Policy aims at the education of the whole man, the total man with commitment to higher values.
3. **Synthesis.** The New Education Policy is built on the foundations of ancient spirituality, modern culture and technical sophistication; history being its past experience and modern knowledge its present instrument to achievements in the future.
4. **Framework.** By linking education to development, on the one hand, and to national unity and integration, on the other, it has provided a framework which is of current relevance and urgency.
5. **National Pattern.** The New Education Policy continues to be within the existing national pattern of 10 + 2 + 3.

6. **Developmental.** The design of education is truly developmental in character, enabling the students to discover, develop and discipline their talents, abilities and skills.
7. **Core Curriculum.** While emphasizing the need for a national curriculum, it provides for a core curriculum to give adequate scope for accommodating local and regional needs.
8. **Minimum Standards.** The new system of education provides for a national minimum standard of achievement for the different stages and levels from primary to the university, including professional education.
9. **Targets.** By stressing the need of defining minimal national standards in terms of competence and learning outcomes in all subjects and for the different stages, it has focused our attention to have clear targets to attain, both for teachers and students.
10. **Performance.** It stresses performance accounting at every level, from the individual school to the highest level.
11. **Decentralisation.** Decentralised educational supervision as proposed is likely to provide more impetus to local initiative.
12. **Check on Standards.** It will decrease the present undue stress on getting marks in public examinations, by fair or unfair means and help the supervising institutions to keep a check on standards and performance.
13. **Self-Employment.** The new education policy aims at overhauling the educational systems in such a way that the students are able to practise their own vocations instead of looking for Government jobs.
14. **Anti-Prejudice.** The new education policy intends to remove narrowmindedness from pupil's mind.
15. **Vocational.** There is the much needed thrust on vocational education under the New Education Policy. Practical and workable suggestions have been made to change the contents of education so as to make youth an instrument of evolving a new developed, self-reliant, socialist and democratic India.
16. **Equalisation.** The New Education Policy has suggested important measures for minimising inequalities of opportunity of education on account of status and wealth.

17. **Job Opportunities.** The new system of education has proposed planned linkages with real job opportunities and the world of work.
18. **Delinking of Degrees.** The New Education Policy has rightly accepted that degrees have no longer remained pious documentary proof of one's learning and knowledge. Degree or diploma is not considered a last word of educational achievements.
19. **Reduction in Rush for Degrees.** The recommendations regarding 'Delinking of Degrees from jobs' that is to refrain employing agencies from prescribing the degrees as essential qualification for a job is likely to reduce the mad rush and craze for higher education. When 'workability' and 'performance' are given preference to degrees, degrees will automatically lose their lustre attractions and false values attached. Jobs like doctors and engineers for which degrees are essential as a basic qualification will be identified and set aside as exceptions.
20. **Women Development.** The New Education Policy has accepted the need for infusing a spirit of boldness and self-confidence among women.
21. **Population Education.** The New Education Policy has identified the role of population in the development and needs of the society.
22. **Open Universities.** Open Universities for higher education are to be expanded besides formal educational institutions through distance education, self-studies, correspondence courses, evening classes, Open University/Mobile University, special studies institutes, etc.
23. **Integration with Culture.** It is for the first time that the policy lays down that integration of culture in education will be a must.
24. **Primacy of Learner.** The New Education Policy envisages a place of primacy to the learner in the learning process. Self-learning and learning by doing have been recommended. Inter-active teaching and relating the process of learning with environment have been emphasised to promote a spirit of discovery and inventiveness.

EIGHT BOLD STEPS

1. **National System of Education.** National system of education to provide access to education of a comparable quality to all students, to have a common educational structure with national curricular framework containing a common core.
2. **Navodaya Schools.** Pace setting Navodaya Schools to be started which will be residential and free of charge.
3. **Vocational Targets.** Vocational courses to cover 10 per cent of higher secondary students by 1990 and 25 per cent by 1995.
4. **Delinking Degree from Jobs.** Beginning to be made in delinking degrees from jobs in selected areas.
5. **Performance and Accountability.** To ensure that all teachers should teach and all students study.
6. **The Management of Education.** Evolving a strategy of decentralization and the creation of a spirit of autonomy for educational institutions.
7. **Indian Education Service.** Constitution of this Service is likely to bring a national perspective in education.
8. **Raising Resources.** Resources to be raised through (i) asking beneficiary communities to maintain school buildings, (ii) raising fees at the higher levels of education, and (iii) levying cess or charge on the user agencies.

Missing Links and Limitations of the New Education Policy

1. **Confined to Privileged.** A lion's share of the benefit of education is cornered by about six per cent of students who have been fortunate to join colleges. It is this privileged section which comers 99 per cent of Government jobs. Educational expenditure has become a mechanism of transferring resources from rural sector to urban sector or in other words from poor to the rich.
2. **Neglect of Neighbourhood Concepts.** The New Education Policy has completely ignored the 'neighbourhood' concept of school system advocated by the Kothari Commission. It is interesting to note that the Kothari Commission considered that the 'neighbourhood school' was a step towards eliminating the segregation that now takes place between the schools for the poor and the underprivileged classes and those for the rich and the privileged one.

3. **Wrong Basis of Reservation.** The New Education Policy should have suggested reservation not on the basis of merit but on the basis of economic conditions.
4. **Need of Basic Education.** The Education Policy does not refer to Basic Education although it has an important place in the ideology of freedom struggle and procedures were finalised as long back as 1937.
5. **No Reference to Working Days.** The New Education Policy should have recommended increased number of working days in educational institutions. There should be about 300 working days instead of about 200 at present.
6. **No Check on Minority Institutions.** Some suitable checks on the working of the schools run by the minority communities should have been proposed so as to prevent them from exploiting the staff working in these institutions.
7. **No Check on Nursery Schools.** The New Education Policy has not mentioned concrete steps to curb the mushroom growth of nursery schools charging high fees and meant only for the rich.
8. **No Check on Public Schools.** The New Education Policy has, by and large, evaded the issue of the 'loot' by so-called public schools which take money only and do not give good education.
9. **No Supervision.** The New Education Policy does not include specific measures for supervising and monitoring Government and Central schools properly. There is an urgent need to ensure that, 'All teachers should teach and all students study'.
10. **Lack of Teachers and Equipments.** The emphasis on teaching and learning through discovery has little meaning as the nation has thousands of schools without adequate teachers and equipment.
11. **No Research Basis.** There is practically no proposal in the documents which is based on authentic research.
12. **Multiplication of Authorities.** Setting up State Advisory Boards of Education, District Institutes of Education and District Boards of Education is not likely to serve any useful purpose. Already there is a multiplicity of authorities in the field of education.

13. **Lack of Funds.** There is very little hope of obtaining community funds for educational purposes as there is a growing tendency on the part of the rich members of the community to contribute liberally to political parties due to obvious reasons. People, in general, are not motivated to donate funds for welfare services.
14. **No Fixed Target.** It is very unfortunate that no target has been fixed in different areas of reforms.
15. **Financial Side Ignored.** Financial implications of the implementation of educational reforms have not been worked out.

EVALUATION AND IMPLEMENTATIONS OF THE POLICY

1. **Programme of Action.** In order to be workable any effective plan of action must be backed by financial and personnel resources otherwise it will remain a 'paper' plan or theoretical statement of intent, just an idealistic empty document. In an article entitled *Education: A Development View* in *The Hindustan Times* dated March 22, 1986 Manmohan Singh observed, "So much has been said, suggested and recommended that when it comes to implementation, the budgetary constraints make a mincemeat of our educational aspirations. We have to be perhaps ruthlessly realistic about our economic and budgetary constraints. There is no point in trying to apply one cubic inch of butter to a square mile of bread. Such an attempt would imply a realignment of priorities in educational investment and discarding a part of the bandwagon. Unfortunately the document, Programme of Action, has completely overlooked this basic fact."
2. **Evolving the Correct Order of Priorities.** After determining the availability of funds, one must draw out the order of priorities in the field of educational reforms and fix our targets in physical terms.
3. **Command, Control and the Management of Education.** Some areas of educational reforms do not require any additional funds. One such area is the management of education. Two factors play a major role in the effective implementation of any programme: identification and stability. Both are wanting in the present system of educational administration, management and planning.

In almost all the States and the Union Territories in India, the two key posts of the Secretary of Education and the Director of Education are conventionally entrusted to persons belonging to the I.A.S. cadre. The story is no different at the Ministry of Human Resource Development, Government of India and in the Planning Commission. These incumbents are not committed and change hands frequently. Their stay is usually so short that by the time they acquaint themselves with the working of the Education Department they are transferred. Thus they are unable to make any substantial contribution. They do not provide effective professional guidance and inspiration to teachers, principals, education officers and supervisors. Nor do they have needed interest or commitment and motivation, and they are keen to move up or away before the consequences of their vague efforts come to roots, to become milestone around them or their successors' necks. The framers of the National Policy on Education and the Programme of Action have completely ignored this aspect. The recommendation for the constitution of an Indian education service is heartening, but the programme of action does not hold out any hope for its early implementation. The technocrats should be immediately replaced by dedicated contractual teachers in the administration, management and planning of education so as to provide the much needed confidence, grassroot professional competence, guidance, inspiration and motivation to the academic staff working in the field of education. The proven men and women of classroom and field experience will be able to implement the break through transformation needed.

Educational administration, management and planning must be professionalised. India is amidst new ideas and attitudes. By ignoring this vital reform needed in education the nation has already paid a heavy price since independence. This reform does not involve any additional fund. The nation can ignore this only at its peril. The missions and committees have failed at the implementation stage on account of neglect of this aspect of the personnel of educational administration, management command and control. Educators not bureaucrats can provide the needed thrust for success.

4. **Strengthening Elementary Education.** The crucial role of universal elementary education for strengthening the fabric of democracy through the provisions of equal opportunities to all for the development of their inherent individual potential has been accepted from the very birth of Indian Republic in the form of Article 45 under the Directive Principles of State Policy in the Constitution. Government have failed miserably to fulfil obligations to achieve universal elementary education within ten years of the enactment of the Constitution.

   Thus one finds neglect of primary school education and the undue emphasis on university education. Numerous departments have been opened in the universities without due regard to financial aspects. In some cases, the members of the faculty outnumber the number of students. Proliferation of departments and bifurcation of universities are alarming signals of intellectual bankruptcy. Primary school education has to be strengthened and given top priority in the field of educational reforms. Most of this ill is existing in the domain of Indian education. The provisions of outlays required for achieving the constitutional goals in respect of elementary education should be considered a national responsibility.

5. **Operation Black-board.** Operation Blackboard should be given priority. All primary schools (Class I to V) with about five sections each should be supplied with three black-boards preferably green chalk-boards, per school. All single teacher schools should be provided with at least one black-board. Provision should be made for about 4 lakh black-boards for 1.3 lakh schools without black-boards. 70,000 black-boards would be needed for about equal number of teachers schools without black-board. Similarly, definite targets may be fixed in respect of the supply of 'tatpattis', furniture, buildings, etc., to primary schools. Priority to the 'Operation Black-board' will give the satisfaction that Government has met the basic minimum needs of all elementary schools in the country.

6. **Retention of Students at the Elementary Stage.** It has been estimated that out of 100 students enrolled in Class I only

23 children reach Class VIII. The rest return to the mass of illiterates in the country. One of the important reasons of dropouts is the detention of a student in a class. Non-detention policy must be effectively implemented up to Class VIII. This reform envisages no financial burden. Incentives and support services should be provided for girls and boys of the economically weaker sections of society subject to availability of funds.

7. **Review of Institutions like Jawaharlal Nehru University and the Indian Institute of Management.** While thousand of primary schools are without buildings, blackboards and chalks, Government are spending huge sums on institutions like J.L. Nehru University, Indian Institutes of Technology (IITs) and Indian Institutes of Management (IIMs).
8. **Institutional Plans.** The Education Commission, 1964-65, emphasised that no comprehensive programme of educational development can ever be put across unless it involves every educational institution. Planning for each institution provides important and basic links in the planning process. Keeping in view the resources for a period of one year every institution must plan its growth and development in the beginning, and long range plans after ensuring sound footing. Institutional plan should form the basis of District, State and Central plans. Implemented of the plans must be closely associated with the formulations of plans.
9. **Review of the Work of the National Organisations like the NCERT.** The document *'Challenge of Education — A Policy Perspective, 1985'* issued by the Ministry of Education, Government of India has observed, The three major expert bodies at the national level which should play some role in educational planning are the National Council of Educational Research and Training (NCERT), the National Institute of Educational Planning and Administration (NIEPA) and the University Grants Commission (UGC). If the preceding paragraphs have any validity, the conclusion that these bodies have not so far met with the expected

response becomes inescapable. Their efforts to improve the content and quality of education, modifying priorities and objectives and correlating the qualitative output of educated manpower with the requirement of these for various tasks connected with national production and development, have not succeeded, mainly because the real initiative for planning is entirely in the hands of State Government. However, it would be wrong to put the blame on the State Governments alone. Programmes of these organisations have hitherto lacked reality and practical purpose. Their approach has been devoid of a sound pragmatic outlook, with some useful exceptions like the core curriculum.

Organisations like the NCERT, NIEPA, SCERT have contributed very little to the development of education in India. They flourish in complete isolation in their 'Ivory Towers', as 'White Elephants'. The money and resources used on them would very profitably be spent on practical target oriented important priority programmes which should be assigned for them by professional field-teachers. If these organisations do not change their style of working, they will prevent successful educational transformation in India. They should be improved by establishing monitoring cells for the implementation of the National Policy on Education, by motivated and experienced personnel manning the educational controls. These national organisations have become 'False Public Utilities'. There is no machinery to evaluate the work of these national organisations as they enjoy a fair amount of autonomy. In launching various projects which have no relevance they can virtually do anything they please. Their autonomy and freedom must be accompanied by accountability.

10. **Adult Education Programmes to be Financed by Industry and Voluntary Organisations.** It has been observed in the 'Challenge of Education' that 'the Adult Education Programme has, thus been far from impressive'. If past performance is any index, it is likely to remain unimpressive in Mure also. The reasons are quite obvious. Government should undertake a radical review of this performance

before granting money. A percentage of the resources earmarked for adult education may be diverted towards the expansion and enrichment of elementary education and over the urgently needed vocationalisation of education. There is need to establish linkages between the Adult Education Programme and Non-formal Education, and Vocational Education through Industry. Big business establishments may be asked to take up literacy programmes for their workers. Autonomous organisations could look after the literacy needs of their employees. Voluntary organisations may be provided more support for taking up adult education programmes. Village panchayats could be allowed to augment their resources for shouldering this responsibility of educating the illiterate villagers.

11. **Consolidation of Higher Education.** Only 4.8 per cent of the relevant age group is enrolled in higher education in India and the proportion is even more adverse in some categories, particularly for women, scheduled castes and scheduled tribes. It would be suicidal to go on absorbing scarce resources without attaining even the minimum standards laid down by the University Grants Commission. Proliferation of non-viable educational institutions will have to be discontinued as resources are limited.

    The drop-outs and failures which account for more than 59 per cent of the students enrolled, represent a colossal waste of human and material resources. This must be checked. Suitable direction should be issued so that results of the annual examinations are moderated appropriately. It has been found that examination results depend on chance and environmental factors. When tools of assessment are not fully objective and valid, students should not be allowed to suffer. The number of effective working days and hours in a year should be increased.

    Priority in research to only those programmes should be given which will lead to the practical application of technology, the needs of villages and rural areas.

12. **Rethinking on the Present System of Inspection and Supervision.** The recommendations of the Secondary Education Commission (1952-53), the Kothari Commission

(1964-66), the Study Group (1969) and other committees have made no impact on the system of inspection and supervision. It has neither achieved the objective of frightening the teachers into putting in their best nor even the objective of inspiring and providing professional guidance to teachers. It has failed to apprise the work of the educational institutions objectively and scientifically. It has also failed to provide constructive guidance to teachers and principals. District Inspectors of Schools have become 'educational post offices' which receive letters and instructions from the headquarters and 'pass' these on to the institutions, and *vice-versa.* The present system of inspection and supervision hardly makes any substantial contribution to the promotion of educational standards. A majority of the inspecting staff may be diverted to other priority areas like actual teaching and field-institutionally based supervision with set deadlines and targets.

13. **Less Emphasis on Seminars, etc.** There is a wide gap in India in educational theory and practice. Most of the failures in education are due to this unfortunate gulf. Utopian ideas are given to the teachers during full-time and even in-service training courses, through educational conferences, seminars, training courses and workshops. The participants find it very difficult to spend the scheduled time fruitfully. Programmes related to the dissemination of the information on the National Policy on Education amply demonstrate their futility. The participants were not even supplied with a copy of the National Policy on Education.

    The 'fad' of bringing about reforms through speeches and sermons should be discarded. There should be down-to-earth involvement in in-service training of teachers so that they grow in stature. Optimum use should be made of limited financial resources. Each available rupee must be spent in providing the essential facilities to educational institutions and not on meeting travelling and dearness allowance of government officials and self-styled experts.

14. **Delinking of Degrees from Jobs.** Immediate steps must be taken to delink degrees from jobs, as everyone wants to join the queue for university education due to the high premium

on degrees. By delinking degrees from jobs, more funds would be available to be spent on school education.

15. **Navodaya Vidyalayas.** It is a right step towards egalitarianism. In it rural areas have been given adequate attention in providing quality education. A detailed strategy must be worked out to provide requisite staff and equipment to these schools from the very beginning. Half-hearted attempts are likely to lead to frustration. Lack of sufficient funds shall lower the target of setting up of one of such Vidyalaya in each district.
16. **Better Scales of Pay and Service Conditions of Teachers.** Immediate steps must be taken to ensure that the teachers enjoy a reasonable status and get emoluments commensurate with it. Recommendations of the National Commission on Teachers should be implemented immediately.
17. **Privatisation of Education.** The demand for the closure of public schools is not justified on two counts. First, the Government does not have the required funds to take over the schools. Secondly, the public schools maintain reasonably good standards. They may be asked to provide free education to at least five per cent of the students belonging to economically weaker sections.
18. **Vocationalisation of Education.** One of the important objectives of the 10+2+3 pattern of education was vocationalisation of education. It is regrettable that even after 11 years of the introduction of the scheme, the present intake of vocational programmes at the plus two level is covering only 2.5 per cent of the students population. It is not understood on what basis the programme of action has fixed the target at 10 per cent. No financial implications have been worked out. As *The Hindustan Times* observed in one of its editorials, it is time to find out why the earlier steps in that direction have come to grief. In view of new policy the target is to divert 10 per cent of the plus two stage students to the vocational stream by 1990. Vocationalisation means proper training for students in selected fields so that they can take up certain vocations without going in for purposeless higher education. Unless qualified teachers and adequate equipments are available, the training programme

will hardly succeed. Moreover, job opportunities should be provided for those who complete the training. It is hoped that the authorities have become wiser by the failure they have faced in vocationalisation of the education. It will be no mean achievement if the Government achieves the limited targets it has set in education.

19. **Accountability of Organisations.** The examination boards must realise that to conduct examinations and declare results as their sole function is not being responsible for the performance of students. The officers/officials of the boards should not consider themselves as 'Overlords' in the educational set-up. A review in their working is overdue.

20. **Optimum Utilisation of Existing Resources and Raising of Additional Funds.** India spends much less on education in terms of the proportion of gross national product in comparison to many countries. Expenditure on education in India is just three per cent. The proportion of gross national product spent on education in many countries ranges between six and eight per cent. Resources must be raised by mobilising donations, asking the beneficiary communities to maintain school building and supplies of some consummables, raising funds at the higher levels of education and effecting some saving by the efficient use of buildings. Institutions involved with research and the development of technical and scientific manpower should be asked to mobilise some hinds by levying a cess or charge on the user agencies. An estimate of the availability of such funds must be made immediately. These funds may be used for programmes falling in the second priority areas.

No new organisation with new staff should be set up for carrying out various programmes like the delinking of degrees from jobs, developing an alternate system of evaluation, vocalisation of education, opening of Navodaya Vidayalayas, etc. Most of the staff of NCERT, NIEPA, SCERT, etc., may be used for implementation and the monitoring of these schemes.

REVISED POLICY FORMULATIONS, MAY 1992

The National Policy on Education (NPE), 1986 is a landmark in educational development of the country. A review of the NPE, 1986 was conducted during 1990-92. The Central Advisory Board of Education (CABE) in its 47th meeting held on May 5-6,1992 considered the report of the CABE Committee on policy set-up to make an in-depth study of the report of the Committee for review of NPE, 1986. While broadly endorsing the policy, it recommended certain modifications in the light of the developments during the last few years and the experience gained in the implementation of the policy. The revised policy formulations containing these modifications recommended by the CABE were tabled in the Parliament on May 7,1992.

Following the adoption of the revised policy formulations in May 1992, a revised POA was prepared. The POA 1992 was tabled in the Parliament on August 19, 1992.

Universalisation of elementary education, equalisation of educational opportunities, women's education and development, vocationalisation of school education, consolidation of higher education, modernisation of technical education, improvement of quality content and process of education at all levels continue to be the themes of national endeavour in the field of education.

Elementary Education

The programme of universalisation of elementary education has been accorded the highest priority to fulfil the constitutional directive of providing universal, free and compulsory education to all children up to the age of 14 year. The revised Programme of Action, 1992 of the National Policy on Education, 1986 resolves to ensure free and compulsory education of satisfactory quality to all children up to 14 years of age before we enter the 21st century. Various Centrally sponsored schemes in the elementary education sector have been initiated to supplement the effort of States for achieving this target. 'Operation Blackboard' was started in 1987-88 to provide physical facilities in primary' schools all over the county. The revised Programme of Action, 1992 of the National Policy on Education, 1986 enlarged the scope of Operation Blackboard to provide three teachers in every primary school and to cover the upper primary schools. In order to operationalise the revised policy of the Government, the following three sub-schemes are proposed under Operation Blackboard during the Eighth Five-Year Plan: (i) Continuation of the on-going scheme to cover all the remaining schools identified in the Seventh Plan; (ii) expanding the scope of the scheme to provide three rooms and three teachers in primary schools; and (iii) extending the scope of the scheme to upper primary schools.

To achieve the goal of universalisation of elementary education, the Non-formal Education Programme has been put into operation in 1979-80 to provide education of a quality comparable to formal system to children who do not/cannot attend school, school drop-outs, girls who cannot attend whole-day schools and working children. This scheme was reorganised and expanded in 1987-88. The scheme covers ten educationally backward States *viz.* Andhra Pradesh, Assam, Arunachal Pradesh, Bihar, Jammu and Kashmir, Madhya Pradesh, Orissa, Rajasthan, Uttar Pradesh, West Bengal and areas of urban slums, hilly desert and tribal areas and areas of concentration of working children in all other States and Union Territories. Under the scheme, assistance is given to the States/Union Territories in the ratio of 50:50 and 90:10 for running general (co-educational) and girls centres respectively. Hundred per cent assistance is given to voluntary agencies for running non-formal education centres and undertaking experimental and innovative projects. About 2.55 lakh centres have been sanctioned so far. The programme of NFE are proposed to be continued and revised in the Eighth Plan.

In elementary education the focus has been shifted from enrolment *perse,* to retention and achievement. The focus also shifted from exclusive concern with schooling to a holistic perception which stressed the need of providing alternative system of education of comparable quality to working children and girls whom the school cannot reach. The concepts of participative micro-planning and local-level capacity building were given wide currency and tested as well as tried through experimental projects. They are today important elements of the strategy to achieve universalisation of elementary education.

Sector-Wise Plan Outlay/Expenditure on Education

(Rupees in Crores)

Sector	Sixth Plan Expenditure				Seventh Plan Expenditure				Eighth Plan Qutlay			
	Centre	State	Total	Percentage	Centre	State	Total	Percentage	Centre	State	Total	Percentage
Elementary Education	72.40	768.99	841.39	32.01	723.80	2142.07	2865.87	37.05	288.00	6065.46	8936.36	45.06
Adult Education	61.75	91.01	153.36	5.09	309.15	380.65	609.80	8.00	1400.00	394.44	1799.44	9.06
Secondary Education	16.75	517.64	534.39	20.04	558.31	1093.59	1651.90	21.60	—	—	—	—
Higher Education	242.82	317.58	560.40	21.04	631.46	460.13	1091.59	14.30	—	—	—	—
Others	92.02	164.29	256.31	9.08	198.54	250.32	448.86	5.90	—	—	—	—
Technical Education	135.80	137.06	272.86	10.04	615.40	349.91	349.71	12.70	824.00	1962.38	2786.38	14.20
Total Education	621.54	1997.17	2618.73	100.00	3036.66	4596.47	4596.47	100.00	7443.00	12156.73	19599.73	100.00

Source: Ministry of Human Resource Development

In pursuance of the provisions of NPE on teacher education a Centrally-sponsored scheme of Restructuring and Reorganisation of Teacher Education was launched in 1987-88. So far 334 DIET, 44 CTEs and 18 IASEs have been established throughout the country to impart good quality or pre-service and in- service training to teachers.

Secondary Education

Education is free up to secondary stage (Class X) in Andhra Pradesh, Arunachal Pradesh, Assam, Bihar, Goa, Himachal Pradesh, Jammu and Kashmir, Karnataka, Kerala, Nagaland, Sikkim, Tamilnadu, Tripura, West Bengal, Andaman and Nicobar Islands, Dadra and Nagar Haveli, Daman and Diu, Lakshadweep and Pondicherry. In Jammu and Kashmir, Sikkim, Tripura, West Bengal, Andaman and Nicobar Islands, Dadra and Nagar Haveli and Pondicherry, free education is provided even up to the higher secondary stage. Gujarat offers free education up to class XI for boys and class XII for girls. In Haryana, Punjab, Madhya Pradesh, Manipur, Orissa, Rajasthan, Uttar Pradesh, Delhi and Chandigarh, education is free up to class VIII for boys and girls. However, Haryana, Maharashtra, Rajasthan, Uttar Pradesh and Dadra and Nagar Haveli offer free education for girls up to class XII. In Maharashtra, education is free up to class VII for boys in Government schools. Meghalaya and Mizoram offer free education for boys and girls up to class VI and class VII respectively.

10+2 Structure of School Education

Starting from the Calcutta University Commission (1917-19), the 10+2 structure of school of pre-university education was recommended. This common structure was made a part of the National Policy on Education (NPE) 1986 also. All the States/UTs have adopted the 10+2 structure. However, the recommendation made in the NPE for a uniform pattern of duration in respect of the three sub-stages of first 10 years of schooling *i.e.* five years of primary (classes I-V), three years of upper primary (classes VI-VIII) and two years of secondary stage (classes IX & X); is yet to be implemented by all the States/UTs. In some States, the + 2 stage (*i.e.* classes XI & XII) is a part of the college system partly. The NPE has stipulated that the +2 stage should be brought within the school system gradually.

VOCATIONALISATION OF SECONDARY EDUCATION

Various committees and commissions on educational reforms have stressed the need for diversifying secondary education by introducing knowledge and skills that may prepare students for remunerative work without necessarily having to go in for higher education.

A Centrally-sponsored scheme of Vocationalisation of Secondary Education was started from February 1988. Under the scheme, financial assistance has been provided to State governments/UT administrations for introduction of vocational courses in schools at the + 2 stage. It has many components including conduct of area vocational surveys so that vocational courses to be introduced in selected institutions are need based, preparing curricula and course material, organising training of teachers, providing apprenticeship training and modification of recruitment rules to enable students from vocational stream to find employment in the organised sector.

Under the scheme, a Joint Council of Vocational Education (JCVE) has been set up at the national level for laying down policy guidelines, planning and coordination of vocational programmes conducted by different agencies and organisations. Two meetings of Joint Council of Vocational Education have been held on August 8,1990 and January 6,1993. A Standing Committee of the JCVE has also been set up under the chairmanship of the Union Education Secretary to ensure that the tasks laid down by JCVE are effectively performed. Two meetings of the Standing Committee of the JCVE have been held on September 12,1990 and June 29, 1991.

Up to 1993-94 16,450 vocational sections have been approved by the Central Government creating facilities for diversion of 8.22 lakh students to vocational streams at + 2 level. During 1992-93, till February 10, 1993, 1,623 vocational sections have been approved creating additional facilities for diversion of 0.81 lakh students to vocational streams. Job-linked vocational courses have been started in General Insurance, Life Insurance and Railway Commercial. Some health-related vocational courses have also been started. Certain State Governments/UTs have also started some vocational courses.

NATIONAL OPEN SCHOOL

'Open School', Delhi, the first of its kind in the country, was started by the Central Board of Secondary Education (CBSE),

Delhi in 1979. Based on a Project Report, the Government of India decided to establish the National Open School (NOS) as a registered society and an autonomous body under the administrative control of the Department of Education, Ministry of Human Resource Development in November 1989 and amalgamated the Open School with it. In October 1990 through a resolution of the government of India, the NOS was vested with authority to conduct its own bridge, secondary and senior secondary examinations and issue certificates. The NOS offers an alternative open learning system through distance education made to a heterogeneous clientele comprising the rural people, the urban poor, women, SC/ST, working adults and school drop-outs vs ho are unable to attend the formal school system. It takes education to the doorsteps of the motivated learners and allows them to study at their own pace at places and time convenient to them. The NOS has recently introduced a variety of vocational courses. During 1993-94, 17 vocational curriculum were started.

Currently, the National Open School has a cumulative active enrolment of over two lakh students, literally from every State and UT oflndia. In the last registration year of 1992-93, 57.14 per cent students were from educationally and socially disadvantaged categories, comprising women (37.29 per cent), scheduled castes and scheduled tribes (18.78 per cent), ex-servicemen (0.3 9 per cent) and handicapped (0.68 per cent) who are also provided fee concessions. In the NOS scheme of work, accredited institutions (AIs) have a central place and they provide various types of student services including personal contact programmes. Presently, the NOS has 339 AIs (300 for general education and 39 for vocational education) all over the country.

INTEGRATED EDUCATION FOR DISABLED CHILDREN

It has been established scientifically that disabled children with mild handicaps make better progress academically and psychologically if they study with the normal children. To integrate these children with others in common schools, a revised scheme of Integrated Education for Disabled Children was started during 1987-88. Under it, cent per cent financial assistance is given to State Governments/UT administrations/voluntary organisations for creating necessary facilities in schools. Admissible items of expenditure are books and stationery allowance, transport allowance, uniform allowance, readers allowance (for blind children), escort allowance (for orthopaedically handicapped with lower extremity disabilities), equipment allowance and wherever necessary hostel charges. Besides, the scheme also provides, among other things, to meet cost of salary and incentives for teachers, setting up of resource rooms, carrying out assessment of disabled children, training of teachers, removal of architectural barriers in schools, development and production of special instructional material for them. Assistance is also given through the University Grants Commission to the selected universities/ institutions to run training courses in special education for teachers of handicapped children. Training facilities are also provided by NCERT and four regional colleges of education. The scheme is at present in operation in Andhra Pradesh, Bihar, Goa, Gujarat, Haryana, Jammu and Kashmir, Himachal Pradesh, Karnataka, Kerala, Madhya Pradesh, Maharashtra, Manipur, Mizoram, Nagaland, Orissa, Punjab, Rajasthan, Tamilnadu, Uttar Pradesh, Delhi, Andaman and Nicobar Islands and Daman and Diu. By the end of 1993-94 about 40,000 disabled children in over 9,000 schools were covered under the scheme.

EDUCATIONAL CONCESSIONS TO CHILDREN OF ARMED FORCES PERSONNEL KILLED OR DISABLED DURING HOSTILITIES

The Centre and most of the State Governments and Union Territories offer educational concessions to children of the defence personnel and paramilitary forces killed or permanently disabled during Indo-China hostilities in 1962 and Indo-Pakistan operations in 1965 and 1971.

During 1988, these concessions were extended to children of IPKF/CRPF personnel who were killed/disabied during action in Sri Lanka and children of the armed forces personnel killed/ disabied in action in 'Operation Meghdoot' in Siachen area.

PROMOTION OF CULTURE/ART/VALUES AND INNOVATIVE PROGRAMMES

Assistance to Agencies/Educational Institutions

The National Policy on Education, 1986 calls for bridging the schism between the formal system of education and country's rich and varied cultural traditions. The policy also resolves to enrich the processes of education by cultural content, enable the children to develop sensitivity to beauty, harmony and refinement and to promote a Value Education to help eliminate obscurantism, religious fanaticism, and violence. In order to supplement the curricular inventions already made to actualise these goals, a Central plan scheme for assistance to agencies for strengthening culture/art/values in education and for assistance to educational institutions implementing innovative programmes was formulated in 1987 for providing assistance to Government agencies, educational institutions, Panchayati Raj institutions, registered societies, public trusts and non-profit making companies. Under the scheme, assistance is provided for (a) strengthening cultural/art input in the educational content and process; (b) strengthening of value education in the school system; and (c) implementation of pioneering and innovative programmes at the school stage.

During 1993-94, financial assistance of ₹ 75 lakh was provided to the 67 organisations. A decision has been taken to reformulate the existing scheme in order to make it more purposeful. The scheme has been reformulated to have the following two components: (i) strengthening culture and values in education; and (ii) strengthening the in-service training of art, craft, music and dance teachers.

Navodaya Vidyalayas

In order to provide good quality modern education to the talented children predominantly from the rural areas, Government of India launched in 1985-86 a scheme to establish Navodaya Vidyalaya on an average one in each district. 342 Navodaya Vidyalayas covering 24 States and seven Union Territories have been established in the country up to January 31,1994. Another 17 Vidyalayas have been sanctioned and are likely to be established during 1993-94.

Admission of Navodaya Vidyalaya is at the level of Class VI. In view of the fact that most of the students so admitted would have been taught earlier through the medium of the mother-tongue/regional language, instruction is provided through the same medium up to Class VI or VIII, during which time intensive teaching of Hindi/English both as a language subject and co-media is undertaken. Thereafter, the common medium would be Hindi/English. At this stage, there is a migration of 30 per cent students in Class IX from one Navodaya Vidyalaya to another Navodaya

Vidyalaya in a different linguistic region. The migration is mainly between Hindi and non-Hindi speaking districts.

Break-up of the students selected so far in 321 Navodaya Vidyalayas is as follows, as on January 31, 1994:

Boys	Girls	Rural	Urban	Genl.	SC	ST
84,548	35,755	93,058	27,245	81,438	24,772	14,093
70 per cent	30 per cent	77 per cent	33 per cent	67 per cent	21 percent	12 per cent

Navodaya Vidyalayas are residential, co-educational and primarily for children from rural areas. Hence, admission of children from urban areas is restricted to a maximum of one-fourth. Efforts are made to ensure that at least one-third of the students in each Navodaya Vidyalaya are girls. Reservation of seats in favour of children belonging to the scheduled castes and scheduled tribes is provided in proportion to their population in the concerned district, provided that in no district such reservation is less than the national average. At present, the overall percentages of SC/ST students admitted so far are 20 and 11 respectively. Girls accounted for 29 per cent.

Kendriya Vidyalayas

The scheme of Kendriya Vidyalayas was started in 1963-64, primarily for catering to the educational needs of the children of transferable Central Government employees including defence personnel, whose education was disrupted owing to transfer of the parents from one linguistic region to another and the resultant change in courses of study.

In 1965, the autonomous organisation, Kendriya Vidyalaya Sangathan, was established to handle the task of opening and managing Kendriya Vidyalayas. The organisationis wholly financed by the Government of India. Initially, 20 regimental schools, then functioning at places having large concentration of defence personnel, were taken over as Kendriya Vidyalayas during 1963-64. The number of Kendriya Vidyalayas at present is 796 in which 7 lakh students are studying. The number of employees sanctioned as on April 30, 1993 was 41712.25 Kendriya Vidyalayas were sanctioned during the academic session 1993-94.

Kendriya Vidyalayas have also distinguished themselves in co-curricular activities including games and sports, out-door activities, environmental educational programmes and fine and performing arts. Kendriya Vidyalaya students have been winning prizes every year in international and national competitions, essay competitions held by the Department of Environment, Government of India, besides awards and prizes in local and regional competitions. Most of the Kendriya Vidyalayas run nature and adventure clubs which are affiliated to the World Wild Life Fund of India and the National Adventure Foundation of India, respectively. About 10,000 students are trained in rock-climbing and about 550 are sent for trekking to glaciers every year. Kendriya Vidyalaya Sangathan has been given a status of a state by the School Games Federation of India and also of the Bharat Scouts and Guides.

EDUCATIONAL TECHNOLOGY PROGRAMME

An Educational Technology Programme was started in the Central sector during the Fourth Plan period in 1972 for widening access to and bringing about qualitative improvement in education. Under the scheme a Centre of Educational Technology was set up in the NCERT and cent per cent assistance was provided to 21 States for setting up of Educational Technology (ET) cells.

In view of the expansion of broadcasting facilities with the advent of INSAT and concommitment demand for educational software, the Ministry of Education decided to take on the responsibility of production of educational television programmes for relay through satellites. Accordingly, a scheme was prepared by the Ministry of Education for creating Educational Television (ETV) programme production facilities within the education sector on a decentralised basis by setting up Central Institute of Educational Technology (CIET) in the NCERT and State Institutes of Educational Technology (SIETs) in six States *viz.* Andhra Pradesh, Bihar, Gujarat, Maharashtra, Orissa and Uttar Pradesh and strengthening of ET cells in other States.

To meet the objectives of the National Policy on Education, 1986, the Educational Technology Scheme was revised in 1987 with the broad objectives of strengthening of both ETV and audio programme production capabilities and providing wider access to the same by supplying one lakh colour television (CTV) sets and five lakh radio-cum-cassette players (RCCPs) to primary schools during the Seventh Plan.

Programme production has commenced in CIET and all the six SIETs. In fact, from the academic year 1988-89, responsibility for programme production which was hitherto being shared between CIET and Doordarshanon 50:50 basis has been taken over by CIET and SIETs. The satellite based ETV service presently provides educational programmes of 45 minutes duration in each of the five regional languages *viz.* Gujarati, Hindi, Marathi, Oriya and Telugu telecast on time-sharing basis. The programmes for children are telecast from Monday to Friday and for primary level teachers on every Saturday. There are separate programmes for the children in the age group of 5-8 and 9-11 years on each day.

The ETV programmes are relayed by all high and low power transmitters in the six INSAT States. The programmes in Hindi are relayed by the other five Hindi speaking States also, namely Haryana, Himachal Pradesh, Madhya Pradesh, Punjab and Rajasthan and the Union Territory of Chandigarh.

The CIET has produced 715 ETV programmes up to September 1992 and 914 language versions. It has also produced 450 capsules for the programme of mass orientation of teachers during the summers of 1986, 1987, 1988 and 1989. The NCERT has set up a Committee to evolve modalities for involving outside producers to produce video films for CIET. As many as nine ETV video programmes commissioned to outside producers have been completed and another eight programmes are nearing completion.

Improvement of Science Education in Schools

In order to improve the quality of science education and promote a scientific temper as envisaged in NPE, a Centrally-sponsored scheme of Improvement of Science Education in Schools was started during the last quarter of 1987-88. Under this scheme, financial assistance is provided to States/Union Territories for provision of science kits to upper primary schools, upgrade and strengthen science laboratories in secondary and higher secondary schools, upgrade libraries in secondary and higher secondary schools, set up district resource centres for science education, development of instructional materials and training of science and mathematics teachers. It also provides assistance to voluntary organisation active in the field of science education for undertaking innovative projects and resource support activities in science education.

With a view to identifying and nurturing talent in mathematics at the school level, the International Mathematical Olympiad (IMO) is held every year. India has been participating in this Olympiad since 1989. An eight-member delegation comprising six student contestants, a team leader and a deputy team leader participated in IMO held in Moscow during July 1992. India ranked 22nd out of 64 participating countries. The Indian team won one silver and four bronze medals.

Environmental Orientation to School Education

In order to promote integration of educational programmes in the schools with environmental conditions, as envisaged in the NPE a Centrally-sponsored scheme of Environmental Orientation to School Education was started in 1988-89. Under the scheme, 100 per cent assistance is provided to the States, Union Territories and voluntary agencies on project basis. The project activities include review of curricular material preparation of textbooks/ instructional material/informative books/booklets/brochures/ posters/audio-visual material on environment, organisation of seminars for creating environmental consciousness and orientation of teachers. Voluntary organisations are assisted for taking up of various kinds of experimental and innovative programmes in this field.

Computer Education in Schools

A pilot project on Computer Literacy and Studies in Schools (CLASS) was initiated in 1984-85 in 248 selected secondary/higher secondary schools jointly by the Department of Electronics and the Department of Education to acquaint students and teachers with the range of computer applications and its potential as a learning medium. Till 1989-90,2,598 schools were covered under the project. 61 Resource centres were set up to train school teachers and provide logistic support to the participating schools. Installation of hardware and its maintenance continued to be the responsibility of Computer Maintenance Corporation (CMC). NCERT continued as the nodal agency for software development, academic support and organisation of teachers training. The Steering Committee for the project was jointly headed by the secretaries of the Department of Electronics and the Department of Education. Up to 1986-87, the schools received a set of two BBC micros, which was increased to five from 1987-88. Since the last financial year, a decision has been taken to provide an additional three BBC micros to 1,249 schools which have so far only two computers each. The evaluation of the project was done in 1986 by the Space Application Centre, Ahmedabad.

In pursuance of the objectives laid down in the NPE, an expanded programme was prepared in 1987-88 to cover 13,000 higher secondary schools all over the country. However, due to paucity of funds this was not finalised. The project is being reviewed for further expansion.

QUESTIONS FOR EXERCISE

1. Why was the National Policy on Education formulated? Describe its main provisions.
2. Explain briefly the educational philosophy of the New Policy on Education.
3. State the aims and functions of education as contained in the New Policy on Education.
4. State the main features of the National System of Education as envisaged in the National Policy on Education, 1986.
5. Explain the merits and limitations of the New Policy on Education.
6. Evaluate critically the recommendations of the New Education Policy and Programme of Action. Suggest suitable measures for the implementation of the policy.

CHAPTER 21

PROGRESS AND PROBLEMS OF PRIMARY AND BASIC EDUCATION

COMMITTEE ON PRIMARY EDUCATION (1951)

Introduction

The report of the Central Advisory Board of Education on post-war educational development in India (1944) (popularly known as the Sargeant Committee Report), had stated that the State governments should forthwith resume all educational powers and that school boards for smaller areas be set up in order to retain local interests, where some people with the requisite knowledge, enthusiasm, integrity and standing were available. In 1948 at the 18th meeting of the Central Advisory Board of Education, the Government of Bihar raised the question of relationships between the State governments and local bodies in respect of administration of elementary education. The Ministry of Education, therefore, appointed this Committee in 1951 with Shri B. G. Kher, Chief Minister, Bombay as chairman to examine, in detail the present set-up of local administration of education in the different States, the experiments carried out in some of the States in the assumption of more powers by the State Governments, the requirements of different State governments in this regard and to recommend a more or less uniform pattern which may, with a few variations, be adopted in all the States of India.

Major Recommendations

1. **Association of Local Bodies with the Administration of Primary Duration.** It would be an advantage to associate local bodies with the administration of primaiy education in some form or other.

2. Creation of Educational Bodies:

(i) ***Village Panchayats and Smaller Municipalities.*** In all village panchayats and smaller municipalities which have been given only a limited control over primary education, the local body should be required to elect a school committee and to delegate to it the task of supervising the local school or schools.

(ii) ***District Boards and Bigger Municipalities.*** In district local boards and in bigger municipalities which exercise wider powers over primary education, a school board be constituted and charged with the responsibility of looking after its educational powers as well as an administrative officer having adequate authority to carry on the day-to-day administration of its primary schools.

(iii) ***State Governments.*** The State governments should adopt the independent system of associating educational bodies with the corresponding local authorities generally.

(iv) ***Administrative Officers.*** The appointment of administrative officers should be obligatory under the statute in the case of all district school boards and the larger municipalities. They should be servants of the State Government.

3. Division of Authority on a Functional Basis:

(i) ***Inspection.*** Inspection should be regarded as a duty of the Government and should be carried out by government officers. All inspecting officers should be directly under the Government and the local bodies should have no control over them.

(ii) ***Training Institutions for Primary Teachers.*** State governments should be solely responsible for maintaining or aiding the requisite number of training institutions for primary teachers.

(iii) ***Authority to Define Curricula on Primary Level.*** The authority to define curricula or courses of study at the primary level should continue to vest in the State governments. But the local bodies should also be authorised, with the previous approval of the Director of Education, to introduce such variation in the prescribed curricula as they may deem necessary in view of local conditions.

(iv) ***Authority to Recruit and Control Primary Teachers.*** Every major municipality was authorised to administer primary school within its area. In every district school board the authority to recruit and control the teaching staff should vest in the Staff Selection Committee, the Administrative Officer, and the Appellate Tribunal constituted on lines similar to those adopted in Bombay.

(v) ***Service Conditions of Primary Teachers.*** The service conditions of primary teachers should be determined by the local bodies concerned with the sanction of State governments and as far as possible these should be uniform throughout the State.

(vi) ***Status of Primary Teachers.*** The primary teachers should continue to be treated as servants of local bodies as at present.

(vii) ***Text Books.*** State governments should prescribe, on the advice of official and non-official experts in the subject, the books to be used in primary schools. Where more than one book happens to be prescribed in a subject, the local body should have the freedom to choose any one of the prescribed books for use in schools under its control.

4. Division of Authority on the Basis of the Local Body Associated:

(i) ***City Corporations.*** The general policy should be to devolve as large an authority upon city corporations as possible.

(ii) ***Authorised Municipalities.*** The larger municipalities may be designated as 'authorised municipalities'. They will differ from corporations in three ways. First, the Government will actually conduct inspections instead of merely reserving the right to do so. Secondly, the general control of the Government will be a little more detailed and thirdly, the administrative officers should preferably remain the servants of State governments.

(iii) ***Non-Authorised Municipalities.*** The small municipalities which cannot be permitted to administer primary education in their areas will have to be treated at a still lower level.

(iv) ***Villages.*** The powers and duties of village school committees should be divided into two groups: the first group will include all those powers which a village school committee will have as soon as it is formed, and the second group will include all those powers which can be conferred on it by the District School Board, in view of its efficiency.

(v) ***District School Boards.*** The powers and duties of these bodies should be similar to those of the municipal school boards with two main differences; first the administrative officers of district school boards should necessarily be Government servants and secondly, there would be a greater indirect control by the Government through its financial sanctions that will be more frequently required here than in the case of municipal school boards.

5. Finance:

(i) The Union Government should assign specific grants for universal and compulsory primary education in the States.

(ii) A sum not less than 60 per cent of the total educational expenditure of the State should be spent on primary education.

(iii) State grants to local bodies on account of primary education should be based on a combination of the proportional grant (used to secure a broad equalisation as well as to provide for rapid expansion), a special grant for backward or necessitous areas, and specific purpose grants.

(iv) Grants for all primary education—whether voluntary or compulsory— should be statutory.

(v) The Municipal Acts should be amended so as to make the levy of all education cess obligatory on all municipalities. Where this is not possible, it would be in the interest of education to make it obligatory on municipalities to earmark a specified proportion of their total revenue for primary education. All funds thus earmarked for primary education should be entitled to receive grants-in-aid according to rules.

(vi) In village panchayats a portion of the total revenue should be earmarked for primary education.

6. Approved Schools:

(i) Local bodies associated with the administration of primary education should ordinarily be in charge of all primary schools in their area, whether maintained under their direct control or managed by private agencies.

(ii) The authority to control and guide the private primary schools in their areas should generally vest in the local bodies themselves.

(iii) The State Government should retain a few powers to themselves with a view to seeing that no hardships are caused to private enterprise.

(iv) Authority to make rules, regulations and by-laws regarding private schools should vest concurrently in the State governments, local bodies and the managements.

(v) Regarding grant or withdrawal of recognition to a private school, it is suggested:

(a) that the inspecting officers of the department should be required to cany out, in the first instance, an investigation into every proposal for the grant or withdrawal of recognition to a private primary school; and

(b) that the school board concerned should consider the report of such investigation and then decide whether recognition should or should not be granted, or should be withdrawn; and

(c) that any Party aggrieved by the order of the School Board should have the right to prefer an appeal to the Director of Education or to any other specified officers.

(iv) The authority to grant recognition should also be the authority to sanction grant-in-aid.

PROBLEMS OF PRIMARY EDUCATION AND THEIR REMEDIES

The Central Government has been giving the financial help to the provincial government for the expansion of primary education. The States which intend to expand primary education are given 34 per cent of the total annual expenditure in the form of financial help. Thus, the primary education has made a great progress, but due to certain reasons it cannot be said to be encouraging and satisfactory. This is due to the following problems:

1. **Defective Education Policy.** It was laid down in the Constitution of the independent India in 1950 that within a period of 10 years from the commencement of the Constitution, States shall endeavour to provide free and compulsory education to all children until they complete the age of 11 year It is regretted that the Government has not achieved complete success in this regard. The main cause for this is that the policy of the Government is based on idealism. Basic education has been accepted as the form of national education. Being inspired with this aim, work has been started to convert primary schools into basic schools. But in a country like India which has a vast population and where there is too much shortage of money, the implementation of the expensive schemes of basic schools is difficult. They admitted that it is not possible to implement the scheme of basic education in the whole of India within a short period. And yet the Government have been spending most of the money on basic education. Thus Government policy is based on idealism and is not taking active steps to expand primary education by adopting a practical and realistic attitude.

   Remedy: Definite Education Policy. The Government should first evolve a definite education policy. The best policy can be this that expansion of compulsory education and basic education should be separated from each other. Education in primary schools should be made compulsory. Slowly and gradually according to convenience that education may be converted into basic education.

2. **Political Difficulties.** Since the attainment of independence Indian Government had to face many problems and many of them still exist, *e. g.* the problem of native States, the problem of the refugees, the problem of Kashmir, the problem of different linguistic States, the problem of food, etc. These have to be removed for adequate growth of education.

   Remedy: Close Attention of Government. The political problems are such which may continue to exist for a long time. The government may have to face some more problems in the near future. However, if the government is responsible to solve the political problems of the country, it is also duty-bound to solve the problem of public education.

Even the political situation demands that the Government should implement the scheme of compulsory, free and universal education within the shortest possible time. To quote K. G. Saiydain, "While the political situation demands the immediate introduction of the scheme, the politicians are not keen enough to take it up." Therefore, the Government should devote proper attention and perform their duties towards the expansion of primary education.

3. **Defective Administration of Education.** The responsibility of the primary education is on the municipalities and the district boards. In most of the States of India, when the responsibility and the work of primary education was entrusted to these institutions, it was hoped that these institutions will speed up the work of the expansion of primary education. In due course, however, it became clear that these institutions have not risen equal to the occasion. Ordinarily there is lack of working capacity, interest and money in these institutions. The Acts relating to compulsory education have become out of date. There is no central institution or power which may compel these institutions to implement these Acts.

   Remedy: Reform in the Administration of Education. It is the responsibility of the nation to educate its citizens. The Government of India should take upon itself the sacred work of primary education. If the Government cannot shoulder the responsibility, then it should establish a powerful central institution, which may compel the district boards and the municipalities to start the work of compulsory primary education in their respective areas within a definite period.

4. **Dearth of Teachers.** It was estimated that to make the education compulsory 28 lakhs of teachers will be required. By the year 1979-80, only 86.8 per cent of teachers were trained. As compared to the city schools, there is great shortage of teachers in village schools.

   Remedy: Supply of Teachers. It cannot be a wise step to wait for making the education compulsory till the time when the desired number of trained teachers may be available. It is rather more essential that the salaries of the teachers should be increased. They should be provided more facilities and they should be attracted towards teaching work by conferring upon them more honour and respect. In the beginning, the teachers with essential qualifications can be selected as teachers, no matter whether they are trained or not. Thereafter, a definite number of teachers from among these teachers may be sent to training schools to undergo the training on Government expenses.

5. **Low Standard of Teaching, Untrained Teachers are not properly acquainted with Teaching Methods.** Only five per cent of the total teachers have qualifications of high school and middle pass; the rest of them are educated only up to primary stage. The primary schools are not using necessary implements of teaching due to shortage of money. Hence the education is uninteresting and its standard is low. Therefore it fails to attract children and their guardians.

   Remedy: Teacher's Training and Grant-in-Aid. Only trained teachers should be appointed in primary schools. The number of training schools should be increased. The training schools should be established not only in the urban areas but also in the rural areas so that men and women of the neighbouring places, may be attracted to receive training in them at less expenses.

   It would be the best if the government or local boards meet the whole expenditure of the training of the teachers. Enthusiastic and trained teachers find themselves unable to do much due to lack of the necessary means of education. The primary schools should be given liberal grant-in aid to enable them to purchase teaching equipments.

6. **Dearth of Money.** During the British period the Government met 30 per cent of the total expenditure incurred on primary education. In the independent India, this amount was increased to 34 per cent. This scanty help, however, is not adequate for making education compulsory.

   The expansion of primary education is not taking place properly due to shortage of money. It has been estimated that if compulsory basic education for the children of 6 to 14 years of age in the whole country is made, it will require an annual expenditure of ₹ 269.5 crore. To spend so much money on education is beyond the capacity of this poor country. Rupees 93 crore were spent on primary education in the First Five Year Plan but this amount was reduced to

₹ 89 crore in the Second Five Year Plan because of the need of money for other development work. In the Fourth Plan ₹ 241.3 crore were spent while the proposed outlay for the Fifth Plan was ₹ 743.0 crore.

Remedy: Our aim should not be to achieve qualitative increase in primary education but rather efforts should be made to educate as many children as possible so as to make them literate. G. K. Gokhale has rightly remarked, "Primary purpose of mass education is to banish illiteracy. Quality of education is a matter of importance that comes only after illiteracy has been abolished."

The expenditure of primary education can be met by reducing the term of primary education up to four year Australia, Germany, Japan, Egypt, China and Russia expanded primary education among the common people by fixing the term of primary education for four year Sri Desai has suggested that in order to reduce the expenditure on compulsory education, fees should be charged from the children of rich persons. Private primary schools should be allowed to take fees from the students.

7. **Establishment of Schools.** India is a rural country. There are 2,40,048 villages where there are no schools. The establishment of primary schools is necessary in nearly four lakh villages including the villages having a population less than 500. It is not easy to provide money to establish so many schools. Moreover, it would not be beneficial to establish schools in the villages having population less than 500.

Remedy: Problem of the lack of buildings of schools can be solved through shift system. In the shift system, different students can be called to receive education into two shifts. The first shift can be run from 7.30 to 11.30 a.m. and the second Shift can run from 1.00 p.m. to 5.00 p.m. Different countries of the world have adopted shift system in their early stage of expansion of education. The more prominent of such countries are Germany, France, Portugal, United States of America, Japan, etc. Even today, this system is prevalent in Australia, New Zealand, Turkey, Egypt, China, Ceylon, Denmark, etc. This system should be made prevalent in India also. If the time of the shifts is kept, keeping in view of the season and the needs of the farmers and the workers, then the problem of buildings can be solved in India. Of course the teachers will have to work more in this system. But if they are given more salaries they will have no difficulty in taking up this additional work.

The Indian educationists have suggested that the number of students in each school should be increased, in order to speed up the progress of compulsory education. At present, the teacher has to teach on an average 35 students in each class. In many Western countries, each teacher had to teach more than 36 students in the early stages of education. For example, till 1922, the number of students in each class was 60 students in the primary classes of China. Therefore, in those primary schools of India where one teacher teaches the students of one class only the number may go up to 60 in a class.

8. **Buildings of Schools.** At present in India there are only 30 per cent buildings of schools which can be called proper and adequate. The rest of the schools are being run in houses, temples, buddings of rich persons, residences of teachers, etc. These schools lack sufficient space for seating all the children much less to talk of their games and sports. Many schools are situated in a very busy locality and undesirable environment. Moreover, these buildings are such that they adversely affect the health of the students because of inadequate supply and provision of the sun and the air. These problems can be solved only by building new buildings which require a huge amount of money but it is very difficult to collect the amount needed for buildings schools.

9. **Narrow and Unsuitable Curriculum.** The curriculum of the primary school is narrow and unsuitable to the local needs. In it emphasis is given on bookish knowledge. The principle of 'learning by woric' to develop the constructive powers of the student is disregarded and ignored.

   Remedy: In order to remove these defects of the curriculum, the Government have decided to convert primary education into basic education. This will remove the defects of the curriculum but the expensive scheme of basic education cannot be enforced at onetime in the whole country.

The education of crafts should be given in the primary schools in accordance with the local needs and requirement. This will increase the interest of the children in education. They will also be benefited by the knowledge they thus acquire.

10. **Wastage and Stagnation.** Another great obstacle in the expansion of primary education is wastage and stagnation. Many children leave studies either after their failure in the examinations or in order to assist their guardian in earning their livelihood.

    Remedy: The problem of wastage and stagnation can be solved through the following ways and means:

    (i) Educational system should be reformed.

    (ii) Teaching methods should be made interesting.

    (iii) Good school buildings should be built.

    (iv) The environment inside and outside the school should be reformed.

    (v) The curriculum should be reformed.

    (vi) Efforts should be made to develop the health of the students.

    (vii) The guardians or the parents should also be educated.

    (viii) Social problems relating to education should also be solved.

11. **National Obstacles.** In India there are natural obstacles in the way of expansion of compulsory education. Due to spare population in Himalyan region, Kashmir, Garhwal and Almora, etc., the villages in these areas are situated at distant places. So is the case with Rajasthan. There are many areas in Madhaya Pradesh and South India, which are covered with forest and the population of these places is scattered in small and distant villages. Due to lack of means of transport in the above-mentioned regions and due to the severe cold, heat or heavy rains, their difficulties further increased.

    Remedy: It is difficult to conquer natural obstacles mentioned above in a big country like India. However, there has been some increase and progress in the means of transport under the Five Year Plans. Roads have been built in many distant villages and the work at large scale is still being done in this connection. It would be more desirable to entrust the responsibility of the education on some local persons in order to avoid the problem of children going to distant places to receive education.

12. **Social Evils.** In India everywhere there are social evils such as superstitions, illiteracy, faith in outmoded conventions and customs, child marriages, untouchability, Pardah system, etc. These social evils create innumerable obstacles in the expansion of compulsory primary education. Harijan students are still not admitted in many schools. Hindus and Muslims believe that girls should be given only little education. Due to Pardah system there are many persons, who oppose the system of co-education in primary schools.

    Remedy: Despite the prevalence of these evils, the work of the expansion of education should not be slackened. Education develops the mind of the man and his logical power. It will itself root out social problems which appear to be formidable at present. The Government and the social workers should try to bring about consciousness among the people against social evils through the means of pictures, speeches and other such works. Educated young men and women should volunteer themselves to remove the social evils in their neighbourhood.

13. **Multiplicity of Languages.** There are 826 languages and 1952 dialects in the country. It is a serious problem before the educationists as to which language should be the medium of instruction for the children speaking different languages, and dialects.

    Remedy: The establishment of special schools is necessary in the areas where there are the people of scheduled castes and tribes and de-notified tribes. The Government have been taking every possible step to establish special schools for the students of such tribes and to provide facilities of free education, scholarship, books, etc.

ASSESSMENT COMMITTEE ON BASIC EDUCATION (1955-56)

The scheme of 'basic education' enunciated by Mahatma Gandhi has been an epoch-making event in the history of primary education in modern India. However, from time to time there have been many misunderstandings and prejudices at various quarters. This called for a careful orientation of teachers' ideas, aptitudes and techniques. Therefore, The Ministry' of Education, Government of India, appointed the Assessment Committee on Basic Education under the Chairmanship of Shri G. Ramachandaran to survey the existing situation regarding basic education in the various States and to think out ways and means of bringing about effective improvements.

The Committee travelled throughout the country and made certain recommendations for the promotion of basic education in the country. The Committee gave its recommendations under the following seven headings:

1. The Government of India.
2. The Government of the States.
3. The Universities.
4. The Administration.
5. Basic Teacher's Training.
6. Basic Schools.
7. The Public.

Major Recommendations

1. The Government of India

1. The Government of India should take appropriate steps to make it clear to all those concerned that the elucidation of basic education given by the Basic Education Standing Committee of the Central Advisory Board of Education has their concurrence.
2. All India and regional conferences on the basic education should be arranged periodically.
3. A Central Research Institute of basic education should be established.
4. A small special committee of educational experts should be set up to lay down the criteria to evaluate the achievements and progress of pupils in basic institutions.
5. The establishment of full fledged Postgraduate Basic Training Colleges can no longer be delayed.
6. Post-basic education should get due recognition and place in the present schemes for the reorganisation of secondary education.

7. The Union Government should insist that any financial aid given by it directly or indirectly to improve or spread elementary education is strictly earmarked by the States for basic education.

2. The Government of the States

1. State governments should no longer delay to make a clear unambiguous declaration of policy that all elementary schools will be converted into basic schools and that all teacher training at this level will become basic teacher training within reasonable time limits.
2. The compact area method of developing basic education should yield place to the whole of elementary education becoming basic.
3. State governments should take effective steps for the supply of raw materials, equipment, for repairs and for marketing of surplus produce.
4. Steps should be taken to effect economy in basic education. Craft equipment whose cost is to be met by the pupils themselves must essentially belong to them. Whatever is produced should, as far as possible, be consumed by the teachers and pupils at reasonable rates and only the surplus need be taken over by the State for marketing.

3. The Universities

Universities should recognise post-basic education for purposes of admitting pupils passing out of post-basic schools into colleges.

4. The Administration

1. Inspecting staff connected with basic education should be fully trained in basic education.
2. English should be offered as an optional subject from the 6th grade onwards, wherever knowledge of English is considered necessary for entrance into high schools and other similar institutions.
3. It is of the utmost importance to guarantee proper dovetailing of basic education with secondary education in such a manner that equal years of study in different types of institutions will be considered as of equal value for purposes of admission into institutions of higher education.

5. Basic Teachers' Training

1. It is urgently necessary to make teacher's training more efficient and real. Improvement is called for in craft training in handling the technique of correlated teaching and in a new and dynamic approach to the study of Psychology. Any craft for basic education must be a whole craft and not split into pieces, nor isolated in isolated parts.
2. The staff of basic training schools and the pupil-teachers should prepare manuscripts of reading books for basic school children.
3. Every basic training school should plan and execute appropriate extension programmes.
4. Basic training schools should be residential for the purpose, among other things, of giving day-to-day training in actual living and practising ofthe principles of a cooperative democratic community work and learning together and producing much of what is necessary for daily life.
5. Sanitation, common kitchen and cultural and recreational activities based on community self-government will be the vital centres of such cooperative community and, therefore, of basic education.

6. Basic Schools

1. Unless the following requisites fulfilled, no school may be considered a basic school or assessed as such:
   - (i) If it provides for an integrated course of eight years of basic education and where there are only the junior five grades, such a school should necessarily be the feeder for a senior basic school.
   - (ii) Supply of adequate quantities of needed raw materials in time.
   - (iii) Provision of adequate craft equipment and repair material.
   - (iv) Availability of minimum land and in no case less than three acres for a senior basic school of eight grades.
   - (v) The majority of teachers at least of basic standards, with the untrained teachers getting training under them all the time.

(vi) Community living and work based on democratic student self-government under the guidance of teachers.
(vii) Systematic and not truncated craft work.
(viii) Correlated method of teaching, with correlation not restricted to productive work only, but also extending to the natural environment and the social environment.
(ix) Commensurate extension work linking the school with the community and *vice versa.*
(x) Congregational prayers.
(xi) A library with suitable books.
(xii) Cultural and recreational activities.

2. Wholly internal examinations based on assessment of continuous progress of students and cumulative records.
3. Application of basic education equally to urban and rural areas.

7. The Public

The Central and State Governments must consider ways and means of convincing the public about basic education and securing their cooperation for its rapid development. The education of the public in regard to all the relevant issues in and for basic education should be undertaken in all seriousness without delay.

THE CONCEPT OF BASIC EDUCATION (1957)

The term 'basic education' has been interpreted and sometimes misinterpreted, in a variety of ways. This is, so because it is a comparatively recent development and its concept and technique are still in the making. Different people had different interpretations of basic education. This called for a clarification of its concept. The Basic Education Standing Committee of the Central Advisory Board of Education prepared the document entitled. The Concept of Basic Education'. Its clarifications were as follows:

1. **As Defined in Zakir Hussain Committee.** The concept of basic education is the same as defined in the Report of the Basic National Education Committee (The Zakir Hussian Committee) and elucidated by the Central Advisory Board of Education. The basic principles and techniques, as made

out in the Report, should guide and shape educational reconstruction in India. About the provision of eight years of compulsory universal schooling and the use of mother-tongue as the medium of instruction, there is no difference of opinion about them.

2. **An Education for Life.** Basic education, as conceived and explained by Mahatma Gandhi, is essentially an education for life. It is an education through life. It aims at creating a social order free from exploitation and violence. Productive, creative and socially useful work is placed at the very centre of basic education, in which all boys and girls may participate, irrespective of any distinction of the caste or class.
3. **Teaching of Basic Craft.** The effective teaching of a basic craft is an essential part of basic education. Productive work, done under proper conditions, makes the acquisition of much related knowledge more concrete and realistic. It gives a powerful contribution to the development of personality and character and instils respect and love for all socially useful work. The sale of products of craft-work will meet some part of the expenditure incurred in running the school. The products will be used by the school children for getting a mid-day meal or a school uniform or help to provide some of the school furniture and equipment.
4. **Development of Total Personality.** The fundamental objective of basic education is the development of the child's total personality which will include productive efficiency as well. The articles made should be of good quality, as good as children at that stage of their development can make them socially useful and, if necessary, saleable. The acquisition of skills and the love for good craftsmanship have deeper educative significance than merely playing with the tools and raw materials which is usually encouraged in all good activity schools. It contributes to the all-round development of the child. It sets up before children high standards of achievement and gives them the right kind of training in useful habits and attitudes like purposeful application, concentration, persistence and thoughtful planning.
5. **Choice of Basic Craft.** In the choice of basic crafts which are to be integrated into school work, such crafts should be selected

as have significance from the point of view of intellectual content, provide scope for progressive development of knowledge and practical efficiency. The basic craft should fit into the natural and social environment of the school and hold the maximum of educational possibilities within it.

6. **Knowledge Related to Activity.** In basic education knowledge must be related to activity, practical experience and observation. To ensure this, the curricular content shouldbe intelligently related to three main centres of correlation, *viz.* craft-work, the natural environment and the social environment. However, any mechanical 'associations' which pass for correlation in many schools should be carefully avoided.
7. **Value of the Book.** The emphasis on productive work and crafts in basic schools should not be taken to mean that the study of books can be ignored. The value of the book cannot be denied. A good library is as essential in a basic school as in any other type of good school.
8. **Integration of School and Community.** The basic scheme envisages a close integration between the schools and the community so as to make education as well as the children more social-minded and cooperative.
9. **In Urban Areas also.** Basic education should be introduced in urban areas as well, both because of its intrinsic suitability and also to remove the impression that it is an inferior kind of education designated only for the village children.

COMMITTEE ON INTEGRATION OF POST-BASIC AND MULTIPURPOSE SCHOOLS (1957)

In their sixth meeting held in August 1957, the Standing Committee of the Central Advisory Board of Education on basic education felt that the multilateral schools and post-basic schools should not be regarded as two parallel systems but each should be regarded as an integral part of the other. The Education Secretary was requested to set up a small committee of experts from the Ministry of Education and the local education units for undertaking a comparative study of the syllabi of the multilateral and the existing post-basic schools and finding out common points which would help in bringing the two types nearer to each other. In pursuance of the recommendation of the Standing Committee on Basic Education, the Union Ministry of Education appointed a committee in November 1957 with Dr. P.D. Shukla, Deputy Educational Adviser as chairman, the following recommendations were made to undertake a comparative study of the syllabi of the multilateral and the existing post-basic schools and to find out common points with a view to bringing the two types nearer to each other:

1. **Standard of Evaluation.** The study of craft in post-basic schools should be considered equivalent to the study of the electives in the multipurpose schools and for doing this, proper standards should be laid down for both.
2. **Assistance.** Necessary assistance should be provided to every post-basic school to enable it to raise its standard of study in humanities and sciences to the same advanced level as is provided for them as electives in every higher secondary school.
3. **Post-Basic Schools.** While selecting schools for conversion to multipurpose schools, the post-basic schools should be given the same consideration for this conversion, wherever possible, as other higher secondary schools.
4. **Common Examination.** For both the post-basic schools and the multipurpose schools a common scheme of examination should be instituted by the State Board of Secondary Education after giving due cognizance to the special features of the work done in post-basic schools. The same certificate should be issued to students of the post-basic schools as to those of other higher secondary schools.
5. **Recognition to Post-Basic Final Examination.** During the interim period the governments should recognise the final examination of the post-basic schools as equivalent to the certificates awarded to the students of other higher secondary schools for purpose of employment and urge upon the universities to accord the same recognition to that examination for purposes of admission to institutions of higher learning.
6. **Same Financial Assistance.** In order to enable post-basic schools to improve the quality of their teachers and strengthen their laboratory, library, etc., the same financial assistance and guidance should be made available to the post- basic schools as is being done to the higher secondary and multipurpose schools.

7. **Same Preference to Products.** As a matter of policy the products of post- basic schools should be given preference in the matter of employment on those special jobs for which their training has specially equipped them.
8. **Implementation of Recommendation.** The recommendation of the All-India Commission for Secondary Education regarding the study of crafts as a compulsory subject should be implemented in all higher secondary and multipurpose schools with due emphasis on the productive aspects of that work.
9. **Technique of Correlation.** The technique of correlation should be specially emphasised in all higher secondary and multipurpose schools and utilised as an effective technique of teaching to the extent it is normally possible to do at that stage of education.
10. **Higher Secondary.** Every post-basic school should suitably add the words 'higher secondary' to its name.

SEMINAR ON PRIMARY AND WORK-ORIENTED EDUCATION (1970)

The National Seminar on primary and work-oriented education was organised by the National Council of Educational Research and Training, as a part of the programme for the celebration of the International Education Year. It was organised to take stock of the trends of development in the field of pre-primary and primary education during the sixties and to formulate programmes and policies for its improvement in the seventies. The seminar was organised in New Delhi from November 9 to 11, 1970 with Prof S.V.C. Aiya, Director, National Council of Educational Research and Training as the Chairman of the organising committee. It made the following major recommendations:

1. The programmes of pre-school education should be closely related to the home and community environments of the child.
2. The expansion of the programmes of pre-school education may be left to the care of voluntary agencies. The agencies engaged in pre-school education should try to develop less costly equipment with the help of indigenous materials. Community resources should be fully utilised.

3. Necessary' additions/modifications in the primary school teacher training programmes should be made to include principles governing child care and preschool education so as to enable the primary school teachers to look after pre-school programmes in mixed schools.
4. The State governments should be in a position to provide funds for the purpose of training teachers and specially trained supervisors for pre-primary education.
5. Special attention should be paid to the promotion of the following Gandhian values in primary schools:
   (i) The dignity of manual labour through the use of work, as a part of the educational programme.
   (ii) A sense of social awareness and social responsibility through involvement of pupils in community service.
   (iii) Secular outlook and respect for other religions through an understanding of the fundamental unity of all religions.
   (iv) Fearlessness, truth, non-violence (universal love), purity, service and peacefulness through participation in curricular and co-curricular activities, and through stress on songs, stories and dramas based on Gandhian life and values.
6. While taking steps for providing work-experience at the primary stage the following details have to be spelled out:
   (i) Formulation of the operational concept of work-experience.
   (ii) Types of work-experience programmes to be introduced during 1970's in our country.
   (iii) Minimum work-experience programmes to be introduced in all the schools in the country with stress on structured activities to be introduced in selected schools.
   (iv) Action programmes pertaining to production of curriculum materials.
   (v) The pre-service and in-service training geared to work-experience to be provided to teachers and supervisors.
   (vi) Steps to be taken for the mobilisation of public opinion in favour of work-experience.
7. Work-experience should be socially meaningful. It should be realistic physical work, without overemphasis on economic aspects at the cost of learning outcomes and it should lead

to the development of productive abilities and the total personality of the child.

8. Individual schools might be encouraged to develop their own programmes of work-experience and the results of their programmes might be made available to the various agencies and institutions in the country.
9. The agencies for curriculum development at the Centre and State level may start a continuous dialogue on programmes and techniques of curriculum development.
10. In order to improve the competence of teachers, the following steps may be taken:
    (i) Suitable in-service and pre-service training courses may be developed by each State Government.
    (ii) Suitable materials as help books and teacher guides may be developed by State Institutes of Education.
    (iii) NCERT should take up programmes on development of good techniques of teaching for the primary classes and make the same available to the State level agencies.
11. Efforts may be made to institute the programmes of close supervision of schools to provide guidance to working teachers.
12. The teachers, supervisors and parents may be made conscious of the rate of wastage and stagnation and efforts may be made for identification and proper treatment of potential cases of wastage and stagnation in the school.
13. The possibility of implementing syllabi on health education for the age group of 6-11 and 11-14 along with that of primary teacher training schools developed by the Central Health Education Bureau and the Ministry of Education jointly may be explored.
14. As there were a large number of pupils who were unable to take advantage of the use of full schooling facilities the possibility of providing some part-time education as a temporary measure for such children may be examined. Shift system may be accepted only as a measure of expediency and not as a principle.
15. The Government grant policy should develop an incentive to exploit one's own resources of finance, even though by the large the Government has to be the main source of financing the primary education in future.

16. The local bodies should exploit the sources of revenue fully for primary education.
17. There is a need for evolving a suitable curriculum for the schools functioning in tribal areas. This curriculum may be science-oriented but culture-based.
18. Steps to improve the Ashram school education may be taken. The teacher-community relationship may be improved.

SEMINAR ON GANDHIAN VALUES IN EDUCATION (1970)

Introduction

This National Seminar was organised by the Ministry of Education and Youth Services in collaboration with the Maharashtra Government and the Hindustani Talimi Sangh to discuss some important facts of the problems relating to Gandhian values in Indian education. It was inaugurated by Prof V. K. R. V. Rao, Union Minister of Education and Youth Services. It was presided over by Shri Shriman Narayan, Governor of Gujarat. It was convened at Seva Gram, where Gandhiji first put forward his concept of Nai Talim. It was blessed by the benign presence of Acharya Vinoba Bhave. It was held from February 9 to 11, 1970.

Major Recommendations

1. **Fundamental Values.** The ultimate objective which Gandhiji had in view was the evolution of a non-exploitative, non-violent society conducive to the welfare of all. To this end, it is essential to emphasise three fundamental values in education, *viz:*
   (i) dignity of manual labour through the use of work as a part of the educational programme;
   (ii) a sense of social awareness and social responsibility through the involvement of students and teachers in meaningful programmes of community service; and
   (iii) the promotion of a secular outlook or sarvadharma samabhava through an understanding of the fundamental unity of all religions.
2. **Programmes of Implementation.** Suitable programmes should be involved in their planning and implementation. These programmes should cover all stages of education and may for instance include:
   (i) Safai and maintenance of campus;

(ii) Participation in sowing and harvesting operations through suitable adjustment of vacations;

(iii) Participation in productive work in agricultural operations in the school, family farms or the neighbourhood;

(iv) Teaching of crafts;

(v) Cultivation of hobbies;

(vi) Adoption of new methods of teaching which provide opportunities for work with hands to the maximum extent possible in every subject;

(vii) Establishing close contacts between the educational institutions and the community through programmes of mutual service and support;

(viii) Participation in programmes of relief in times of famine, flood, epidemics and other natural calamities;

(ix) Beginning the school day by an assembly with a silent and/or common prayer and provision for teaching of moral and social values;

(x) Organising suitable programmes of adult education, including the spread of literacy;

(xi) Involvement of students in programmes which will train them in responsibility.

In view of the special problems involved, the Ministry of Education and Youth Services may set up a study group to make concrete proposals for their introduction in urban areas.

3. These programmes have an obvious significance at the primary stage because about 70 million children are involved.
4. At the secondary stage, the programmes of work-experience should be highlighted.
5. At the university stage, the national service programme should be generalised.
6. It is essential to produce books for children to teach sarvadharma samabhava.
7. All students should be introduced to the life and message of Mahatma Gandhi through suitable courses.
8. The success of these programmes will largely depend upon the efficiency and proper orientation of training institutions for teachers, the quality of leadership provided by the

State Education Departments, and the extent to which the programme becomes a movement undertaken by the community of teachers themselves.

9. The realisation of Gandhian values in education needs an elastic and dynamic system of education for its proper development.
10. The efforts of the educational system to realise these values will need support from parents and the community in general. An appropriate *Lokeshikshana* programme to this end should, therefore, be simultaneously developed.

QUESTIONS FOR EXERCISE

1. Describe the terms of reference and major recommendations of Committee on Primary Education (1951).
2. Enumerate and explain the present problems of primary education in India and suggest remedies.
3. Describe the recommendations of Assessment Committee on Basic Education (1955-56).
4. Discuss the concept of Basic Education outlined in the document on the concept of Basic Education (1957).
5. Explain the recommendations of the Committee (1957) on Integration of Post-Basic and Multipurpose schools.
6. Describe the major recommendations of the National Seminar on Primary and Work-oriented Education (1970).
7. Describe the recommendations of the National Seminar on Gandhian Values in Education (1970).

CHAPTER 22

PROGRESS AND PROBLEMS OF SECONDARY EDUCATION: THE MUDALIAR COMMISSION (1953)

PROBLEMS OF SECONDARY EDUCATION

1. **Aimlessness.** To counter this problem the following aims should be listed.
   (i) Development of democratic citizens.
   (ii) Increase in professional skill.
   (iii) Development of personality.
   (iv) Development of leadership.
2. **Unsuitable Curriculum:**
   (i) Single Track. The curriculum of secondary schools is unsuitable because of being single track. All the students have to study one pre-fixed curriculum. The students do not get opportunity to select subjects according to their interests and desires.
   (ii) Impractical. The curriculum is not related to the environment and practical life. Education in general and secondary education in particular has failed to keep pace with the changes.
   (iii) Mercenary. The pupils read the traditional curriculum without interest, understanding or appreciation. Their immediate aim is to get through the examinations.

   Remedies. The Secondary Education Commission recommended the diversification of courses and made the following suggestions:
   (i) The curriculum should be such as may develop the different abilities and capability of the students.

(ii) The curriculum should be diversified and flexible so that it may be according to the needs and interests of the students.

(iii) The curriculum should be closely related to the social life of the students.

(iv) The curriculum should be such so that the students may not only be encouraged to work but also to make proper use of leisure.

(v) The curriculum should not include such subjects as are not related to each other. All the subjects of the curriculum should be interlinked with each other.

3. **Indiscipline.** The present educational system, examination system, aimless education, etc., are the factors responsible for the indiscipline among the students. Chief causes of them are as follows: 1. Loss of higher spiritual values, 2. Political changes, 3. Defective mode of examination, 4. Wretched economic condition of teachers.

   Remedies. To remove widespread indiscipline among the students, proper attention should be given to the above-mentioned factors which are responsible for growing indiscipline among the students. This can be achieved only when the Government, people and guardians co-operate to take active and constructive measures in this connection.

4. **Undesirable Growth of Private Schools.** After the attainment of independence, there has been an unprecedented increase in the number of private secondary schools in the name of expansion of education. Most of these schools are the private properties of some particular caste, political party or capitalist. Casteism, nepotism and favouritism are rampant in these schools.

   Remedies. As nationalisation of the entire secondary education does not appear practicable, the Government should regulate the management and administration of private institutions. Raghukul Tilak Committee had recommended that in order to improve the management of private institutions, the managing committees must include one representative of teachers and three members nominated by the Education Department.

5. **Low Standard of Teaching.** Low standard of teaching is also one of the chief problems of the secondary education.

Unless the teachers are given proper facilities and are given the place of respect in society, these cannot hope to perform. There are many schools which do not have sufficient funds to make proper provision of buildings and other necessary things connected with education. These shortcomings have adversely affected the standard of teaching.

Remedies. The standard of teaching can be raised by taking into consideration many factors, which have been mentioned earlier. The Government should appoint such Inspectors who would make necessary suggestions. The teachers should be sent to training colleges from time to time in order to acquaint them with latest teaching methods. Only enthusiastic persons and the persons who wish to dedicate themselves for the service of the society should be selected for the teaching work.

6. **Defective System of Examination.** The system of examination of our secondary education is full of defects. There is the domination of Matriculation examination over the whole secondary education. A school, its teachers and its students are tested in accordance with their success in the examinations. According to R.N. Mukerjee, "Worse than India's community ridden, social and political system is her examination ridden educational system. In fact, the Matriculation examination dominates the entire work of our secondary schools. The prestige of a school depends entirely upon Matriculation results and very little on real educational merits of the institution." Mass copying is a glarive defect of examination system.

   Remedy. Change in the examination system. The Secondary Education Commission made the following suggestions to reform the present examination systems:

   (i) Number of external examinations should be reduced.

   (ii) The method of the questions asked in the examination should be changed in such a way so that they may not remain merely essay type.

   (iii) While making the final evaluation of the work of the students along with the internal examinations, proper importance be given to the periodical test and schools' records.

(iv) The public examination of the students should be taken only after the completion of the whole curriculum of the secondary schools.

7. **Absence of Community Life.** There is absence of well-organised community life in the secondary schools of the modern period. Sports and games, excursions, physical exercises, social activities, etc, are not sufficiently organised in the schools. There is total absence of religious and moral education in the schools.

   Remedy. To make schools the centres of community life, Mudaliar Commission has rightly remarked, "School is a small community within a large community and the attitude, values and modes of behaviour which have currency in national life are bound to be reflected in the school."

8. **Lack of Vocationalisation.** Secondary education is single track. There is no diversification in its curriculum. It has not given any importance to vocationalisation.

   Remedy. About the need of vocationalisation of secondary education, the Secondary Education Commission has remarked, "Secondary Education should be vocationalised in a large measure and enrolment in vocational course rest to 20 per cent of total enrolment at the lower secondary stage and 50 per cent of total enrolment at the higher secondaiy stage by 1986." The following suggestions may be given in this connection:

   (i) Money should be taken from all the rich persons of the country in the form of education cess.

   (ii) Fifty per cent of the money thus obtained should be contributed by the Central Government and the rest 50 per cent contributed by the State Government.

   (iii) In order to impart education of vocational subjects, persons of different professions of the district and the country should be invited from time to time.

   (iv) The student should be given opportunities for acquiring practical knowledge in the professions which are carried on in the neighbourhood of the school.

9. **Wastage and Stagnation.** In 1992 while the high school pass percentage in U.P. Board Examination was only eight per cent, the intermediate pass result was 14 per cent. This shows the grave waste and stagnation which may be checked by

restricted admission on merit-base and improvement of teaching.

10. Management of Secondary Schools. At present three types of secondary schools are imparting education at the secondary stage:

(i) Government schools.

(ii) District Board and Municipal schools.

(iii) Schools run by private bodies.

As compared to the government schools, the condition of the District Board and Municipal schools is very miserable. Schools managed by private bodies are run on the principle of business and to augment the income of their managers. As they are run on profit basis, they cannot be expected to render the real service for the cause of education.

Remedy. The above mentioned problem can be solved if the Government take the management of all the non-Govemment schools by making necessary law in this connection.

THE MUDALIAR COMMISSION (1953)

Secondary Education Commission (1953) was appointed with Dr. Lakshman Swami Mudaliar as the Chairman of the Commission. Therefore the Commission is known as Mudaliar Commission.

Aims and Terms of Reference

1. "To enquire into and report on the present position of secondary education in India, in all its aspects.
2. To suggest measures for its re-organisation and improvement with particular reference to:
   (i) the aims, organisation and content of secondary education.
   (ii) its relationship to primary task and higher education.
   (iii) the inter-relation of secondary schools of different types, and
   (iv) other allied problems so that a sound and reasonable uniform system of secondary education suited to our needs and resources may be provided for the whole country."

Method of Enquiry. The Commission prepared a questionnaire dealing with various aspects of secondary education. This was sent out to various educational experts, teachers and educational institutions of India. On the basis of the replies received a good deal of information was collected. The members of the Commission took an extensive tour of the various parts of India and acquired a first-hand knowledge of the various problems faced in the secondary education in the country. The commission presented a report running in 250 pages on August 29,1953.

Defects of the Secondary Education

Mudaliar Commission pointed out the following defects existent in the secondary education of the day:

1. **Bookish.** The Commission felt that the secondary education was bookish, mechanical, stereotyped and uniform. It does not cater to the different aptitudes of the pupils or to pupils of different aptitude.
2. **No Qualitative Development.** Secondary education does not develop the essential qualities of discipline, co-operation and leadership in the pupils to enable them to become useful citizens of the country.
3. **Examination Oriented.** It was pointed out that there was too much stress on examination. Curriculum was overcrowded. Methods of teaching are not scientific and up-to-date. There is lack of proper material aims.
4. **Unilateral Scheme.** The scheme of education is unilateral. It concentrates its attention on preparing students to enter the university. It fails to bring out the best in the teachers and the students.
5. **No Diversification.** 'It does not have provision for diversified courses. Students, after completion of their education, due to this defect, fail to secure suitable Jobs.
6. **No Scope for Self-Expression.** A rigid time-table, unsuitable text-books and unduly detailed syllabus don't give the teacher sufficient opportunity for self-expression.
7. **No Scope for Close Contact.** The number of students in each class is so large that it becomes impossible for the teachers to establish close personal contacts with their students.
8. **No Proper Atmosphere at Home.** Many children, now seeking education, come from homes where there is little of an educational atmosphere. Hence, they get little or no

opportunity for supplementing the education given at schools.

9. **Lack of Good Teachers.** The teaching profession does not have the right type of men. They have not entered the profession with a mission. They don't possess the requisite personal qualities, aptitude and devotion for teaching, due to defective method of recruitment of the teachers.
10. **Lack of Facilities for Play and Recreation.** There is no proper provision for playgrounds, group games and other recreational activities. Therefore the school work does not have the atmosphere, vitality and joyousness. Hence the total personality of the children does not grow.
11. **Lack of Co-curricular.** Like the dearth of above facilities, there is inadequacy of co-curricular activities in the schools. Mind, emotion and aptitude of the students and their physical welfare are not very much looked after in the institutions.
12. **Impractical.** Education imparted in secondary schools is isolated from life, while it should be in perfect consonance with the requirements of life. Hence the students do not develop a proper insight into the life.
13. **Unbalanced.** The education imparted is unbalanced, narrow and one-sided. Hence the all-round development of the personality of the child is not achieved.
14. **Unbalanced Emphasis.** Where much importance has been given to subjects which are not important from the view of the society, subject that have social importance, are not given due attention.
15. **Defective Emolument System.** The emoluments of the teachers are not lucrative. Therefore competent and experienced persons do not care to enter this profession.

OBJECTIVE RECOMMENDATIONS

1. **Development of Democratic Citizenship.** India can be a democratic republic if the citizens uphold and practice the values of discipline, tolerance, patriotism, cooperation, equality in thought, speech and writing. The essence of the world citizenship is inculcated and developed through education. According to Mudaliar Commission, schools should maintain and develop all these qualities in the

students. Citizens with these qualities can grow into ideal citizens capable of making the democracy a success.

2. **Development of Personality.** The secondary education must aim at the development of the personality of the students. The creative energy in the students should find proper expression. They should acquire constructive and valuable interest. They should be trained to preserve and conserve their cultural heritage.
3. **Education for Leadership.** The secondary education must impart education for leadership. Students should also be trained to be able to own the responsibilities of leadership in various fields of life, namely, social, cultural, political, industrial, etc.
4. **Improvement of Vocational Capability and Efficiency.** In all the secondary schools, proper emphasis should be laid on crafts and productive work. This can be achieved through diversification of the courses of study at the secondary level. The students may take up agriculture or some other technical or commercial course to add to the productive capability of the country.
5. **The Concept of World Citizenship.** The students should not only be encouraged and taught the qualities of patriotism and citizenship, as citizens of their motherland but they should also be taught to acquire the aims of as a citizen of the entire world.

1. Reorganisation

1. **Age-limit.** The period of secondary education should be seven year It may start at the age of 11 and finish at 17 or 18 years.
2. **Division of the Period:**
   (i) *The Middle or Junior Secondary or Senior Basic Stage.* It should cover a period of four years.
   (ii) *The Higher Secondary Stage.* This should cover a period of four years.
3. **Abolition of Intermediate Classes.** The Commission has suggested the abolition of the present Intermediate classes. The Senior Intermediate or 12th class should be attached to the university and the Junior Intermediate class or 11th class should be added to the High School. Thus it has pleaded for

a three years degree course with one year of pre-university course for the students who pursue higher education.

4. **Diversification of the Courses.** Multipurpose schools should be established. Agricultural schools, technical schools, commercial schools should be established to enable the students to acquire education, according to their diverse aims, interests and abilities.
5. **Emphasis on Agricultural Education.** Much greater opportunities for agricultural education should be provided. Horticulture and Animal Husbandry should also be taught.
6. **Technical Schools.** The Commission has put forward that technical schools should be established in industrial centres in large number. These schools may either be independent or connected with multipurpose schools. Technological institutes should also be started in big cities. The technical schools located at the industrial centres should function in close cooperation with industry with which they are concerned. Legislative measures should be taken to enable every industry to take a certain number of apprentices for training. Cess may be levied in industrial establishment. The proceeds of this cess may be utilised for the development and improvement of technical education.
7. **Public Schools and Residential Schools.** Public schools should be allowed to function for about five year During the period, they may also organise education in accordance with the education in other schools imparting secondary education.

   Residential schools may be established at the places where there are suitable opportunities for them. These should provide for greater opportunities for teacher-taught contact, recreation and extra-curricular activities to enable the students to have an all-round development of their personality.
8. **Home Science for Girls.** The Commission has recommended for special facilities for the study of Home Science by the girls.
9. **Study of Three Languages.** The Commission has recommended that the following groups of languages should be taken into consideration while taking up the question of teaching of the languages:

(i) Mother tongue.
(ii) Regional language when it is not the mother tongue.
(iii) Official or Federal language.
(iv) Classical languages — Sanskrit, Arabic, Persian and Latin, etc.
(v) English as an international language.

10. **Medium of Instruction.** The medium of instruction at the secondary stage of education should be either the mother tongue or the regional language. Linguistic minorities may be given special facilities in this regard. At middle schools every student must be taught at least two languages—Hindi and English. While teaching these languages, it should be kept in view that the teaching of both these languages should not start in the same year. At the higher secondary stages of education, the student must be taught at least two languages, one of them should be the mother tongue and the other one regional language.

11. **Place of Hindi.** The study of Hindi should be compulsory in schools. The Commission has made the following suggestions in this regard:
    (i) Hindi has been adopted in the Constitution as the official language of the Centre.
    (ii) After some time, the Hindi will become the language of official correspondence between the Central Government and the States, and will also become a means of communication of large number of people.
    (iii) As a common language, Hindi will promote national unity and solidarity.
    (iv) Those who do not study Hindi may be handicapped if they shall enter service or communicate with people where Hindi is spoken.

12. **Place of English.** The Commission suggested revision of English, as a subject of study at the Secondary stage of education as follows:
    (a) English is widely known among the educated classes of the country.
    (b) Much of the national unity in political and other spheres of activity in India has been brought about through the study of English.

(c) The present position of India in the internal sphere is particularly due to the command that educated Indians have acquired over English.

(d) If, guided by national sentiment, English is removed from the curriculum of Secondary Schools, its effects will be harmful for India.

2. Curriculum

The Commission has pointed out the following defects in curriculum:

(i) The present curriculum is narrow.

(ii) It is bookish and theoretical, it is overcrowded and does not provide rich and significant contents.

(iii) There is no adequate provision for practical and other kinds of activities that should find place in any curriculum at this stage of education. Hence, the curriculum is not able to bring about the education of the whole personality of the child.

(iv) It does not cater to the various needs and capacities of the adolescents.

(v) Technical and vocational subjects are very much needed for India today, but the curriculum does not find room for these subjects.

(vi) Curriculum is too much dominated by the examination.

Suggestions for Improvement

(i) The curriculum should touch the life of the students at all points. It should help in the evolution and development of balanced personality.

(ii) It should have enough of variety and elasticity. Such qualities would enable the individual itself, to find satiable adaptation. Individual needs and interests should also be properly accommodated.

(iii) It should be related to the community life.

(iv) It should train the students to work for leisure.

(v) The curriculum should not be split up into a number of isolated, uncoordinated watertight subjects, but all the subjects should be inter-related.

Suggested Scheme of Curriculum

1. Middle Class and Senior Basic Schools, and
2. High and Higher Secondary Schools.

The present Intermediate stages should be replaced by the Higher Secondary stage which would be of four years duration. One year of the present Intermediate should be included in it while the second year should be included in the Degree Course of the University. The Commission has laid down following different curriculum for these two stages in the secondary stages of education.

Curriculum of the Middle Schools. The Commission has recommended the inclusion of the following subjects:

(a) English.
(b) Social Studies.
(c) General Science.
(d) Mathematics.
(e) Art and Music.
(f) Craft.
(g) Physical Education.

The Curriculum for High and Higher Secondary Schools. For this stage of education, the Commission has suggested that there should be a diversified course. The subjects of the curriculum have been divided into two:

(a) Compulsory subjects or main subjects; and
(b) Optional subjects.

A. **Compulsory Subjects.** The compulsory subjects shall include the following:

1. Mother tongue or regional language or composite course of the mother tongue and a classical language.
2. One other language to be chosen from among the following:
   (i) Hindi for those whose mother tongue is not Hindi.
   (ii) Elementary English for those who have not studied English in the middle stage.
   (iii) Advanced English for those who have studied English at the earlier stage.
   (iv) A modern Indian language, other than Hindi.
   (v) A modern foreign language, other than English.

(vi) A classical language.

(vii) *(a) Social Studies.* General course for the first two years only.

(b) General Science, Including Mathematics. General course for the first two years only.

3. One Craft to be chosen out of the list given below:
   (i) Spinning and Weaving.
   (ii) Wood Work.
   (iii) Metal Work.
   (iv) Gardening.
   (v) Training.
   (vi) Typography.
   (vii) Workshop Practical.
   (viii) Sewing, Needle Work.
   (ix) Embroidery.
   (x) Modelling.

B. Optional Subjects. The optional subjects have been divided into three groups. They have been diversified and the Commission has left option to the students to offer three subjects from any of the groups:

Group I — deals with humanities.
Group II — deals with Science.
Group III — deals with Technical subjects,
Group IV — includes Commercial subjects.
Group V — consists of Agricultural subjects.
Group VI — includes Fine Arts.
Group VII — includes Home Science, which is specially meant for girls.

3. Selection of Text-Books

1. High Power Committee should be constituted for selecting text-hooks, for study at different stages. It should comprise a high dignitary of the judiciary of the State, preferably a Judge of the High Court, a Member of the Public Service Commission of the Region, a Vice-Chancellor of the region concerned, a-Head Master or Head Mistress of the State, two distinguished educationists, to be coopted and the Director of Education.

2. This Committee should lay down the criteria for the books.
3. A fund should be maintained from the amount realised from the sale of publication which may be utilised for awarding and providing books illustrations.
4. The Central Government should set up a new institution or help some existing Art Schools, to develop training in the technique of book illustrations.
5. The Central and State Government should maintain libraries and collections of blocks of book illustrations which could be loaned to Text-Book Committee and publishers in order to improve the standard of book illustration.
6. Single text-book should not be prescribed for any subject of study. Reasonable number of books should be recommended, which satisfy the standards laid down, the choice should be left to the schools concerned.
7. In case of languages, definite text-books should be prescribed for each class, to ensure proper gradation.
8. No book prescribed as a text-book or a book for general study, should contain any passage or statement which might offend the religious or social susceptibility of any section of the community or might indoctrinate the minds of the young students with particular religion or political ideology.
9. Frequent changes should be discouraged in text-books and books prescribed for study.

4. Method of Teaching

1. The method of teaching should not merely aim at imparting knowledge in a thorough manner. It should also aim at inculcating desirable values and aim, attitude and habit of work in the student.
2. It should try to create in the students real attachment of work and a desire to do it as efficiently and honestly as possible.
3. Emphasis should shift from verbalism and memorisation to learning through purposeful, concerted, realistic situation, and for this purpose, the principle of activity method and project method, should be used in school work.

4. The method should provide opportunities for students to learn actively and apply mechanically the knowledge acquired in the class-room.
5. Clear thinking and expression, both in writing and speech, should be stressed upon in all subjects. It should aim more on teaching the student in the method of acquiring knowledge through personal effort. It should not make them only passive listeners.
6. The student should be trained to acquire the qualities of group-life and cooperative work.

5. School Administration

1. **Teachers Responsibility.** The education of character should be the responsibility of all teachers. Every single aspect of school programme should aim at providing education of character.
2. **Close Contact.** In the interest of discipline, it is very much desirable that close personal contact between the teacher and the pupil must be established and strengthened.
3. **Self-Government.** The Commission has also recommended the introduction of Self-Government in all schools. This Government may be in the form of houses system with perfects or monitors of student's council. Under the scheme of Self-Government the student leaders should be made responsible for drawing up a code of conduct and enforcing it among their brethren.
4. **Extra-Curricular Activities.** Extra-curricular activities must form a part of the education programme. Every teacher should be asked to devote definite time to such activities.
5. **Congenial Atmosphere.** "If all school works and activities are made psychologically interesting and exacting and if students are trained to take them up in the right spirit, the most congenial conditions will be created for the right training of character."
6. **Legislation.** Legislation should be passed making it an offence to utilise students at the early age of 17 for the purpose of political propaganda and election campaign.
7. **Financial Aid.** "State should give financial assistance to the Scout movement and help to secure suitable sites for Scout camps, N.C.C., First Aid, and Junior Red Cross should be encouraged in all schools."

8. **Religious and Moral Education.** The Commission also felt that religious and moral education plays an important part in the building up of character. Since the Commission was of the view that education for character must be imparted, it recommended the following things in regard to religious and moral instructions:
   (a) Religious instructions may be given in schools but these instructions should be voluntary and optional. These instructions should not be within the time-table or the regular school hours.
   (b) These instructions should be confined to the children of the particular faith concerned. While imparting these instructions the consent of the parents and management must be obtained.

6. **Examination System**

In the opinion of the Commission, "The subject of examination and evaluation occupies an important place in the field of education. It is necessary for parents and teachers to know from time to time how the public are progressing and what their attainments are at any particular stage." The Commission has made the following recommendations:

1. The number of external examinations should be reduced by introducing objective tests.
2. School records should be maintained indicating the progress of each pupil from time to time.
3. For the final evaluation of the pupil, due credit should be given to interval tests and progress records. There should be only one public examination at the completion of secondary school course.

7. **School Building and Libraries**

1. The building of the school should be planned with a definite aim in view. Preferably they should be outside the noise and bustle of the city life. There should be adequate arrangement of air and light, and class-rooms should be spacious enough to accommodate 40 students.
2. In the secondary schools there should be arrangement for class library and general library.
3. In all the libraries, there should be special comer for the students so that they may benefit by it.

4. From the point of view of the people at large and the students, the library should also open during holidays.
5. Trained librarians should be there in all secondary schools. Teachers should also be given some training in the basic principles of library work. Arrangement for this training may be made in the training colleges and through refresher course.

8. Guidance and Counselling in the Secondary Schools

1. "Educational authorities should give greater attention towards educational guides."
2. "In order to improve the pupil's understanding of the scope, nature and significance of various occupations and industries, films should be prepared to show the nature of work in various industries, and this should be supplemented by actual visits.
3. "Trained *Guidance Officers* and *Carrier Masters* should be appointed in secondary schools.
4. "The Government should undertake the responsibility of opening training centres of Guidance of Officers and Carrier Masters. Each State should send a number of teachers and suitable persons for training at these centres. After that when they acquire the requisite training, they may be deputed for work in the secondary institutions."

9. Physical Education and Welfare of Students

1. All the students should be thoroughly medically examined every year.
2. Properly organised school medical services should be there in all the States.
3. In order to keep the students healthy, they must be encouraged to undertake physical and manual labour.
4. Teachers should be given facilities for physical training. Some of the teachers should also be trained in the principles of First-Aid.
5. Proper nutritional and balanced diet should be arranged for the students.
6. Complete record of physical activities of the students should be maintained.
7. Training in physical training should include all the aspects of Health Education.

8. Facilities for physical training should be extended and new colleges of physical education be started.
9. Teachers of physical education should be associated with the teaching of subjects like Physiology and Hygiene.

10. Teachers' Selection, Welfare and Training

1. The method of selection and appointment of the teachers should be uniform throughout the country. In the schools run by the private bodies, the selection of the teachers should be made by a Committee, which must include the Principal of that institution.
2. As far as possible only trained teachers should be appointed.
3. The period of probation for a trained teacher should be one year.
4. The teachers of same qualifications should get the same salary and emoluments. They should also get provident fund and pension, etc.
5. The Commission also recommended the appointment of a special committee to suggest improvements in the salaries of the teachers concerned.
6. The teachers who teach in High School, should be graduate and possess a degree in education as well.
7. The teachers who teach technical subjects should be graduates in the subject concerned.
8. The teachers in the Higher Secondary Schools should possess the qualifications that are required for the teachers of Intermediate colleges.
9. The system of triple benefit fund scheme, pension, provident fund and insurance should be introduced for teachers in all the States.
10. Teachers who are physically fit and competent should be allowed to work up to the age of 60.
11. Arbitration Boards should be established. These Boards should look into appeals and grievances of the teachers and consider the matters in regard to dismissal, suspension, etc.
12. Teachers and the children of the teachers should be given free education.
13. Teachers should also be provided with quarters in neighbourhood of their working place.

14. Teachers who wish to go to health resorts or hold camps or intend to attend educational conferences, seminars, etc., should be given travel concessions and leave facilities.
15. They should be given free medical aid and treatment in hospitals and dispensaries.
16. The teachers should also be given opportunities to go abroad on study leave for higher education.
17. The practice of taking up private tuitions should be abolished.
18. Teachers who wish to acquire educational degree while they are in service, should be given leave with full pay.

11. Training of the Teachers

1. The Commission has suggested for the establishment of only two types of institutions to train teachers.
   (i) Such institutions that train teachers who wish to enter into the profession after taking higher secondary school leaving certificate. Such people should be given two years training.
   (ii) There should be institutions for training persons who wish to enter profession after graduation. The training period for such people should be one year. But this period should also be extended to two years in due course of time.
2. No fee should be charged in training colleges.
3. Those who intend to enter teaching profession should also be given training in one or more of the various extra-curricular activities.
4. Training colleges should arrange refresher courses, short intensive courses in special subjects and practical training in workshops.
5. Training colleges should also conduct research in various branches of education.
6. For the Master's Degree in Education, only trained graduates who have normally done a minimum of three years' teaching should be admitted.
7. To meet the shortage of women teachers, the Commission has recommended for conduct of special part-time course. This would solve the problem to a great extent.

QUESTIONS FOR EXERCISE

1. Discuss the problems of secondary education in India. Suggest remedies.
2. Critically examine the recommendations of the Mudaliar Commission for the re-organisation of the secondary education in India. How far these have been implemented?

CHAPTER 23

PROGRESS AND PROBLEMS OF HIGHER EDUCATION: DR. RADHAKRISHNAN COMMISSION

PROBLEMS OF UNIVERSITY EDUCATION

1. **Impractical Aims.** The aims of university education in India are praiseworthy but most of them are based on idealism. These aims have neither been achieved to this date nor are they expected to be ever achieved. The aims determined by the University Education Commission are very good but it is not easy to provide facilities to achieve them.
2. **Wastage.** This is clear from the results of various institutions of higher education.
3. **Faulty Curriculum.** The curricula of higher education are full of defects. The subjects of study are old and out of date. The curricula fail to fulfil the interests of different types of students.

   Remedy. There should be diversification of courses in curriculum of the universities as determined by the Mudaliar Commission for the curriculum of the secondary schools. The curriculum of the universities should be flexible so that it may adapt with the changing conditions and needs of the society. The University Education Commission has rightly remarked, "Educational systems are built for the time and not for all time. There are no changeless ways of educating human nature. A curriculum which was prevalent in the Vedic period of the renaissance cannot continue unaltered in the 20th century."
4. **Emphasis on Specialisation.** In university and higher education in India emphasis is given on the specialisation

in different subjects. When the students complete the university education they acquire special knowledge and skill in some particular subjects but their viewpoint remains unbalanced and narrow.

Remedy. Different branches of knowledge should be interlinked and harmonious relations established among them. Along with the education of art and science, provision should also be made for imparting general education so that the students may acquire the knowledge of other subjects. Thus, the defect of narrow specialisation can be removed by establishing harmony between general education and specialisation. This will also help the development of personality of the students. The subjects and curriculum of the general education should be selected in accordance with students of particular fields. University Education Commission has suggested the inclusion of general education in the curriculum of the universities. This has been accepted by many universities, including Aligarh, Andhra, Banaras, Baroda, Jadavpur, Karnatak, Kerala, Mysore, Poona, Rajasthan, Sagar, S. N. D. T., Bombay, Sri Vankateshwara, Utkal and Vishwa Bharti, etc.

5. **Lack of Guidance and Counselling.** There is no provision for giving proper guidance and counselling to the students. Hence, the students select their courses either according to their own choice or with the advice of some inexperienced persons. Many students select subjects which are either against their interests and tendencies or which they are not capable of studying.

   Remedy. There should be a provision of experienced and trained persons to provide guidance and counselling to the students from beginning to the end. The suggestions given by Mudaliar Commission and Kothari Commission hold good for the higher education also.

6. **Low Standard of Teaching.** In his book *A New Deal for Our Universities*, K. R. S. lyenger has remarked, "Ours standards whether in scholarship or teaching, never very high of exacting, are now fast racing to the bottom."

   Remedy. Suggestions for raising the standard of teaching include increase in the salaries of teachers; more than 18 hours of teaching work in a week; improvement in the condition of their service; provision of tutorial classes; well-organised libraries and laboratories and encouragement to debates and discussions. The Kothari Commission has recommended professional training to junior lecturers organisations or Re-orientation Courses for new lecturers, etc.

7. **English as Medium of Instruction.** India's subservience to the British for a long time has created so much reverence and love for English that even now English has not been replaced as the medium of instructions with some other Indian language or national language.

   Remedy. The University Education Commission has suggested the use of regional language as medium of instruction. Some of the universities of the country have been endeavouring to give practical shape to the suggestion of making regional language the medium of instructions. It would be convenient to conduct the examination of All India Services in the federal language.

8. **Defective System of Examination.** The Indian University Commission in 1902 pointed out "The greater evil from which university education in India suffers is, that teaching is subordinate to examination, and not examination to teaching." The University Education Commission of 1949 also pointed out, "If we are to suggest one single reform in university education, it should be that of examinations."

   Remedy. Examination system can be reformed by including scientific methods in the examination of students by progressive test, preparation of objective progressive test and determination of 70, 55 and 40 per cent marks for awarding first, second and third division to the students. Abolition of internal examination, starting internal assessment or evaluation system and training of teachers in new system of assessment may remove many of the defects of the present examination system.

9. **Indiscipline.** Prof. N. K. Siddhant, former Vice-Chancellor of Calcutta University, has mentioned the following types of activities coming within the indiscipline: (1) Financial irregularity, (2) Minor misconduct, (3) Disorderly misconduct, (4) Theft and burglary, (5) Sex misconduct, (6) Misuse of privilege, and (7) Cheating in

examination. In his book *Indian University Administration* Prof. N. K. Siddhant said, "The problem of maintaining discipline in the seats of higher education is assuming greater importance every day."

Remedy. According to Prof. Siddhant the best way of solving the problem of indiscipline is to divert the activities of the young students into healthy channels including sports, games, co-operative living in hostels, self-management of messes, debates and symposia. He has also made the following suggestions for solving the problem of indiscipline among the students:

(1) In each centre of higher education the statistics of different types of indiscipline should be maintained.

(2) The family and social life of the students and records where the student has studied earlier should be studied.

(3) The cause of each crime committed by the students should be discovered.

It has rightly been suggested by the Education Commission that not only the teachers but the students, their guardians and parents, society, government and the political parties will have to work in order to solve the problem of indiscipline among the students.

10. Student Unions. The student unions in educational institutions of higher education pose serious problems before us. The harms which these student unions cause to the students are well known. The leaders of these unions interfere in each and every work of the college. If the teacher, principal or manager of the college does any work which is against their wish they strongly oppose such works. They want that the appointment of the teachers, their teaching work and all the policies connected with the college should be done with their advice.

Remedy. V. K R. V. Rao has pointed out, "Unfortunately, we have in our universities certain very undesirable elements, many of whom are in contact with embassies, planning trips abroad and obtaining money from outside sources. All these have a demoralising effect on the student-community and should be stopped. I should like to suggest that legislation be introduced for the registration of university or college societies to ensure that they observe certain rules in elections, method of keeping accounts and similar other things."

REASONS OF FALLING STANDARDS

1. **Rapid Growth in the Number of Students.** The number of students receiving higher education in India is constantly increasing and it is likely to increase more in the near future. Hence it is not possible to provide them with necessary facilities. The number of able teachers is not increasing with the same proportion.

   Remedy. Kothari Commission has recommended that selective system of admissions should be adopted in the universities. The number of students should be determined by the facilities available in the institutions. The university should prescribe necessary qualification for admission. The best students should be selected from among them desiring to seek admission in the universities. Modern method should be adopted while selecting the students. Each university should establish a Board of University Admission which should resolve all the problems concerning admission. The University Grants Commission should establish Central Testing Organisation in order to help the students to select different subjects of higher education.

2. **Lack of Necessary Facilities.** In Indian universities the students do not have the same facilities which are provided in other countries of the world. They have to face the shortage of books. The libraries are not properly equipped. The environment is likely to lower the standard of education. There is not even proper seating arrangements for the students. Many degree colleges do not possess even playgrounds.

   Remedy. A high level committee should be appointed for providing necessary facilities to the students. The Government's efforts alone will not solve this problem. Private institutions should also come forward and make as much contribution as possible in this field. The rich class of the society should spend as much money as possible to raise the standard of higher education.

3. **Poor Condition of the Teachers.** The teachers of Indian degree colleges and universities get so meagre salaries that they adopt other means in order to meet their expenses. Hence, they are not able to devote themselves heart and soul into the teaching work.

Remedy. The Kothari Commission has recommended that the salaries of the teachers at different stages should be improved. Mehrotra Commission has recommended new grades for university teachers.

4. **Working Conditions of the Teachers.** The teachers have been burdened with too much work. Their working conditions are such that they are not able to perform their teaching work properly.

   Remedy. In order to remove the above mentioned defects, the working hours of the teachers should be reduced. They should be encouraged to devote sufficient time in the research work. Each teacher should be given one year leave with salary after a period of five years of service for increasing his knowledge and for travelling to foreign countries. They should be provided with concessional tickets. They should have complete freedom in performing the teaching functions. The suggestion made by Kothari Commission in respect of the promotion of the teachers, improvement in the conditions of their service and other works, etc., should be implemented.

5. **Wide Gulf between the Teachers and Students.** There is a wide gulf between the students and the teachers. The number of students in each class is so much that the teacher is not able to recognise each student. There exists a wide gulf between the teachers and the students.

   Remedy. It is necessary to adopt tutorial system to establish close relationship between the teachers and the students. Debates and discussions should be organised to establish close relations between the teachers and the students.

6. **Defective Examination System.** Radha Krishnan Commission pointed out that if only one suggestion is made to reform university education, it should be in respect of present examination system. As too much importance is given to the essay type of examinations, the students think that they will achieve success by studying some selective questions and hence do not devote themselves heart and soul into the studies throughout the years.

   Remedy. From essay type examination emphasis may be shifted on internal assessment or evolution. To get first, second and third divisions respectively the percentage of marks should be increased to 70, 55 and 40 respectively.

7. **Party-Politics.** The prevalence of party-politics is responsible for the decline in the standard of education in Indian universities. Different political parties and persons are ever eager to establish their control over universities. The groupism of the teachers also lowers the standard of teaching as they remain busy in group party-politics and do not get sufficient time for teaching work.

   Remedy. The politicians should not be appointed Vice-Chancellors in the universities. Rather they should be appointed from among the prominent educationists of the country. They should keep themselves away from party-politics and the influence of prominent politicians.

8. **Indiscipline.** Growing indiscipline among the students is one of the chief causes responsible for the decline in standards of higher education. The prominent among its causes are the social and economic difficulties; growing unemployment; non-availability of educational facilities, group party-politics; lack of interesting subjects in the curriculum, etc.

   Remedy. Kothari Commission has suggested that not only the teachers but the students, parents or guardian's society, Government and political parties should work together to solve this problem. Programmes should be organised in colleges and universities to keep the students busy in constructive work away from party-politics. Every effort should be made to solve the problem of unemployment.

INDIAN EDUCATION COMMISSION OR RADHAKRISHNAN COMMISSION (1948-1949)

Inter-University Board of Education and Central Advisory Board of Education recommended to Government of India that an All India Commission on Education should be appointed to inquire into the requirements of the higher education in India and put forward recommendations for re-organisation of the University Education in the light of requirements of the country and its traditions. On November 4, 1948 the Government of India appointed University Education Commission with Dr. Sarvapalli Radhakrishnan as Chairman. Hence, it is also known as 'Radhakrishnan Commission'. There were 10 members of the Commission.

Aim of Appointment. The Commission was appointed, to report on Indian University Education and suggest improvements and extensions that may be desirable to suit present and future requirements of the country.

Terms of Reference. The terms of reference of the Commission were ways and means for the improvement and re-organisation of the University Education, problems of the teachers, curricula, medium of instruction, religious education, problem of discipline, health and residence of the students and such allied problems in the perspective of the national and international conditions.

Method of Study. The Commission made a thorough study of the problems of Higher Education in India. It toured the country extensively.

It prepared a questionnaire which was sent over to about 600 persons who mattered in the field of education. It interviewed administrators, organisations of the students and other educationists. Thus, it tried to gather information in regard to almost all the aspects of university education. Its report runs into two volumes. The first part of the report contains 18 chapters and about 747 pages. The second volume contains the statistics in regard to institutions and other educational problems and the evidence tendered by the witness examined by the Commission.

RECOMMENDATIONS

1. Aims and Objectives

(i) The universities have to provide leadership in politics, administration, education, industry and commerce.

(ii) The university should be organised as centres of civilisation to train intellectual pioneers of civilisation.

(iii) The aim of university education should be to produce intellectual adventurers.

(iv) Universities should produce such wise persons who may disseminate learning to make democracy successful and who may make an incessant search for new knowledge and unceasing effort to plug the mission of life.

(v) Contents of education must accept the best of what the modern advancement has to offer but without neglecting our cultural heritage from the past.

(vi) One of the main functions of universities is to bring about the spiritual development of students.

(vii) Universities should preserve the culture and civilisation of a country. To be civilised, we should sympathise with the poor, respect women, love peace and independence, and hate tyranny and injustice. The university education should infuse these ideals into the youths.

(viii) Education should discover the innate qualities of a person and develop them through training.

(ix) Attention should be paid not only to the mental but also to the physical development of students in universities.

(x) University should give the most important place to the mother tongue in general education.

(xi) We are engaged in a quest for democracy through the realisation of justice, freedom, equality and fraternity. Hence it is necessary that our universities should be the emblems and protectors of these ideals.

In regard to the importance of the teachers in the scheme of education, the Commission has laid down the following points:

(i) "The teacher occupies a very important place in the field of education. The success of educational process depends on the character and policy of a teacher."

(ii) "The primary responsibility of the teacher is to arouse the interest of the pupil in the field of study for which he is responsible. He should stimulate the spirit of inquiry and criticism so that his pupils may acquire the habit of exercising independent and unbiased judgment."

(iii) "A good teacher desiring to achieve the results in the intellectual field, must instil into his pupils responsibility for right values and truth. He must inculcate habits and modes of behaviour through which their life may be moulded to the realisation."

2. Unsatisfactory Condition of the Teachers

(a) "Teachers do not possess sufficient knowledge of their subject. Hence, there is a constant fall in the standard of teaching. For this, the teachers are not so much responsible as the universities and the Government. The teachers have no facilities of research and libraries. If they are provided these facilities, they can become masters of their subjects."

(ii) "With the introduction of democratic control and elections in our universities, there has grown a tendency among the teachers to interest themselves more in the administrative affairs of the universities than in their legitimate duties."

(iii) "The salaries of the teachers are low. The conditions of their services are not attractive. Hence they have no incentive to throw themselves heart and soul into their work."

Suggestions for the Improvement

(a) Provident Fund, Residential Accommodation and Age of Retirement

1. "Teachers should have better facilities of provident fund. To this teacher should contribute 10 per cent of the salary and the University 10 per cent."
2. "University should provide residential accommodation on rent to the teachers in the neighbourhood of their buildings and hostels."
3. "The age of retirement of teachers should ordinarily be 60. But working could be allowed up to 64 in case of proficiency."

(b) Working Hours and Leave, etc.

1. " There should be provision for study leave. One year's leave at a time and three years leave in total service should be available to any teacher who wants to devote his time to study."
2. "Eighteen periods a week including tutorial classes is the maximum that any teacher should be required to put. Those who are in charge of Master's Degree classes and have to guide research students should have between 12-15 periods."

(c) Salary Scales of the Teachers

(i) Scale of the University Teachers

Professors	...900-50-1,350	per month
Readers	...600-30-900	"
Lecturers	...300-25-900	"
Instructors or Fellows	...250-25-500	"
Research Fellows	...250-25-500	"

(ii) *Scales for the Teachers of the Affiliated Degree Colleges*

(a) Principal	...600-40-800	per month
(b) Senior Teacher, at least two in every College	...400-25-600	"
(c) Lecturers	...200-15-320-20-400	"

(iii) *Scales for Teachers of the Post-Graduate Degree Colleges*

(a) Principal	...800-50-1,000	per month
(b) Senior Teachers, at least two in every College	...500-25-800	"
(c) Lecturers	...200-15-330- ...200-20-400-25-500	"

(d) Status of the Teachers

(i) The importance of the teachers and his responsibility should be recognised.

(ii) The conditions in the universities which are suffering from lack of finance and consequent demoralisation should be greatly improved.

(iii) There should be four classes of teachers *viz.*, Professors, Readers, Lecturers and Instructors.

(iv) Each university should have some Research Fellows. Promotion from one category to another should be solely on grounds of merits.

(v) Care should be taken in selection of proper teachers.

(vi) Proportion of Lecturers and Instructors to Professors and Readers should be 2:1.

(vii) Conditions regarding provident fund, leave and hours of work should be definitely laid down.

(viii) Other than casual leave there should be provision of study leave as well.

(ix) A tribunal to settle a dispute that may arise between the teachers and the administrators of the university.

3. Standards of Teaching

In this regard the Commission remarked, "The standards of teaching, examinations and experimental works are low. Hence, they need a great deal of improvement. Unless it is done, the Degree conferred by our universities will not be recognised in the advanced countries of the world."

(a) Causes of Failures

As the failures were the real proof of the low standards of education, the Commission suggested that "30 per cent to 60 per cent students failed every year in the University examinations. This means a good deal of wastage. Our universities should realise that every student who is admitted to a university has a right to assume that the university is prepared to see him through it, he has ordinary ability and works diligently."

The Commission has assigned the following three reasons for the failures:

(i) low standards of teaching,

(ii) lack of restrictions on students coming to seek admission to universities, and

(iii) the students are not instructed in the work as they really should be.

(b) Suggestions for Improvement in the Standard of Teaching

(i) "The standards of admission to the university courses should correspond to that of the present intermediate examination. This means that the students should be admitted to the university courses only when they acquired 12 years of study at school and an intermediate college."

(ii) "For raising the standard of education and teaching, the Commission felt that education at intermediate level should also be better equipped. It has suggested that a large number of well-equipped and well-staffed intermediate colleges should be established in each and every province."

(iii) Good number of vocational institutions should be started in order to divert students to various vocations after their schooling of 10-12 years.

(iv) Refresher courses should be organised by the university for the teachers of high school and intermediate colleges.

(v) The maximum number in the Arts and Science faculties of a teaching university should be fixed at 3000 and in an affiliated college, the number of students should not go beyond 1,500.

(vi) There should be 180 working days in a session in a university or a Degree College not including the days of examinations.

(vii) The session should be divided into three terms; each term should be of 11 weeks duration.

(viii) Lectures should be carefully planned and supplemented by tutorial, library work and written exercises.

(ix) The Commission has said that there should be no prescribed text-books for any course of study.

(x) Attendance at lecture should be compulsory for under-graduate students.

(xi) Only certain categories should be allowed to appear at public examinations privately.

(xii) Evening colleges should be started for working people.

(xiii) Tutorial system should be developed in all the institutions of higher education. Libraries in these institutions should be improved.

(xiv) Buildings, laboratories, fittings, equipments, work-shops, etc., of the institution of higher education should be improved.

(xv) Seminars should be organised for the development of post-graduate students pursuing work for Master's and Doctor's Degrees.

(xvi) Pass percentage should be improved. The minimum number of pass marks at all First Degree Examinations should be raised to 40 per cent and marks for the Second Division should be 55 per cent and for the First Division 70 per cent.

4. Curriculum of Courses of Study

(a) Functions of Courses of Study

Courses of study are essential expedients of formal education, but it should be recognised as nothing but an arbitrary though useful contrivance. Unless the vital inter-connections of all pieces of experience are kept in mind the convenient devices of courses of study may become barriers, which prevent our realising the unity of knowledge and experience."

(b) Phases of Education

(i) General Education. This includes information and experiences of varied nature. Its business of general education is to make available to the student, to inspire him to master, wisely selected information as to fact and principles, so that he will have representative and useful data, on which to base his thought, judgement and action and will be aware of the fields of interest and importance.

(ii) Liberal Education. It is preparation of the students for independent thinking for critical inquiry and appraisal and for creating the constructive thought and action.

(iii) Occupational Education. It prepares the students for his life work or for other specialised interest.

(c) Suggestions for Improvement of the Courses of Study

(i) General education should be so planned as to give varied experiences of life to the student and to enable him to feel that the elements of his environment have meaning and interest to him.

(ii) There should not be over specialisation. Rigidly fixed curriculum should be avoided as far as possible.

(iii) Students should be admitted to colleges and universities in the faculties of Arts and Science and to such provisional schools as do not require more advanced preparation for successful completion of 12 years of schooling or its equivalent.

(iv) Master's Degree should be given to Honours' students after one year of study, beyond the pass Bachelor's Degree and to pass students after two years beyond the pass Bachelor's Degree.

(v) The study of the theory' as well as practice of General Education should be undertaken both at the universities and the secondary schools.

(vi) The Commission has suggested to do away the overemphasis on specialisation.

(vii) The relations of general and special education should be worked out for each field keeping in mind the general interest of the student as personality and a citizen and his other special occupational interest.

(viii) As no improvement in the curriculum and syllabus of the University education can take place unless improvement is made in the curriculum and syllabus of the secondary education, the Commission suggested the following subjects:

(1) *Courses of Study at the Secondary Education*

(i) Mother tongue.

(ii) Federal language or a classical or modern Indian language (for those whose mother tongue happened to be Federal language).

(iii) English.

(iv) General Sciences (Physics and Biology or Social Studies including elements of Economics and Civics).

(v) to (vii) Not less than two of the following subjects:

(a) History (Indian, European, World).

(b) Geography and Geology.

(c) Economics.

(d) Civics.

(e) A classical language (Sanskrit, Persian, Arabic, Latin, Greek).

(f) Modern Indian languages (Hindi, Urdu, Bengali, Marathi, Gujarati, Tamil, Telugu, etc.).

(g) Modern European languages (English, French, German, etc.).

(viii) Logic, Psychology, Music, Science, Home Science, Hygiene, Mathematics, Physics, Chemistry, Biology, Elements of Accountancy and Book-keeping, Elements of Business Method, Economics, History and Geography, Stenotyping, Industrial Organisation, Commercial Arithmetic, and Elements of Soil Science.

(2) *Courses of Study at the First Degree Course.* First Degree Course should be of three years duration. In addition to the courses of general education and religion, arts and science students, whether for the 'Post or Honours courses' will have to study:

(i) Federal language, or if that happens to be the mother tongue a classical or modern English language,

(ii) English, and

(iii) For Arts students not less than two subjects preferably one from each group.

Group A — *Humanities*

(i) A classical or a modem Indian language.
(ii) English.
(iii) French or German.
(iv) Philosophy.
(v) History.
(vi) Mathematics.
(vii) Fine Arts.

Group B — *Social Studies*

(i) Politics.
(ii) Economics.
(iii) Sociology.
(iv) Psychology.
(v) Anthropology.
(vi) Geography.
(vii) Home Economics.

For Science students, not less than two special subjects from the following:

(i) Mathematics.
(ii) Physics.
(iii) Chemistry.
(iv) Botany.
(v) Zoology.
(vi) Geology.

5. Post-Graduate Teaching and Research

(a) Importance

"Human civilisation has derived great benefits from the efforts of specialists, for penetrating into the secrets of nature and motives and principles of human behaviour, individual and social. To a constantly increasing extent, modern life is the outcome of research. To quote Whitehead, 'A progressive society depends on its inclusion of three groups — scholars, discoverers, inventors'. "While the scholars re-discover the past and set before us ideals of wisdom, duty and goodness, discoverers find out new truths and inventors apply them to the present need. Universities are the agencies for producing these types of men who will fuse progressive activities into an effective instrument. Universities are responsible as much for extending the boundaries of knowledge as for the training of citizens; in fact, the differentiation of knowledge is a necessary condition of continued vitality of their teachings for unless a study is rooted in research, it will die."

(b) Utility

(a) "In humanities, research concerns itself mainly with the past history of man-of-his-thought as well as his experiences. The understanding of a man as a whole and the integration of the past with the present."

(b) In the Natural Science, research takes the form of an attempt to find out the undiscovered properties of nature and their application to the material needs of mankind.

(c) Training and research are equally valuable for administrators and men of affairs. The administrator imbued with the spirit of research will tackle a problem more thoroughly with greater directness than one who has had no training in research.

(c) Recommendations

(i) ***Post-graduate Studies.*** "At this stage the student must be trained in hard intellectual endeavour which must form an essential feature of any good higher education worth the name. In this regard it has suggested that there should be a standardisation of the courses prescribed for the post-graduate degrees in the various universities of the country. A candidate for the M.A. or M.Sc. Degree, should show high degree of scholarship and achievement in an examination, which should be conducted by papers and *viva voce* test, to be supplemented by a practical examination for science subjects.

Great care should be exercised in admission of students to the M.A. and M.Sc. classes. The whole of the students' record from the High School to B.A. and B.Sc. should be scrutinised before admitting them to the Second Degree course. Emphasis should be placed on the capacity and quality of the student and not on their number."

(d) Research

(i) ***Selection.*** Students for research leading to Ph.D. degree should be selected on all India basis. Only such students

should be allowed to carry on research who have attained not only a proper background in the fundamentals of their subject, but who have a certain innate originality of mind apart from mere learning, that is essential for a research worker.

(ii) ***Subjects.*** The Ph.D. course is that of specialisation in which the training and achievement should be such as to ensure that the student has successfully explored as a field study and has appreciably advanced knowledge of that subject by his own research.

(iii) ***Supervision.*** "A supervisor who should be a specialist in the subject and a successful researcher should meet his students about once a week during the term for the discussion of difficult points and the criticism of rough drafts of part of their thesis."

(iv) ***Facilities.*** For poor and meritorious and deserving students, the Commission suggested creation of certain 'studentship' so that the researcher may not suffer on account of economic reasons.

(v) ***Rules of Residence.*** There should be no strict rule about the residence in regard to research students. They may be allowed leave or absence for purpose of work at recognised institutions.

(vi) ***Requirement for the Award of Degrees.*** "The Training or Ph.D. Degree should extend over a period of two year The candidates should show ability to study the problems systematically and to relate his results to the general body of the subjects. He should present a thesis embodying his original contribution to knowledge set forth in such a manner as to be fit and ready for publication."

(vii) ***Examinations.*** "The educant should be examined ordinarily by three examiners, two external and one internal. There should always be a *viva voce* examination, which should test his general knowledge of the whole field of the subject to which his thesis refers."

(viii) ***Publication.*** The greater stimulus to produce good work is the publication of the thesis awarded with a degree of Ph.D. The University should assist in the publication of really good work through financial aid.

(ix) ***Research Fellowships.*** The Commission suggested the establishment of research fellowships in the various branches of knowledge in the universities in order to further the cause of research and knowledge. The universities should provide atmosphere as well as apparatus for higher study and encouragement to research. "Research should be primarily, if possible, the sole work of the holders of these fellowships and not mere adjuncts to a life consumed in teaching. They would generally divide their time between their own investigations and the training of other research workers.

(x) ***D. Litt, and D.Sc. Degrees.*** "D. Litt. and D.Sc. Degrees should be conferred on persons whose work show conspicuous originality, ability and distinction. They should be awarded entirely on published work of outstanding quality. Published work for these degrees should be adjudged by external examiners alone.

(xi) ***Research by College and University Teachers.*** The teachers of the universities and colleges should not only be encouraged to carry on the research but made to do so. They should be given ample opportunities for this task. The teachers should not only impart existing knowledge but should also be in a real sense creators of new knowledge.

(xii) ***Research in Humanity and Classical Languages, Fine Arts, etc.*** Government should try to aid to the research in these various branches. In this regard important roles could be played by the universities.

6. Professional Education

Professional Education is the process by which men and women prepare for existing responsible service in the professional spirit. The term may be restricted to preparation of fields requiring well informed and disciplined insight and skill of high order.

(i) Teaching of Agriculture

1. Agricultural education should be recognised as a major national issue.
2. Agricultural policy must rest on the understanding and participation of those engaged in agriculture. The study of agriculture in primary, secondary and higher

education should be given top priority in national economic planning.

3. Agricultural education, agricultural research and formulation of agricultural policy should be in the hands of persons and groups or associations of persons, who have first hand knowledge of agricultural life.
4. Agricultural education should be given a rural setting so that it may include experience of agricultural life.
5. The present agricultural colleges should be strengthened in equipment and teaching staff. New agricultural colleges, should be opened and agricultural education may be supported and enriched by contacts with other fields.
6. Experimental farms should be developed by the Central and Provincial governments.
7. Every basic elementary school, every secondary school and every rural university should have its own small experimental farm so that the spirit of research and experiment should pervade on rural life.
8. The existing agricultural laboratories should be supported and expanded to the full extent.
9. The Indian Council of Agricultural Research should be supported and developed as a clearing house and coordinating agency for all advanced agricultural research centres. An Institute of Agricultural Policy should be established to study the long-time agricultural policy of India.

(ii) Education of Commerce

1. Practical work should be given in the education of Commerce. The student should be given opportunity to undergo practical training in three or four forms of various kinds.
2. When the students have achieved graduation, some of them should be advised to become specialised in a particular profession like Accountancy and receive the practical training.
3. The Commission did not like the idea of making the studies at the Master's Degree in Commerce as bookish. On the other hand it suggested that very few students should be encouraged to go in for such a degree.

(iii) Medicine or Medical Education

1. "The maximum number of admissions to a Medical College should be 100.
2. All the departments of study which require hostel facilities, should be located in a single campus. There should be 10 beds per student admitted to a college.
3. Training in a rural centre should be required both in the under-graduate and graduate stages.
4. History of Medicine should be taught in the First Degree Course in Medicine with special reference to Indian system.
5. Facilities for research in indigenous system should be provided.
6. Public Health, Engineering and Nursing should be in colleges taking into account the personnel and the equipment essential for the purpose."

(iv) Education of Engineering and Technology

1. "The existing Engineering and Technological institutes of the country should be regarded as national assets, and steps should be taken to improve their usefulness.
2. The number of Engineering schools of different trades should be increased for training Foremen, Craftsmen, Draftsmen, Overseers, etc.
3. The First Year or more of Engineering Courses should be generally common to all branches of Engineering.
4. The existing Engineering and Technological colleges should be upgraded for post-graduate training and research in selected subjects.
5. Steps should be taken to start without delay the higher technological institutes for training Engineering Scientists, and design and development engineers.
6. Enquiries should be made to find out possibilities for training of Graduate Engineers and Engineering Scientists as employees in American and other institutions.
7. While establishing new Engineering colleges or institutions, inquiries should be made as to the types of Engineering services needed in India.
8. Engineering colleges should not be controlled by Ministries or Government Departments. They should be closely associated with universities.

9. Faculties of Engineering should be called the Faculties of Engineering and Technology."

(v) Education of Law or Legal Education

1. Legal Education should be thoroughly recognised. Since there is lack of uniformity in the set-up of Legal Education, the Law colleges should be reorganised.
2. Law should be taught on the pattern of teaching of other subjects at the university level. The staff of the Law faculties should be recruited and controlled by the universities in a fashion similar to Arts and Science faculties.
3. There should be restriction on admission of the students into the Faculties of Law. For admissions to Law course, there should be a three-year Degree course in pre-legal and general subjects as a requisite.
4. The students pursuing Degree courses in Law should not be permitted to carry other Degree courses simultaneously.
5. The teachers of Law should be whole-time as well as part-time. The duration of teaching should be like the regular hours of teaching of other subjects.
6. Opportunities for research should be available in every Law Faculty.

7. Teaching Profession

1. The courses of training colleges should be re-modelled. It has also recommended that more time should be given to school practice. More weight should be given to practice in evaluating the performance of the students.
2. The students should be encouraged to fall in with the current practice of school teaching and make a test of it.
3. Suitable schools should be used for practical training.
4. The staff of the training colleges should be recruited from people who have first-hand experience of school teaching.
5. The courses on the theory of education should be flexible and adaptable to local circumstances.
6. The students should be encouraged to proceed to the Master's Degree only after some years of experience of teaching. Original work by professors and lecturers should be planned on all-India basis.

8. Religious Education

1. All educational institutions should start working with a few minutes of silent meditation.
2. That in the first year of the Degree course, lives of great religious leaders like Gautam Buddha, Confucious, Zoraster, Socrates, Jesus, Shankar, Ramanuj, Madhva, Mohammad, Kabir, Nanak, Gandhi may be taught.
3. That in the second year, some selection of the universalist character of the scriptures of the world be studied.
4. That the central problems of philosophy of religion be considered.

9. Education of Women

The Commission observed, "There cannot be educated people without educated women. If general education had to be limited to men or women, that opportunity should be given to women, for then it would most surely be passed on to the next generation." The Commission had made the following recommendations:

1. The education of women should be in conformity with the requirements of women. They should be imparted education that may make them successful and good housewives.
2. Women should be given maximum facilities for education.
3. Women should be encouraged to the maximum to acquire education of Home Economics and Home Management.
4. In the institutions where co-education is prevalent due attention should be paid to the general facilities of co-education. Due regard should be paid to behaviour towards ladies as well.
5. Lady teachers should be given the same pay as the male teachers get.

10. Rural Education or Rural Universities

1. Radhakrishnan Commission surveyed rural education as prevalent in the various countries of the world. It recommended a programme for the reconstruction of the Indian villages. It suggested for the establishment of rural universities. The number of the students studying in rural colleges and universities should not exceed 2,500.
2. The aim of these rural colleges and rural universities should be to provide general education to the boys and girls of the

rural areas and to bring about the development of their individual interests.

3. There should be provision for separate teachers and teaching in the various rural colleges and universities. But they may be brought to one place for laboratory work and for the use of libraries.
4. While the students are getting education for the undergraduate classes, they should be encouraged to go in for a curriculum of some professional or occupational institutions. This will bring about greater development.
5. Arrangement for research facilities should also be made in these rural universities.
6. An all India institute of rural education should be established.

11. Medium of Instruction

1. Hindi was likely to be the language of the Union or the Federal language and so it was suggested that steps should be taken for its enrichment and development at the earliest.
2. In order to develop Hindi not only new words should be acquired but such words that are prevalent since olden days in other Indian languages should be acquired and owned.
3. In order to get the fullest benefit of the higher education, English as the medium of instruction should be at the earliest replaced by some other Indian language.
4. At the secondary stage of education and the university stages as well, the students should be taught by regional language or the mother tongue: national language or the Federal language and English as well.
5. Regional language should be the medium of instruction of higher education. But the Federal language should be made a medium of instruction of one or more subjects.
6. Constructive steps should be taken to develop regional languages and the Federal language.
7. The Commission was in favour of the use of Devanagri script. It suggested that its defects should be removed at the earliest.
8. The Commission did realise the importance of the Sanskrit language but it did not agree with the idea to make the Sanskrit as the medium of instruction.

9. The Commission recommended a uniform list of technical and scientific terms for all the Indian languages. It also recommended the establishment of a body to discharge this duty. It was in favour of taking over of international technical and scientific terminology, of course, by changing its sound and pronunciation in accordance with the sound and pronunciation of the Indian languages. Thus it suggested their Indianisation.
10. The Commission suggested the teaching of English as before, in secondary schools, colleges and universities.

12. The System of Examination

The Commission observed, "For nearly half a century the examinations, as they have been functioning, have been recognised as one of the worst features of Indian education. Commissions and committees have expressed their alarm at their pernicious domination over the whole system of education in India. The obvious deficiencies and harmful consequences of the most pervasive evil in Indian education have been analysed and set out clearly by successive University Commissions since 1902, by a Government Resolution as far back as 1904 and by a Committee of the Central Advisory Board of Education in recent years."

The Commission recommended:

1. Objective type of examinations held instead of the present essay-type of examinations. The Ministry of Education and the universities should try to study the problem with a view to apply the results of this study in Indian educational practice.
2. Every University should have a permanent full-time Board of Examiners with a small staff of assistants who can do clerical and routine work. The members of this Board should have at least five years of teaching experience and at least one of them should be a highly expert person in this field. This Board should advise the university or college instructing staff in regard to techniques in devising and constructing objective tests for the class examinations. They should also make periodic and thorough inspections by use of progress tests in affiliated colleges which should be required to maintain certain academic standards in addition to the quantitative criteria now required for affiliation.

3. Experts of the techniques of examination should be in the Ministry of Education, who may carry on the experiments in this field.
4. University Degree should not be required for Administrative Services. Special State examinations for recruitment to the various services should be organised and should be open to whosoever cares to take them.
5. Class work should be given due credit and importance. At least one-third of the marks allotted to a particular subject should be reserved for the class work of the boy.
6. Only such persons should be appointed examiners who have five years teaching experience of the subject.
7. Every examining authority should have a careful study made of the work done in other countries to discover methods of minimising the outstanding defects of essay-type examinations and other such things.
8. Uniform standard of marking should be observed in various universities. A candidate should get 70 per cent or more marks to secure the first class, 55-69 per cent for second class and at least 40 per cent for a third class.
9. The practice of giving grace marks should be abolished for the first-degree and all higher examinations.
10. *Viva voce* examinations should be employed only for post-graduate and professional degrees. They should be designed, however, to test the candidate's competence in the fundamentals of the field of study to which the problem of his research belongs.

13. Students

1. **Selection of the Students.** Students should be admitted to the universities without any distinction of caste or creed. They should be selected on the basis of achievement tests. Those who have capacity for higher education should be selected. Opportunity for higher education should be based on ability, character and industry. No favour should be given to student belonging to a particular caste or creed.
2. **Scholarship to Equalise Opportunity.** For the boys and girls with slender resources, scholarships should be available. Tests should be held for scholarships and those who succeed at them should be given scholarships to pursue their higher education.

3. **Health and Medical Care of the Students.** Due care should be taken of the health of the students.

   (i) ***Medical Examination.*** There should be medical check up of the students coming up for education in the university or the colleges.

   (ii) ***Hospital and Medical College.*** All residential universities should have a medical college and there should be at least a hospital or infirmery with a competent staff of doctors, technicians and nurses, established in each and every university. In regard to colleges situated in the Muffassils, doctors should be brought from city for physical examination. The members of the staff should also be medically examined. Due care should be taken for the treatment of mental and physical elements.

   (iii) ***Recreation and Physical Education.*** Physical education is necessary for good health. Programmes of physical education and exercises should be arranged. Universities should be equipped with teachers of physical education, gymnasias, play-grounds, etc.

   (iv) ***National Cadet Corps.*** Scheme of National Cadet Corps should be introduced in all the colleges and universities. The entire expenditure on this scheme should be made by the Central Government. Those students who do not join it should be made to undergo a two years physical education.

   (v) ***Social Services.*** Students should be encouraged and inspired to take up social services.

   (vi) ***Residences.*** In the universities and the colleges, there should be good arrangement of the hostels. No hostel should have more than 50 boys and in every hostel there should be good arrangement of the facilities for games and physical exercises, etc.

   (vii) ***Proctorial System.*** Proctorial system should be introduced in order to encourage the students to take part in administration and to develop administrative abilities.

   (viii) ***Student Unions.*** Authority should not interfere with the students' unions. The students' unions should also have nothing to do with the politics and other political activities.

(ix) *Discipline.* Every effort should be made to maintain the discipline amongst the students. With this aim in view the students should be encouraged to take part in constructive activities.

(x) *Development of Corporate Life.* Development of corporate life is an essential part of higher education. The teachers should mingle with the students freely and bring about development of corporate life.

(xi) *Dean of the Students Welfare.* Dean of the Students' Welfare should be appointed in every university. A Board of Students' Welfare should be established in universities where there is no such body.

SECONDARY EDUCATION

1. The Director of Education should be the main officer responsible to advise the Minister of Education.
2. A committee should be constituted at the Centre as well as at the States, entrusted with the task of drawing up new plans of education and giving thought to educational problem.
3. There should be a Board of Secondary Education to deal with the matters of education at the Secondary stage. The Director of Education should be the Chairman of this Board, and there should not be more than 25 members.
4. The Board should appoint a sub-committee, specially to deal with and conduct examinations.
5. There should also be a Board for the teachers' training. This Board should lay down the necessary conditions for the proper training of those under-graduates who wish to enter the teaching profession.
6. There should be clear-cut conditions for the recognition of the schools.
7. Inspectors should be responsible for studying the problems of the institutions under them.
8. The Managing Committees of the institutions, run by private bodies should be registered bodies.

MERITS OF RECOMMENDATIONS

1. **Original.** The Commission studied the secondary education from an original point of view.

2. **Aims.** The aim of secondary education should be to inculcate and develop democratic qualities in the students. With this aim in view, the Commission has recommended that education for building up of the character of the students and discipline, moral and religious instructions should be imparted in the schools.
3. **Diversification.** The Commission has suggested for the diversification of the courses, at this stage of education, in order to satisfy the individual interests and aptitudes of the students going in for this stage of education.
4. **Multi-purpose Schools.** It has also recommended for the establishment and development of multi-purpose schools.
5. **Improvement of Teachers Status.** The Commission has suggested the improvement in the salary scales and conditions of service of the teachers.
6. **Examination.** Recommendations in regard to examinations and evaluation of the work done by the Commission shall really be very useful for our education, where implemented.
7. **Counselling and Guidance.** Educational counselling and guidance shall help the students to know their interests, capabilities and aptitudes. This thing will help them to be successful in their future life.
8. **Physical Welfare.** The suggestions of the Commission in regard to physical welfare of the students are also very valuable.

DEMERITS OF RECOMMENDATIONS

1. **Repetitions.** The suggestions of the Commission lack originality. They are only repetitions of the old ones.
2. **Unbalanced.** The recommendations in regard to administration are incomplete and unbalanced.
3. **Women Education.** The Commission has not given any important suggestion in regard to education of women.
4. **Curriculum.** It has not made any important distinction between the curriculum prescribed for the boys and the girls, although the requirements of the two are quite different from each other.
5. **Abolition of Intermediate.** The suggestion of the Commission to abolish the Intermediate classes is not very justified.

6. **Three-Language Formula.** By recommending the study of the three languages, the Commission has burdened the curriculum of the students.

QUESTIONS FOR EXERCISE

1. Discuss the main problems of university and higher education in India and suggest remedies.
2. What are the chief reasons for the falling of standard of higher education in India? How can the difficulties in this direction be removed?
3. What are the problems of Indian universities? What proposals have been offered by Radhakrishnan Commission to solve those problems?
4. In what way is the educational programme laid down by Radhakrishnan University Commission practicable for the development of the rural system of education in India?
5. State the views of the Radhakrishnan Commission on reforms of examination and medium of instruction.
6. What reforms have been suggested in the university education in this country by the Radhakrishnan Commission?
7. Describe briefly the recommendations of Radhakrishnan Commission in regard to various types of education, medium of instruction, teaching profession and students' welfare.

CHAPTER 24

ACHARYA NARENDRA DEV COMMITTEE (1939, 1953)

ACHARYA NARENDRA DEV COMMITTEE (1939)

Appointment of the Committee. With the aim to study the problems of education and its re-organisation a committee under the chairmanship of Acharya Narendra Dev was appointed. This is called Acharya Narendra Dev Committee Report in the name of its Chairman, Acharya Narendra Dev.

RECOMMENDATIONS

1. The present system of education is incapable of bringing about alround development of the personality of the child.
2. The aim of the secondary education has become only to prepare the students for the universities.
3. The curriculum of the Intermediate classes should be complete and independent.
4. The period of education should be from 12 years to 18 years.
5. All the Secondary institutions should be called 'Colleges' and their standards of education should be higher than the standards of the present Intermediate classes.
6. The course of the First-year of the new colleges should be the same as that of the last two years of the basic primary schools. English should be a compulsory subject of study. A good deal of emphasis should be laid on handicrafts.
7. The following subjects should be included in the curriculum:
   (i) Language, Literature and Social Studies.
   (ii) Natural Sciences and Mathematics.
   (iii) Art.
   (iv) Commerce.

(v) Industrial and Vocational education.

(vi) Home Science for girls only.

8. Only those students who have finished seven years curriculum or have passed the Basic Primary Examination should be admitted into college.
9. The names of High Schools and Intermediate ones should be done away with.
10. The medium of instruction should be Hindustani.
11. Curriculum should be real and practical. They should be drawn up by the experts, keeping in view the conditions, requirements and needs of the country.
12. Teaching of Physiology and General Science should also be made compulsory. Advisory Boards for the establishment of all types of institutions should be formed.
13. Home Science colleges should be established for the girls.
14. Adequate arrangement should be made for the women education.
15. Technical, occupational and industrial education should be encouraged.
16. Reforms in the text-books, system of education and organisation of education should be made at the earliest.
17. It should be made binding to have well-equipped library in every educational institution.
18. Adequate arrangement should also be made for the training of the teachers. Their conditions of service, security, pay scales, etc., should also be improved. They should also be required to fill in agreement forms.
19. With a view to bring about the character building of the students and inculcate the spirit of patriotism, self-reliance, citizenship, capable of standing on their own legs, feeling of social service, etc., in them, extra-curricular activities should be organised in every institution from time to time.
20. Scouting, co-opertive societies, debating societies, first-aid, social service, etc., should be properly organised in the institutions.
21. A Central Pedagogical Institute should be established in the province.

ACHARYA NARENDRA DEV COMMITTEE (1953)

Terms of Reference

1. To determine the new scheme of secondary education made operative from July 1948.
2. To examine the various groups, A, B, C and D laid down by the Board of High School and Intermediate Education.
3. To determine how far boys and girls have been directed to take up different types or courses according to their predisposition and aptitude.
4. To determine the extent to which success has been achieved in the introduction in Government schools as well as non-Government institutions of the new groups 'C' and 'D':
   (a) to assess the utility of introducing the subject in a particular area,
   (b) to examine the extent to which suitable provision by way of staff and equipment has been made for the successful teaching of these subjects.
5. To examine how far the practical and industrial subjects have helped those who have taken up these courses to make them choose professions related to these activities.
6. To suggest ways and means in which improvements can be effected in making the *Secondary Education Scheme* successful, as a whole.
7. To consider if and in what way technical education can be coordinated with general education.
8. To examine the working of continuous classes in Government and non-Government schools and to determine how far the objectives expected have been fulfilled. To make recommendations about the syllabus legibility for admission and the award of a certificate to successful candidates and the equivalents of such a certificate.
9. To consider the recommendations of the *"Holiday and School Hours Committee"*.
10. To examine the existing system of selection of text-books and to suggest ways and means for the production of text-books for the use of students and to consider how far frequent changes in the text-books could be avoided.
11. To inquire into the present system of conduct of High School and Intermediate Examinations.

12. To consider the existing system of management of non-Government institutions and to suggest changes which might remove the various defects.

REPORT OF THE COMMITTEE

Defects in the Secondary Scheme of Education

1. The scheme of secondary education as suggested by the first Acharya Narendra Dev Committee was not preplanned. It had been implemented without giving a proper examination of it before implementing it. Because of this lacuna it had to face various problems and defects, and therefore it did not achieve the desired success.
2. The division of the subjects into compulsory and optional and subsidiary led to various difficulties for the teachers as well as students.
3. No result was achieved by making general knowledge a compulsory subject for the students. Although Elementary Hindi was made a compulsory subject, but because its marks were not added to the result, it was looked at with negligence and Hindi could not get the proper encouragement.
4. Although the scheme had very specifically provided for guidance and counselling of the students, no steps were taken to provide this facility to the students.
5. The number of students in secondary schools is going up so fast that it is not possible for the Government to keep control over it. Not only there is dearth of trained teachers, but there is also inadequate provision for the training facilities in the newly established training institutions.
6. Since classes III, IV and V have been taken away from the Secondary schools, many guardians educate their children up to V class at their own and then get them admitted into VI class.
7. The Secondary Education schools do not possess good buildings, necessary educational and teaching material, good libraries and laboratories.
8. The condition of the teachers is also not satisfactory They not only receive inadequate and low salaries but they also do not receive it in time. The Managing Committees are free to dispense with the services of the teachers as and when they like. There is no security of service for the teachers of

these secondary schools, and the Managing Committees are in no way in the control of the administrative authorities of the Education Department of the State.

RECOMMENDATIONS

1. Syllabus

1. Hindi with Sanskrit should be a compulsory subject for all the four years of the secondary education, namely 9-12 year There should be two papers for Hindi, carrying 25 marks and the third paper should be Sanskrit with 30 marks. It should be compulsory to secure pass marks in Hindi as well as Sanskrit separately.
2. A modern Indian language as enumerated in the Schedule VIII of the Constitution of India, other than Hindi or modern foreign language should also be a compulsory subject at the Secondary stage of education.
3. General English should be taken out of the curriculum.
4. Mathematics should be a compulsory subject in class IX and X and an optional subject in XI and XII classes for the boys. It should be an optional subject for the girls. On the other hand, Home Science should be a compulsory subject for the girls at the Higher Secondary stage of education. The boys should not be allowed to offer this subject.
5. For the first two years *i.e.* classes IX and X, six subjects should be taught, in classes XI and XII five subjects should be taught. The students may offer certain additional subjects.
6. The division of the subjects into main and subsidiary should be done away with.
7. Particular attention should be paid to the aptitude of students for offering optional subjects. Facilities for educational guidance and counselling should be provided all over the State at the earliest.
8. While granting recognition in commercial, agriculture, aesthetic, constructive and scientific groups, the needs of the areas or the local needs should always be kept in view.
9. No institution should be given recognition in agriculture, unless it has 10 acres of farm attached to it for agriculture work. Institutions should also have agricultural implements and equipments for those students who wish to take scientific group in classes IX and X.

10. In order to have a co-ordinated scheme of education, the Committee suggested that necessary change should be effected in the syllabus of Basic, Primary and Junior High schools.
11. The College of Home Science for Women at Allahabad should be improved in all respects. It should be equipped from the point of view of personnel, method of teaching and other requirements.

2. Text-books

1. Education Department should recommend a few books as help and guide. These books should be properly written and produced. Selection of the text-books should be left to the Head of the Institution, who may do so in consultation with the subject teachers.
2. Syllabus for each subject should be laid down by the Education Department. This task may be accomplished with the help of the experts and senior teachers who are actually engaged in the task of teaching those subjects.
3. Like America and England, societies and associations should be formed for production of standard text-books, a book once selected should be allowed to stay at least for three years.
4. Government should take up the task of production of good and standard textbooks. Eminent authors and teachers should be encouraged and requested to write standard text-books on various subjects. For this task, monetary assistance may be given. The Government should undertake the responsibility of printing and publishing of text-books.

3. Examinations

(i) ***Three Years Course.*** There should be a three-year Secondary course as well as University course. The Committee recommended the abolition of the Intermediate classes and suggested that XII class should be added to the University course and the XI class to the Secondary education. There should be only one public examination and this should be held at the end of three years of Higher Secondary stage education.

(ii) ***High School Examination.*** High School Examination should be conducted only for private candidates. Regular candidates may be promoted from class X to XI class. Those

regular students who want to get a High School certificate may appear at a High School Examination.

(iii) ***Minimum Age for Appearing at this Examination.*** In order to be able to appear at the High school Examination as a regular student, one must have attained the age of 14 years and 16 years for Intermediate examination. In case of a private candidate, he should have attained the minimum age of 16 years for High School and the girl candidate should have attained the age of 15 years.

(iv) ***Percentage of Attendance.*** A regular candidate in order to be able to appear at the High School or Intermediate examination should have attended 75 per cent of the classes held.

Those students who have not put in at least 90 per cent of the total attendance, should not be promoted to the next higher class in the whole examination.

No student should be admitted to class IX unless he had passed class VIII of a Higher Secondary school or secured a Junior High school certificate.

Suitable attainment test should be prepared for Junior High School Examinations. This would add to the efficiency of the examinations.

Objective tests, in order to test usual intelligence and general knowledge should be conducted and also, attainment of Hindi and Mathematics should be assessed in these scholarship examinations.

4. Technical Education

1. Technical schools should provide for medium of general education with, of course, technical subjects.
2. Technical schools should be administered by the Education Department.
3. A Board should be appointed to co-ordinate the activities of the Industries Department and the Education Department.
4. While openings schools, an industrial survey should be conducted.
5. Many of the existing technical schools should be made polytechnics.
6. After Junior High schools, the curriculum should be bifurcated.

7. In Higher Secondary schools, constructive subjects should be taught in a way that they encourage the student to take up practical activities in the field.
8. Education in industrial and technical schools should be free.
9. In the institutions run by the Industries Department there should be two years and four years' courses. The minimum educational qualification to these schools should be VIII class.
10. In Junior Technical Schools, Hindi and one other modem Indian or foreign language. Science, Physics and Chemistry should be the compulsory subjects of study. The educational standard of theses schools should be that of High School. The curriculum or the courses of study of the Senior Technical Schools should not include subjects prescribed for general education.
11. For girls arrangement for teaching suitable crafts should be made in the schools meant for them. These subjects are book-craft, tailoring, embroidery, laundry work, needle work, dyeing and printing, applied economics and fruit preservation, etc.
12. Metal crafts, ceramics, industrial chemistry, etc. should not be taught in Higher Secondary schools. They should be left to the industrial and technical schools.
13. Higher institutes should be provided with facilities for industrial research. Various institutions of this nature might join together in this task to carry on the work in a co-operative manner.
14. One year course of general education must be given to the boys who wish to come over from technical schools to literary schools after completing their two years' course.

5. Testing and Guidance of the Students

1. The Committee recommended the standardisation of the test in the following fields:
   (a) Stanford Binet test of individual intelligence should be adopted in Hindi.
   (b) Group test of work, mental abilities should also be standardised.
2. There should be psychological centres in every district.
3. Government should establish a Council of Psychological Research in Education and Psychology.

4. The syllabus of the training colleges and the degrees in education of the various universities may be modified, as to include the guidance aspect and psychology. The branch of study may be included in the papers of experimental Psychology. The school should maintain a record of each student right from the basic stage. Such a record is helpful in providing guidance to the students.
5. Teachers of Junior High School classes in the Secondary schools should be required to watch the aptitude of the children with great care. The guidance should be an optional facility only. The heads of the institutions and the guardians of the students should be encouraged to avail of this advice and facility wherever it is available.

6. Working Days and Hours

1. The institutions should work for at least 200 days. These days should not be more than 235 inclusive of examination days and the days fixed for certain extracurricular activities.
2. During summer, the schools should run four hours in the morning, but during other months they should run for five hours. This time should not include recess.
3. Every institution must open on July 8 and if that is a holiday it should open the day next to it.

7. Religious and Moral Education

1. The moral and humanist education should form an integral part of our education.
2. The school should begin its work by an assembly of at least 10 minutes' duration and a prayer selected by the Principal should be recited.
3. There should be a periodical discourse, say, once a week or fortnight, on a topic concerning moral and spiritual values.
4. The lives of the leaders of great religions of the world and moral leaders of humanity of all ages should be prescribed as rapid readers.

8. Discipline and Good Manners

1. In order to secure an intimate contact between the teacher and the taught and the guardian, the students should be divided into groups of 20-30.
2. Institutions that have a very good discipline or excellent discipline should receive some sort of recognition from the Government.

3. Occasional meetings of the guardians and the teachers should be convened and the case of indiscipline may be discussed at these meetings and remedies thought about.
4. There should be a Students' Advisory Committee to help the Head in the maintenance of the discipline. Prefectual system should be introduced in educational institutions.
5. The Head of the institutions should have powers for expulsion, rustication and corporal punishment.
6. The age prescribed for different classes should be reduced by two years in each case.
7. In order to include a sense of dignity of labour and to impress upon the students the importance of social service, every student should be required to devote 40 hours in a year to manual work and social service.
8. One full-time physical training instructor should be provided in every school which can afford to do so and every teacher of the recognised institution should be made to undergo a short refresher course in physical training to be prescribed by the department.
9. The school records giving a number of details about the students (namely, academic attainment, conduct, participation in extra-curricular activities, health) should be regularly maintained in the schools by the principal with the help of class teachers and columns for discipline and good manners should be provided in the scholar register.
10. The students should be discouraged for going to the films that have an adverse effect on the mental health and discipline of the students.
11. The Committee has also suggested for further classification of the students, keeping in view the requirements of the students.
12. Cinema advertisements should not be allowed within the premises of the schools.
13. The programme of radio broadcasting by All India Radio should be given a proper orientation.

9. Better Management of Non-Government Institutions

1. The Committee suggested that the reforms should be conducted immediately. The Managing Committee of an institution should not have more than 12 members, to be elected after every three year Every Managing Committee

should have the Head of the institution and representative of the teachers in it. These Managing Committees should not be formed on the basis of religion or caste.

2. Every Managing Committee should have a sub-committee of five members for the appointment of teachers. The Head of the institution must be a member of the committee. After the appointment the approval of the District Inspector of Schools must be obtained on it.
3. Within four months of the appointment, the teacher should be asked to fill in the agreement form and arbitration board should also be established to decide the disputes between the teachers and the Managing Committees.
4. Transfer Board for the transfer of the teachers of non-government institutions should be formed.
5. Efforts should be made to bring about reforms and improvements in the emoluments and service conditions of the teachers.
6. If a management or a board controls more than one institution, situated in different districts, then separate managing bodies should be created for each school or district or town. The committee should hold its meeting in the district or in the town in which the institution is situated.
7. Donors of educational endowments should get examined from the Income-tax authorities on that donation.
8. All well-managed institutions are received at the hands of the Governments.

10. State Bureau of Psychology

The Committee realised that the State Bureau of Psychology, U.P. was doing useful work. It therefore suggested that the Bureau should be encouraged and better equipped.

Evaluation of the Recommendations

1. The Committee has made a very valuable suggestion for the reorganization and reorientation of Secondary Education in free India.
2. The Committee has made a comprehensive study of the Secondary Education in the State and made suggestions and recommendations for the overall development and reorganisation of Secondary Education.

3. The classes and regrouping of the subjects have been made in a practical and scientific manner.
4. The suggestions of the Committee in regard to Psychological tests and guidance and counselling are very valuable.
5. The suggestions in regard to text-books are useful and practical.
6. Recommendations in regard to better management of non-government educational institutions and the emoluments and conditions of service of the teachers are useful.

QUESTIONS FOR EXERCISE

1. Describe briefly the recommendations of Acharya Narendra Dev Committee (1939) Report and examine them critically.
2. Describe briefly the recommendations made by the Acharya Narendra Dev Committee (1953) for the re-organisation and improvement of the educational set-up in the State. Critically examine the recommendations as well.

CHAPTER 25

THE 10+2+3 SYSTEM

The Historical Background

10+2+3 concept of educational structure is not an altogether new idea of the eighth decade of the current century. It originated from the Calcutta University Commission of 1917-19, which recommended the introduction of matriculation, intermediate and the first degree examinations. This Commission recommended that the first degree course should be of three-year duration. But the three-year degree course could not be introduced due to certain factors. The Radhakrishnan University Commission of 1948-49 repeated the idea of 10+2+3 pattern contained in the Calcutta University Commission. It expected that the introduction of the three-year degree course will raise the standard of higher education.

The Secondary Education Commission (1952-53) pondered over the problem of 10+2+3 educational structure. But it introduced a new pattern of 8+3+3. The first eight years term of education was called junior classes. After this the three-year duration was to be of higher secondary and three years for the first degree course. This structure could not be accepted by the whole country. For example, in U.P., till very recently the first degree course continued to be of two years duration.

At the time of the Kothari Commission (1964-66) there were four patterns of educational structure in the country *viz.*, 10+2+3,10+2+2,11+3,11-12+1+3. The Commission, therefore, emphasised the necessity of introduction of a uniform educational structure of 10+2+3. Teachers, students and various educational bodies of the country accepted this pattern. It was planned that by the end of the Fifth Five Year Plan this educational pattern should be adopted in the whole country. The Government of India also recommended the introduction of this uniform educational structure. Andhra Pradesh, Maharashtra, West Bengal, M.P., Rajasthan, Punjab, Haryana, Himachal Pradesh, Bihar and Orissa adopted this educational structure. U.P., also adopted the three-year degree course pattern since the academic session of 1987-88. but it continues to hold High School and Higher Secondary (Intermediate) examinations separately.

The Meaning of 10+2+3

Under the 10+2+3 structure of education, general education is imparted to the child for the first ten year This education is common to all the children in the country. In the two year or 'plus two' education plan an attempt was to be made to identify the individual differences, such as abilities as physical, intellectual and emotional, etc. This was in order to do the needful for their further development to enable them to stand on their own legs when their formal education is over. The 'plus three' plan means the first three years degree course only for those students who were really able for the same.

Towards the close of the seventh decade of the current century this system was recommended to obtain a similar pattern of education throughout the country, as the various States differed from each other in their pattern. Till very recently in U.P. the system has been that of 10+2+2. In Rajasthan, Bihar and M.P., and in some other States has been 11+3, and in some places 10+2+3.

Content of Education

10+2+3 structure of education is an attempt to introduce a uniform pattern of education throughout the whole country. In it enough scope has been provided to make necessary adjustment according to local requirements. This new pattern has not been an imposition. During the first ten years of education the teachers were given freedom in adopting teaching methods for the curriculum in consonance with the needs and aspirations of the people of various areas concerned. Work- experience was chosen as the principal means of learning under this new structure of education during the first ten years of education. The child was taught so much of science that he was able to understand its importance in modern life. Along with teaching of science, the children were taught social sciences as well. Simultaneously, they were given education in aesthetic experience and physical culture. The students were embued with the idea that education is not restricted to the four walls of the school. They clearly understood that it is related with all the social unity and that it has to be continued throughout one's whole life and not during the school life alone. This view of obtaining education from wherever it is possible could keep an individual alive to his surroundings and improve his behaviour through all possible and available means.

The study of three languages, mathematics and social sciences was made compulsory' for each student during the first ten years of education. History, geography, civics, economics and psychology were included in the group of social sciences. In the curriculum of science importance was attached to the study of physics, chemistry and biology.

The Three Language Formula

Under the three-language formula primary education was to be imparted through the mother tongue of the child. Mother tongue was to be regarded as the first language. Where the mother tongue was not Hindi, the second language should be Hindi. The third language should be either English or any other foreign language. Sanskrit or Persian may be accepted either as a part of the first or second language or it may be included as subject. It was assumed that by the end of the first ten years of education a student should be expert in the first language. He should be able to understand and express himself in the second language and he should be able to understand the printed pages of the third language.

The Semester System

It was recommended that the various aspects of the curriculum should be split into units in such a manner that each one is related with another in a natural manner. It is after the study of one unit that another one will be taken up. It was suggested that under this scheme the academic session will be split into two or three semesters during the year. The work of students will be evaluated through an examination at the end of each semester. Each semester will be of about four months duration. Thus the load of the curriculum will be equitably distributed within the span of two or three semesters.

No Hurry to Finish the Course

It was hoped that the teachers and students will not be in a hurry to finish the course anyhow. The process of learning was to be so guided that students assimilate the rudiments of the various courses properly and effect improvements in their behaviour accordingly. It was not important for the students to memorise the various aspects of the curriculum. The teaching method was to be such that the students get inspired to learn things themselves. It was expected that the school will become conscious of the ever-arising new needs of the society and will make students better able to meet them successfully.

The Plus Two Education

After the first ten years "The plus two" year education was for those students who wanted to continue their formal education further. During "plus two year" education the emphasis was laid on 'vocational' and 'academic' courses. Facilities were available for a student to get himself transferred from one course to another if he feels so inclined. The plus two year education was to relieve universities of the burden of over-crowdedness, as those studying vocational courses are likely to opt themselves for vocational lines and not run for university education for the sake of a degree. After completing the 10+2 education of 12 years, the aspiring student was to go for the first degree course of three years run by a University.

Suggestions for Success

For a successful implementation of the above 10+2+3 structure the following suggestions were made:

1. A suitable machinery should be evolved for analysing and interpreting the various aspects of the curriculum for the different levels, *i.e.* '10', '2' and '3' levels. This machinery should indicate as to how to make the process of learning practical and more useful to life situations.
2. Necessary investigations must be made for organising work experience for students of various levels in order to enable them to obtain really useful experiences.
3. Necessary changes should be introduced in the teachers education programme in order that newly trained teachers may be able to meet the requirements of this new educational structure.

4. Co-operation should be obtained from the society. For this purpose, a group of well-trained workers should be organised for propagating the view in the society that the school is for the people (or society) and it cannot be successfully run without their co-operation and that parents have to play a vital role in education of their children.
5. The university education system should be reorganized in order to make its courses suitable for those students who come for higher education after successfully completing the 10+2 education.
6. A constructive revolution should be peacefully brought out in our educational structure so that the primary, secondary and university education become geared to help all-round development of our students.

QUESTIONS FOR EXERCISE

1. Explain, discuss and evaluate 10+2+3 system.
2. Bring out the basic points implied in the 10+2+3 structure of education.
3. How is the 10+2+3 policy of education likely to improve the existing system of education in the country? Explain.

CHAPTER 26

THE OPEN UNIVERSITY AND ASC

Explanation of the Concept

The concept of Open University or University of their Air was originated in 1963 by Mr. Harold Wilson, the opposition leader of Great Britain. In 1967 a plan for 'open university' was formulated and in 1969 a Committee was appointed in U.K. to implement the idea. From 1971 an open university was started in U.K. under the campus of Walter Hall of Milton Kans. Open university is an attempt to make higher education available to people of distant places in their own homes through correspondence, T.V. and Radio programmes, and sometimes through seminar and contact programmes wherever possible and necessary. In India for the first time during 1970 the University Grants Commission, the Government of India, Ministry of Education and the Ministry of Information and Broadcasting organised a seminar on 'open university'. However, the idea could be given a concrete shape only in 1982 when an open university was started at Nagarjun Sagar in Andhra Pradesh.

Functioning

An open university does not hold formal classes as the traditional universities do. An open university may have a number of regional centres. Each regional centre is put under a Director. It is hoped that an open university will remove the crowd from universities, it will be able to impart education to those youths who have not been able to obtain higher education due to some reasons. There is no age-limit for obtaining this higher education which costs much less than what a formal university student has to pay for his studies. An open university is not required to appoint a number of teachers. Instead, it may choose to appoint some part-time teachers for working at its regional centres. In order to assist the Vice-Chancellor in his administrative duties a pro-Vice-Chancellor, Registrar and Deans of various faculties and Subject-Heads of Departments are appointed.

INDIRA GANDHI NATIONAL UNIVERSITY

Establishment

By an Act of the Indian Parliament the Indira Gandhi National University was established on September 20,1985. Its foundation-stone was laid on November, 19, 1985 within 100 acres of land in the southern surrounding of New Delhi by Prime Minister Rajiv Gandhi who said, "Our endeavour is that in India, the poorest, the most backward children received best possible education, and in this direction, today, we are here to take a step forward. This open university will extend educational opportunities to all the corners of the country."

Teaching Methods

The Indira Gandhi National University proposed to use modern communication technologies for giving education. It adopted a number of methods which consist of 1. Broadcasts through Radio and T.V., 2. Audio and Visual materials, 3. Specially printed materials, 4. Face-to-face contact between the tutors and students at the established study centres.

Programmes

From the beginning of 1987 a number of academic programmes were started such as courses in diplomas in management, distance education, computer science, and rural development etc. Undergraduate courses in arts, science and commerce have also been started from August and September, 1987 under certain regional centres. Application-oriented courses for developing skills of students in such areas as management studies, energy resources, local self-government, horticulture and computer science, etc., were opened at various centres. There was no rigidity in the choice of subjects. There was no minimum qualification for admission to the undergraduate courses. But those who did not pass the intermediate examination or the first year of the three-year degree course were to pass an entrance examination to be conducted by the university.

Evaluation

Evaluation in the Indira Gandhi National University is like conventional examination conducted at the end of an academic session. It is a continuous process. A self-assessment by a student and continuous assessment by the university makes the student ever-alert. To maintain high standards, there is external examination also.

Contact Sessions at Study Centres

Contact session at study centres are organised for rendering academic and personal help to students The students are given carefully prepared materials which is supplemented by lectures and demonstrations during contact sessions at study centres. The study centres provide a common forum to students for interaction with each other and also with the tutors. Each study centre is equipped with audiovisual materials, reception and information service and a library. At this study centre there are counsellors for giving expert guidance to the needy students. A part-time co-ordinator with a supporting part-time staff is available at the study centre for giving the necessary help to students.

Regional Centres

For better co-ordination and administration of this open university the country has been divided into several regions. A Director is appointed as the head of each region. He is assisted by an academic and administrative staff. The State Government concerned is required to provide housing accommodation for the regional centres under its jurisdiction. Other liabilities are the responsibility of the Central Government. The regional centre negotiates with the State Government and other universities under its region for developing local facilities and for promoting goodwill amongst the students and staff, for organising contact sessions and for creating public awareness about distance educational orientation programmes. A regional centre has a well equipped functional library having books on distance education and course material.

PROGRESS OF I.G.N.O.U.

Indira Gandhi National Open University (I.G.N.O.U.) was established for the introduction and promotion of open university and distance education systems in the educational pattern of the country and for the coordination and determination of standards in such systems. The major objectives of the university include widening of access to higher education by providing opportunities to larger segments of the population, particularly the disadvantaged groups, organising programmes of continuing education and initiating special programmes of higher education for specific target groups like women, people living in backward regions, hilly areas, etc.

The I.G.N.O.U. provides an innovative system of university level education, flexible and open in regard to methods and pace of learning, combination of courses, eligibility for enrolment, age of entry, methods of evaluation, etc. The University has adopted an integrated multi-media instructional strategy consisting of printed materials and audio-video aids, supported by counselling sessions at a network of study centres throughout the country . The evaluation system followed by the university consists of both continuous evaluation as well as term-end examinations.

The I.G.N.O.U. introduced its academic programmes in 1987 and has so far launched 55 programmes. These include a certificate course in guidance (for primary school teachers), food and nutrition (in seven languages) and rural development, the preparatory programme for the bachelor's degree, diploma programmes in management, rural development, higher education, distance education, creative writing in English and Hindi, computers in office management and operations management; the bachelor's degree programmes in arts/science/commerce and library and information sciences as well as the master's degree in business administration and distance education.

The total number of students registered for various programmes of study in the I.G.N.O.U. during 1993-94 is over 83,000. The University has established an extensive student support services network consisting of 16 regional centres and 229 study centres situated in different parts of the country. A Distance Education Council (D.E.C.) has been established by the University as a statutory authority under the I.G.N.O.U. Act for performance of its function as an apex body for coordination and determination of standards in Distance Education. D.E.C. have formulated guidelines for providing support to state open universities during the Eighth Plan.

Doordarshan commenced telecast of I.G.N.O.U.'s programmes in May 1991. The Bombay and Hyderabad stations of the All India Radio started broadcasting selected audio programmes of the I.G.N.O.U. from early 1992. At present, there are six other openuniversities functioning in the country. These are the B.R. Ambedkar Open University at Hyderabad, the Kota Open University at Kota, Rajasthan, Nalanda Open University, Bihar, Yashwant Rao Chavan Maharashtra Open University at Nasik, Maharashtra, the Madhya Pradesh Bhoj Vishwavidyalaya (M.P.B.V.), Bhopal and Ambedkar Open University at Ahmedabad.

ACADEMIC STAFF COLLEGES (A.S.C.)

As a result of the Academic Staff Colleges Report of the Mehrotra Committee on the new pay scales of various categories of teachers in the country the University Grants Commission (New Delhi) chose to establish about 50 Academic Staff Colleges (A.S.C.) for retraining of university teachers. The new national policy on education clearly emphasised the improvement of teachers performance. It was thought that utility of education cannot be elevated without the same. In its recommendations the Mehrotra Committee clearly stated that promotion from one scale to another higher one should depend upon the university teachers obtaining training in an academic staff college to be organised by an open university or any other university in the country. A few academic staff colleges were established during 1987.

Some Basic Problems

The functioning of an academic staff college poses certain problems which must be solved in advance. Of course, there is no financial problem, as the U.G.C. meets all the financial liabilities. The main problems pertain to the following aspects:

1. Organisation of the programme of retraining of university teachers.
2. Size of the staff for this purpose.
3. The quality on the basis of which instructors should be chosen.
4. The motivation that should be specified for these instructors in order to enable them to perform their task faithfully.
5. The mode of support to be obtained from the administrators of the concerned university may become ticklish at times if not irritating and difficult to comply with.

6. The particular issues, aspects and content that should form the core and basic substance of the instructors' classroom deliveries before the university and college teachers that will come for retraining.

A successful tackling of the problems involved in the above aspects indicates that the academic staff college has been a success. While forwarding this scheme of Academic Staff Colleges to some of the universities in the country, the U.G.C. indirectly anticipated these problems, so it gave ample freedom to an A.S.C. to make its programme flexible and to make the teachers aware of the intellectual, social and moral environments in which they have to fulfil their responsibilities. The U.G.C. cautioned that the programmes must be in consonance with the Indian condition.

The Alternative—The following alternatives were suggested:

1. The A.S.C. should function as a separate entity within a university.
2. It may be regarded as a separate Department of Continuing Education.
3. It may be accepted as a working of the College Development Council which the U.G.C. has established in each affiliating university bearing its hill cost itself, and
4. An A.S.C. may ultimately be transformed into a State Institute of Educational Planning and Administration.

The U.G.C. has made a university free to adopt any of the above four alternatives and act accordingly.

The Major Objectives—Following are the major objectives which the U.G.C. seeks to realise through an A.S.C:

1. To help the university and college teachers understand the unavoidable link that should be maintained between the university education and economic and social development with particular reference to Indian democracy as envisaged in the Constitution.
2. To understand how the university and college teachers may help in establishing a secular society in which society, economic and political rights and privileges will be the birth-right of all citizens.
3. To acquire and improve the basic skill of teaching.
4. To grasp the fundamentals of the organisation, management and administration of colleges and universities.

The Curriculum

Keeping in view the above objectives an A.S.C. is expected to develop its own curriculum. It should not be difficult to do so, because each of the above objectives dearly point to the contents that should be prepared for the instructors' lectures for the retraining of university and college teachers.

The Staff

Choice of the staff or instructors for an A.S.C. is an issue to be considered with all seriousness. An A.S.C. has been left free to choose its own instructors from wherever it wants or do so. Generally, they are to be chosen from the inside of the university. Working as a member of the core staff of an A.S.C., one is likely to enjoy some better conditions of service. This allurement is likely to promote an opposition and other unhealthy 'isms' which may work as a disease for eating out the very vitality and health of an A.S.C. So the necessary steps must be taken to protect this healthy institution of A.S.C.

QUESTIONS FOR EXERCISE

1. Explain the concept and form of Open University envisaged in our country.
2. What are the basic postulates of the new education policy as initiated in 1985?
3. How will the new education policy of 1985 improve the condition of education in India?
4. What are the academic staff colleges? Why have they been started? Discuss their utility and possible success.

CHAPTER 27

THE KOTHARI COMMISSION 1964-66

Historical Review

In inaugural address of the Commission, Mr. M. C. Chagla, the Education Minister of India, said about the appointment of Kothari Commission:

"If we look at the Resolution that steps up this Commission you will find that the Commission has been requested to formulate national system of education. There are two broad approaches to education prevalent in world today. The first emphasis the worthwhileness of the individual – it holds that every individual is unique and he must be permitted and assisted to develop to the best that is possible for him. If this is done, it is claimed the national good and the national system of education will take care of themselves. In the other approach, a greater emphasis is laid on the society into which the individual will have to live and work and it is claimed that, if education helps to create a new social order the good of each individual member will be automatically looked after. We, in India, will have to choose a path which lies between these two extreme approaches to education."

Object of the Appointment and Members. Amongst the several objectives of the appointment of this Commission were evaluation of the different stages of education and to evolve a National System of Education. In his address to the inauguration of the Commission on October 2, 1964: Dr. S. Radhakrishnan, the President of India and an eminent educationist said, "I am glad to know that the new Education Commission which was set up recently will hold its inaugural session on 2nd October. It is an auspicious day for our country. It is my earnest desire that the

Commission which includes representatives of progressive areas in the world will survey all aspects of education – Primary, Secondary, University and technical and make recommendations which will help to improve our education system at all its levels."

The Commission was appointed under the provisions of a resolution of the Government of India setting up the Education Commission, dated July 14, 1964 under the chairmanship of Dr. D.S. Kothari, Chairman, University Grants Commission, New Delhi.

Terms of Reference

1. **National System of Education.** To evolve a national system of education keeping in view the values and traditions of India as suited to the needs and aspiration of a modern society. This fact is very well evident from the following extract of the resolution of the Government of India:

   "In view of the important role of the education in the economic and social development of the country, in the building of any truly democratic society in the promotion of national integration and unity and above all, for the transformation of the individual in the endless pursuit of excellence and perfection, it is now considered imperative to survey and examine the entire field of education in order to realise within the shortest possible period a well balanced, integrated and adequate system of national education capable of making a powerful contribution to all spheres of national life."

After the attainment of freedom a new era was ushered in. Following are the requisites of this new era:

(i) Adaptation of secular democracy.
(ii) Eradication of illiteracy.
(iii) Ensuring a reasonable standard of living for all.
(iv) Rapid development of industries.
(v) Adoption of modern science and technology and their harmonising with traditional spiritual values.
(vi) Establishment of a socialistic society based on equitable distribution of wealth and equality of opportunity for all in education, employment and cultural advancements.

All these requisites can be fulfilled only through education, and unless education is re-organised, nothing can happen. The Commission was appointed to suggest the means for the fulfilment of the requisites mentioned above. The following lines from the resolution of the Government of India justify the statements:

"The attainment of independence ushered in a new era of national development founded upon; the adoption of a secular democracy, not only as a form of Government but also as a way of life, the determination to eliminate the poverty of the people and to ensure a reasonable standard of living for all, through modernisation of agriculture and rapid development of industry; the adoption of science and technology their harmonising with traditional spiritual values; the acceptance of a socialist pattern of society which will secure equitable distribution of wealth and equality of opportunity for all in education, employment and cultural advancement. Great emphasis came to be placed on educational development because of the realisation, that education, especially in science and technology, is the most powerful instrument of social transformation and economic progress and that the attempt to create a new social order based on freedom, equality and justice can only succeed if the traditional education system was revolutionised both content and extent."

2. **Qualitative Improvement in Education at All Levels.** Since the Commission was appointed with all these tasks in view of the resolution of the Government of India, dated July 14,1964 it stated:

   "Quantitatively, education at these levels has shown aphenomenal development in the post-independence period. In spite of this expansion, however, there is widespread dissatisfaction about several aspects of educational development. For instance, it has not yet been possible to provide free and universal education for all children up to 14 years of age: the problem of mass raise in standards adequately at the secondary and university stages. The diversification of curricula in secondary and higher education has not kept pace with the times so that the problem of educated unemployment has been intensified on the one hand while, on the other, there is an equally acute shortage of trained manpower in sectors.

The remuneration and service conditions of teachers leave a great deal to be desired and several important academic problems are still matters of intense controversies. In short, qualitative improvements in education have not kept pace with quantitative expansion and national policies and programmes concerning the quality of education even when these were well-convinced and generally agreed to, could not be implemented satisfactorily."

3. **Giving Place to Education as the Key of National Prosperity and Welfare and as Productive Investment.** "The Government of India are convinced that education is the key to national prosperity and welfare and that no investment is likely to yield greater returns than investment in human resources of which the most important component is education. Government have also decided to mobilise all the resources of science and technology which can only be done on the foundation of good and progressive education and, to that end, to increase considerably their total investment in the development of education and scientific research. The nation must be prepared to pay for quality in education and from the value attached to education by all sectors of the people it is clear that they will do so willingly."
4. **Survey the Entire Field of Education and Recommend the Ways and Means for Looking Education as a Whole and not Fragmented into Parts and Stages.** "It is desirable to survey the entire field of educational development as the various parts of the educational system strongly interact with and influence one another. It is not possible to have progressive and strong universities without efficient Secondary schools and the quality of these schools is determined by the functioning of Elementary schools. What is needed, therefore, is a synoptic survey and an imaginative look at education considered as a whole and not fragmented into parts and stages. In the past several Commissions and Committees have examined limited sectors and specific aspects of education. It is now proposed to have a comprehensive review of the entire educational system."
5. **Benefiting from the Experiences of other Countries of the World.** Blaming for education in India can be

done only by keeping in view the experiences and the conditions of this country but it was felt desirable to draw from the experiences of other countries. It was, therefore, decided to invite educationists from other countries of the world to help the education Commission and serve on it Educationists from England, Russia, Japan, America, etc., helped the Commission to draw up its recommendations and suggestions.

RECOMMENDATIONS

The Committee studied the problems of education in India and submitted its 1600-page report to the Education Minister of India on June 29,1966. It is a comprehensive report and expected to have far reaching political repercussions.

1. **Education and National Objectives.** Education should be related to the life and needs of the person so that national objectives may be achieved. Following are the five objectives which should be achieved through a five point programme:
   (i) Increase in production.
   (ii) Social and national integration.
   (iii) Consolidation of democracy.
   (iv) Speeding the process of modernisation.
   (v) To build the character through the development of social and spiritual values.
2. **Educational Structure and Standard.** General education should last for a period of 10 years (four years of lower primary, three years of higher primary and three years of lower secondary education). Prior to the general education, primary education from one to three years should also be given. The theme of higher secondary education should bc fixed for two year. After it the degree course should be of three year The Graduate course should be extended from two to three years.
3. **Teacher Status.** It is necessary to improve the economic, social and professional status of the teachers. The scale of pay of teachers of Government and non-Government schools should be the same. A suitable increase should be allowed in the scales of the pay of teachers. The following scales of pay to teachers at different stages of education are recommended:

SCALES OF PAY OF TEACHERS

	Teachers	Pay
1.	Secondary Course passed, untrained teachers of primary schools.	Minimum Salary ₹ 100/-
2.	Above mentioned teachers after 5 years of service.	Minimum Salary ₹ 125/-
3.	Secondary course passed and trained (having completed two years training course) teachers of primary schools.	Minimum Salary ₹ 125/-
4.	Above mentioned teachers after 5 years of service.	Minimum Salary ₹ 150/-
5.	Teachers having passed Secondary course and two years' training.	Minimum Salary ₹ 150/-
6.	Above mentioned teachers after 20 years of service.	Minimum Salary ₹ 250
7.	15 per cent teachers selected from category 6.	Minimum Salary ₹ 250-300
8.	Graduates having completed one year's training course.	Minimum Salary ₹ 220/-
9.	Above mentioned teachers after 20 years of service.	Minimum Salary ₹ 400/-
10.	15 per cent teachers selected from category 9.	Minimum Salary ₹ 400-600
11.	Untrained graduates so long as they do not complete their training.	Minimum Salary ₹ 220/-
12.	Teachers working in Secondary schools conducting graduate course.	Minimum Salary ₹ 300-600
13.	Above mentioned teachers, after completing their training.	One year's increment in their existing salary.
14.	Heads of the Secondary schools.	Their salaries will depend upon their respective abilities and the size of schools.
15.	Teachers of affiliated colleges.	1. Lecturer Jr. Scale 400-25-600. 2. Lecturer Sr. Scale 400-30-640-40-800. 3. Senior Lecturer or Reader 700-40-1100.

		4.	Principal I. 700-40-1100. II. 800-50-1500. III. 1000-50-1500.
16.	University teachers.	1.	Lecturer 400-40-800-50-950.
		2.	Reader 700-50-1250.
		3.	Professor 1000-50-1300-90-1600.

There should be no discrimination and distinction between the teachers of Government and non-Government schools in regard to pay scales and conditions of service. Proper facilities of residence, etc., should be provided to the teachers working in rural areas. The teachers should have complete freedom to take part in election. They should be provided proper facilities of receiving education through correspondence courses.

4. **Teachers' Education.** Isolation of teachers' education should be removed and extension service department should be established in each training institution. Comprehensive colleges should be established wherein provision should be made for giving training at different stages of education. A State Board of Teachers' Education should be established in each State. It should be the responsibility of this Board to make proper provision of teacher education at all stages. Curriculum of teaching institution should be so changed and reorganised that the teachers may become more practical. The period of training of the teachers with secondary course should be two years. The period of the training of the graduates should continue to be one year but later on it should be increased to two year. The course of M.Ed. shouldbe 1-1/2years. The teachers of the training colleges should have two degrees namely the Master's Degree and the Degree in Education. Summer institutions should be organised for the training of the teachers There should be provision for their education through correspondence course. The students of the training institutions should be given free education. There should be the provision for

granting leave and scholarship to them. Keeping in view the rise in the number of teachers training facilities should be expanded.

5. **Equalisation of Educational Opportunities.** In India two types of inequalities are found in the field of education:
   (a) In the education of boys and girls, and
   (b) In the education of developed and backward classes.

   In order to remove these inequalities, lower secondary education should be made free up to the end of the Fifth Five Year Plan and thereafter in the period of 10 years, Higher Secondary and University education should be given free to the poor and meritorious students. There is need of reducing the cost of education. Sufficient number of text-books should be kept in the libraries of educational institutions. Meritorious students should be granted financial help to enable them to purchase the text-books.

   Fifteen per cent students should be granted scholarships at the Secondary education stage. By the year 1976, 15 per cent of the students of pre-graduate courses should be granted scholarship. By the year 1986 this percentage should be increased to 25. A system of University scholarships should be started, 500 scholarships should be granted to the students, who are selected to receive education in foreign countries.

6. **Expansion of School Education.** School education needs to be greatly expanded. Centres should be opened in each district and State. With a view to expand primary education, managers of the private schools shall be encouraged to expand primary education. By the year 1975-76 and by the year 1985-86 proper provision should be made for primary education of all the boys and girls up to the age of five and seven years respectively. 20 per cent and 50 per cent of the students at Lower Secondary stage and Higher Secondary stage respectively should be given professional education. The number of students should be regulated at this stage.

7. **School Curriculum.** The Commission recommended the following curriculum for the different classes:

1. Lower Primary (Class I to IV)

(i) One language — mother tongue or regional language.
(ii) Mathematics.

(iii) Study of environment – science and social studies should be taught in class III and IV.
(iv) Creative activities.
(v) Work-experience and social service.
(vi) Health education.

2. Higher Primary (Class V to VII)

(i) Two languages:
(a) Mother tongue or regional language.
(b) Hindi or English.
(ii) Mathematics.
(iii) Science.
(iv) Social Studies (or History, Geography and Civics.)
(v) Art.
(vi) Work-experience and social service.
(vii) Physical education.
(viii) Education in moral and spiritual values.

3. Secondary (Class VIII to X)

(i) Three languages in non-Hindi speaking areas, generally there should be the following languages:
(a) Mother language or regional language.
(b) Hindi in higher or lower standard.
(c) English in higher or lower standard.
In the Hindi speaking areas, generally there should be the following languages:
(a) Mother language or regional language.
(b) English (or Hindi if English has been taken as mother tongue).
(c) One modern Indian language besides Hindi.
(ii) Mathematics.
(iii) Science.
(iv) History, Geography and Civics.
(v) Art.
(vi) Work-experience and social service.
(vii) Physical education.
(viii) Education of moral and spiritual values.

4. Higher Secondary (XI to XII Class)

(i) Any two languages which should include any modern Indian language, any modern foreign language and any classical language.

(ii) Any three subjects to be selected from the following subjects:
  (a) One additional language.
  (b) History.
  (c) Geography.
  (d) Economics.
  (e) Logic.
  (f) Psychology.
  (g) Sociology.
  (h) Art.
  (i) Physics.
  (j) Chemistry.
  (k) Mathematics.
  (l) Biology.
  (m) Geology.
  (n) Home Science.

(iii) Work experience and social service.
(iv) Physical education.
(v) Arts and crafts.
(vi) Education in moral and spiritual values.

Amendment in the Three Language Formula:

The three-language formula should be amended on the basis of the following principles:

(i) Hindi as national language of the Union should occupy an important place after mother tongue.
(ii) The knowledge of English would be a language for the students.
(iii) The most suitable stage for learning the three languages is the lower secondary stage.
(iv) The teaching of Hindi or English should be started from that period when utmost inspiration and need is experienced for it.
(v) The teaching of four languages should be made compulsory at any stage.

On the basis of above mentioned principles, the Commission amended the three-language formula in the following manner:

(a) Mother tongue or regional language.

(b) National language or the Union or associate national language so long as it exists.

(c) One modern Indian or European language, which should not be selected from the curriculum of the students and which should not be the medium of education.

5. Place of Hindi

English will continue to be used as a language of intellectual exchanges in higher education. However, English cannot be a medium of exchange of views for the majority of the Indian people. In the course of time, this language will certainly be Hindi. Hence efforts should be made to spread education of Hindi in all parts of the country.

6. Place of Different Indian Languages

The study of Indian languages is defective on account of difference in their script. Some lectures on modern languages should be published in Devanagri or Roman script. The formulation of new policy of the study of languages in schools has become necessary. English will be used in the form of associate language for an indefinite period. Besides this, proper language policy is necessary for national integration. Therefore, the mother tongue should be made the medium of education at the stages of schools, colleges and higher education. In addition to Hindi, all modern Indian languages should also be developed so that they may become the medium of exchange between the States.

7. Place of English

English should be used as the medium of instruction in all India educational institutions or universities. The study of English should be started from the school stage. Six universities should be developed wherein English should be the medium of education. These six universities should be selected from amongst the existing universities, one of which should be a University of industrial science and one should be University of agriculture.

8. Place of Classical Languages

Sanskrit language occupies a special importance and position in the national education system. However, the Commission does not agree with the view that Sanskrit or any other classical language should be included in the three-language formula. Only modern Indian languages should be included in the three-language formula. A mixed curriculum of mother tongue and Sanskrit should be formed. However, as public opinion is not in its favour, the Indian classical languages can find their place only as optional subject in the curriculum. Such optional subjects should be started in classes higher than VIII class.

9. School Administration and Supervision

Provision should be made for common school system of public education. Administration should be kept separate to the supervision and teaching. Up to the district stage, it should be in the hands of District School Board. The work of supervision should be conducted by the Education Department in the Secondary schools. A State Board of Schools should be established in each State in order to perform the work of the prevalent Secondary Educational Board. A National Board of Education should be established in the Ministry of Education in order to advise the Government in regard to school education.

10. Higher Education

The University Grants Commission should develop six universities from among the existing universities into major universities wherein best type of graduation, teaching and research work should be performed. Clusters of advance courses should be started in each major university. The teachers imparting education in universities and schools should be sent to major universities to acquire knowledge relating to their subjects. The teachers as well as students should not be allowed to leave one institution and to join the other institution during the session of the education. In order to admit the students in the University, the system of selective admission should be adopted. Regional language should be the medium of pre-graduate courses. English should be the medium of post-graduate courses. The examiners should not be given any remuneration for examining the answer-books. Wherever there are degree colleges, they should be organised into universities.

11. Education of Agriculture

Dr. D.S. Kothari, has remarked, "It is important to observe that in our system of education agriculture has not received the importance that is to be given today." Each State should have at least one Agriculture University. At least 25 students should be granted scholarships to study in such universities. New universities should be established. The knowledge of agriculture should be made a part of general education in primary schools. Agriculture should also be included in the curriculum of secondary schools and universities. Agricultural polytechnics should be established.

12. Vocational, Technical and Engineering Education

Having completed school education, the students should be provided facilities of short courses, correspondence courses and short extensive courses. A special provision should be made for the engineering education to the girls. The students receiving education in engineering colleges should be given practical training in the third year. Provision should also be made for imparting education in chemical technology, aeronautics and astronautics.

13. Education of Science

Study centres should be established for the higher education of science and mathematics. The number of students taking such subjects in the university should be increased. Famous Indian scientists working in foreign countries should be invited to return to India. Science and technology should be made an indivisible part of educational system. Efforts should be made to develop the study of chemistry and physics. A new degree should be started higher to M.Sc. Its courses should be started on optional basis. This course should be of one year or even lesser period. The curriculum of such courses should be organised in such a way that it may fulfil the needs and requirements of the present time. Summer institutes of science should be established. Efficient teachers of secondary schools and universities should be invited to impart education of science in such institutes.

14. Adult Education

Illiteracy should be ended in all the corners of India within a period of 20 year To achieve this, schools should be converted into the centres of community life. Comparatively more efforts should be made in the rural areas to end the illiteracy. The curriculum of the educational institution should be organised in such a way that the adults may acquire general knowledge and experience. Correspondence courses should be started for the expansion of adult education. A network of libraries should be spread throughout the country. The newly literate persons should be supplied with books and other materials according to their interests. The programmes for teaching the adults should be organised in the universities also. A National Board of Adult Education should be established for organisation and administration of adult education. Such board should also be established in the national level and district level.

The Government of India have welcomed the suggestion of different Commissions. It has already implemented some of the suggestions and the efforts are still being made to make important the rest of the suggestions.

Problems of Indian Education increased with the development of Indian education. Some of the problems are as old as the modern education system itself. Following are the chief problems of Indian Education:

1. **Aimless Education.** There is no definite aim before the Indian students. Innumerable young men and women are receiving education in schools and colleges having no definite aim before them. Most of the young students consider jobs as the ultimate aim of their education. Kothari Commission has remarked in very clear words that the most important reform in the education is to change it so that it may be related to the life of the people, their needs and aspirations. Education development should be as a powerful weapon for bringing about social, economic and cultural changes, which are necessaiy for the achievement of national objectives. The development of education should be made in such a way that it may secure social and national unity, modernisation, social change and moral values. In short, modern education should aim at the fulfilment of the needs of the citizens and develop the feeling of universal brotherhood among them. Structural changes are needed in the present system of education.
2. **Defective Curriculum.** Indian education has a defective and imbalanced curriculum. It emphasises only bookish knowledge. It has no relation with life. Consequently, many young persons who have received higher education are facing the problem of unemployment.

The Secondary Education Commission has pointed out the following defects of the curriculum:

(i) The present curriculum is very narrow.

(ii) It is bookish and theoretical.

(iii) It includes more subjects than are required and many of them are useless and unnecessary.

(iv) Emphasis is not given to teaching the boys practical subject and other types of activities, which may help development of the versatile personality of the child.

(v) It does not fulfil the different needs and interest of the students.

(vi) It lacks technical and professional subjects.

The Kothari Commission has pointed out that in the background of the important efforts that are being made in the foreign countries in the development of curriculum, the basis of the curriculum in India is very narrow and out of date. It emphasises bookish knowledge and cramming. It has no provision for practical activities and internal examination. Since adequate importance is not given to the development of the skills, proper aptitude, tendencies and values, it is not complete to keep pace with the lives of the people. There is urgent need of improving the curriculum, raising its standard and for reforming it.

3. **Conventional and Out of Date Teaching Methods.** Our teaching methods have not been changed in accordance with the change of time and circumstances. Even now the education is not child-centred in India. While other countries of the world have been adopting new methods of teaching, even today we are using the conventional and out-of-date teaching methods. In view of the needs and circumstances of the present time new teaching methods should be adopted with immediate effect.

4. **Defective Examination System.** The aim of Indian education is to pass examination. Mostly, only one examination is held in a year with the result, that students are not able to acquire proper and real knowledge. The number of the examiners is so much that no correlation can be established in their decisions. It depends upon the mood, individual ability, knowledge of the subject and environment to award marks to the examinees. Mostly, essay type of examinations are organised, which are completely unpsychological. The University Education Commission has remarked that although the seriousness and complication of this problem has been increasing with great speed, constructive steps have not been taken to reform it. The Mudaliar and Kothari Commissions also have pointed out the seriousness of this problem. Therefore necessary all out efforts should be made to solve this problem as early as possible.

5. **Wastage and Stagnation.** It is unfortunate that the problem of wastage and stagnation exists in the field of education since very long time. The problem of wastage and stagnation exists at all stages of education. There are some students, who leave education in the middle and there is a large number of students, who fail every year in the examinations. Lakhs of students fail every year, due to the defective administration, defective environment, defective curriculum and defective examination system. Kothari Commission has expressed the view that the rate of wastage is from 1/3 to 1/2 in class 1.
6. **Defects of Control and Management.** In India, the education up to primary and junior high school is organised by the local district board and municipalities. Some schools are directly under the control of the State government. Our institutions are under the control of private managements. Some institutions are under the control of religious institutions. Secondary schools are under the control of local boards or private or religious institutions. There are also government schools. Most of the schools are non-government and they are managed by the management committees of the schools concerned. The members of the managing committees make the institutions serve their personal interests. Even the higher officials of the State Education Department hesitate to take any action against them. The Education Boards of the State are not able to function properly because of groupism and party politics. Groupism, favouritism, corruption, etc., are rampant in primary as well as secondary schools. Teachers are also the victims of anger of the members of the management committees. Casteism, communalism, linguism, regionalism, rivalry, jealousy, groupism and corruption are rampant in the management committees of the non-government schools.

   Most of the universities in India are under the control of State Governments. Only five universities are under the control of Central Government. The problem of control in the affiliated colleges of the universities has become so serious that its solution seems to be very difficult. Many colleges are run by private and religious institutions. There exist all those defects which exist in the field of Secondary education. There are very few institutions at present which are run with the aim of public welfare. Most of the teaching institutions have become the means of earning money. The condition of the government schools and colleges is far better than the non-government institutions.

Kothari Commission has made important suggestions in regard to the management, administration and control of education at different stages. If these suggestions are properly implemented, the problem of control, management and administration of education at different stages can be solved.

7. **Indiscipline.** Indiscipline is increasing among the Indian students. It has attracted the attention and anxiety of all the scholars and educationists of the country. It is absent at the primary stage. It is rampant at the secondary stage. The prominent among these many causes for the prevalence of indiscipline among the students are — (a) defective examination system, (b) defective economic system, (c) impracticable curriculum, and (d) wastage and stagnation. According to Kothari Commission, the modern social and economic systems are to a great extent, responsible for the indiscipline among the students. The chief cause of indiscipline among the students is the interference of the politicians in the schools, colleges and universities.

   Explaining the causes of unrest among students, Kothari Commission observed that "There is a variety of causes which has brought about these ugly expressions of uncivilised behaviour *e.g.,* the uncertain future facing educated youngmen leading to a sense of frustration which breeds irresponsibility, mechanical and unsatisfactory nature of many curricula programmes, the totally inadequate facilities forteaching and learning in the large bulk of institutions; the poor student-teacher contact, the inefficiency and lack of scholarship on the part of many teachers and their failure to involve themselves in students problems; the absence of imagination and tact combined with firmness on the part of heads of institutions; the prevalence of what has come to be known as teachers politics, the attempt by political parties to interfere in their work, and by no means the least, the impact of the conditions of public life in the country, the falling standards of discipline among the adults and a weakening of their civic consciousness and integrity."

It is necessary to remove the above mentioned causes to solve the problem of indiscipline. The number of students in classes should be reduced. The curriculum should be reformed. Aimlessness of education should be finished. Sports, games and cultural programmes should be organised. Well-trained teachers should be appointed. Teachers should be kept away from party politics.

Kothari Commission has classified the remedies for student indiscipline into two categories, *viz.* removal of educational deficiencies that contribute it and setting up of consultative and administrative machinery to prevent the occurrence of indiscipline.

The remedies of the first group is regarded as the core of the problem. To quote the Commission "The incentives to positive discipline have to come from the opportunities that the institution presents and the intellectual and social demands it makes on the students." As regards second remedy, it has been suggested that polarisation between teachers, students and administration should be removed. All this should create a spirit of comradeship between the teachers and the students. The Commission hopes that if this "spirit could be created, many of the problems of discipline which bedevil our academic life at present, will become easier to solve and will be hoped to disappear in course of time."

8. **Defective Medium of Instruction.** Since the beginning of 19th century, the medium of instruction has remained a controversial issue. In 1956, the State Organisation Commission defined the frontiers of all States while giving rise to the controversy of language issue. In 1957, the Official Language Commission suggested that Hindi should be developed as the obvious linguistic medium for mass Indian purpose and ruled out English as the language of India's mass medium. Then Radhakrishnan Commission recommended that the medium of instruction should be any Indian language except Sanskrit. In 1966, Kothari Commission recommended that the regional language should not be made the medium of instructions at the primary and secondary stages only but they should

also be made the medium of education at the university stage. Hence, Hindi should be developed as a link language and the use of English should also be continued. This was severely criticised as a conspiracy to continue the use of English in India.

At present education is imparted through the medium of regional languages at the primary and secondary stages in different states. At the higher stages also, endeavours are being made to make the regional languages as the medium of education. But the influence of English has yet not declined at this stage. English language continued to be the medium of education in different universities. Thus, the problem of language still defies solution. It is very urgent that this problem should be solved and the language controversy should be laid at rest for ever.

9. **Defective Women Education.** The Constitution of India has preserved the principle of equality of men and women. However, women of India still lag behind in many respects. In 1932, as compared to 100 boys, only 55 girls were receiving education at the primary stage. At the secondary stage, this number was only 26. Therefore, the education of women has greatly expanded but still the percentage of women is very low. The main cause of this limitation is the failure to understand the importance of education. Indian Government are conscious of its responsibility towards the education of women and taking every possible step to encourage it. The Kothari Commission has emphasised that for some time priority should be given to the education of women in our educational system and only then the problem of education of women can be solved.
10. **Difficulties in Adult Education.** The efforts that have been made by the Indian and State Government in regard to education of adults have not met with much success. Proper curriculum and proper teaching method should be adopted for the education of the adult and able sufficient teachers should be appointed to make the scheme of adult education a success. The Kothari Commission has made some very important suggestions to achieve these goals. The prominent among such suggestions are the establishment of 'National Adult Education Council', establishment of Adult

Education Department in Universities', proper provision of libraries and the establishment of Social Welfare Councils. The Government should act according to the suggestions of the Commission and solve the problem of adult education in India, so that the problem of illiteracy may be solved in India in near future.

11. **Difficulties in the Education of the Workers.** Industrialisation is progressing with great speed in India and the number of working persons is constantly increasing. The education of these workers poses serious problems before us. Although Government have been emphasising the education of the workers in the programmes of the expansion of adult education yet sufficient success has not so far been achieved in this field.

12. **Education of Disabled Persons.** There are mainly two types of disabled persons in India (a) mentally retarded persons, and (b) physically disabled persons. Mentally retarded children are those, whose I.Q. is below 55. At present about 33 per cent of school going children are mentally retarded in varying degrees. According to Kothari Commission the number of disabled children in India was 25 lakhs out of which 14 to 18 lakhs were said to be mentally retarded children.

    With the expansion of civilisation, mental diseases are also increasing. Poverty, bad company, lack of opportunities to education, cruel and apathetic behaviour of the parents, family quarrels, etc., are the causes of mental diseases. There are also lakhs of physically disabled children in India. The Government have made many efforts for the education of disabled persons. However, so far sufficient arrangements have not been made for the education of all types of disabled persons.

13. **Difficulty of Technical and Professional Education.** No special provision was made for the professional and technical education before independence. Great efforts have been made in this direction after the achievement of independence. Despite tremendous increase in the number of schools and the students, there is still shortage of skilled craftsmen and trained persons in the field of different professions. It is true that many engineers and overseers

are facing the problem of unemployment but in other professions there is still shortage of skilled and trained persons.

14. **Education System in Accordance with Political, Social and Economic Conditions.** Last but not the least problem that Indian education is facing is that our education system is not in accordance with the political, social and economic conditions of the time. Education should be reorganised in order to solve this problem.

QUESTIONS FOR EXERCISE

1. Describe briefly the recommendations and suggestions of National Education Commission, 1964-1966.
2. The appointment of the Education Commission, 1964 has been criticised on the ground that there was no need for the appointment of a Commission so soon after the Report of the University Education Commission (Radhakrishnan Commission) and the Secondary Education Commission (Mudaliar Commission). State what can be said in defence of the appointment of the Commission?
3. Give critical estimate of the recommendations and suggestions made by Kothari Commission.
4. "The Indian education is facing manifold problems which are to be tackled." Discuss.

CHAPTER 28

EDUCATION IN INDIA TODAY

Resume

The structure of educational services in India was somewhat loose and undefined in the early British period. With the issue of Woods Despatch in 1854, about 20 years after Macaulay's minute advocating the use of English language and Western literature as the main form of education in India, Departments of Education were set up in the various provinces. They undertook the supervision of schools established by the Government or private agencies as also the gradual conversion and absorption of indigenous primary institutions in the system of education. The training of teachers, often drawn from the indigenous schools themselves, and the preparation of a few basic texts to be used in these schools were undertaken in this connection, In 1857, three universities were established at Calcutta, Bombay and Madras in order to undertake the work of examining the teaching done in Government as well as private, mostly missionary, institutions, at the high school, F.A. and B.A. levels. This set the essentially examination-dominated tone of Indian education for the succeeding century. The affiliating character of the universities enabled private enterprise, primarily missionary, in the first instance, but local Indian managements from about 1880 onwards, to organise a large number of institutions. While adhering to the formal syllabus for purpose of instruction and examination, it had thus become possible for different institutions to have their own specific religious or cultural climate. After the Indian Education Commission, 1882 (Hunter Commission), had recommended withdrawal of active Government leadership in opening schools and encouragement of private enterprise, this trend became even more predominant. However, poor state support in terms of finance did very often lead to poor quality in instruction.

One consequence of the emergence of private managements and simultaneous grants to graduates of franchise in university elections towards the end of nineteenth century, was an increasingly Indian composition of university bodies and strong reflection of nationalist sentiments in the fields of education and culture.

Early in the 20th century, the Swadeshi Movement in Bengal, as also the reformist as well as the radical trend of the nationalist movement in Maharashtra, represented by Ranade-Gokhale and Tilak, respectively had their reflection on education. A little later, Arya Samaj in Punjab also called for the development of a national system of education under which the gurukuls were formed and Vedic learning was emphasised. The Bengal movement for national education led to the establishment of technical institutions, the strongest of which today constitutes the Jadavpur University at Calcutta. Muslim and Hindu sentiments led to the establishment of the Muslim University (growing out of the earlier Muslim Anglo-Oriental College at Aligarh) and the Banaras Hindu University founded by the late Pt. Malaviya.

The next big wave of nationalist activity in education came after Gandhiji's call for a boycott of British educational system in 1920 The rebel Jamia Millia Islamia at Aligarh, which was later transferred to Delhi, the Gujarat Vidyapeeth, Kashi Vidyapeeth, Tilak Vidyapeeth and an earlier National University sponsored by Mrs. Annie Besant and some liberal educationists, along with a large number of national schools, were efforts to liberate education from official control and to change its content.

Emphasis on practical activity related to national reconstruction and on study of the indigenous and national problems and culture were the two key points in the programmes of the various national movements in education. However, the great bulk of educational activity continued along the broad lines of the officially sponsored university and school education even as they influenced the content of education in a somewhat nationalist direction.

Policy-making and Legislation in Education

Education being a State subject in the Constitution, annual meetings of the Central Advisory Board of Education and the Conference of State Ministers of Education, supported by Conference of State Secretaries of Education, have been important media for formulation of educational policy. As is understandable, these policies are framed within the broad limits laid down in the Five-Year Plan where not only the rough magnitude of resources available for education, but also the general direction of growth is set out. Plan proposals for educational development are formulated by a working group set up jointly by the Planning Commission and the Ministry of Education and discussed with State Governments. On the other hand, the Central Government has a number of advisory boards in the field of women's education, secondary education, education of the handicapped and the blind, etc.

The Government of India have set up the National Council of Educational Research and Training to develop improvement activities in the whole range of school education such as production of new model text-books for adoption by States, devising of improved techniques of examinations for adoption by the State Boards of Secondary Education and by schools, research in appropriate areas, *e.g.*, testing, guidance, school organisation, supervision and inspection of schools, etc., which may lay the basis for better practices in education. The Central Ministry of Education also supports the creation of State Institutes of Education and other agencies like Bureaux of Educational and Vocational Guidance, Institutes of Science Education, Institutes of English, and Examination Reform Bureaux to bring about improvement in their respective fields.

The most important pieces of legislation in the field of education have been the Primary Education Acts passed about 1961 in various States where such Acts were not already enforced. This enables States to employ compulsion. The approach, however, has been not punitive, but one of providing schools to all children and persuading parents. The regulation of secondary education and of private education in most States is through State Acts, setting up Boards of Secondary Education which lay down examination curricula, conditions of recognitions of institutions, etc. In many cases, States have undertaken supervisory functions *vis-a-vis* private managing bodies of institutions largely in order to protect the interest of teachers in respect of security of service and conditions of management.

Universities are set up by Acts and receive grants from the State Governments though there has recently been some feeling that they (the governments) might, on the one hand, be encroaching too much on the autonomy and privileges of academic institutions and, on the other, setting up universities without due consideration of the resources available and educational needs. It has, therefore, been felt that the State Governments should consult the University Grants Commission which provides grants for developmental purposes and which has itself been set up by an Act of Parliament to exercise the Union Government's responsibility for maintenance of standards in higher education. Education is not yet a justiciable right, that is, no citizen can claim education from the State in a court of law. The provision of education upto the age of 14 has been mentioned in the Directive Principles chapter of the Indian Constitution.

Some legislation has impinged on the privileges of private bodies, particularly, religious and the denominational groups. The Constitution permits the minorities to set up institutions of their own choice and the State's right to legislate is limited to that extent.

International Contacts

International organisations involved in education in India have been mainly the United Nations Educational, Scientific and Cultural Organisation (U.N.E.S.C.O.) and the United Nations Children's Emergency Fund (U.N.I.C.E.F.). The International Labour Organisation (I.L.O.) pay attention to technical and vocational training and the Food and Agricultural Organisation (F.A.O.) have recently paid attention to agricultural education and some farm-oriented literacy programmes in connection with increases in agricultural productivity. U.N.E.S.C.O. started as the continuation of an earlier International League of Intellectual Co-operation which mainly stressed extension among the intellectual contacts of the world. However, during the past 6 years, with the growth in the numbers of new under-developed nations, which have become independent, and with increasing attention to the growth gap between the rich and the poor nations of the world, the activities of U.N.E.S.C.O. have been taken a developmental character. Thus, technical support in educational planning, improvement of methods and curricula, teacher-training, equalisation of access to education and women's education have figured in its programme.

The main point to note about the activities of most of the U.N. Organisations is that a great part of their assistance is available in the form of services of experts, equipment and training fellowships. Substantive support for the programme in the country has still to be found necessarily from national finances, except in cases like U.N.I.C.E.F. mid-day meals programme. This is also a characteristic of all the activities of the United Nations Special Fund, now United Nations Development Programme, whose activities may be treated as pre-investment programmes preparing the ground for fruitful investment of capital in economic development programmes of under-developed countries. The support of Special Fund has mainly been available to programmes of technical training on the job training, etc. The activities of U.N.I.C.E.F. have covered a wider ground besides supporting U.N.E.S.C.O. work in the fields already mentioned. It has been willing to sponsor assistance programmes for school-meals, school medical services and recently, studies in problems of wastage, and greater co-ordination of school programmes with the community's life and needs, etc.

There is also a certain amount of bilateral assistance mainly from the United States through its Agency for International Development and the U.S. Educational Foundation in India, and also through Colombo Plan and other agreements with other countries. The Colombo Plan, in particular, is a programme of mutual assistance among nations so that India not only receives but also gives help of a technical nature to countries which need it. The Soviet Union has co-operated mainly in technical and higher scientific education by providing staff and consultants in this area and joint publication of text-books for schools as well as higher technical institutions.

Control Over Education

In India today, while the various States of the country are made responsible for progress of education in their respective areas, the Centre also shares some responsibility in some fields of education. According to 1976 Constitution amendment some of the subjects of education have been placed under joint responsibility of the States and the Centre. The Centre is responsible for determining the standard of higher research, science education, technical education and higher education. Aligarh Muslim University, Banaras Hindu University, Hyderabad University, Jawaharlal Nehru University, Delhi, Visva Bharati University, Shantiniketan and North Eastern Hill University, Shillong and some other centres of higher learning come under the direct control of the Central Government. All educational institutes, scientific and technological institutes of national importance are run on the finances obtained from the Centre. Hence these are under the control of the Central Ministry of Education. Educational planning and education of the backward classes are also the responsibility of the Centre.

Central Bodies of Education

In order to carry out its responsibilities in the area of education the Central Government has established the University Grants Commission, I.T.I.'s (Indian Technological Institutes), N.C.E.R.T. (National Council of Educational Research and Training), etc. For education and research in engineering the Central Government has established live national technological institutes. Besides, there are 15 regional engineering colleges, four management institutes, four technological teachers training institutes and about 350 Central schools run by the Central Government.

THE NATIONAL EDUCATION POLICY

In July 1978 a conference of State education ministers was held at Delhi. The conference unanimously decided that the following fields of education should be developed:

1. To make primary education universal.
2. Structure of education.
3. Adult education.
4. Arts and culture.
5. Physical education and Sports.

The Central education ministry appointed *ad-hoc* committees for each of these fields of education. The work is being done on the recommendation of these committees.

EDUCATIONAL STRUCTURE

The Education Commission of 1964-66 recommended the implementation of the 10+2+3 system of education *i.e.,* ten years of high school, two years of higher secondary and three years of undergraduate education. In 1968 this pattern has been recognised as the national pattern. Andhra Pradesh, Assam, Bihar, Gujarat, Kamatak, Kerala, Maharashtra, Tamilnadu, Orissa, Nagaland, Sikkim, Manipur, Meghalaya, Tripura, Andaman Nicobar Islands, Chandigarh, Dadra, Nagar Haveli, Delhi, Goa, Daman, Diu, Lacca Islands and Mizoram have accepted this pattern. Himachal Pradesh, Rajasthan, Uttar Pradesh, Punjab, Haryana and Madhya Pradesh, too, have accepted this pattern in principle and they need some more time to implement it.

Primary Education

In all the States of the country primary education has been made free and compulsory. Primary education is taken care of both by the Government and the local institutions run by private organisations and local bodies. Except in U.P., Orissa and West Bengal education up to the VIII class, too, is free. In these three States education up to the VIII class is free for girls only. In Bihar, Manipur, Meghalaya, Nagaland, Tripura and Sikkim the free education law has not yet been passed. In all the centrally governed areas this law has been passed and implemented also.

Middle School

In the beginning of the Sixth Five Year Plan, *i.e.* by 1978-79 special efforts were made for making primary education for the children between 6 and 11 years of age compulsory, instead of trying for making the junior high or middle class education *(i.e.* from classes 5 or 6 to 7 to 8) compulsory. It was decided that during the Sixth Five Year Plan, *i.e.* from 1978-83, primary education and middle school education would be made universal within ten year Informal and part-time education was considered necessary for those children who have not taken admission in schools for some reasons. So it was planned that the Centre would give financial assistance to those States in which there were about four crores and 18 lakhs unregistered children.

Secondary Education

In Tamilnadu, Kerala, Gujarat, Andhra Pradesh, Arunachal Pradesh, Andaman and Nicobar Islands and Lacca Islands, Secondary education has been declared free. In Nagaland, Jammu and Kashmir, Dadar and Nagar Haveli and Pondicherry no fees are charged in Government Secondary schools. In Madhya

Pradesh, Manipur, Orissa, Rajasthan, Tripura and Uttar Pradesh Secondary education for girls has been made free. For the children of scheduled castes and tribal classes Secondary education is free in all the States of the country. Their children are given stipends also for their education.

Higher Education

All education including higher education has, in response to a recognisable tendency in the Indian national movement for over half a century, been considered to be the constitutional prerogative of the States. Universities are set up by law, by State legislatures with formal as well as much practical autonomy. However, in the special powers of the State Governor as Chancellor, in the State's control of Government grants to universities and, recently, in certain States through reconstitution of university bodies as well as on account of the private as well as Government management of colleges affiliated to them, their autonomy suffers some limitations. The essential feeling of national unity is, in this matter, properly expressed in the provision of our Constitution that the maintenance and improvement of standards of higher education will be the responsibility of the Government of India. For discharging this responsibility, the Government has neither resorted to straight control by itself as, for instance, is the case in U.S.S.R., Germany and even France, nor gone to the American extreme of leaving it to voluntary accreditation associations of higher institutions. Somewhat on the British model, it has set up a University Grants Commission (U.G.C.) to disburse central finances to universities and to discharge the responsibility regarding maintenance of standards. Unlike the British Committee, however, the Commission in India has a somewhat greater affinity to Government styles and methods, presumably on account of general predominance of such styles and methods in our society. Similarly, the Indian U.G.C. has, among its members, heads of universities, *i.e.* Vice-Chancellors, in contrast to University professors who sit on the British University Grants Committee. Research grants from bodies like the Indian Council of Medical Research, the Council of Scientific and Industrial Research, the Research Programmes Committee of the Planning Commission, the National Council of Educational Research and Training, etc., also affect the control and the morale of higher institutions. Disbursement of funds and formulation of policy also come, in their respective fields, from the All-India Council for Technical Education, the Indian Council of Agricultural Research, etc. The Indian Medical Council inspects medical institutions but does not disburse grants for which the State Governments make appropriate arrangements.

EXPANSION OF EDUCATION

Primary and Secondary

Phenomenal expansion has taken place in the field of education since Independence. The number of schools increased from 5,30,000 in 1950-51 to 8,21,988 in 1992-93. The enrolment in schools increased from about 2.4 crore in 1950-51 to about 16.07 crore in 1992-93. Since Independence the gross enrolment ratios have gone up many times and have reached 105.5 per cent in classes I-V and 67.5 per cent in classes VI-VIIL. The number of universities (including deemed universities) has increased from 25 at the time of Independence to 207 and the number of colleges from about 700 to 8545 by 1992-93. In addition there are 1040 polytechnics. The student enrolment in universities and colleges increased from about two lakhs at the time of Independence to 44.18 lakhs in 1991-92. The literacy rate as per the 1991 census is 52.11 per cent compared to 20 per cent in 1947.

With quantitative expansion of educational facilities, there is now a greater emphalsis on qualitative improvement. Before 1976, education was largely the responsibility of States, the Central Government being only concerned with certain areas like co-ordination and determination of standards in technical and higher education, etc. In 1976, through a Constitutional Amendment education became the joint responsibility of the Centre and the States.

Universalisation of elementary education, eradication of illiteracy in the age group of 15 to 35 and strengthening of vocational education (VE) so as to relate it to the emerging needs in the urban and rural settings are the major thrust areas of the Eighth Plan in the education sector. Utilisation of formal, non-formal and open channels of learning would be the strategy for this purpose. The changed approach, improved methodology of teaching, increased participation of NGOs and student volunteers have infused a new vitality into the literacy programme and have given it a fresh momentum. The aim would be to impart a similar vitality and momentum to the universal elementary education programme with a definite edge in its favour. The Eighth Five Year Plan strategy for universalisation of elementary education envisages adoption of disaggregated target setting and decentralised planning. District specific plans for universalisation of elementary education are proposed to be drawn within the strategy frame of micro planning through people's participation and introduction of minimum levels of learning.

Higher Education

At present higher education is imparted through 137 universities of which 12 are under Central and the rest under State administration. The total number of colleges in the country is 8210. Besides, there are 34 institutions deemed as universities. The number of students is 50.07 lakhs and the number of teachers is 2.86 lakhs.

VOCATIONAL AND TECHNICAL EDUCATION

The Government has established the following four institutes for meeting the requirements of specialised workers:

1. Higher Training Institute, Madras.
2. Foreman Training Institute, Bangalore.
3. Central Employees Training and Research Institute, Calcutta.
4. Institute of Higher Training in Electronics, Hyderabad.

The progress of Primary and Secondary education in India may be assessed from the following Table.

INCREASE IN ADMISSIONS

In lakhs

	Primary	Secondary
1960-61	350	07
1968-69	544	125
1970-80	716	193
1982-83	795	236
1984-85	856	262
1986-87	900	288
1987-88	929	300

1988-89	957	309
1989-90	973	322
1991-92	1016	345
1992-93	1054	387

Seven Central Training Institutes have been opened for preparing teachers under the Directorate of Employment and Training. In 750 polytechnics 90,000 trainees are admitted every year for acquiring practical experience regarding production, construction, experimentation and development. The successful trainees are awarded diplomas in engineering, technology and some non-technical areas. These institutes give three years' training. For the part-time trainees the period of training is four years.

Upto 1983-84 about 30 polytechnics have opened for giving training in engineering and technology to those women who are leading poor life due to unfavourable social and economic conditions.

Engineering colleges teaching courses leading to degrees in engineering to those persons who want to serve as engineers in engineering and technological vocations. Today there are 300 such engineering colleges in which about 65,000 students are receiving education in various branches of engineering. For postgraduate education in engineering there are 76 institutes in which about 11,000 students are admitted every year. For part-time students these institutes offer four years course. In the engineering colleges affiliated to some universities graduate and post-graduate degree courses in management and vocational administration are taught. The State Technical Education Board evaluates the working of the various industrial training institutes and polytechnics spread in the respective States.

There are six national institutes known as I.I.Ts. (Indian Institute of Technology) established at six places, *viz.,* Bombay, Bangalore, Kanpur, Khadakpur, Madras and Delhi. In the Bangalore I.I.T. 2,000 post-graduate students and 1,500 research scholars are admitted every year. In the remaining five institutes about 7,200 students are admitted every year. In addition to these five institutes there are 70 other engineering colleges and engineering faculties of universities admitting 3,500 students every year for education in engineering. For giving training in various branches of engineering and technology there are 15 regional colleges, technical institutes and polytechnics. There are various centres giving training in the various branches of mining and metallurgy. Some institutes give training also along with work. These institutes offer 5/½ years degree course and 3/½ years diploma course. Four training centres have been opened for training of teachers of engineering.

TEACHING IN EDUCATION

Four Years Degree Course in Education

A new direction has been given to teachers' training by introducing a four years degree course in Education on the pattern followed in U.S.A. There are four regional colleges of education in the country situated at Mysore, Bhubaneshwar, Bhopal and Ajmer, besides the Kurukshetra University in Haryana (which has been discontinued now) where too this degree course has been introduced with the object of turning out efficient teachers. This move has been started on the plea that nine months' teachers' training imparted to graduates and post-graduates is not adequate to make the trainee an efficient teacher. Consequently, a four years degree course after High School has been introduced in education with the hope that the future teachers will be fully trained to become efficient teachers. This degree course is divided into three main parts which are as follows:

1. General and Liberal Education,
2. Specialised Education, and
3. Professional Education.

1. General and Liberal Education

The object of this part of education is to develop in the future teacher such qualities as may help him to develop the personality and character of his students in a manner which may enrich their country and the humanity at large. To achieve this proficiency he will have to study the following subjects:

1. Languages – regional and the English language.
2. Social Sciences.
3. Mathematics.
4. Natural Sciences.
5. Arts and Crafts.
6. Health and Physical Education.

2. Specialised Education

The future teacher must acquire a thorough knowledge of the subject which he intends to teach his students. The teachers of High School standard have to teach more than one subject. So any teacher of this standard must possess a knowledge of a number of subjects. They are, therefore, given specialised education in some subjects.

3. Professional Education

Under this part the future teacher is taught subjects of educational psychology, educational philosophy, social science, history of education, problems of education and principles of guidance and evaluation.

2. CORRESPONDENCE SCHOOL AND COURSE

There are many persons in India who had to give up education due to certain circumstances beyond their control, although they possessed a strong desire to pursue their studies further. Correspondence schools are meant for persons of this category. In Delhi a Directorate of Correspondence Course was opened in 1962 for the first time in the country and in this way a way was opened to make higher education available to any citizen who desired to be educated. Such schools exist in countries like Japan, U.S.A., Russia, England and some other countries. They have proved a success there. In these schools lessons are prepared by very able teachers. The answers to these questions are carefully examined and improved and then returned to the students along with the next lesson. The Directorate has declared that the curriculum, examination and degree awarded will be the same as is given to the students of Delhi University. We need such correspondence schools in large number in the country. Himachal Pradesh University, Simla, too, has started correspondence courses for B.Ed., M.Ed. and other subjects. Many other universities in the country are now planning to start correspondence courses for degree classes.

3. REGIONAL COLLEGE OF EDUCATION

Four regional colleges of education have been set up at Ajmer, Mysore, Bhubaneshwar and Bhopal in order to prepare teachers for multi-purpose schools. These colleges have been opened on the recommendation of Secondary Education Commission of 1953. The colleges started functioning in July 1963.

Aims of Regional Colleges

1. To prepare teachers for multi-purpose schools.
2. To train teachers for science, agriculture, commerce, home-science, sculpture, arts and crafts.
3. To provide in service training to teachers and supervisors engaged in teaching profession in multi-purpose schools.
4. To run a Model Demonstration Multi-purpose schools.
5. To function as regional centre for extension services.
6. To conduct research for improving teaching methods.
7. To conduct research in teachers education and implement new methods of teaching evolved as the result of research.

Expansion of Regional Colleges

The regions covered by different regional colleges are given as below:

Mysore	— Southern regions—Kamatak, Kerala, Tamilnadu and Andhra Pradesh.
Bhopal	— Western regions—Madhya Pradesh, Gujarat and Maharashtra.
Ajmer	— Northern regions—Rajasthan, Delhi, Himachal Pradesh, Uttar Pradesh, Punjab, Haryana, Jammu and Kashmir.
Bhubaneshwar	— Eastern regions—Orissa, Bihar, Assam, West Bengal, Manipur, Tripura, NEFA and connected regions.

Programme of Regional Colleges

1. Four years course for training science and technology teachers.
2. One year course for training teachers in commerce, art and crafts (in colleges in Bhopal and Bhubaneshwar), agriculture, science, home science (for colleges in Mysore and Ajmer) and technology.
3. In-service training programme.
4. One to two years diploma course and two years degree course for the teachers of sculpture.

CENTRAL SCHOOLS

These schools have been opened for the children of those Union Government employees whose jobs are transferable (who are transferred from one place to other). These schools have been opened on the recommendations of Second Pay Commission. These schools prepare students for the Higher Secondary Education curriculum and examinations, as prescribed by the Central Board of Secondary Education, Delhi. In these schools the children of the following categories of people are admitted:

1. Those employees of the Union Government who are often transferred from one place to another.
2. Defence personnel.
3. Employees of the All India Services.
4. Employees of the autonomous bodies aided by the Union Government.
5. Floating and local population.

Finances at Central Schools

The Union Ministry of Education is responsible to bear the expenditure incurred over these schools. Education is free up to eighth class. The fee for classes IX, X and XI is ₹ 6, ₹ 7 and ₹ 8 respectively. No fee is charged from the boys of scheduled castes. The medium of instruction is both English and Hindi in these schools. These schools exist in all the States in the country.

At present there are 796 Central Schools with seven lakh students and 41712 employees. During 1993-94 additional 25 schools were sanctioned.

N.C.E.RT.

The National Council of Educational Research and Training (N.C.E.RT.) was established in September 1961 in New Delhi as an autonomous body. Qualitative improvement and excellence in school education and teacher education are some of its major objectives. To achieve them, the N.C.E.RT. undertakes programmes related to research, development, training, extension and dissemination of educational information through its constituent departments — the C.I.E.T., the Regional Colleges of Education at Ajmer, Bhopal, Bhubaneshwar and Mysore and 17 field offices located all over the country.

The N.C.E.RT. continued to coordinate and monitor activities related to the U.N.I.C.E.F.-assisted projects in elementary and non-formal education and U.N.F.P.A.- assisted National Population Education Project (school and non- formal education).

The N.C.E.RT. maintains effective liaison with State education authorities and State level institutions for providing academic inputs to school education system.

During 1992-93, major achievements of N.C.E.RT. were directed towards Early Childhood Care and Education (E.C.C.E), Universalisation of Elementary Education (U.E.E.), Minimum Levels of Learning (M.L.L.), orientation of content and process of education at the school stage, improvement of science education in school, computer literacy, vocationalisation of education, teacher education, education of SCs/STs and minorities, education for women's equality, education of the disabled children, utilisation of educational technology, educational survey and data processing, National Talent Search Scholarship, promotion of educational research and publication of textbooks for C.B.S.E. affiliated schools in the country.

N.C.E.R.T. develops curricula, syllabi and prepare text-books for classes I-XII. The syllabi prepared by the N.C.E.R.T. from the basis for prescription of scheme of studies by Central Board of Secondary Education (C.B. S.E.) for the students of schools affiliated to the Board. The syllabi and text-books so prepared by N.C.E.R.T. are given to State/UT agencies for use in their schools after adoption/adaptation. It also develops instructional material for childhood education and training packages for teacher educators and supervisory personnel. N.C.E.R.T. organises Jawaharlal Nehru National Science Exhibition every year in which a large number of school students from all over the country participate. The Council produces science kits for the use of school students. It prepares comprehensive guidelines for curriculum evaluation and school-industry linkages as well as for pre-service and in-service education of teacher on vocationalisation of education. Training courses for the officials involved in the Integrated Education Programme for Disabled Children are also conducted by the N.C.E.R.T.

SPECIAL RESEARCH ORGANISATIONS

Indian Council of Historical Research, New Delhi, set up in 1972, enunciates and implements a national policy on historical research and encourages scientific writing of history. It operates research projects, provides financial support of research projects by individual scholars, awards fellowship and undertakes publication and translation work.

Indian Council of Philosophical Research which started functioning from 1981 with offices in New Delhi and Lucknow, reviews the progress of research in philosophy from time to time, sponsors or assists projects of programmes of research in philosophy, gives financial assistance to institutions and individuals to conduct research in philosophy and allied disciplines.

Indian Institute of Advanced Study, Shimla, set up in 1965, is a residential centre for advanced research in humanities, social sciences and natural sciences. It is a community of scholars engaged in exploring new frontiers of knowledge aimed at making major conceptual development and offering interdisciplinary perspectives on questions of contemporary relevance.

Indian Council of Social Science Research, New Delhi, is an autonomous body for promoting and coordinating social science research. Its main functions are to review the progress of social science research, give advice on research activities in Government or outside, sponsor research programmes and give grants to institutions and individuals for research in social sciences.

THE U.G.C.

Co-ordination and determination of standards in Higher education is a subject in the Union List and, hence, a special responsibility of the Central Government. This responsibility is discharged mainly through University Grants Commission (U.G.C.)., which was established in 1956 under an Act of Parliament to take measures for promotion and co-ordination of university education and determination and maintenance of standards in teaching, examination and research in universities. To fulfil its objectives, the Commission can enquire, among other things, into financial needs of universities, allocate and disburse grants to them; establish and maintain common services and facilities, recommend measures for improvement of university education and give advice on allocation of grants and establishment of new universities. U.G.C. has approved 111 colleges for autonomous status—23 in Andhra Pradesh, 44 in Tamilnadu, 30 in Madhya Pradesh, 5 each in Rajasthan and Orissa, 2 each in Gujarat and Uttar Pradesh.

According to 1991 census the literacy rate in India increased to 52.2 per cent in 1991 from 43.56 percent in 1981, an increase of 8.65 per cent. Where the literacy among males increased 13 per cent literacy among women increased by 6.45 per cent. The number of literates (aged seven and above in 1991 at 3,593 lakhs compares very well with the number of literates at 2,357 lakhs in 1981. The number of illiterates in 1991 was 3,289 lakhs which is a marginal increase from 3,053 lakhs in 1981. The increase in the number of literates in 1991 over 1981 was 1,236 lakhs whereas the corresponding increase in the number of illiterates was 236 lakhs only. Kerala (82.8 per cent) tops the literacy rate followed by Mizoram (82.27 per cent), Lakshadweep (81.78 per cent) and Chandigarh (77.81 per cent). At the end of the ladder are Bihar (38.48 per cent), Rajasthan (38.55 per cent) and Dadra and Nagar Haveli (40.71 per cent). The increase in female literacy rate has been very significant in the States/Union Territory of Sikkim (19.29 per cent), Lakshadweep (17.59), Nagaland (14.45 per cent), Daman and Diu (12.90 per cent), Haryana (13.57 percent), Manipur (13 percent), Andaman and Nicobar Islands (12.26 per cent), Pondicherry (12.63 percent), Tripura(11.65 percent), and Kerala(10.47 per cent). The literacy rate is above the all India level of 52.21 per cent in case of 22 States/UTs but eight States *viz.* Bihar, Rajasthan, Arunachal Pradesh, Madhya Pradesh, Uttar Pradesh, Andhra Pradesh, Meghalaya, Orissa and Union Territory of Dadra and Nagar Haveli are still below the threshold level of literacy *i.e.* 50 per cent. All these States/UTs except Meghalaya are also below the all India level in case of female literacy.

ADULT EDUCATION

The National Literacy Mission (NLM) was launched in 1988 with the objective of imparting functional literacy to 800 lakh adult illiterates in the age-group 15-35 by 1995. The implementation of programmes under the NLM has showed that eradication of illiteracy is not a utopian idea but possible, feasible and achievable. The most important development that has taken place under the NLM is the near ascendancy of the campaign mode in the adult education programmes in the country. After experimenting with successive number of alternative models of adult education programmes we have finally settled down to one which has given us hope and faith that literacy can be overcome in a time bound manner with planned and coordinated efforts and with mobilisation of people belonging to all sections of the society.

Campaigns for total literacy constitute the major thrust and initiative in the mission, they also constitute the principle strategy. In the heels of success of Emakulam and Kerala experiments for achieving full literacy, these campaigns for total literacy have generated certain characteristic features which make them unique and distinguish them from other programmes. They are area specific, time-bound, voluntary-based, cost-effective and outcome-oriented. Total literacy campaigns have been launched in 258 districts of the country covering over 520 lakh illiterate persons. Eighty districts have commenced post-literacy campaigns.

The thrust in all programmes of adult education is now on adoption of area approach, continuous environment building for literacy through Jathas, street plays, nukkad nataks, T.V., radio, newspapers, folk art forms, etc. and use of motivation-oriented teaching/learning materials produced under the new technique of Improved Pace and Content of Learning (I.P.C.L.).

NATIONAL POPULATION EDUCATION PROJECT

The objective of inculcating the message of small family norms and other population related issues in the minds of school and college students and the clientele of adult and non-formal education is being achieved through National Population Education Project. The National Population Education Programme is now being implemented through three projects of School and Non-Formal Education, Higher Education and Adult Education.

Since its inception in 1980, National Population Education Project (N.P.E.P.) has covered much ground towards achieving its main objective of institutionalising population education in the school education system. During the second cycle (1986-90), the main focus has been on consolidation of project's multidimensional activities and further expansion of its network. The project is currently running in 29 States/UTs. During the Seventh Plan, it is proposed to direct substantially and systematically the N.P.E.P. activities towards the non-formal sector.

SCHOLARSHIPS

The Department of Education funds several scholarship/ fellowship programmes for Indian students for Higher education including some offered by other governments. These include the National Scholarship Scheme, a special coaching scheme for Scheduled Castes and Scheduled Tribes students, a scheme of scholarships to help students of non-Hindi speaking States studying Hindi, research scholarships for Indian classical languages and scholarships to enable talented rural children to continue Secondary education. These programmes are administered through the State governments. A new programme of prestigious fellowships for Post-graduate studies in India and abroad named Jawaharlal Nehru Fellowships have recently been introduced.

Scholarships for advanced or specialised studies are offered under the provisions of cultural exchange programmes, bilateral agreements, Commonwealth scholarships/fellowships plan and *ad hoc* scholarship offers received from different countries. These scholarships are mostly for Ph.D (Doctoral) and Post-doctoral specialisation for which the minimum eligibility requirement is a Master's Degree.

BOOKS

National Book Trust

The National Book Trust (N.B.T.), India, an autonomous organisation under the Department of Education, Ministry of Human Resource Development, plays an important role in book promotion programmes. The National Book Trust publishes low priced books on a variety of subjects including physical environment and culture of India, folklore, popular science, biographies and books for children, adults and neo-literates. Publishing translations of significant creative writings in various Indian languages is a major activity. The trust has published over 6,000 titles in 13 languages. During 1993-94 the trust published more than 300 titles.

The N.B.T. subsidises publication of economically priced books for higher education. Besides subsidy to the publisher, the trust pays an attractive royalty directly to the author. Under this scheme, the N.B.T. has subsidised about 800 titles. The trust also provides financial assistance to private publishers and voluntary agencies for producing quality low-priced books for children, neo-literates and school drop-outs.

N.B.T. organises book fairs, festivals and exhibitions, seminars, symposia and workshopstopromote interaction amongst readers, writers, intellectuals, publishers, booksellers, etc. During the year 1993-94 the trust has organised children's book fairs at Guwahati (October 10-18,1992) and New Delhi (January 2-10,1993); book festivals at Bhubaneshwar (October 31 - November 8,1992) and Visakhapatnam (November 28 - December 6, 1992); and the National Book Fair at Bangalore (January 30 - February 7, 1993).

Since 1989, the trust has been promoting the celebration of National Book Week on all-India scale. The trust has taken up pilot projects for establishing Readers' Clubs in schools of Bangalore, Guwahati and Bhubaneshwar. On behalf of the Ministry' of Human Resource Development, the National Book Trust participates in various international book fairs and exhibitions and puts up exhibits of contemporary Indian books.

Import Policy for Books

Under the new policy announced by the Ministry of Commerce with effect from April 1, 1992, any person/organisation is free to import books on educational, scientific and technical subjects without any restrictions.

Copyright

Copyright protection is governed by the Indian Copyright Act, 1957. The Copyright Act has been amended thrice in 1983,1984 and lastly in 1992 to extend the term of Copyright from 50-60 year A comprehensive review of the Act has been made and two Bills— the Copyright (Second Amendment) Bill, 1992 and the Copyright Cess Bill, 1992 — were introduced in the Lok Sabha in July 1992 to amend the Act further.

Raja Rammohan Roy National Agency for I.S.B.N.

The International Standard Book Numbering System (I.S.B.N.) is an international system by which a distinct identifying number is assigned to each book. The I.S.B.N. system introduced in 1985 is still in its infancy in India but is already proving useful to the book trade, libraries, information systems and research scholars. Since 1985 up to March 31, 1994 more than 2367 publishers have been registered under the system. The National Agency also brings out National Catalogue of I.S.B.N. titles annually.

PROMOTION OF LANGUAGES

The Government encourages development of all Indian languages including classical, modern and tribal. Its policy lays emphasis on training of teachers in relation to adoption of the three-language formula and production of university-level text-books with a view to facilitating media switch over from English to regional languages. In order to assist non-Hindi speaking States/Union Territories to effectively implement the three-language formula, support for provision on facilities for teaching of Hindi in these States/UTs is provided by sanctioning financial assistance for appointment of Hindi teachers in schools and for establishment of Hindi teachers training colleges in these States/UTs, under a Centrally-sponsored scheme. The grant-in-aid is provided mainly to assist the consolidation and further development of Hindi teacher training colleges in non-Hindi speaking States/Union Territories and to a limited extent, to assist the setting up of a new institution in such areas which are in need of such assistance. Assistance is also given to voluntary organisations for enabling them to hold Hindi teaching classes, conducting research on methodology of its teaching and providing Hindi books to various organisations. Various schemes are in operation to promote and develop tribal, classical, modern Indian languages and prepare and publish books, dictionaries, research and instructional material besides training of teachers in Hindi. Through the Kendriya Hindi Sansthan, Agra, the Government of India promotes development of improved methodology for teaching Hindi to the non- Hindi speaking students. Central Hindi Directorate runs programmes relating to purchase and publication of books and their free distribution to non-Hindi speaking States and to the Indian missions.

The Commission for Scientific and Technical Terminology, New Delhi, prepares and publishes definitional dictionaries and terminology in various disciplines and Pan-Indian terminology. Hindi-English glossaries in basic sciences, humanities, social sciences and applied sciences, university level text-books in agriculture and engineering and other subjects are also published. Fifty scholarships are awarded every year to foreign students for studying Hindi in Kendriya Hindi Sansthan, Agra.

Modern Indian Languages

Financial assistance is given to voluntary organisations and individuals to bring out publications like encyclopaedias, dictionaries, books of knowledge, original writing on linguistic, literary, indological, social anthropological and cultural themes, critical editions of old manuscripts, etc., for the development of modern Indian languages. Grants are also given for holding literary conferences, seminars and exhibitions besides, purchasing copies of printed publications. States are given special help for the production of university level books in the regional languages. The Bureau for Promotion of Urdu was set up in 1969. Apart from working as a secretariat to the Taraqqi-e-Urdu Board which advises the Government on development of Urdu, it also develops educational literature in Urdu. It has established 39 calligraphy centres where training is given to students in Kitabat.

Government also provides facilities for study of languages other than mother tongue. For this, the Central Institute of Indian Languages (C.I.I.L.), Mysore, conducts research in the areas of language analysis, language pedagogy, language technology and language use. Study of tribal languages is one of its important functions. It runs six regional language centres at Bhubaneshwar, Mysore, Patiala, Pune, Solan and Lucknow to help meet the demand for traineid teachers to implement the three-language formula and one extension centre at Guwahati to do research for development of tribal languages of north-eastern region.

English and Foreign Languages

The Central Institute of English and Foreign Languages (C.I.E.F.L.), Hyderabad, set up as an autonomous body in 1958 is engaged in bringing out qualitative improvement in teaching of English. Subsequently, teaching of major foreign languages, *viz.* Russian, German, French and Arabic and their literatures was also included in its activities. In 1973 it was declared to be an institution of higher learning deemed-to-be a university. It has two regional centres at Shillong and Lucknow.

Financial assistance is also provided to States for setting up C.I.E.F.L.'s district centres for English with a view to improving the standard of English language, teaching and learning. These centres aim at imparting training to teachers of English in their areas through orientation courses. Under another scheme, financial assistance is given to regional and State institutes of English for strengthening their programmes of training with respect to improving standard of English language teaching.

Sanskrit and other Classical Languages

There are many schemes for propagation, popularisation and development of Sanskrit and other classical languages like Arabic and Persian. These include schemes for financial assistance to State governments and voluntary Sanskrit organisations, development of Sanskrit institutions run by voluntary organisations into Adarsh Sanskrit Pathshalas, for incentives to retired scholars as Shastra Chudamani Pandits, for publication of original writings of contemporary authors, editing and publication of rare manuscripts and catalogues of manuscripts, reprinting of important out-of-print Sanskrit texts, promotion of oral Vedic tradition, vocational training to products of Sanskrit Pathshalas, national awards to eminent Sanskrit, Arabic and Persian scholars and preparation/publication of Sanskrit dictionaries.

Registered organisations engaged in the development and propagation of Sanskrit are given recurring and non-recurring grants for salary of teachers, scholarships to students, construction and repair of buildings, library books, research projects, etc., up to 75 per cent of the approved expenditure. About 700 voluntary institutions conducting courses on traditional Sanskrit education and about 200 institutions working in the field of propagation and promotion of Arabic/ Persian are benefited under this scheme every year. Institutions having potential for greater development are identified and brought under the scheme of Adarsh Sanskrit Mahavidyalayas and Shodh Sansthans. At present, such Mahavidyalayas and Shodh Sansthans are being assisted. Under the scheme of Certificate of Honour to Sanskrit, Arabic and Persian scholars, 15 eminent Sanskrit scholars and three each in Arabic and Persian are honoured by the President every year. They are also given a grant of ₹10,000 per year for life.

Department of Education also conducts an all-India Vedic convention (through R.V.V.P.) and an all-India Sanskrit elocution contest every year where scholars in different Shastras and a team of eight contestants from all States are invited with a view to identifying the rare Veda Shakhas and their repositories, devising ways and means for preserving the oral traditions and encouraging *ex tempore* speech on classical subjects. As a special measure to preserve oral tradition of Vedic studies, a scheme was introduced in 1978 under which each Swadhyayin is expected to train two students each below 12 years, one of them being his own son or near relative in a particular Veda Shakha. The scholar gets an honorarium of ₹ 1,250 and the student ₹ 175 per month. In all, 21 such units are receiving assistance. Seven of them were set up after the Vedic convention held in Indore in November 1987. Rashtriya Veda Vidya Pratishthan has been set up with the objective of preserving and developing all aspects of Vedic studies. For this, the Pratishthan undertakes various activities such as supporting traditional Vedic institutions and scholars by providing fellowships, scholarships, etc. Similarly, there are 26 institutions which are given 95 per cent grant for popularising Vedic education. Government is also providing financial assistance to eight Veda units which are engaged in the preservation of oral tradition of Vedic recitation.

Under Shastra Chudamani scheme, young scholars are given in-depth coaching in Kendriya Vidyapeethas/Adarsh Sanskrit Mahavidyalayas, etc. in various disciplines by utilising services of eminent elderly scholars. These scholars are appointed on a monthly honorarium of ₹1,000.

Rashtriya Sanskrit Sansthan, an autonomous organisation under the Ministry with its headquarters at Delhi, exercises academic and administrative control over seven Kendriya Sanskrit Vidyapeethas at Jammu, Allahabad, Guruvayoor, Puri, Jaipur, Lucknow and Sringeri where Sanskrit education in traditional Shastras and research in various fields is conducted. Vidyapeethas of Delhi and Tirupati, were declared deemed-to-be universities in 1987. The Sansthan also conducts examination from Prathma to Vidyayaridhi (Ph.D) and Vachaspati (D. Litt.) and in addition to its own institutions over 50 other institutions all over the country are affiliated to it.

Under the Centrally-sponsored scheme of Development of Sanskrit 100 per cent grant is given to the State governments/ UTs for (a) financial assistance up to ₹ 4,000 per annum to eminent Sanskrit scholars in indigent circumstances; (b) for appointment of teachers for teaching selected modem subjects in the traditional Sanskrit Pathshalas; (c) for providing facilities for teaching Sanskrit in High and Higher Secondary schools; (d) for scholarships to students studying Sanskrit in order to attract good students in IX to XII classes; and (e) for their own schemes for promotion of Sanskrit.

Resources for Education

Promotion of quality and equity are no less resource initiative than quantitative expansion of institutions. The budgetary outlays on education, of the Centre and States, had steadily increased from 1.2 per cent of GNP in 1950-51 to 3.5 per cent

MAHILA SAMAKHYA

A Central scheme 'Mahila Samakhya' was launched in April 1989. This programme seeks to mobilise rural women for education through Mahila Sanghas in each of the village concerned. This is a Central scheme where full financial assistance is provided to Mahila Samakhya societies in Karnataka, Uttar Pradesh, Gujarat and Andhra Pradesh set up under the chairmanship of the concerned State Education Secretary. The Minister of Education in the State is the president of the society. As an Indo-Dutch programme, it receives cent per cent assistance from the Government of Netherlands. Essentially, the programme revolves around Mahila Sanghas where women are mobilised around issues like access to health, education, water, information about development programmes, general information about their immediate environment, and above all, issues related to their personality and self-image in society. The programme tries to facilitate critical reflection and analysis which would encourage women to take active interest in issues that affect their daily life. The focus of the programme is on generating demand for education and introducing innovative educational inputs for pre-school, non-formal, adult and continuing education.

BIHAR EDUCATION PROJECT

The Bihar Education Project (B.E.P.) is a programme of educational reconstruction for bringing about fundamental change in the education system in Bihar. As a comprehensive basic education project, it covers the elementary school system; the non-formal education system; early childhood care and education; women's education and development; and post-literacy, continuing education and inculcation of basic skills for survival and general well being. It is a joint project of Central and

State Government which U.N.I.C.E.F. is also assisting. The project is implemented through an autonomous State level society with the partnership of State Government, the Centre, U.N.I.C.E.F., teachers representatives and N.G.Os. active in the field. The Chief Minister is Chairman of the society. The executive responsibility vests with the State Project Director. The project is currently under implementation in Ranchi, Rohtas, Chatra, Sitamarhi, Muzaffarpur, West Champaran and East Singhboom district.

LOK JUMBISH: PEOPLE'S MOVEMENT FOR EDUCATION FOR ALL

An innovative educational project called 'Lok Jumbish: People's Movement for Education for All, Rajasthan with assistance from Swedish International Development Authority (S.I.D.A.) has been taken up in Rajasthan. The basic objective of the project is to achieve education for all by the year 2000 through people' s mobilisation and their participation. The project presupposes that creation of a people's movement would generate a stimulus for human development which, in turn, would lead to a basic socio-economic change. Lok Jumbish concentrates on primary education.

SHIKSHA KARMI PROJECT

The Shiksha Karmi Projectis being implemented since 1987 in Rajasthan with the assistance from the Swedish International Development Authority (S.I.D.A.). Its aim is universalisation of primary education in selected remote and socioeconomically backward villages of the State.

The project identifies teacher absenteeism as a major obstacle in achieving the objective of universalisation. It accordingly, envisages substitution of the primary school teacher in single teacher schools by a team of two locally resident educational workers called 'Shiksha Karmi'.

U.N.E.S.C.O. AND INTERNATIONAL COOPERATION

Since the inception of the United Nations Educational Scientific and Cultural Organisation (U.N.E.S.C.O.), India has been in the forefront in promoting the ideals and objectives of the organisation. The Indian National Commission for Cooperation with U.N.E.S.C.O. set up in 1949 in compliance with Article 7 of the Constitution of U.N.E.S.C.O., is the apex advisory, executive, liaison, information and coordinating body at the national level. It has been playing an active role in U.N.E.S.C.O.'s work particularly in the formulation and execution of its programme in collaborating with national Commissions of Asia and the Pacific region.

During 1991-92, India extended its co-operation to U.N.E.S.C.O. and its regional offices through participation in numerous workshops, symposia and conferences, organising national, regional and inter-regional activities in the country in area of competence of U.N.E.S.C.O., arranging placement of U.N.E.S.C.O. fellows in Indian institutions, implementing projects under the participation programme of U.N.E.S.C.O. and administration of U.N.E.S.C.O. Coupons scheme.

External Academic Relations

External academic relations both bilateral and multilateral performa significant role in international diplomacy. With a view to deepen India's academic interaction with important countries, the educational component of the cultural exchange programmes and other bilateral arrangements is being explored to encourage studies regarding India and Indology in foreign universities. A dialogue has been established to concretise new ideas in this area with our missions in China, Pakistan, Japan, U.S.A., Germany, Bhutan, France, etc.

U.N.E.S.C.O. Clubs and Associated Schools

The U.N.E.S.C.O. clubs, constituted mainly in educational institutions, are voluntary bodies engaged in the promotion of aims and objectives of the organisation. The associated schools are educational institutions which are directly linked with U.N.E.S.C.O. Secretariat for participation in the Associated School Project for undertaking activities relating to education for international understanding, co-operation and peace. Thirty-seven schools and teacher training institutions from India are enlisted with U.N.E.S.C.O. under the project.

BORDER AREA DEVELOPMENT PROGRAMME (B.AD.P.)

Border Area Development Programme (B.A.D.P.) is implemented in the border States of Gujarat, Jammu and Kashmir, Punjab and Rajasthan covering 18 border districts and 79 border blocks. Financial assistance was rendered to the States under this programme in all priority areas of education such as universalisation of Elementary education, improvement of Secondary education, vocational education, culture and sports besides establishment of ITIs and polytechnics.

EDUCATION OF WOMEN

Enrolment of girls as a ratio of total enrolment during 1991-92 is only 39 per cent at primary stage, 33 per cent at middle stage and 28 per cent at Higher education stage. All out efforts were made during the period for improving girls/women's participation in education. Under the Scheme of Operation Blackboard, Government has provided assistance since 1987-88 for creation of 1,22,890 posts of primary school teachers mainly to be filled by women. According to the latest reports, 1,02,587 posts of teachers have been filled up of which 48.52 per cent are women teachers. Ninety per cent assistance was given for N.F.E. centres meant for girls. The cumulative number of N.F.E. centres for girls is 82,000. The 'Mahila Samakhya' (Education for Women's Equality) Project has been under implementation. By conscious action, admission of girls to the extent of 28.44 per cent in Navodaya Vidyalayas has been ensured. Special attention was given to enrolment of women in adult education centres. In the Total Literacy Campaigns (T.L.Cs), the theme of empowerment of women is receiving special focus. The women learners under T.L.Cs outnumber male learners.

EDUCATION OF SCHEDULED CASTES AND SCHEDULED TRIDES

The year 1990-91 was the centenary year of Dr. B.R. Ambedkar. The National Committee which was set up under the chairmanship of the then Prime Minister, decided that the programmes for the development of SCs and STs would continue up to the year 1993-94. Department of Education has issued instructions to organisations under its control to take up programmes and activities for celebrating the birth centenary in a befitting manner and extend these activities to the current year also. The programme includes panel discussion, seminars, essay competitions, publications of Dr. Ambedkar's biography and anthology of his works, creation of chairs of Baba Saheb Dr. B.R. Ambedkar, philosophy and thoughts in universities, inclusion of Baba Saheb's thoughts in the text-books, etc.

The thrust on removal of disparities and equalisation of educational opportunities by catering to specific needs of SCs and STs continued. Under the schemes of 'Operation Blackboard', non-formal education, adult education, etc., States were advised to give high priority to selection of blocks which have large concentration of SCs and STs.

The revised Programme of Action (P.O.A.) 1992 prepared in pursuance of the modified National Policy on Education (N.P.E.), 1986 provides for continuance of the existing education programmes for SCs and STs with stress on improving literacy increasing enrolment and reducing drop-out rates among SCs/STs. The scheme of upgradation of merit of SC/ST students started in 1987-88 continued to be implemented through States/UTs. Under this scheme, remedial coaching is given to SCs and STs in classes IX-X, and special coaching in classes XI and XII for preparing them for competitive examinations.

Other facilities like reservation of seats in educational institutions (15 per cent for SCs and 7.5 per cent for STs), relaxation in qualifying marks in entrance examinations, reservation in pre-Matric scholarships, freeships in Kendriya Vidyalayas, reservation in university level research fellowships, research associateships, teacher fellowships, etc. were continued.

The Indian Institutes of Technology operate a scheme under which candidates belonging to SCs and STs, who fail in the Joint Entrance Examination by very slender margin of marks are given further training and admitted to relevant courses.

EDUCATION OF MINORITIES

Under 15-Point Programme, University Grants Commission continued to implement the scheme of providing assistance to universities and colleges for coaching students from educationally backward minorities. The scheme is being revamped. It will be expanded to cover minority concentration areas as well as non-minority concentration areas for remedial and enrichment coaching. One of the proposals under consideration is to get the minority students coached for the higher studies through reputed private coaching institutions as is being done in the case of SC/ST students. The programme of review of text-books from the point of view of communal harmony, secularism and national integration is being implemented by the National Council of Educational

Research and Training (N.C.E.R.T.) and State governments. All the 41 minority concentration districts identified by the Programme of Action (1986), have been covered by community polytechnics and their extension centres under 15-Point programme.

The revised Programme of Action 1992 envisages several short, medium, and long term measures for the improvement of minorities' education. In pursuance of these programmes, a scheme of financial assistance to voluntary organisations for modernisation of Madrasa education has been prepared to encourage traditional institutions like Madrasas and Maktabs by giving financial assistance to introduce science, mathematics, social studies and modern Indian languages like Hindi and English.

Another new scheme of Area Intensive Programme for educationally backward minorities has also been prepared to provide assistance to State governments and voluntary organisations for taking up programmes for educationally backward minorities, not covered by the on-going programmes. The Eighth Five Year Plan provision for the scheme is ₹ 16.27 crore.

Upto March 1993 the facility of coaching was availed by 41002 candidates under the coaching scheme for competitive examinations started in 1984 and at present being carried on in 21 universities and 32 colleges. During 1992-93 the number of successful candidates was 2650. The scheme was modified in March 1993. In the programme of teachers' training for minorities, so far 450 principals and 950 teachers have been trained.

STIPENDS FOR FOREIGN STUDENTS

The Central Government grants various stipends to foreign students for education and training in India. Under the general cultural scholarship programme every year about 200 stipends are given to foreign students of Asia and Africa. Scholarships to foreign students are generally given in the areas of engineering, agriculture, medicine, technology and humanities. According to the 1972-73 plan it has been decided to award stipends to about 100 students of Bangladesh every year. During 1983-84 about 300 students of Bangladesh have been studying in India. There is a provision for granting stipends for studies to foreign students of those countries which maintain friendly relationship with us. Under this provision the following are the plans worth-mentioning:

1. The plan of exchange of stipendship.
2. The plan of Commonwealth fellowship or stipendship.
3. Technological co-operation and stipendship under the Colombo Plan.

YOUTH SERVICES IN INDIA

In India there are many Youth Services which work towards promoting physical, mental, social and cultural development of our youths. Below we are hinting at some of these services:

Nehru Youth Centre. There are about 255 Nehru Youth Centres in the various States and Union Territories which engage student and non-student youths in activities leading to national reconstruction. Constructive work for youths between 15 and 35 years of age, informal education, competitive sports and games, physical training, spreading literacy, health education and cleanliness, community service work and land improvement work are the main activities of these centres.

National Service Scheme. This scheme was enforced in 1969 for under-graduate boys and girls. Their chief activities are co-operation in spreading literacy, constructive work through free labour (Shramadan), planting trees, cleaning dirty colonies, first-aid and organising hospitals.

All India Board of Sports and Games. This Board has been established for promoting physical, mental, moral and social developments of the youths. This Board has appointed a Committee of sports and games which sends suggestions to universities, schools of various States, State Boards of sports and games and federations of sports and games. It is on the advice of this national Board that players are sent to foreign countries to participate in international games and sports. The Board also advises to invite foreign teams to play in our country. Competitions and training camps for national championship are organised by this Board. The State Boards of sports and games are given grant on the advice of this Board. Physical training facilities and centres for games and sports in rural areas are organised by the Board. This Board determines the national policy regarding sports and games. According to the Parliament Directive of 1968 sports and games programmes are organised occasionally throughout the whole country.

Besides the above Board at the Centre, there is another National Organisation of Sports which gives training in sports and games to the selected youths of universities and colleges in the country. This Organisation holds camps also. The University Grants Commission and Indian University Organisation exercises some control over the National Organisation of Sports and Games. The following two institutions are playing leading roles in the field of physical development of youths of the country:

(1) The Netaji Subhash National Institute of Sports, Patiala.

(2) Lakshmibai National College of Physical Education, Gwalior.

The Netaji Subhash National Institute of Sports at Patiala runs two years postgraduate diploma in sports and games in addition to a graduate course in the same. Foreigners also obtain training in sports and games at this institute. The Nehru Youth Centre and the National Board of Sports and Games co-operate with this institute in running national training plans at various regional centres of sports and games.

The College at Gwalior offers three years graduate course in physical education, sports and games. For employees a three years summer course is also run by this college.

In 1959 a National Physical Efficiency programme was instituted. Afterwards this programme was called the national capacity programme. Those participating in this programme are grouped into four classes — sub-junior, junior, senior and adult. The Gwalior College runs this programme through various training institutions.

QUESTIONS FOR EXERCISE

1. Write an essay on Education in Modern India.
2. Write short note on (i) N.C.E.R.T., (ii) Central Schools, (iii) Education of Women, and (iv) The U.G.C.